NEW WAYS OF
MANAGING CONFLICT

NEW WAYS OF MANAGING CONFLICT

Rensis Likert

Chairman of the board, Rensis Likert Associates, Inc.; director emeritus, The University of Michigan's Institute for Social Research; and professor emeritus of Psychology and Sociology, The University of Michigan.

Jane Gibson Likert

Writer and editor, former teacher, vice-president of the League of Women Voters of the United States, project director and counselor, The Center for Continuing Education of Women, The University of Michigan.

McGraw-Hill Book Company

New York   St. Louis   San Francisco   Auckland   Düsseldorf
Johannesburg   Kuala Lumpur   London   Mexico   Montreal
New Delhi   Panama   Paris   São Paulo   Singapore
Sydney   Tokyo   Toronto

53749

Library of Congress Cataloging in Publication Data

Likert, Rensis, date.
  New ways of managing conflict.

  Bibliography: p.
  Includes indexes.
  1. Management. 2. Social conflict. 3. Organization.
I. Likert, Jane Gibson, joint author. II. Title.
HD38.L48   658.4   75-23216
ISBN 0-07-037842-8

   567890 KPKP 7854321098

The editors for this book were W. Hodson Mogan and Margaret Lamb, the designer was Elliot Epstein, and the production supervisor was George E. Oechsner. It was set in Baskerville by University Graphics, Inc.

Printed and bound by The Kingsport Press.

Contents

Preface

Persons seeking to resolve any kind of conflict except that within a single individual should find this volume of value. It applies major research findings concerned with organizations and their effectiveness to the management of conflict.

The authors have drawn extensively on the important research of the staff of The University of Michigan's Institute for Social Research and of many other social scientists. The numerous citations and quotations provide evidence of the value of their contributions.

Many helpful suggestions have been made by the staff of Rensis Likert Associates, especially by Charles Araki, Robert W. Bauer, and Albert F. Siepert. Others who have read and criticized the chapters include David G. Bowers, Dan Caldwell, Kermit Hanson, Roy Leffingwell, James Marshall, Borje O. Saxberg, Stanley E. Seashore, Donald C. Stone, Charles A. Waters, and Barbara Won. Mary Lou Holdren, Roberta Dash, and Pamela Deasy have given invaluable help in the preparation of the manuscript. The assistance of all these persons is deeply appreciated.

Rensis Likert

Jane Gibson Likert

1
A new resource for conflict management

There is ample evidence in the mass media and elsewhere that bitter, unresolved conflict is widespread and increasing in frequency. It occurs at all levels of society: among nations and within nations, among organizations and within them. What is causing this trend?

Human values as legitimate rights

In the United States and throughout the world, important human values, for the first time in history, are being widely recognized as legitimate rights. This is an exciting worldwide trend. But recognizing these rights does not provide the sophisticated social, political, and business institutions needed to put them into operation.

New graduates from high schools and colleges, employed in both blue-collar and white-collar jobs, expect to be involved in decisions to a much greater extent than they actually are. The decision-making processes of most business organizations fail to provide the involvement that these new employees expect and feel entitled to. This is a growing source of frustration and dissatisfaction among employees. It is also true of unions and is leading some of the new, younger members to challenge the established union leadership and occasionally to take over.

Many other rights, in addition to the right to be involved in decisions affecting oneself, are being legitimized and are creating new expectations. Civil rights have been given general public support and have been affirmed by our high courts. These rights and others, such as political, educational, and economic rights, and rights to decent housing and suitable jobs, have been supported strongly by top governmental officials and national political leaders.

In the United States, in recent decades, every President has endorsed these rights and expressed the belief that they can and should be realized by all persons. Arthur M. Ross (1967), when Commissioner of Labor Statistics in 1966, said:

> A new view of the manpower goal, which concentrates on human aspirations and possibilities, as well as accumulated skills and jobseeking endeavors, is emerging. (p. 57)

> Recent policy declarations state that rewarding, self-respecting and self-fulfilling employment, not merely something which qualifies statistically as a job, should be the birthright of every American. (p. 58)

The Congress and some state legislatures have passed bills affirming these rights and seeking their implementation, but again there often has been a failure to build the more sophisticated institutions required to implement the stated goals. For example, in the legislation creating the Office of Economic Opportunity (OEO), the Congress stated explicitly that the programs at the community level were to be carried out with the full and active participation of the persons affected. Unfortunately, the legislation failed to recognize that effective participation requires an appropriate structure as well as the skills that a sizable proportion of the population lack. If effective participation is to occur, an interaction-influence network is required that is more complex than most persons have experienced or have the skills to function in. Little or no provision was made in the legislation for the coaching and training of the persons affected by the OEO Act to enable them to participate successfully and effectively in the decision-making process. As a consequence, the more sophisticated and complex form of organization required to provide the called-for participation never emerged, and the persons at the local level who tried to participate found the experience unsuccessful, ineffective, and highly frustrating. Bitter, destructive conflict resulted and defeated the important objectives of the legislation. It also led to wasteful use of the appropriated funds.

University students are keenly aware that there is widespread acceptance of their rights to be heard and to influence decisions affecting them. As a consequence, their more active members are demanding an influential role in all decisions which affect students, such as housing, curricula, faculty selection, and the quality of instruction. More broadly, they want a voice in solving society's problems.

The National Commission on the Causes and Prevention of Violence stated in its summary (1969):

> We urge that young people must be given a greater role in determining their own destiny and in shaping the future course of our society. Responsible participation in decision making may, for many, be a substitute for the violence that is born in frustration. (p. 2)

Although recognizing that our society has legitimized as accepted values the rights which the students claim, few universities have modified their administrative structure and their decision-making processes to provide the interaction-influence network required to translate these values into successful action. Students find that they cannot exercise these recently legitimized rights since the existing interaction mechanisms, especially in large universities, generally are incapable of providing them with the opportunity. Participation is urged, but no mention is made of the need to develop the more effective social system required for genuine participation to occur.

This same situation exists in the public schools. There is a frustration gap between the students' expectations of being involved in decisions affecting them and the extent that they are. This gap is small at the 5th grade, but it increases each year. It is sizable in middle schools and even larger in senior high schools. School systems have not yet changed their administrative and decision-making processes to meet the changed expectations of their students.

Unrealized expectations as a source of conflict

All these developments concerning newly legitimized or reaffirmed human rights are creating strong expectations that they can be and will be realized now or very soon. Even though improvement may be occurring in such areas as housing, education, job opportunities and employment, administration of justice, and civil liberties, expectations among the deprived are often increasing faster than the improvements are occurring. This results in unfavorable attitudes and reactions since attitudes reflect *experience in relation to expectations* rather than experience alone.

When new, cherished values or rights are legitimized and new expectations are created, failure to fulfill these expectations at least as fast as they are created causes unfavorable attitudes and frustrations. These unfavorable reactions are magnified when underprivileged persons fail not only to experience the better jobs, pay, and living which they are led to expect but also find themselves unable to exert any influence on decisions concerned with implementing these newly legitimized rights which are so important to them.

Here, again, impressive progress has been made in affirming rights and legitimizing them as basic human values, but the more complex and sophisticated social systems required to give full operational meaning to them have not been established.

On the international scene, a similar phenomenon is taking place which affects particular cultural groups, minorities, and developing nations. In recent decades, the nations of the world have legitimized as a right the basic value of self-determination. Woodrow Wilson stated it earlier as one of his Fourteen Points. But here, again, although the value is being legitimized as a right, the interaction-influence networks required to make the right operational are not being established.

Throughout the world, especially in developing countries, persons are embracing with enthusiasm the newly won right to be involved in decisions affecting them. But their enthusiasm changes to frustration, bitterness, anger, and aggressive behavior when their successive attempts to be involved in decisions important to them are unsuccessful. As the world is witnessing, these frustrations are so great that they often lead to hostile acts, even though the consequences may be suicidal for those involved.

Frustrations, aggressions, and conflicts are likely to continue and to grow even worse until the United States and other nations develop and make widespread use of social systems and institutions which provide the degree of participation that the new rights require.

Other causes of modern conflict

Research in the physical and biological sciences and in engineering is increasing in rate and magnitude throughout the nations of the world. To benefit from research, a nation must undergo a variety of social and economic changes. Change almost always is accompanied by tension, anxieties, resistance, and conflict. Since more, not less, is being spent everywhere on research and development, the application of the results of research is causing faster and faster change in industrial nations and in developing countries as well. Research, therefore, although essential to progress, is in itself producing conflict.

Research in business firms also heightens conflict within the organization. If research findings are to be applied as they emerge, changes are required in the way production, sales, and other departments do their work. These changes create intradepartment and interdepartment problems and conflict. At present the conflict generally is handled by "win-lose" problem solving that yields costly consequences for the firm. Research increases the magnitude of the problem and makes more important than ever the use of a "win-win" model of problem solving rather than the "win-lose" method.

Modern technology is contributing in additional ways to the magnitude of present-day conflict. When individuals are struggling hard to survive, they have neither the time nor the inclination to press for involvement in decisions affecting them. But as per capita income is increased in industrialized and industrializing nations, persons have both the time and the resources to press for rights not yet achieved and for the realization of unfulfilled values.

There are, of course, many other sources of conflict. In addition to the newer sources created by modern society, all the older causes continue unabated: struggles for power, the desire for economic gain, the need for status, and the exploitation of others. For many reasons, consequently, present-day society can be expected to experience more conflict, not less. The need to manage conflict constructively will increase in importance each year.

Tensions are inevitable and are necessary for creative thinking

A common orientation toward conflict is to seek to handle the problems which conflict creates by reducing the tensions producing conflict. This was the focus some years ago of a major project of UNESCO. This approach has serious limitations in its ability to cope with conflict for two reasons: (1) it is not likely to succeed, and (2) in many situations, more, not less, differences and tensions are desirable.

It would be unrealistic to seek to resolve conflict by trying to turn the clock back and denying newly legitimized rights. It would be equally unrealistic to seek to halt all improvement in the level of living in order to remove the tensions created by the social changes accompanying technological change.

For many if not all conflicts, the need is to find a way to resolve them constructively without eliminating the differences which led to the conflict. Differences and tensions often yield a productive outcome. Studies of creativity and innovation show, for example, that diversity of research field and diversity of prior experience among scientists who interact frequently bring differences which contribute significantly to increasing their scientific productivity (Pelz & Andrews, 1966). Research on small groups indicates that they are more productive when dissenters are present than when there is no difference of opinion (Cartwright & Zander, 1968). The highest levels of creativity are found in those organizations which deliberately stimulate innovative-mindedness by encouraging diversity and differences among persons engaged in tasks where imaginative thinking yields valuable results. Pelz calls this stimulation the "dither effect." It shakes people out of their comfortable ruts and makes them think anew (Pelz, 1967). It gives them new frameworks, new assumptions, and new points of view from which innovative solutions may emerge.

The following statement, adapted from Harlan Cleveland (1972, pp. 17–29), discusses the need for the public executive to "understand the web of tensions":

> I would not deny that every agency has to get its staff and its constituents to cooperate. But I would argue that in a modern large-scale organization, just getting people to cooperate is by no means the most pressing problem. You can always get cooperation, after all, by eliminating the real issues that divide people from each other.
>
> Every one of you who works for the government knows of the process by which the boss is screened off from real problems. The assistant director will get the branch chiefs together and say, "Now fellows, you don't seem to be agreeing with each other. Why don't you come into my office and we'll work it out." After the first ten minutes, it becomes clear that two of the branch chiefs are diametrically opposed on a matter of fundamental policy. Yet the last thing anybody suggests is to go to the boss and say, "How will we work this out?" Instead, the assistant director says, "Let's go through the document paragraph by paragraph." For

everybody knows that even the most acrimonious disagreements can be effectively buried if attention is paid to language rather than to principle.

It is too easy just to get people to cooperate. People are, if anything, too conformist. This is why the executive's most difficult task is almost precisely the reverse of inducing cooperation. It is to maintain an adequate degree of tension within the organization—enough fruitful friction among its members so that all possible points of view are weighed before important decisions are made. No executive worth his salt wants staff members that are so bored with the agency's work or so undifferentiated in function that they never argue with each other or with the boss.

Diversity of orientation and differences in point of view—"fruitful friction"—are essential if one seeks creative and effective organizations. Differences, of course, can result in irreconcilable, costly conflict unless the interaction-influence network and the problem-solving processes of organization channel the differences to productive and not destructive ends. There is need to develop more sophisticated social institutions and organizations that have the capacity to deal constructively with the conflicts caused by change or by diversity.

Social science research is aiding conflict management

Learning to cope with conflict successfully is a social science problem. Progress has been limited because the social sciences have been supported niggardly. In the United States, for example, less than 2 percent of all the funds for research and development from 1945 to 1970 went to support the social sciences. In most other nations, the social sciences have received even less support. It is ironic that large sums are spent on research on the technical aspects of such problems as water supply, the energy crisis, overpopulation, food supply, and pollution, but virtually nothing is spent on finding ways of overcoming resistance to change, of gaining acceptance of the soundest technical solutions, and of putting them into practice. In spite of this imbalance in support, social science research is yielding new, promising approaches to conflict resolution.

The contribution from social science research to conflict management is often a by-product, as, for example, the results emerging from research on the human dimensions of an organization. This research has revealed the principles used by the highest-producing managers in comparison with those used by managers who achieve average or poor results. When the principles used by the highest-producing managers are integrated into a management system, there emerges a more complex, sophisticated, and socially evolved system (System 4) than those used by most managers today (Likert, 1961, 1967).

The basic principles and concepts of System 4 and the organizational theory upon which the system is based can be applied to any human organization or institution. In addition to improving performance, this theory provides new insights and strategies for resolving conflict more constructively.

Apply organizational theory to managing conflict

The focus of this volume, as the preceding paragraphs indicate, is on applying the emerging, powerful, research-based principles and theories of organization and management to the resolution of conflict. The success of a corporation or governmental agency is influenced greatly by its capacity to achieve cooperative coordination rather than hostile conflict among its functional departments and also to stimulate differences and then to capitalize on them by productive problem solving leading to creative and acceptable solutions. The knowledge and skills yielded by current research concerned with organizations and organizational theory clearly have much to contribute to improving humanity's capability of successfully managing the wide array of conflicts occurring today. This becomes particularly evident when the causes of recent violence and conflicts are examined.

Institutions based on traditional organizational theory, such as most business firms and universities, lack the capacity to deal successfully with the conflicts created by the new demands which recently legitimized values are placing upon them. These kinds of conflicts usually cannot be solved by the methods suggested in the current literature for dealing with conflict. Repressive action brings costly backlash. These conflicts are dealt with most constructively when the most sophisticated and effective form of organization is applied to them.

To facilitate applying a more effective system of organization to the management of conflict, several major aspects of System 4 will be discussed more fully than they have been previously. These aspects are examined in general as well as in relation to resolving conflict. They are:

- linking pins and the linking process

- the nature of System 4 leadership

- the contribution of supportive behavior, integrative goals, deemphasizing status, and use of consensus to productive problem solving (win-win)

- principles of System 4 organizational structure

Conflict defined

As the preceding sections of this chapter show, conflict is viewed as the active striving for one's own preferred outcome which, if attained, precludes the attainment by others of their own preferred outcome, thereby producing hostility.

It is well to differentiate between two kinds of conflict: *substantive* conflict and *affective* conflict. Guetzkow and Gyr (1954) define substantive conflict as "conflict rooted in the substance of the task." They define affective conflict as "conflict deriving from the emotional, affective aspects of the . . . interpersonal relations" (p. 369). We are concerned in this volume with how to handle substantive conflict successfully even in situations where the presence of affective conflict makes this task more difficult.

A conflict is viewed as resolved when all opposing parties are satisfied with the outcome. A conflict remains unresolved as long as any party is dissatisfied with the outcome.

When differences exist, conflict may or may not be present. Differences, particularly differences in values, often lead to conflict. Whether differences actually do lead to conflict depends on the character of the interaction processes.

Meeting human yearnings and needs more adequately

As a society applies modern organizational theory and principles to the management of conflict, the changes produced in the society will enable it to meet deep-seated but unsatisfied human needs and yearnings much more adequately than at present. These yearnings were expressed well by a student leader quoted by Wierzynski (1969) when he said:

> We want to return society to a human scale, a scale small enough for us to participate in the decisions that affect us. We want a society in which our place is not preordained by birth and circumstance. We want a society that tolerates candor and spontaneity. We want to retain control over our own lives. (p. 114)

Individual freedom, which is being restricted more and more in highly industrialized societies under their present form of government, decision making, and conflict management, can be regained without returning to the simple agricultural society of our forebears and the small town meetings of the early days of New England. Satisfactory control over one's life and destiny can be achieved in large industrial societies. A more complex form of social organization is required that gives all people a substantially greater capacity to influence the decisions affecting them. This is now a possibility. New knowledge available from social science research can be used to create more socially evolved and more effective social and political institutions than we now have. If this knowledge is used, these institutions will be based on the more effective organizational theory produced by research. They will have the structure and decision-making processes to enable all persons in the institution to exert influence commensurate with their contribution upon decisions affecting them. In political institutions, all citizens, consequently, will be able to exert sufficient control over the political processes and the social environment within which they live to satisfy their yearning for freedom. Persons who live in a more complex and socially evolved society can enjoy the health and wealth benefits of a highly industrialized society while simultaneously retaining substantial control over their own lives.

Subsequent chapters describe the structure and interaction characteristics of a social system capable of managing conflict in any situation much more constructively than can present practices. In our judgment, the proposed system of social organization based on an organizational theory (System 4) derived from extensive research in business and government is the best now available for coping with conflict; it can be used profitably until better formulations based on further research are discovered.

It is hoped that this book will encourage additional research on System 4 and the principles underlying it, particularly on ways of applying those principles to the important task of managing conflict.

Some readers may be interested in applying System 4 to improving organizational effectiveness as well as to conflict management. They will find that the chapters on leadership, organizational structure, linking pins, problem solving, and consensus present a much more complete description of System 4 principles and operating characteristics than has appeared previously.

2
The relation of conflict strategies to a society's values and organizational theories

If we define human nature as those qualities present at birth, such as inherited capabilities and motives, human nature has changed little, if at all, in tens of thousands of years. But there has been tremendous change in what humans have learned and passed on from one generation to another. Moreover, these changes continue as experience and insights enrich learning.

A major aspect of human history has been the continuous struggle to learn how to live and work productively and constructively with others. Acquiring new knowledge by trial and error has been extremely slow. Its use often has been delayed by the refusal of those in power to permit new insights to be applied since any change might diminish the power and control of these individuals. Slowly, however, progress has been made in knowledge and skill in building more effective social institutions.

The reorganization of the Jewish people under Moses represented an important forward step. Ernest Dale (1960) describes this event as follows:

> When Jethro saw that Moses "stood by the people from morning unto evening," he said:
>
>> "The thing that thou doest is too heavy for thee . . . thou and thy people will surely wear away."
>
> Moses, as leader, had all the departments reporting to him. Figure 2-1 shows the structure. . . .
>
> Organization counsel, in the person of Jethro, prescribed the remedy. Figure 2-2, straight from the Bible, shows the new organization he devised. . . . Moses no longer needed to settle all the details himself; he was provided with staff assistance. This is the earliest example of a general staff.[1]

[1]From Ernest Dale, *Organization: An Illustrated Outline.* Copyright 1960 by Ernest Dale. Reprinted by permission of the author. Adapted in Ernest Dale, *Management: Theory and Practice* (3rd ed.). New York: McGraw-Hill, 1973, pp. 193–194.

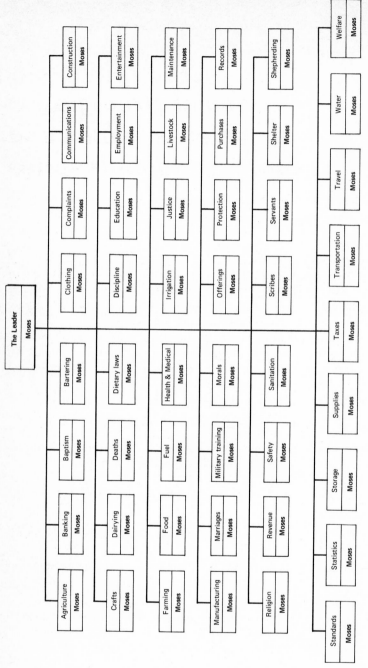

Figure 2-1 The Leader: Chart No. 1.

Progress over the centuries

The concepts which Moses introduced in this reorganization represented a big step forward in the understanding and skill of organizing activities. This step was from an amorphous tribe to a structured organization with staff and a workable span of control. Since then, people have learned to live and work successfully in larger and larger social units. This transition has been from primitive villages to city-states to states to nations. In business, it has been from individuals to partnerships to corporations. At each stage, as success has been achieved, the learning acquired has been taught to the next generation through the process of socialization.

For a long period of human history, the use of naked power by individuals or small social units was common. Whenever a disagreement or conflict occurred, a solution would likely be forcibly imposed by one of the parties if it had sufficient power to settle the dispute in the way it wished, had no qualms about using this power ruthlessly, and felt that it could live safely with all the consequences of the increased hostility and bitterness which its behavior would be likely to create. The defeated party may have been motivated to strike back whenever the opportunity occurred, but for the moment the conflict was "settled."

Power appears to be unbearable when used in this ruthless and unchallengeable way. Over many centuries, people have sought, fought for, and largely won the establishment of checks and balances as a safeguard against the abusive use of power in political, industrial, and governmental systems. Related major social inventions such as majority rule and parliamentary procedures also were created in the struggle for freedom and justice. Gaining the acceptance of each was a major step forward in social evolution.

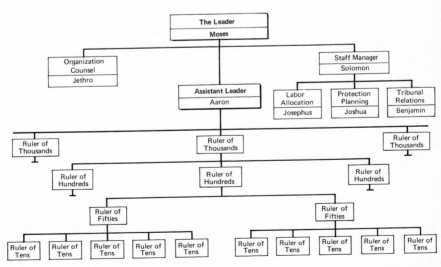

Figure 2-2 *The Leader: Chart No. 2.*

There is need, however, for further progress since checks and balances, majority rule, parliamentary procedures, confrontation, bargaining, negotiation, and the advocacy concepts of the law are all based on the win-lose approach to resolving conflicts. Since the win-lose approach is seriously inadequate for managing present-day conflict, as we shall see in Chapter 4, any system—political, industrial, or other—that is based on this approach is equally inadequate and needs to be revised or replaced by more effective ways.

Progress usually starts in one area of human activity

Progress over the centuries has not occurred at a uniform rate or in a uniform manner. Improvement in such different areas as (1) political, legal, and governmental activities; (2) business and commercial activities; and (3) military activities typically has not occurred simultaneously, equally, or in a parallel fashion. Sometimes the progress has occurred first in one area of activity. At another time and, perhaps, in a different society, it has occurred in one of the other areas.

Rome represented a great step forward in human capacity to organize military activity as well as to rule through governors whose operations were coordinated but decentralized. The French and American Revolutions and the political thinking of that period was an era of important progress in political life. The principles of Adam Smith and the Industrial Revolution and, much later, the American corporation were major developments in commercial and business activities.

In every society, however, there seems to be a general trend toward establishing and maintaining a basic consistency in values, principles, and procedures among all its different areas of activities—political, legal, governmental, educational, business, and military. When any one area of activity, for whatever reasons, develops a significantly better mode of operation, this improvement and the underlying concepts and philosophy upon which it is based is generalized sooner or later and applied to all the other activities of that society. This may require a considerable span of years, but the trend toward an internal consistency appears to occur.

The nature of a society is reflected in its management of conflict

This general trend toward a consistent pattern means that the strategies and principles used by a society and all its organizations for dealing with disagreements and conflict reflect the basic values and philosophy of that society. A primitive society uses primitive procedures for coping with differences and conflict; a feudal society employs feudal concepts and principles. A modern, industrialized nation's approach to the management of disagreements and conflict reflects its more sophisticated philosophy, values, and social system as do all the other principles and procedures employed by organizations within that society.

This same consistency also is found within large organizations. All the component activities within an organization, such as its leadership, decision making, communication, motivation, and control, tend to be consistent, one with the other, as well as to reflect the values and organizational concepts of the society of which it is a part. A large number of organizational studies of leadership, management, and organizational performance demonstrate that every organization in all its operating characteristics, including its customary procedures for resolving disagreements and conflicts, displays orderly, internally consistent patterns. (See Likert, 1967, chap. 7 and app. 1, for a report on these data.) This is true of conflicts within the organization and of conflicts between it and other organizations. Since organizations tend to maintain internally consistent procedures, progress by an organization in developing and using more effective organizational theory and systems will lead to improvement in its handling of conflict.

The management of conflict is a major function of every organization including business firms and governmental agencies. Research in these organizations which brings improvement in their organizational theory and management systems brings with it corresponding improvement in the way conflict is managed. An important contribution of organizational research is, consequently, better principles and strategies for managing conflicts more constructively.

Quantitative research accelerates development of improved social systems

Social science research is accelerating the social evolution of appreciably more effective but more complex organizational systems. This research, using quantitative methods (e.g., Likert & Willits, 1940), was started about four decades ago shortly after the basic methodology (Likert, 1932; Thurstone, 1929) required for it became available. It substitutes rigorous quantitative measurement for crude judgment and trial and error. Since 1945, the volume of this research on leadership, management, organizational performance, and organizational theory has increased greatly.

The bulk of the published research has been done by universities, and most of it has been conducted in business enterprises because precise measurements of performance are more often available there. Studies, however, have been undertaken in governmental agencies, hospitals, and other nonbusiness organizations.

Probably the most extensive and sustained research on organizational systems and theory since 1945 has been done by The University of Michigan's Institute for Social Research. The central objective of this research has been to discover more effective ways for a human organization to establish its objectives and to achieve them efficiently. Several hundred studies have been completed and have obtained data from more than 20,000 managers and 200,000 employees (e.g., Taylor & Bowers, 1972).

The Institute for Social Research's studies show that on the average, in widely different industries and for widely different kinds of work, the same basic principles for managing human activity are used by the managers who achieve the highest production, lowest cost, and most financially successful operations. These principles differ significantly from those used by those managers who achieve below-average productivity, costs, and earnings.

Although *the principles used by the highest-producing managers are essentially the same from industry to industry or for different kinds of work, the specific methods for applying them usually differ markedly from situation to situation.* These principles are applied in what might well be called a culturally relative manner (Likert, 1961, chap. 7). Able managers apply the basic principles by using methods which are appropriate to that particular industry, job, and personnel and which are consistent with the traditions of the individual firm.

System 4

The basic principles used by the highest-producing managers have been integrated into a general organizational system called System 4. A brief description follows:

> The human organization of a System 4 firm is made up of interlocking work groups with a high degree of group loyalty among the members and favorable attitudes and trust among peers, superiors, and subordinates. Consideration for others and relatively high levels of skill in personal interaction, group problem solving, and other group functions also are present. These skills permit effective participation in decisions on common problems. Participation is used, for example, to establish organizational objectives which are a satisfactory integration of the needs and desires of all the members of the organization and of persons functionally related to it. Members of the organization are highly motivated to achieve the organization's goals. High levels of reciprocal influence occur, and high levels of total coordinated influence are achieved in the organization. Communication is efficient and effective. There is a flow from one part of the organization to another of all the relevant information important for each decision and action. The leadership in the organization has developed a highly effective social system for interaction, problem solving, mutual influence, and organizational achievement. This leadership is technically competent and holds high performance goals.

The preceding description of System 4 paraphrases that which appeared in *New Patterns of Management* (Likert, 1961, p. 99). It was not labeled System 4 at that time. This description is not sufficiently precise to enable a manager or other persons in an organization to know whether or not they are using this system in their operations. System 4 needs to be defined in dimensions that can be measured quantitatively. A quantitative definition of System 4 is presented in this and subsequent chapters.

In comparison with the management systems used by most firms today, System 4 is a more highly developed and complex system and represents a more advanced social evolution. It requires those using it to learn more complex leadership and interaction skills. As might be expected, however, it displays all the characteristics of a more effective form of organizing human interaction and efforts. A rapidly growing body of research findings shows that it is appreciably more effective in enabling an organization to decide upon its objectives and to accomplish them efficiently.[2] When an organization shifts to System 4 from a traditional organizational theory, performance improves, costs are reduced, and improvement occurs in the satisfaction and health of the members of the organization (Caplan, 1971; Coch & French, 1948; Likert, 1973b; Marrow, Bowers & Seashore, 1967; Rensis Likert Associates, 1971; Seashore & Bowers, 1963). In addition, the System 4 theory provides more effective processes than do traditional organizational systems for successfully handling all the different kinds of conflicts arising in organizations.

Recent results reveal, moreover, that the greater effectiveness of System 4, in comparison with more traditional organizational theories, is much more clearly demonstrated when *trends over time* in productivity, costs, earnings, and other end-result variables are examined rather than when all variables are measured simultaneously (Likert, 1973b; Likert & Bowers, 1969). More and more research findings support the view that System 4 is applicable to every kind of organization, such as schools, hospitals, and governmental agencies.[3]

Human organizations can be described quantitatively

The extensive research over the past quarter of a century that has produced the System 4 theory has yielded methodology for measuring organizational sys-

[2]See research summaries, references, and reports in Bowers & Seashore, 1966; Habibullah, 1967; Jerovsek, Mozina, Tannenbaum, & Likert, 1970; Katz & Kahn, 1966; Likert, 1961, 1967; Likert & Bowers, 1969; Misumi & Shirakashi, 1966; Misumi & Tasaki, 1965; Roberts, Miles, & Blankenship, 1968; Tannenbaum, 1968, 1971; Taylor & Bowers, 1972.

[3]For example, see Bernhardt, 1971; Byrnes, 1972; Carr, 1971; Ferris, 1965; Georgopoulos & Mann, 1962; Gibson, 1973; Gilbert, 1972; Haynes, 1971; Johnson, 1968; Ketchel, 1972; Lepkowski, 1970; Rensis Likert Associates, 1971; NTRDA, 1970; Thompson, 1971; Wagstaff, 1969; Warwick et al., 1975; White, 1971a, 1971b, 1971c, 1971d.

tems. Any management or human organizational system, consequently, can be measured and described in terms of well-defined variables. Moreover, the scores of an organization on these variables can be related to measurements of its performance, its success in achieving its goals, and its capacity to resolve conflicts constructively.

The management system of an organization can be described in two-dimensional space. These dimensions can be applied to any organization in an industrialized or moderately industrialized nation. They have been used successfully for this purpose in such areas of the world as the United States, Western Europe, Eastern Europe, Asia, and Latin America.

Employing the customary x and y axes, organizations are arrayed on the y axis according to the degree to which they employ the concepts of functionalization or differentiation. Organizations at the very low end of this axis are relatively amorphous masses. There is little differentiation in function, an excessive span of control, considerable confusion about each person's role, and, in extreme cases, chaos and anarchy. These organizations, as shown in Figure 2-3, are viewed as using System 0 (zero).

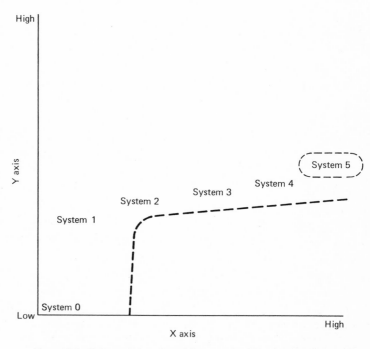

Figure 2-3 *Schematic location of Systems 0 to 4 in relation to degree of functionalization and the motivational forces used. The Y axis shows the extent to which basic concepts of functionalization are applied through appropriate structure; the X axis, the extent to which major innate motive sources are used in ways that reinforce rather than conflict with one another.*

The *x*, or horizontal axis, is used to reflect the *basic motivational forces which the organization seeks to employ, the manner in which they are used, and the extent to which they are cumulative and reinforcing.* This axis, in essence, reflects the degree of social evolution achieved in the use of the basic human motive sources[4] employed by the organization. In industrialized nations, the more socially evolved the management system is, the greater is the magnitude of the motivational forces mobilized by the organization to accomplish its objectives.

The items in Table 2-1 indicate the nature of the motive sources which different management systems use and the resulting motivational forces and consequences. At the System 1 or left end of the continuum, the motivational forces rely on punitive treatment of members of the organization. At the right end, labeled System 4, the motivational forces are based on supportive treatment and involvement. Punitive treatment yields hostile attitudes and restriction of production. Involvement and supportive treatment yield favorable attitudes and cooperative, responsible behavior which seeks to accomplish the organization's goals.

Prior to the time that Moses, using Jethro's advice, introduced the major reorganization shown in Dale's chart, his organization would have been classified as a System 0 organization. It would fall at the lower end of the *y* axis (see fig. 2-3).

After the reorganization, it would fall much higher on the *y* axis, but since Moses relied heavily upon fear and punishment as major motive sources, his organization would have fallen well over to the left end of the *x* axis, toward System 1. The punitive character of the Mosaic Law reflects this orientation.

Operating characteristics of different management systems

The characteristics of different management systems are revealed in greater detail by the items in Table 2-2. As will be observed, the range along the *x* axis in Table 2-2 varies from the left end of System 1 to the right end of System 4. Each organizational variable in the table displays this same range. Under each system heading, there is a brief statement describing that system for that particular variable.

An examination of Table 2-2 will reveal that any organization with sufficient functionalization and corresponding structure to fall within the System 1 to System 4 band can be categorized readily on that continuum. In a modern nation, the overwhelming majority of business, government, education, and

---

[4]The term "motive source" is used to refer to the inherited, innate sources of motivation. Major motive sources include sex, hunger, thirst, and others derived from biological sources and also such desires as those for physical security and for achieving and maintaining a sense of personal worth and importance. Motive source is used rather than such terms as "motive," "need," or "drive" since these have been defined and used elsewhere in a more specific sense (Atkinson, 1964; Atkinson & Feather, 1966; McClelland, 1961; McClelland, Atkinson, Clark, & Lowell, 1953).

Table 2-1

Motivational forces tapped by different management systems*

Item no.	System 1	System 2	System 3	System 4
1. Underlying motives tapped: a. Desire for physical security b. Economic motives c. Desire to achieve and maintain a sense of personal worth and importance d. Desire for new experience	Major use of *a*. Moderate use of *b*. Slight use of *c* in form of desire for status and power	Some use of *a*. Extensive use of *b*. Some use of *c* in form of desire for status, power, recognition, and achievement	*a* fulfilled. Extensive use of *b*. Moderate use of *c* in form of desire for recognition and achievement and some use of *c* in form of power and status. Some use of *d*	*a* fulfilled. Highly effective use of *b* achieved by involvement in decisions on how best to use economic motivation fully. Extensive use of *c* through group problem solving and resulting desire for achievement and self-actualization. Effective use of *d*

2. Manner in which motives are used

Fear, threats, punishment, and occasional rewards	Rewards and some actual or potential punishment	Rewards, occasional punishment, and some involvement	Economic rewards based on compensation system developed through participation. Group participation in setting goals, improving methods, appraising progress toward goals, etc. Full recognition of achievement. Opportunity for free, responsible behavior in achieving established goals

* Adapted from *New patterns of management* and *The human organization* by Rensis Likert. Copyright © 1961 and 1967 by McGraw-Hill Book Company, Inc. Reprinted by permission of the publisher.

Table 2-1

Motivational forces tapped by different management systems* *(Continued)*

Item no.	System 1	System 2	System 3	System 4
3. Kinds of attitudes developed toward organization and its goals	Attitudes usually are hostile and counter to organization's goals	Attitudes are sometimes hostile and counter to organization's goals and are sometimes favorable to the organization's goals and support the behavior necessary to achieve them	Attitudes usually are favorable and support behavior implementing organization's goals	Attitudes are strongly favorable and provide powerful stimulation to behavior implementing organization's goals
4. Extent to which motivational forces conflict with or reinforce one another	Marked conflict among motivational forces weakening motivation to achieve organization's goals	Conflict usually exists; occasionally some forces will reinforce each other in support of the organization's goals, at least partially	Some conflict, but often motivational forces in support of organization's goals will reinforce each other	Motivational forces in support of the organization's goals generally reinforce each other in a substantial and cumulative manner

	To a very small extent	To a small extent	To quite an extent	To a very great extent
5. Extent to which members of the organization feel they should, on their own initiative, take action when the best interests of the organization require it				
6. Amount of responsibility felt by each member of organization for achieving organization's goals	High levels of management feel responsibility; lower levels feel less; rank and file feel little and often welcome opportunity to defeat organization's goals	Managerial personnel usually feel responsibility; rank and file usually feel relatively little responsibility for achieving organization's goals. Restriction of output occurs	Substantial proportion of personnel, especially at higher levels, feel responsibility and generally behave in ways to achieve organization's goals	Personnel at all levels feel responsibility for organization's goals and behave in ways to implement them.

Table 2-1 *(Continued)*

Motivational forces tapped by different management systems*

Item no.	System 1	System 2	System 3	System 4
7. Attitudes toward other members of the organization	Subservient attitudes toward superiors coupled with hostility; hostility toward peers and contempt for subordinates; distrust is widespread	Subservient attitudes toward superiors; competition for status resulting in hostility toward peers; condescension toward subordinates	Cooperative, reasonably favorable attitudes toward others in organization; may be some competition between peers with resulting hostility and some condescension toward subordinates	Favorable, cooperative attitudes throughout organization with mutual trust and confidence
8. Subordinates' feeling of responsibility for initiating accurate upward communication	None	Relatively little, usually communicates "filtered" information and only when requested; may "yes" the boss	Some to moderate degree of responsibility to initiate accurate upward communication	Considerable responsibility felt and much initiative; subordinates communicate all relevant information

Organizational variable				
9. Forces leading to accurate or distorted upward information	Powerful forces to distort information and deceive superiors	Many forces to distort; also forces for honest communication	Occasional forces to distort along with many forces to communicate accurately	Virtually no forces to distort and powerful forces to communicate accurately
10. Amount of cooperative teamwork present to achieve organization's goals	Practically none	Slight amount	A moderate amount	Very substantial amount throughout the organization
11. Extent to which the decision-making process helps to create the necessary motivations in those persons who have to carry out the decisions	Decision-making contributes little or nothing to the motivation to implement the decision; usually yields adverse motivation	Decision-making contributes relatively little motivation	Some contribution by decision-making to motivation to implement	Substantial contribution by decision-making processes to motivation to implement

Table 2-1
Motivational forces tapped by different management systems* (Continued)

Item no.	System 1	System 2	System 3	System 4
12. Forces to accept, resist, or reject goals	Goals are overtly accepted but are covertly resisted strongly	Goals are overtly accepted but often covertly resisted to at least a moderate degree	Goals are overtly accepted but at times with some covert resistance	Goals are fully accepted both overtly and covertly
13. Extent to which there is an informal organization present and supporting or opposing goals of formal organization	Informal organization usually present and opposing goals of formal organization	Informal organization usually present and partially resisting goals of formal organization	Informal organization usually present and may either support or partially resist goals of formal organization	Informal and formal organization are one and the same; hence all social forces support efforts to achieve organization's goals

Table 2-2

Profile of organizational characteristics*

Organizational variable	System 1	System 2	System 3	System 4	Item no.
1. Leadership processes used:					
a. Extent to which supervisors have confidence and trust in *subordinates*	Have very little confidence and trust in subordinates	Have some confidence and trust	Quite a bit of confidence and trust	A great deal of confidence and trust	1
b. Extent to which subordinates, in turn, have confidence and trust in *supervisors*	Have very little confidence and trust in supervisors	Have some confidence and trust	Quite a bit of confidence and trust	A great deal of confidence and trust	2
c. Extent to which supervisors behave so that subordinates feel free to discuss important things about their jobs with their immediate supervisor	Subordinates do not feel at all free to discuss things about the job with their supervisor	Subordinates feel somewhat free to discuss things about the job with their supervisor but do it guardedly	Subordinates feel quite free to discuss things about the job with their supervisor but with some caution	Subordinates feel very free to discuss things about the job with their supervisor and do so candidly	3

*Adapted from *New patterns of management* and *The human organization* by Rensis Likert. Copyright © 1961 and 1967 by McGraw-Hill Book Inc. Reprinted by permission of the publisher.

Table 2-2

Profile of organizational characteristics (Continued)

Organizational variable	System 1	System 2	System 3	System 4	Item no.
d. Extent to which immediate supervisor in solving job problems generally tries to get subordinates' ideas and opinions and make constructive use of them	Rarely gets ideas and opinions of subordinates in solving job problems	Occasionally gets ideas and opinions of subordinates in solving job problems	Usually gets ideas and opinions and usually tries to make constructive use of them	Virtually always gets ideas and opinions and tries to make constructive use of them	4
2. Communication processes: a. Direction of major flow of information	Downward	Mostly downward	Down and up	Down, up, and with peers	5
b. Extent to which supervisors willingly share information with subordinates	Provide minimum of information	Give subordinates only information supervisors feel they need	Give information needed and answer most questions	Seek to give subordinates all relevant information and answer questions	6
c. Extent to which downward communications are accepted by subordinates	Viewed with great suspicion	Some accepted and some viewed with suspicion	Often accepted but, if not, may or may not be openly questioned	Generally accepted but, if not, openly and candidly questioned	7

d. Accuracy of upward communication via line organization 8

Tends to be inaccurate	Information that boss wants to hear flows; other information is restricted and filtered	Information that boss wants to hear flows; other information may not be complete and is cautiously given	Accurate and complete

e. Lateral communication: its adequacy and accuracy 9

Usually poor because of competition between peers, corresponding hostility	Fairly poor because of competition between peers	Fair to good	Excellent

f. Psychological closeness of supervisors to subordinates (i.e., friendly, sincere, frank interaction between supervisors and subordinates) 10

Far apart	Moderate distance	Fairly close	Usually very close

Table 2-2

Profile of organizational characteristics* (Continued)

Organizational variable	System 1	System 2	System 3	System 4	Item no.
g. How accurate are the perceptions by supervisors and subordinates of each other?	Generally in error	Often in error on some points	Moderately accurate	Usually quite accurate	11
3. Character of interaction-influence process:					
a. Amount and character of interaction	Little interaction and almost always with fear and distrust	Little interaction and usually with some condescension by supervisors and fear and caution by subordinates	Moderate interaction often with fair amount of confidence and trust	Extensive friendly interaction with high degree of confidence and trust	12
b. Extent to which subordinates can influence the goals, methods, and activity of their units and departments:					
(1) As seen by supervisors	Practically none	Slight amount	Moderate amount	A great deal	13

other organizations will be found, of course, to have sufficient functionalization and structure to fall somewhere along the System 1 to System 4 continuum; that is, they will fall within the area above the dotted lines shown in Figure 2-3.

Even in highly industrialized nations, organizations will be found occasionally which, although seriously deficient in functionalization, do not use highly punitive motivation. These organizations are low on the y axis and, consequently, fall well below the dotted line shown in Figure 2-3, especially when the interactions in the organization are consultative in character. These kinds of organizations are relatively rare and generally display internal confusion and poor performance.

In Figure 2-3, System 5 is shown as a dotted ellipse. This is intended to suggest that social science research will help create, in the next decade or two, an even more effective, complex, and socially evolved management and social system. Some experiments already are providing a glimmering of what System 5 may be like. It appears that it will have the structure and interaction process of System 4 but will lack the authority of hierarchy. The authority of supervisors will be derived from their linking-pin roles, from the influence exerted by the groups of which they are members, and from the larger organizational entities that they help link.

Becoming familiar with Systems 1 to 4

To help develop a working understanding of Systems 1, 2, 3, and 4, and their application to the management of disagreements and conflicts, the reader is urged to do the following:

> Please think of the *most* productive department, division, or organization you have known well. Then place the letter h on the line under each organizational variable in Tables 2-1 and 2-2 to describe where this organization would fall. Treat each item as a continuous variable from the left extreme of System 1 to the right extreme of System 4.

> Now that you have completed the forms (Tables 2-1 and 2-2) to describe the highest-producing department or unit you know well, please think of the *least*-productive department, division, or organization you know well. Preferably it should be about the same size as your most-productive unit and engaged in the same general kind of work. (It should fall, of course, in the System 1 to System 4 zone and not be a System 0 organization.) Then put the letter p on the line under each organizational variable in Tables 2-1 and 2-2 to show where, in the light of your observations, you feel this least-productive organization falls on that item. As before, treat each item as a continuous variable from the left extreme of System 1 to the right extreme of System 4.

> After you have completed Tables 2-1 and 2-2 so as to describe your low-producing organization, draw a line connecting your p's which describe that

organization. This line is the organizational profile of your low-producing organization. Now do the same for the *h*'s. This line is the profile of your high-producing organization.

Examine now where the profiles for your high- and low-producing organizations fall on the System 1 to 4 continuum. Based on responses from thousands of managers, the chances are very great that your high-producing organization will fall to the right, more toward the System 4 end, and the low will be to the left, more toward System 1. The chances are sizable also that your profiles will not overlap, not even on a single item.

Relation of interaction-influence networks to conflict management

The profile of an organization obtained by using Tables 2-1 and 2-2 is a quantitative description of that organization's *interaction-influence network* and the manner in which it functions. [The interaction-influence network of an organization is concerned with both structure and interaction processes. These processes include all those dealing with leadership, communication, motivation, control, decision making, coordination, goal setting, and evaluation.]

An essential function of the interaction-influence network of an organization is coping with conflict wherever it may occur either within the organization or between it and others. The manner in which an organization copes with conflict is governed by the operating characteristics of its interaction-influence network and the management system upon which its interaction-influence network is based. Table 2-3 presents many of the variables involved in a conflict situation. This table describes for each variable the characteristic way of behaving in organizations using different interaction-influence networks ranging from those based on System 1 to those based on System 4.

Table 2-3 was prepared in the same manner as were the original versions of Tables 2-1 and 2-2 (Likert, 1961, pp. 223–233). Data from several hundred studies were used. The pattern of relationships among the kinds of items and the relationship of the items to such performance variables as productivity, costs, and earnings were examined. Based on the general pattern observed in the original versions, the specific wording for each item in Tables 2-1 and 2-2 was prepared for each of the different management systems. Table 2-3 is, essentially, a detailed elaboration of the conflict portion of Tables 2-1, 2-2, and longer tables, such as the one in the Appendix. It presents in considerable detail an array of items dealing with conflict.

Data were obtained from administering the original table (Likert, 1961) and longer and shorter versions of it to thousands of managers in several hundred organizations. Analysis shows that the relationships stated in Tables 2-1 and 2-2 and in the Appendix are patterns which, on the average, exist in such organizations as business firms, governmental agencies, and educational institutions.

Table 2-3

*Profile of conflict characteristics**

GENERAL (FORM G)

This questionnaire is designed to describe the nature and extent of conflict within and between organizations or groups. These may be industries, firms, schools, hospitals, voluntary associations, or any other kind of organization.

In completing the questionnaire, it is important that you answer each question as thoughtfully and frankly as possible. This is not a test; there are no right or wrong answers. The important thing is that you answer each question the way you see things.

The responses will be summarized in statistical form so that individuals cannot be identified. To insure *complete confidentiality*, please do not write your name anywhere on the questionnaire.

INSTRUCTIONS

Please indicate your answer to each question by filling in the circle under the choice that, in your experience, most nearly characterizes, at the present time, the aspect of the particular conflict you are describing.

For example, suppose the question were:

	System 1		System 2		System 3		System 4	
	Rarely		Sometimes		Often		Very Often	
How often do the opposing parties cooperate?	①	②	③	④	⑤	⑥	⑦	⑧

If you think they cooperate often, you would fill in ⑤ or ⑥. You would fill in ⑤ if you feel that the situation is closer to "sometimes" than to "very often." You would fill in ⑥ if you think that the situation is closer to "very often."

Table 2-3

Profile of conflict characteristics* (Continued)

	System 1	System 2	System 3	System 4
1. How much does each opposing party try to understand the points of view, needs, objectives, and preferred solution of the others?	Very little ① ②	Some ③ ④	Quite a bit ⑤ ⑥	A very great deal ⑦ ⑧
2. How much does each party seek to use joint problem solving to develop innovative solutions satisfactory to both parties?	Very little ① ②	Some ③ ④	Quite a bit ⑤ ⑥	A very great deal ⑦ ⑧
3. How open, candid, and unguarded is the communication and interaction between the opposing parties?	Extremely guarded ① ②	Quite guarded ③ ④	Some guarded, some candid ⑤ ⑥	Open, unguarded and candid ⑦ ⑧
4. To what extent do the opposing parties seem to deceive or to inform the other correctly?	Parties try hard to deceive ① ②	Parties often try to deceive ③ ④	Sometimes try to deceive, sometimes try to inform correctly ⑤ ⑥	Consistently try to inform correctly ⑦ ⑧

	System 1	System 2	System 3	System 4
5. How many open channels of communication are there for flow of information and influence between opposing parties?	Practically none; if any, through top leaders only ① ②	Relatively few, largely through leaders ③ ④	Several, involving many of the leaders and some rank and file ⑤ ⑥	Great many, involving virtually all leaders and many rank and file through appropriate linking ⑦ ⑧
6. How effective are the channels for the flow of interaction and influence between opposing parties?	Highly ineffective ① ②	Moderately ineffective ③ ④	Moderately effective ⑤ ⑥	Highly effective ⑦ ⑧
7. To what extent are efforts made to build or restrict channels of communication, interaction, and influence between opposing parties?	Extensive efforts to restrict except through top leaders ① ②	Some efforts to restrict; little interest in building ③ ④	Some efforts to build, especially at top levels of organization(s) ⑤ ⑥	Extensive efforts to build at all levels of organization(s) ⑦ ⑧
8. To what extent are innovative, mutually acceptable solutions being sought, or is each party striving to impose the solution it now prefers on the other?	Each striving hard to impose own solution on other ① ②	Primary focus on imposing own solution; some consideration of alternate solutions ③ ④	Initially prefers own, but willingly considers alternate solutions ⑤ ⑥	Earnestly seeks innovative solution acceptable to all parties ⑦ ⑧

Table 2-3

Profile of conflict characteristics* (Continued)

	System 1	System 2	System 3	System 4
9. How much does each party strive to discover and state explicitly the integrating goals and common interests that they share?	Very little ① ②	Some ③ ④	Quite a bit ⑤ ⑥	A very great deal ⑦ ⑧
10. How well can each conflicting party state freely and clearly and with understanding the points of view, needs, objectives, and preferred solution of the others?	Poorly ① ②	Not well ③ ④	Moderately well ⑤ ⑥	Very well ⑦ ⑧
11. To what extent does each opposing party strive to gain power *over* the other party or seek mutually satisfactory solution *with* the other party?	Strives very hard for power over others ① ②	Strives primarily for power over others ③ ④	Seeks some mutually satisfactory solutions but still strives for power over others ⑤ ⑥	Seeks mutually satisfactory solutions through joint efforts with others ⑦ ⑧
12. What methods of resolving conflicts are used?	Suppression ① ②	Some suppression, win-lose confrontation ③ ④	Negotiation, bargaining, and compromise ⑤ ⑥	Creative problem solving using consensus ⑦ ⑧

	System 1	System 2	System 3	System 4

13. To what extent do the opposing parties use a third party to help them find a mutually acceptable solution?

Very little	Little	Considerable	Very great
① ②	③ ④	⑤ ⑥	⑦ ⑧

14. When solutions are reached, how well do the opposing parties accept and implement them?

Strong covert resistance except by victor	Some overt acceptance; appreciable covert resistance except by victor	Overt acceptance, some covert resistance except by victor	Overt and covert acceptance; full implementation sought
① ②	③ ④	⑤ ⑥	⑦ ⑧

15. Do the solutions reached result in favorable cooperative attitudes among the opposing parties or in continued or increased hostility?

Increased hostility	Continued hostility; few favorable cooperative attitudes	Relatively favorable, cooperative attitudes on part of some; lingering hostility on the part of others	Favorable, cooperative attitudes prevail generally
① ②	③ ④	⑤ ⑥	⑦ ⑧

Organizations display a marked consistency. If they fall more toward System 4 on one item, they display the same pattern on all other items. Chapter 7 of *The Human Organization* (Likert, 1967) reports the kinds of results typically found and the magnitude of the correlations among the items.

Examining the relationship of management systems to conflict management

Table 2-3 can be used to examine the relationship between the interaction-influence network used in a conflict situation and the extent to which the conflict is resolved constructively. To use Table 2-3 for this purpose, the reader should consider the table worded in the past rather than in the present and follow these instructions:

> Think of the major conflicts within an organization or institution, or between it and another, which you have observed and known well. Then select the one which in your judgment was resolved *most* constructively.

> Answer the items in Table 2-3 so as to describe the interaction and other processes which occurred in that conflict situation by placing the letter *b* under the appropriate circle.

> Treat each item as a continuous variable from the extreme left (System 1) to the extreme right (System 4).

> After you have finished, think of other conflicts occurring in comparable situations which you have known well and select the one which in your judgment was resolved *least* constructively. Using the letter *w*, answer the items in Table 2-3 so as to describe the interaction and other processes which occurred in that situation.

> Again draw a line from item to item connecting all the *b*'s and do the same with another line connecting all the *w*'s. Each line is a profile showing the pattern of conflict management used in the two situations.

Virtually every reader will find that the profile for the *b* responses in Table 2-3 is appreciably to the right of the *w* profile; i.e., the *b* profile is more toward System 4 and the *w* profile is more toward System 1. Most persons find, as they examine their own experience and observations, that the System 4 approach to conflict management is much more effective than is the System 1 approach.

Conflict managed best in most highly developed social system

There is an orderly progression in the development of social or organizational systems from System 0 to System 4. To date, System 4 is the most socially mature and developed form of human interaction and provides the most highly developed and effective means of managing conflict. System 0, of course, is the most primitive. Without doubt, this development over time will continue, and, as suggested previously, an even more sophisticated, complex, and effective system will emerge gradually in the form of System 5. It will provide even better resources for handling conflict constructively.

Each of these different systems and its corresponding interaction-influence network has its own characteristic way of handling conflict. This relationship is evident when Tables 2-1, 2-2, and 2-3 are compared. System 1 has the least capacity to handle conflict well. Organizations using System 4 and its interaction-influence network are most likely to be successful in managing conflict.

These different patterns of managing conflict and the different outcomes they achieve in resolving conflict illustrate the major propositions of this volume.

1. *Every conflict, other than those internal to a particular individual, involves an interaction among persons, groups, organizations, or larger entities and occurs within a social system.*

2. *The extent to which a conflict is likely to be resolved constructively depends directly upon the effectiveness of the social system used during the conflict.*

3. *The more socially mature, i.e., the more toward System 4, the social system is, both in its structure and in its interaction processes, the greater is the probability that the conflict will be solved constructively.*

4. *Mature and effective social systems based on System 4 can be created and can be used in every conflict situation by those who wish to see the conflict resolved more constructively and successfully.*

    a. *The use of System 4 social systems requires an understanding of System 4 principles and skills in applying them effectively.*

    b. *A period of time is required to build an effective social system and have its full potential ready to use in a difficult, emotion-laden conflict. For this reason, it is desirable to anticipate major crises and create a social system based on the System 4 model before the conflict erupts.*

Obsolete social systems still used in attempts to resolve conflict

Some feeling of the potential for improvement in the management of conflict through the use of more effective interaction-influence networks based on System 4 can be obtained by answering Table 2-3 to show how a particular conflict is being handled *now* and answered a second time to show how you would *like* it to be. This can be done by selecting any major conflict you wish and answering Table 2-3 with an *n* to show how you feel the conflict is being dealt with now. After completing Table 2-3 in this manner, answer it again with an *l* to show how you would like it to be managed. Draw a line connecting all the *n*'s and another line connecting all the *l*'s. You are likely to find your *n* profile much to the left of your *l* profile. If this is the case, *the implication for changes needed to improve the management of the conflict is clear.* When inadequacies become evident in the existing interaction-influence network, substantial improvement can be made in the management of the conflict by strengthening the interaction-influence network at the points of revealed weakness.

It is a sobering and distressing experience to analyze present-day conflicts by comparing their actual (now) profile with the desired (like) profile. The analysis reveals our faith in woefully obsolete social systems and our reliance on them for managing the conflicts that seriously threaten our well-being and even our existence.

Archaic interaction-influence network used in Red China-United States relationships

The interaction-influence network used for two decades by the United States and the People's Republic of China to cope with their differences was so primitive and inadequate that it is surprising the conflict did not worsen seriously. News such as the following extracts from an Associated Press dispatch from Warsaw, Poland, dated January 8, 1970, described the situation at that time:

> Warsaw, Poland (AP)—U.S. Ambassador Walter J. Stoessel, Jr. and Lei Yang, chargé d'affaires at the Communist Chinese Embassy, conversed over tea for two hours at the American Embassy here today, but the session was not classified officially as a formal meeting.
>
> There was immediate speculation that the conversation may have centered around a date for the resumption of full-scale Chinese-American ambassadorial talks, which have been held in Warsaw since 1958 but were canceled by the Peking government in the last two years.
>
> The last session—the 134th—was held exactly two years ago.
>
> The United States and Red China do not recognize each other diplomatically.
>
> Officials in Washington indicated a few days ago that the United States was ready to resume the talks. Asked by a newsman, the U.S. spokesman said today's meeting was not the 135th.
>
> But it was the third contact between Stoessel and Yang since last Dec. 3 when the American sought out the Chinese diplomat at a Yugoslav reception and apparently suggested a resumption of talks.
>
> The two met again Dec. 11 at the Chinese Embassy. The subject matter of these contacts was never disclosed.

Chinese-American relationships relied on these extremely inadequate contacts—a very rudimentary interaction-influence network—until the Chinese changed the situation with their "ping pong diplomacy." Their invitation to the Americans to participate in a ping pong tournament, which was very well publicized, opened the door to the possible creation of a more effective interaction-influence network.

Inadequate interaction-influence networks exist in business and government

When Table 2-3 is used to analyze conflicts between central headquarters and field operations in both business and government, serious deficiencies in the interaction-influence network typically are revealed. The structure may be satisfactory for geographical linkages but poor for functional linkages, or conversely. All too often it is inadequate for both geographical or functional linkages. Moreover, even though the structure is adequate, it may be used with obsolete patterns of interaction, such as Systems 1 or 2.

Union-management conflicts are another example of the use of poor interaction-influence networks in attempts to resolve conflicts. Again, there frequently are serious gaps in the linkages between the two parties combined with obsolete patterns of interaction. This linkage network is often so inadequate that third-party mediation and linkage of the parties is required to deal with the dispute. This condition appears to occur frequently in situations where collective bargaining is beginning for the first time, as, for example, school systems and governmental agencies.

Conflicts between whites and blacks or other minority groups also are greatly aggravated by the absence of effective interaction-influence networks. Customarily, there is a lack of structure linking the blacks and whites and also a lack of structure within each party linking its component parts together for constructive problem solving.

Large universities lack effective interaction-influence networks

A similar picture emerges if we analyze, with the aid of Table 2-3, the interaction-influence networks of our large universities. The scores on Table 2-3 reveal that the formal interaction network between each of the three major sectors of the university—students, faculty, and administration—is seriously deficient. None of our large universities appears to have an interaction-influence network embracing all parts of the university through which efficient communication and problem solving can occur. Moreover, once decisions are reached, the interaction-influence networks of these universities do not create the levels of motivation and felt responsibility among all, or virtually all, students, faculty, and administrators to assure that the decisions will be effec-tively implemented. The present interaction-influence networks of our large universities are as inadequate for creating widespread responsibility as they are in their communication and problem-solving capabilities.

When other kinds of conflict are scored using Table 2-3, especially conflicts resulting in serious disruptions in normal operations, the outcome is the same. In every case, the social system in which the conflict takes place is archaic and woefully inadequate. Since such primitive forms of social systems are being used, it is surprising that the results of these conflicts are not more disastrous than we have experienced to date.

There are, however, grounds for encouragement. The analyses which reveal the serious inadequacies in the social systems point simultaneously to opportun-ities for improvement. The knowledge that enables these analyses to be made can be used equally well to guide corrective action, as we shall see in subsequent chapters.

Macro and micro conflicts

The strategy for resolving conflict more constructively, suggested in this chap-ter and developed more fully in the rest of the volume, is equally applicable to any conflict regardless of its scope, except for conflict within the individual. Intrapersonal conflicts are not discussed in this book. There is, however, an important difference between conflicts that involve relatively few persons, such as those between departments in a small firm, and those at the international level. It is much, much easier to create the needed linking structure and to change the interaction processes in the desired direction when the number of persons involved is relatively small and the structure simple (micro conflicts) than when the conflict involves large numbers of persons and complex institu-tions with strongly entrenched values and traditions (macro conflicts).

Much faster progress in improving the management of conflict, conse-quently, can be expected with micro than with macro conflicts. As persons acquire skill in successfully applying System 4 to the management of micro conflicts, they will become better equipped to use this approach in dealing with the much more complex problems of structure and interaction involved in macro conflicts. They will also have more faith and confidence in the undertak-ing.

3
Readiness for improving conflict management

The invention of the telescope by Galileo was a necessary preliminary to the development of astronomy as a science and as a body of knowledge. Newton had to invent the calculus to derive his laws of gravitation. The invention of the chronometer was essential to modern navigation. Every major advance in understanding the environment and the capacity to cope with it and with the problems of day-to-day living has been anticipated or accompanied by the creation of a methodology to make that step possible.

In addition to methodological resources, the rate of advance in a particular field depends upon two other factors: the availability of valid theory derived from research findings and the willingness of those in control to allocate adequate resources to the application effort. The degree of willingness depends, in part, upon the recognized seriousness and importance of the problem.

The development of polio vaccines and the harnessing of atomic energy are examples of the rapid progress that can occur when three conditions are present: (1) the necessary methodology, (2) a body of generalized knowledge based on research findings, (3) the allocation of adequate resources to the application effort. In each case, the relevant methodology and theory were present and substantial sums were made available for the developmental work and the application. The creation of the polio vaccines required tens of millions of dollars. The development of the first atomic bomb required more than a billion dollars, and many billions more have been spent on the hydrogen bomb and on the peaceful uses of atomic energy.

The management of conflict appears to be reaching a state of readiness for rapid and substantial improvement. As we shall see in this and subsequent chapters, social science research is close to providing the necessary methodology and the research-based theory. *It remains to be seen whether conflicts at local, regional, national, and international levels are felt to be sufficiently serious and threaten-*

ing for the gatekeepers of resources, such as foundations and the federal government, to make available the sizable amounts needed to bring about the rapid progress that now appears possible.

Important dimensions of social systems

In Chapter 2, two dimensions, the x and y axes, were used to define Systems 0, 1, 2, 3, and 4. Research shows that the addition of a few other dimensions enables one to state, with reasonable confidence, the operating chartertistics of any human organization and its level of performance, including its capacity to manage conflict constructively. These dimensions are listed in Table 3-1. Omitted from the table are variables which do not deal with social or human organizational aspects of a system, such as the adequacy of available capital and favorable or adverse geographic factors.

All the variables in Table 3-1 are causal[1] in character. The causal variables shown in Table 3-1 are responsible for a substantial proportion of the variation from organization to organization in the capacity to manage conflict well and to perform effectively (Bowers & Seashore, 1966; Taylor & Bowers, 1972).

Intervening variables, such as peer leadership, motivation, influence (control), and coordination, are not shown in Table 3-1 since the state of these variables in an organization is determined by the causal variables.

All these variables, both causal and intervening, can be measured with reliable instruments now available. These instruments will yield the same scores for a particular organization or unit irrespective of the investigator who does the measuring. (An excellent discussion of some of these instruments can be found in Taylor & Bowers, 1972). The measurement and use of many of the dimensions in Table 3-1 is considered in later chapters of this book when the nature of each variable and its use in the management of conflict is discussed.

Most of the human systems variables in Table 3-1 are unrelated and can vary independently of the others. Supportive behavior and team building, however, are related since team building always requires supportive behavior (see table 2-2). They both are included in Table 3-1 since, in addition to supportiveness, such team-building behavior as group problem solving and cooperative relationships among members are needed to build a System 4 organization.

---

[1]a. The *causal* variables are independent variables that can be altered directly by an organization and its management and that, in turn, determine the course of developments within the organization and the results achieved by that organization. The general level of business conditions, for example, although an independent variable, is *not* viewed as causal since the management of a particular enterprise ordinarily can do little about it. Causal variables include the structure of the organization, and management's objectives, policies, decisions, business and leadership strategies, skills, and behavior.

b. The *intervening* variables reflect the internal state, health, and performance capabilities of the organization, e.g., the loyalties, attitudes, motivations, performance goals, and perceptions of all members and their collective capacity for effective action, interaction, communication, and decision making.

c. The *end-result* variables are the dependent variables which reflect the achievements of the organization, such as its productivity, costs, scrap loss, earnings, and services rendered.

Table 3-1
Dimensions for measuring a human organization
and assessing its performance capabilities

I. Human organizational variables

    A. System 1–4 continuum. This variable is concerned with the motive sources used by an organization, the manner of using them, and the magnitude of effective motivation created. The state of this variable depends upon:

        1. Leadership

            a. Extent of supportive behavior applied in a culturally relative manner.*

            b. Extent of team-building behavior, including work-group problem solving applied in a culturally relative manner.

        2. Structure

            a. Extent to which the structure is compatible with the leadership processes, i.e., is person-to-person when the leadership is System 1-3 in character and is multiple overlapping group when the leadership is System 4 in character.

    B. Additional leadership variables

        1. Extent to which the leader has high performance goals and encourages subordinates to hold high performance goals.

        2. Level of technical competence of leader including both knowledge and skill concerning:

            a. His or her own technical field

            b. The administrative aspects of the job

            c. Interactional processes

                (1) Person-to-person

                (2) Groups

            d. Problem-solving processes

                (1) Cognitive

                (2) Cognitive combined with group building and maintenance.

---

*Members of organizations and units within them differ in their expectations as to the amount of supportive behavior their leaders will display, the extent to which they will involve members in decisions affecting them, and the extent to which the leaders will seek to use group problem solving in resolving work problems thereby building members into cohesive, cooperative teams. Members differ also in their level of skill in responding positively and effectively to their leaders' behavior. When leaders behave in "a culturally relative manner," they are meeting or exceeding the expectations of their members for support and involvement but not in excess of the members' ability to respond favorably.

Table 3-1   (Continued)

    3. Level of help with work (work facilitation) by leader. This combined:

       a. Capacity of leader to provide planning and necessary resources and equipment and to give technical and operational training and help

       b. The motivation to do so (supportive behavior).

  C. Additional structural variables

    1. Extent to which there is a variation from no structure to a structure which provides an optimum amount of differentiation with adequate vertical and horizontal (cross) linkages.

  D. Extent to which well-established working relationships exist among members of each organizational unit.

 II. Time is treated as a variable; i.e., relationships are examined over time among causal, intervening, and end-result variables.

Technical competence

The kind of technical competence that a superior needs varies with hierarchical levels. At low levels, the superior needs to be competent in the technology of the operation he or she is supervising. At higher levels, the superior requires very little of this kind of competence (Mann, 1965). The technological competence needed by persons at higher levels is in the skills required to build highly effective interaction-influence networks capable of efficient problem solving.

Possessing high technological competence, useful to a manager at lower levels, can become a liability as that person moves up the hierarchy. If that manager, upon promotion, "takes the job along," the responsibilities of the subordinates are diminished, if not usurped. As they move up the ladder in any kind of organization, such as business, governmental, educational, medical, and voluntary, superiors need to keep in mind the changing character of their position. They must not try to do the old job in addition to the new one. They must keep to their new role.

The director of a large medical research organization employed a novel reminder to himself that his job had changed. He had spent 30 years at a laboratory bench and was the top scientist in his field. Now he was the director. The executive officer of the organization noticed that this man had a white lab coat on a hanger in his office. He also discovered that the lab coat was laundered every two weeks. Finally, his curiosity overcame his reticence and he said to the director, "I notice that you have a freshly laundered lab coat hanging here, but I never have seen you wear it." The director smiled and said, "That's right. I have that lab coat laundered every two weeks as a nostalgic reminder of the happiest 30 years of my life. But I also have it hanging there as a reminder never to be such a damn fool as to put it on again."

Top leaders of organizations should encourage their high-level managers to be generalists, not masters of technical detail. Boards of directors never should expect top-level managers to have massive detail at their fingertips about all problems that may come to their attention. These details can be supplied, as needed, by persons whose job is to be thoroughly familiar with them. Technical competence is important but must fit the requirements of each level of responsibility. The concentration on minutiae by upper levels of management is an indication that the organization lacks a sufficiently effective interaction-influence network to supply information and technical help where and when they are needed.

Well-established working relationships

One of the variables listed in Table 3-1 has been so unrecognized and neglected that there is need to point to it explicitly and define it. This variable deals with the changes in an organization between the time when positions are filled with new people who do not know each other and the time when the organization has settled down into a smoothly functioning entity. Even if the best-possible structure were to exist for an organization or unit staffed with newly appointed persons, and even if they were the best possible personnel, the initial performance of the new operation would be significantly below its later performance. Working relationships have to be established. Members must come to know each other well enough to understand the communications coming to them from others. They must know what others mean by their comments and by their day-to-day behavior. Each person must learn his or her own role and that of every other member to whom that person must relate. Each work group in the organization has to develop the confidence, trust, loyalties, and favorable attitudes which characterize a highly effective group.

The extent to which well-established working relationships exist among its personnel is an important variable for every organization, whether it is System 2 or System 4 in character. There is, however, an important difference in the character of the working relationships finally established.

Hostility and fear among members will be greatest in System 1 organizations, less in System 2, and even less in System 3. In System 4 organizations and to some extent in System 3, favorable attitudes replace hostility, and working relationships become cooperative. Members of System 4 organizations seek to help one another, and their motivation and capacity to cooperate become substantial as their working relationships are firmly established.

System 4T: The total model

An organization which scores high on all the variables in Table 3-1 will be referred to as a "System 4 Total model organization (System 4T)." Those which score high on the System 1 to 4 scale, but whose scores on the other variables are not known, will be referred to simply as "System 4" organizations.

The System 4T model is concerned with the human aspects of an organization. This includes all the variables in Table 3-1 except time, namely:

1. The System 1 to 4 continuum

2. The levels of performance goals

3. The level of technical competence

4. The level of help with work

5. The nature of the organizational structure

6. The level of established working relationships

It is necessary to know the present state of each of these variables and trends in them to estimate with reasonable accuracy the organization's capacity to manage conflict and its level of performance. An organization must score high on *all* these variables to be highly effective as a social system. If an organization, or a department, scores high on the System 1 to 4 scale and low on one or more of the other dimensions, such as technical competence or level of performance goals, the probabilities are great that it will not be highly effective in conflict management or in performance.

Human system variables successfully differentiate effective from ineffective organizations

One indication of the potential value of the available methodology and theory for improving conflict management is the extent to which the System 4T model proves to be more effective than other social systems. This can be assessed by measuring on the human system variables (table 3-1) several business enterprises that are comparable in technology and size but that differ in their ability to resolve conflicts and also in their productivity, earnings, and other end-result variables. The scores of each organization on human system variables can be used to array them from best to poorest. Their position on this listing and their performance data can be compared by inspection or by multivariate analysis.

When either inspection or the more elaborate statistical tests are used, the results show that the human system dimensions do a consistently good job of differentiating organizations as to the results they achieve in their conflict management and in their performance. As we shall see in Chapter 5 and subsequent chapters, a rapidly increasing body of data shows that the closer a firm, division, or profit center approaches the System 4T model, the more successfully it manages conflict and the higher are its productivity and earnings.

The accuracy of estimating the performance of an organization from the human system dimensions is much greater, moreover, when the trends over time are taken into account. Research findings show that changes in performance may lag as much as one to five years behind changes in the causal variables. The larger the organization, the longer the lag time tends to be. The marked effect of trends over time upon observed relationships between the causal variables and organizational performance is discussed at length in Chapter 5 of *The Human Organization* (Likert, 1967; see also Likert & Bowers, 1969.)

The existence of general principles

Many persons believe that there are no universally applicable principles. This view leads to the conclusion that the System 4T theory and the human systems dimensions cannot be generally applicable. This conclusion, as we shall see, is unwarranted. The view that there are no generally applicable principles is based on an erroneous interpretation of the work of French, Israel, and Aas (1960), Lawrence and Lorsch (1967), Sanford (1950), Tannenbaum (1954), Vroom (1960), Woodward (1965), and many others.

French et al. (1960) repeated in Norway a study done by Coch and French in the United States. Their results overall were similar: Participation improved performance. They found, however, that those workers who felt that it was legitimate for them to be involved in decisions related to their work responded much more favorably than did those who felt it was not legitimate.

These findings are consistent with the view of Lewin (1951) that behavior (B) is a function (f) of the person (P) and of that person's environment (E), i.e., $B = (f)(P,E)$. Before applying Lewin's formula it will be useful to mention some research findings.

Whenever persons in an organization are asked to answer Tables 2-1 and 2-2 so as to describe their organization as it is *now* and then to answer the table describing what they would *like* their organization to be, a consistent pattern emerges. This pattern has been found to occur wherever these questions were asked in the United States, Europe, and Asia. Irrespective of where people see their organization at present, whether System 1, 2, or 3, they invariably would like it to be closer to System 4. Although they want it to be closer to System 4 than at present, they usually want it to be only somewhat closer. They may desire a shift from System 2½ to System 3, but they virtually never want a shift in one jump from System 2 or 2½ to System 4. Persons apparently recognize that they can respond effectively to a modest shift and may view it as legitimate but do not wish a huge jump.

Substantial research shows that if a moderate shift toward System 4T occurs, the persons affected respond favorably in both attitude and behavior, such as performance. A shift is moderate when it falls within the range of the expectations, skills, and interaction capabilities of those persons affected by it. If a shift is greater than the capacity of the persons involved to respond to it effectively, the response will be less favorable than to a moderate shift. There also may be some negative reactions caused by the insecurity produced by a sudden large shift (Likert, 1961; Tannenbaum, 1954). After a moderate shift toward System 4T has occurred, and the personnel affected have become accustomed through socialization to the new management system pattern, they then typically desire a further shift toward System 4T. If this further shift occurs, there will be an additional improvement in attitude and behavior. Each additional shift is found to bring further improvement. As these shifts occur and the organization approaches the System 4T pattern, there tends to be better and better performance. System 4T organizations display typically 20 to 40 percent or more superiority in performance compared with System 2 organizations (see chap. 5).

Every organization socializes its members to desire and expect the kind of management system it employs. System 1 organizations create in their members the skills required to live and perform in that kind of organization. System 4 organizations produce the skills required to function effectively in a System 4 manner. One can expect, consequently, to find in any organization persons who can perform the leadership and other roles required by that kind of an organization, whether it is System 1, 2, 3, or 4.

An example of the way an organization socializes its personnel to fit its characteristics is shown in the data from two assembly plants in the same company and located in the same labor market. One plant was the highest-producing assembly plant in the company; the other was the poorest in all performance dimensions. In the highest-producing plant, which had a System 4 manager, one-third of all personnel at the general foreman level or above scored in the high System 3 or System 4 range as seen by their subordinates. In the poor-producing plant with a System 1½ manager only one-eighth of the personnel at that level scored that high.

Returning now to Lewin's model. A shift by an organization toward System 4 is a favorable change in the environment (E) and yields a corresponding improvement in the behavior (B) of members of the organization. But a second important change also occurs. The change in the environment, i.e., the moderate shift toward System 4, produces also through the processes of socialization a change in the persons (P) in the organization. They become accustomed to the new management system pattern that is closer to System 4. After they have become accustomed to the new pattern, they would like a further shift toward System 4. This process of becoming accustomed to the management system after each change toward System 4 has occurred takes time, usually six months to one year for each shift. The significant fact, however, is that the (P) part of the equation is changing as well as the (E) part. Persons in the organization are progressively shifting closer to System 4 both in what they would like and what they respond to favorably.

The (P) part of the equation in Lewin's model is not fixed and invariable as is so often assumed in contingency models and in the situational view of leadership. Of course, leaders should display a leadership style that fits the expectations, skills, and interaction capabilities of those who are in subordinate positions. Similarly, organizations and departments should use management systems that are within the range of expectations and skills of their members. But to assume that these situational factors are inflexible and incapable of changing is to assume that the system is static and that the expectations, skills, and interaction capabilities are incapable of changing. This is an unwarranted assumption. All organizations and institutions should be viewed as dynamic systems within which the P factors as well as the E factors can change. Socialization processes can change the expectations, skills, and interaction capabilities of the persons in any organization.

Since System 4 organizations achieve substantially better productivity, quality, labor relations, employee satisfaction, and employee health, both physical and mental, it is essential that the dynamic view of organizations be adhered to and that efforts be made to change at appropriate rates both the P and E dimensions in every organization.

When organizations are viewed from a dynamic rather than from a static point of view, the System 4T concepts are applicable. When they are applied in a way and at a rate appropriate to the situation, substantial improvement in performance and other dimensions occurs.

Woodward's findings (1965) have been viewed as demonstrating that principles and management systems such as System 4T cannot be generally applicable. This is based on her studies showing that firms using different kinds of manufacturing processes displayed quite different patterns of organization. For example, batch manufacturing firms have a different structure from continuous-process firms. Studies by the Institute for Social Research and Rensis Likert Associates support this conclusion; we find that assembly plants have different organizational structures from oil refineries. But we also find that within each kind of plant or industry, the higher-performing plant or department is more likely to have a System 4 multiple overlapping-group structure and the lower-producing plant or department a person-to-person System 2 kind of structure (Likert, 1973b; McCullough, 1975; Toronto, 1972; see also Mohr, 1971.) (These kinds of structures are discussed in chap. 10.)

The finding that each kind of industry requires a form of organizational structure that fits its particular need does not mean that each plant's peculiar characteristics alone should determine its unique situational structure and that there are no other general principles applicable to structure. Lawrence and Lorsch's differentiation and integration principles, for example, are applicable as well as other principles of structure.

Lawrence and Lorsch (1967) use concepts of "differentiation" and "integration" as though they viewed them as general principles. They state: "the evidence indicates that high differentiation plus effective conflict resolution leads to high integration, and these are the overall conditions organizations must attain to be effective in this type of environment" (p. 82).

As to differentiation, they say: "Our research indicates that the clear-cut and formal differentiation of organizational units, when based on significant task and environmental differences, contributes to good performance" (p. 213). They stress that differentiation always should be adequate but not excessive. They provide an excellent conceptual framework for analyzing any organization to be certain that the enterprise has an optimum amount of differentiation (pp. 213–218).

Integration is defined by Lawrence and Lorsch (1967) as "the quality of the state of collaboration that exists among departments that are required to achieve unity of effort by the demands of the environment" (p. 11). With integration, as with differentiation, Lawrence and Lorsch describe the general character of the desirable state each organization should strive to achieve concerning that concept. They make clear, as they did when discussing differentiation, that the specific steps and procedures used to achieve integration must be appropriate to that specific situation.

They found that to be successful every firm must apply the two concepts of differentiation and integration, but it must do so in ways that are appropriate to its situation. They point out, for example, that these concepts were applied quite differently in three different industries: plastics, food, and container. They report that the food and plastics organizations are much more differentiated than are the container firms, and they discuss, in terms of the guidelines they propose for applying differentiation, why this should be the case. They also found that in the more successful firms, these two concepts were applied in ways which met the requirements of their particular situation better.

Lawrence and Lorsch's use of these concepts follows the same general orientation toward principles as that stated for the variables proposed in Table 3-1. In each case, *the general concept or variable must be applied in each specific situation in ways that fit that situation in an optimum or appropriate manner.*

Concerning the general applicability of System 4T, it is significant that Lawrence and Lorsch (1967) report findings revealing that the more productive and successful firms in their study apply the principle of supportive relationships more extensively than do the less successful. The statements by the personnel of the high-performing and low-performing organizations, quoted by Lawrence and Lorsch, reveal this to be the case. In the low-performing organizations, for example, punitive behavior ("a guy with a red hot bayonet") and the reliance on hierarchical authority are much more prevalent than in the high. When the reported behavior of managers is scored on the tables shown in Chapter 2, their high-performing organizations score toward System 4 and the low-performing score toward System 1 on the System 1-4 scale.

As Lawrence and Lorsch report, this substantially greater amount of supportive behavior in the high-performing firms contributes to their greater success in resolving cross-function conflicts constructively and in achieving effective integration. Moreover, in dealing with conflict, the high-performing firms made much greater use than did the low of what Lawrence and Lorsch call "confrontation," which they define as "problem solving." Work-group problem solving, properly done, is characteristic of System 4 (see Table 3-1) and contributes to the constructive resolution of conflicts. It is discussed at length in Chapters 7, 8, and 9 of this volume.

There is ample evidence that general principles and models such as System 4T can be applied universally and can be of great value. But if these general principles and models are to yield valuable results in specific situations, they always must be applied in ways appropriate to the situation. The application is made in each instance in a culturally relative manner since there has to be a good fit of principle to situation (Likert, 1961, chap. 7).

System 4T seeks to use general principles in this manner. This is illustrated by the principle of supportive relationships which states that the leader must behave so that *"each member will, in the light of his background, values, and expectations, view the experience as supportive and one which builds and maintains his sense of personal worth and importance"* (Likert, 1961, p. 103). As will be observed, this principle explicitly states that supportive treatment of persons should always be done in a culturally relative manner, i.e., in ways which fit the particular situation.

Principles never should be applied in a rigid, uniform manner regardless of the requirements of the specific situation. All the principles in the System 4T model should be applied in each particular situation in the specific ways which are most relevant and appropriate. One always must "temper the wind to the shorn lamb." A parent would apply the principle of supportive relationships differently in dealing with a four year old than in dealing with an adult. There is a fundamental difference between a principle and an act or technique for applying it.

Human systems dimensions and System 4T are widely applicable

A general organizational theory, if it is universal, should be applicable to the interaction-influence networks of every kind of organization and institution. Confirming these theoretical expectations, data now becoming available show that the human systems dimensions shown in Table 3-1 work well when applied to widely different kinds of nonbusiness organizations, such as governmental agencies, libraries, military installations, hospitals and medical centers, school systems, universities, and voluntary organizations. Even more relevant are the findings now emerging which reveal that the superiority of the System 4T model is as great in nonbusiness fields as in business in enabling an organization to manage conflict and to accomplish its objectives efficiently.[2]

[2]See Alger, 1965; Bernhardt, 1972; Byrnes, 1973; Carr, 1971; Cullers, Hughes, & McCreal, 1973; Feitler & Blumberg, 1971; Ferris, 1965; Georgopoulos & Mann, 1962; Georgopoulos and Matejko, 1967; Gibson, 1974; Gilbert, 1972; Haynes, 1972; Katz & Kahn, 1966; Ketchel, 1972; Lepkowski, 1970; Marchant, 1971; NTRDA, 1970; Rensis Likert Associates, 1972; Riedel, 1974; Smallridge, 1972; Tannenbaum, 1958; Tannenbaum & Donald, 1957; Thompson, 1971; Wagstaff, 1970; Warwick et al., 1975; White, 1971a, 1971b, 1971c, 1971d.

The interaction between an organization and its environment

In applying a general organizational theory, it is important to keep in mind that there is constant interaction between an organization and its external environment. As Gestalt theory and open systems theory remind us, every organization or institution exists in an environment, never in a vacuum. The interaction that occurs is influenced by the management systems of the organization and the management systems of the external environment. When the organizations and their external environments all are using substantially the same management system, there are no problems caused by incompatibility.

When an organization is using a different management system from the external environment, problems are likely to be created. Thus a System 4 organization in an environment whose organizations and institutions are largely System 1 or 2 will experience a variety of pressures to move to a management system similar to the predominant characteristics of the external environment. The System 4 organization simultaneously will be creating forces in the external environment to move it toward System 4.

In this situation, the System 4 organization will experience pressure in a variety of ways. For example, newly employed personnel from a System 1 or 2 environment will expect to use System 1 or 2 leadership behavior if employed as supervisors or managers. This will cause strong resentment and hostile attitudes among those supervised who expect System 4 supportive leadership. Similarly, the competitive rather than cooperative behavior shown by new supervisors from a System 1 or 2 environment will cause friction and stress in their relations with their colleagues. If the new employees were nonsupervisory, they would feel incapable of responding to the System 4 leadership and would feel threatened and insecure.

There also would be some problems of relationships between the System 4 organization and its System 2 suppliers and customers. Dealing with conflicts would be more difficult.

The System 4 organization would have to undertake appropriate steps to meet these problems. In hiring, it should select persons oriented more toward System 4 than is the average applicant. It should provide orientation and training to help new employees experience the System 4 patterns of interaction under favorable conditions so as to help them shift rapidly, easily, and with a sense of accomplishment to this style of behavior.

The System 4 organization should modify its behavior in relation to its customers and suppliers by initially using a System 3 model so that those with whom it deals will feel more comfortable than with a model more remote from their experience. When the persons it deals with are able to make the additional shift, it could move closer to System 4 in its behavior pattern.

Any conflict that might develop between the System 4 organizations and the System 2 institutions in their environment would again create problems. The institutions in a System 1 or 2 environment would be likely to use a win-lose power approach. Skillful, patient efforts on the part of the System 4 organization would be required to convert the conflict-resolution efforts to a win-win pattern.

Comparable, but opposite, problems would be encountered by a System 2 organization in relating to a System 4 environment. Again efforts would be required to establish effective and productive relationships.

Every organization needs to be alert to its environment and its interaction with all parts of that environment. When incompatibilities exist, action should be taken to assure that the interaction yields positive rather than negative results.

Research strategy for improving conflict management

The nature of many of today's most serious conflicts, e.g., urban or racial riots, major strikes, international disputes that reach a bitter or violent stage, is such that research focused directly on them is complex and difficult, and progress is necessarily slow. To make rapid, economical progress in this kind of social science research, the cause and effect cycles should be of short duration and numerous so that a large number of observations are obtained readily. The independent (causal) variables should be clearly recognized, not confused with symptoms, and should be readily measurable. The measurements of the outcome occurring in each cycle should have little error. These conditions for rapid and efficient progress in research are not present in most major conflicts. Studies designed to discover cause and effect relationships make much slower progress and require vastly more data when the cycles are few and long, when causes and symptoms are confused, and when the performance criteria are inadequate, inaccurate, or "rare events" phenomena. Urban riots, for example, are "rare events" phenomena since, fortunately, they occur in any one city infrequently. Under these conditions, starting *de novo* in research on the problem and gradually establishing cause and effect relationships is a slow, costly process requiring a large number of observations over a long period of time.

Studies of organizational theory, interaction-influence networks, and conflict management in business firms do not suffer from the handicaps which make research costly and progress slow in complex, nonbusiness conflict situations. It is always possible to find among business firms situations which offer excellent conditions for conducting organizational research in a highly efficient manner. These conditions include: (1) relatively accurate measurements of performance or outcome, (2) the short time span of the cause and effect cycles enabling observations and analyses to be made without waiting long periods to discover the outcome, (3) the large populations of cause and effect cycles providing a large number of observations and conclusions that are statistically significant even though the differences are only moderate or small in magnitude. Research in business on organizational theory and conflict management can be efficient and make relatively rapid progress.

Organizational research in business sites, consequently, can provide the relevant general principles and social system theory needed to accelerate the progress of coping with serious conflicts in other situations. The fundamental variables dealt with in organizational research in business firms are essentially the same as those involved in serious conflicts elsewhere, namely, such variables as leadership, technical competence, level and nature of goals, decision making, motivation, communication, influence, interaction, and the structure through which interactions occur.

When the research in business organizations has discovered better general principles and more effective social systems, the applicability of these findings to a particular conflict situation can be tested readily by using the wide variety of data usually available or easily obtained. For example, in most conflict situations it is relatively easy to obtain measurements showing the nature of the existing attitudes and the accuracy or inaccuracy of the communications between the opposing parties. One test of the effectiveness of different social systems for managing conflict, therefore, can be made by seeing which social system produces the least hostile, most favorable attitudes along with the most accurate perceptions of each party by the other.

The System 4T model is being tested in some nonbusiness situations and appears to be as effective in dealing with conflict there as it is in business firms. It seems reasonable to assume that further tests will demonstrate it to be generally applicable in all kinds of conflict situations.

The best social system and the soundest principles, however, are of little value in resolving conflict unless knowledge and skills for applying them successfully in a particular conflict situation are present. Fortunately, the same research strategies and procedures that have yielded better principles and social systems can be used to discover and refine better ways of applying them. Research on the principles and methods of changing organizations to improve conflict management can make rapid and efficient progress in appropriate business sites where performance-criteria measurements are accurate and where there are many cause and effect cycles of short duration. Once better principles and methods have been discovered for helping any organization change to a System 4T model of operation, the effectiveness of these principles and methods can be tested in nonbusiness situations in the manner suggested above.

Unfortunately, a substantial proportion of present-day conflicts make use of social systems, such as System 2, which rely on win-lose confrontation as the major means of coping with conflict. Before discussing the use of the System 4T model to improve conflict management, we shall examine the costly consequence of win-lose confrontation.

4

Inadequacies in prevailing methods for coping with conflict

Win-lose, in one form or another, appears to be the prevailing strategy for resolving conflicts. Confrontation, nonnegotiable demands, and ultimatums have become the order of the day as *the* way to deal with deep-seated differences. One party marshals all its forces to compel the other party to do what the first has decided it wants. Confrontation is from a fixed position and seeks to mobilize the power to win. Win-lose strategy is used in a wide variety of situations, such as struggles for civil rights; urban riots; student demonstrations and sit-ins; international conflicts; union-management disagreements; a hearing on next year's budget; a controversy between departments in business, such as sales and manufacturing, or the personnel department and a line department; a controversy between two federal agencies; disagreements between central headquarters and field offices; or controversy between professional staff and the lay board of a voluntary agency. What happens when the win-lose approach to conflict is used? What are its costs and other consequences?

The character of win-lose conflict is revealed by studies of both experimental and actual situations. It is striking to note how successful laboratory and field experiments can be in generating the same hostility and strong emotional reactions as those occurring in real-life, win-lose conflict. (See Blake & Mouton, 1968; Blake, Shepard, & Mouton, 1964; Maier, 1967; Sherif, 1956, 1962, 1967; Sherif, Harvey, White, Hood, & Sherif, 1961; Sherif & Sherif, 1953.) Studies of experimental situations are valuable in being able to reveal in greater detail and clarity than is possible in actual situations the dynamics of win-lose conflicts, the factors contributing to intensifying the conflicts, and the nature of the negative results that usually emerge.

A particularly valuable series of experiments by Blake and colleagues (Blake et al., 1964) has been described as follows:

> The subjects were members of more than 150 almost-identical groups which were matched according to personal characteristics and other relevant dimensions. Each study has been repeated, as necessary, to verify conclusions.

EXPERIMENTAL SETTING

The setting for these industrial experiments can be described as follows: twenty to thirty executives came together for two weeks to discuss interpersonal and intergroup relations in their own behavior as well as those characteristic of their organization. Aspects of interpersonal and intergroup relations were first experienced by the executives in a series of controlled laboratory experiments. The experiments were then evaluated and analyzed as a basis for generalizations about organizational dynamics.

INGROUP PHASE

During the first meetings as each group tackled the conference problems, some degree of ingroup cohesiveness developed, along with some frustration and fears that it was floundering. Concern lest the other group might be doing a better job was expressed in cautious questioning and kidding of members at coffee breaks and meal times. The natural trend of this intergroup comparison was in a negative and invidious direction.

INTERGROUP PHASE

The competitive feelings underlying intergroup comparison created an eagerness in both groups to engage in a contest. Hence, the necessary conditions were present for studying the dynamics of intergroup conflict.

At this point, each group was provided an identical problem for which it was to find the "best" solution. The solutions were then evaluated with one being chosen as the better of the two. Because the atmosphere of the conferences induced deep involvement of the participants, this test of their groups' performance had psychological reality for them. . . .

At the point where intergroup competitiveness emerges in the experiments, the fundamental significance of the win-lose dynamic appears. When the goal "to win" is accepted by a group, it has a spontaneous power to mobilize team effort and to give it character and direction. The consequences for ingroup and intergroup life are substantial when the goal of each side is to win.

The consequences of a win-lose struggle[1]

When intergroup conflict occurs with the orientation of winning, there is a complete loss of interest in any other outcome, such as finding a mutually acceptable solution. Some highly important developments begin to happen rapidly in the embattled groups. There is an immediate increase in group

---

[1]The material in this chapter which describes the win-lose struggle and its consequences draws very heavily upon the work of Blake, Shepard, & Mouton, 1964; it also borrows from the work of Maier (1963, 1967) and Sherif (1967). All these publications present valuable and insightful material and are recommended reading. The material in the chapter is also supported by other research, as the citations indicate.

loyalty and team spirit. It is largely of a superficial rather than of an enduring nature, but it increases substantially. Members close ranks, spirits go up, and everyone starts working hard (Mulder & Stemerding, 1963).

This closing of ranks and the accompanying sharp focus on accomplishing the immediate tasks required for winning has serious costs. Differences of opinion among members, which can lead to new and better solutions, are no longer tolerated. Questioning of decisions and requests for their reexamination are no longer permitted. Any member who is skeptical of the soundness of a decision, however hastily arrived at, is rebuffed, and pressures are put on him or her to conform—or get out (Festinger, Schachter, & Back, 1950; Maier, 1967; Schachter, 1968). All this snuffs out diversity and disagreement and eliminates the processes which lead to the most creative problem solving and the best solutions (Pelz, 1967; Pelz & Andrews, 1966).

A second development in a win-lose struggle is that leadership in the group migrates rapidly to a few persons or to a single person. A clear-cut power structure emerges quite rapidly. All too often it is the aggressive person or the ones who express themselves clearly and well who take over. Sometimes those who like fights emerge in leadership positions. Those members who can provide the best leadership and the most skillful leadership processes often are submerged along with the questioning and sounder thinking which they would foster.

This "steamroller" method of dealing with people lays the foundation for serious internal strife which often backfires after the pressures created by the intergroup conflict subside. This may set the group back seriously in efforts it subsequently may make to become a highly effective group.

Perceptual distortion

Perception is the key to behavior. The way persons see things determines the way they will act. If their perceptions are distorted, the distortions are reflected in their behavior. The experiments by Blake, Sherif, Maier and others reveal that one of the most sinister consequences of a win-lose struggle is the sizable distortions it creates in the judgment and the perceptual processes of the opposing groups. The group members see the work of their own group as superb and downgrade that of the opposing group. Even when differences in quality between the solutions produced by the two conflicting groups is measurable, this distortion still occurs. The members of each group see the product of their work as far superior to that of the other group. All capacity for objective perception is wiped out by the struggle.

The perceptual distortions occur not only with regard to the product each group produces but also are manifest in the perceptions of the other group. The members of each group develop and express hostile attitudes toward the members of the other. This, in turn, increases the hostility as well as the errors in the perceptions as to the feelings and behavior of the other group members.

Confidence and trust in them are obliterated, and only hostile distrust of the other's motives and behavior remains. The perceptual distortion caused in a win-lose struggle greatly aggravates the conflict.

Perceptual errors occur also in the group's views of the representatives they select. Each group tends to select individuals seen as strong, aggressive, and good spokespersons for its solution. These representatives are seen by members of *both* groups as mature, competent, intelligent, and well-intended human beings *before* they start performing their role. But once they start serving in this capacity and start presenting the excellence of the solution of their own group and pointing to the inadequacies in the solution of the other, they are seen as superb by their own group and as incompetent and irresponsible and less than well-intentioned by the other.

Along with perceptual biases which develop as each group and its representatives press the superiority of its solution go other distortions in the intellectual processes of each group. These are manifest in many ways. For example, when each group is asked to study the solution of the other group to the point where it says it knows it well, and when its members are then given an objective test on the content of the solution of each group, important differences are revealed. These differences reflect the intellectual distortions present and the likely effect of these distortions on the capacity for objective thinking. Two kinds of errors occur which tend to magnify the differences between the groups and intensify the conflict.

The members of each group fail to see the similarities in the two solutions and see only the differences between their solution and that of the other group. The most common error shown by the test is that items present in both solutions are seen as occurring only in one. Group members correctly recognize the items in their solution but fail to see that these same elements are present in the other solution. Seeing the solutions as being much different from what they really are magnifies appreciably the size of the conflict. *Areas of agreement are seen much less than is actually the case.*

The other kind of intellectual error shown by the objective test is that each group understands its own solution far better than it understands the other. This occurs even though both groups have studied the solutions until they feel they know them well. The distinctive items, i.e., those which are present in one solution only, are remembered best by all persons, but the members of each group correctly identify more of the distinctive items in their own solution than they are able to identify in the other (Blake et al., 1964).

These cognitive blind spots, demonstrated in this experiment, are similar to those found in research on communication and attitude change. Persons who hold a particular point of view select from the mass media material which supports their own biases and read and remember such material. They tend to ignore information contrary to their point of view. Even when they do read it, they reject it and forget it rapidly (Hovland et al., 1957).

The effect of the win-lose orientation and the attitudes and perceptual distortions which it creates are clearly manifest when the groups start to evaluate the solutions. After the positions of each group have been studied, the groups meet to ask questions through their representative to assure a complete understanding of the solution of the other group. The questions asked, however, soon show that the motivations of the members of each group are to disparage, reveal weaknesses, and in other ways to demonstrate the inferiority of the solution of the opposing group. Although the designated purposes of these sessions is to improve the objective understanding of each solution, the win-lose struggle intensifies the conflict and the questions contribute to heightened distortion, not to objective understanding (Gibb, 1961).

These forces are felt keenly by the representatives. When the representatives are presenting their group's solution and pointing to its superiority, they soon find they dare not take an objective point of view. To do so is seen as likely to lead to defeat for their group's solution. To recognize the strengths in the "enemy's" position and to admit the weaknesses in one's own solution is too hazardous when victory is sought at all costs. There are great and continuous pressures on each representative not to be objective. Even though representatives may feel they are acting with reasonable objectivity, they rarely do so. The group pressure and the perceptual and intellectual distortions prevent objectivity. Despite their efforts to do a competent, unbiased job, most representatives soon engage in attacking, parrying, and probing for weaknesses in the other's position. Winning becomes paramount and objectivity is forgotten.

The representative who wins for his or her group becomes its hero. The one who loses becomes a "heel." If, in the negotiations, the loser has displayed any behavior which could be construed as capitulating to the enemy, that individual is branded as a traitor. Even the slightest admission of weakness or failure to press a point strongly may result in the losing representative's being treated as a turncoat by the group. Thus, the hero, to win, and the loser, to avoid being seen as a traitor, both discard objectivity in their role as representatives and never engage in unbiased problem solving and evaluation of the solutions (Blake et al., 1964).

Impact of win-lose on group improvement

There are additional costs of the win-lose orientation of conflict. The winning group glorifies its leaders under whom it achieved success. The group becomes "fat and happy," coasts, and rests. There is little motivation to strive for improvement. The group members make little or no effort to analyze their performance to see how it could have been done better, nor do they look at their group processes to see how these could be improved. While they smugly glory in their success, all their weaknesses continue unchanged.

The defeated group displays bitterness among members. Internal fighting and splintering occur. Cliques and factions emerge. The aggressive leaders and those who took over early in the consolidation of the group in response to the win-lose battle are rejected. There is a substantial shift in the acceptance and status of different members. The rejected leaders may fight back and heighten the split in the group. This internal struggle may be quite intense, and the group may be so badly shattered that it is never able to recover and develop into an effective group.

Many of the defeated groups, however, after these initial responses, tend to become "lean and hungry." Sober analyses are undertaken to discover what led to the defeat. How and in what way could a better job have been done? As problem solving takes place on how the group should carry out its strategies and its tasks so as to increase the likelihood of victory next time, the cohesiveness of the group begins to return. Often, a defeated group emerges from the conflict much better prepared for win-lose combat than when it started. The "fat and happy" victorious group, on the other hand, may emerge as a less effective group than at the start of the conflict. Its own smugness blinds it to weaknesses that exist in its capacity for effective decision making and group performance in a win-lose struggle (Blake et al., 1964).

The cost of chronic defeat

When a defeated group *continues* to experience defeat, it is often unable to learn from its experience and become more effective. Chronic losers in win-lose struggles suffer a debilitating effect and display a protective response which has serious adverse impact on their capacity to perform useful services for their organization. This has been described well by Shepard[2] (1964):

> One of the major problems with which we have to contend in intergroup relations is that of chronically defeated groups. Many industrial organizations have them. Staff groups, for example, have by administrative design less power than line groups, so the experience of chronic defeat is fairly common in staff groups.
>
> The chronically defeated group develops certain characteristics. Such a group tends to divide into subgroups and to develop both cliques and social isolates. There is also mutual disparagement among the cliques. Rumor, especially gloomy rumor, is usually abundant. The group itself becomes unattractive to its members. Some members leave, and those who leave are usually considered the "good" ones, leaving those who remain to become even more insecure. The group develops a "servant" self-image; it stops initiating ideas, squashes would-be innovators, and does only what it is sure will be wanted by superiors. An increasing bureaucratization takes place, partly to prevent potentially dangerous ideas from getting out to the line and bringing more trouble to the group. The group perceives itself as a weak competitor of groups with related functions. Other groups are no longer seen as entities to be cooperated with, but as more

[2]From *Power and Conflict in Organizations,* edited by Robert L. Kahn and Elise Boulding, © 1964 by the Foundation for Research on Human Behavior, Basic Books, Inc., Publishers, New York, pp. 134–135.

powerful groups with which this group must compete but against which it cannot win. In short, as the group comes to feel less and less valued, its capacity to respond adequately deteriorates.

It is in a vicious downward cycle. Its self-image of defeat leads to inappropriate activities and inaction which confirm its estimate of itself. Stopping at or revising the cycle normally requires active intervention from outside the group. Rarely does initiative arise within. Of course, chronically defeated groups may never occur in an organization which is structured to avoid such destructive cycles. But, once a certain level of defeatism and low self-esteem has been established, deterioration proceeds rapidly unless strategic counteracting forces are introduced.

The chronically defeated group illustrates, again, the personal and social costs of conflicts not constructively resolved.

The win-lose pattern summarized

As we have seen, the win-lose approach to conflict resolution generally creates forces which aggravate the struggle and does relatively little to discover innovative, constructive solutions acceptable to all. In summary, the win-lose approach typically displays the following:

1. As the conflict starts and the group sets out to win, group cohesion mounts rapidly. The group closes ranks against the "enemy."

2. Leadership becomes more concentrated, with the more aggressive or those who express themselves better taking over. The power structure becomes clear and establishes control.

3. The deliberative processes of the group become accelerated with less and less time permitted for disagreements and for questioning the advantages of alternate courses of action. The diversity in outlook necessary for creative problem solving is snuffed out as the group concentrates on achieving unanimity rapidly.

4. The subjugation of differences and refusal to permit disagreements and their constructive resolution lay the groundwork for internal strife after the win-lose battle is over.

5. Judgmental and perceptual distortions occur and become progressively greater. The solution of one's own group is seen as superior; the solution of the other group is seen as distinctly inferior. Even when measurable differences in the solutions demonstrate the superiority of one, the other group fails to perceive and accept them. Heightened conflict eliminates objectivity.

6. These perceptual distortions are extended to each group's view of the other. The attitudes become increasingly hostile. Confidence and trust disappear. As the conflict continues, similar distortions develop and grow in each group's perceptions of the representatives of the two groups. Their own representa-

tive is seen more and more favorably, the "enemy" representative less and less so.

7. Distortions occur in the intellectual as well as in the perceptual processes. Memory biases occur which magnify the conflict: differences in positions are remembered, commonalities are overlooked or forgotten. Each group understands its own proposal better than that of the other group even after careful study of the other proposal.

8. Representatives are put under pressure by each group to win. There are great pressures not to be objective or innovative or to seek the best solution but to win at any cost by parrying, jabbing, and probing for weaknesses in the other's proposal. Representatives who win are treated as heroes by their group; the losers are often viewed by their own group as traitors.

The brilliant experimentation by Blake, Maier, Sherif, and their colleagues, briefly summarized above, shows that, regardless of where conflicts occur and who is involved, all forms of win-lose conflict display the same basic patterns of interaction and have the same impact on intellectual and emotional processes. They heighten commitment by each side to its initial position, block accurate evaluation of other situations, and halt any further search for creative, constructive solutions satisfactory to all.

Each side endeavors to have accepted as the final solution the one at which it had arrived prior to the confrontation. Since disagreements in win-lose confrontation are not resolved to the full satisfaction of all concerned, a substantial residue of unresolved conflict and hostility usually remains. This is true even though a solution has presumably been reached. This residue in the form of hostile, resentful attitudes, especially on the part of the group experiencing the greater defeat, provides a fertile seedbed for the germination and growth of more bitter conflict. Every situation, subsequently, is viewed through hostile and suspicious eyes, and the intentions and motives of the opposing group are always suspect.

The erroneous perceptions that each holds of the other are continued and further distorted by the absence of accurate and reassuring communication. Sometimes there is practically no communication between them. Often what communication takes place is biased. Anxieties stimulated by the continuing hostility and lack of communication lead to reveries which enlarge, exaggerate, and intensify the actual differences and produce even more hostile attitudes. Members of each side feel the need to demonstrate their loyalty by viewing every development with suspicion and by unconsciously exaggerating its adverse significance in discussions with members of their group.

Since there is no mechanism present for the correction of these mutually distorted views and since effective mechanisms are at work to continue and strengthen these distortions, hostile attitudes are always present below the surface. Any event, no matter how trivial, can trigger them into a first-rate conflictual outbreak.

In win-lose conflict, each side seeks to mobilize all the power and authority available to compel the other party to accept its decision. When necessary and possible, coalitions are formed and alliances established by one or both sides to mobilize more power in support of each side's preferred solution. Every effort is made by each side to give the least and gain the most from its original position. Each seeks to outwit the other side and to compel it, against its will, to accept the other's preferred solution.

Powerful motive sources create intense emotional reactions

In win-lose conflicts, the emotional responses are commonly quite strong. Even in temporary groups formed of strangers, whose members are aware of the experimental character of the interaction, strong reactions are elicited. In one experiment using two gangs of boys in a camp setting to test the effects of win-lose confrontation, hostilities became so great that the experiment had to be terminated. Even then, the hatreds remained so strong that the camp had difficulty in proceeding normally for the rest of the summer (Sherif et al., 1961).

Win-lose confrontations intensify the hostile, bitter attitudes that the conflicting parties hold toward each other. This intensification of hostility makes it even harder to resolve a conflict constructively.

It is not surprising that the win-lose approach to dealing with conflict intensifies the hostility between the parties. At least two of humanity's most powerful motive sources are at work in win-lose confrontations: the desire for physical security and the desire to achieve and maintain a sense of personal worth and importance. These motive sources are present in win-lose struggles directly and in the form of such derived needs as those for achievement, status, recognition, power, and affiliation. When such fundamental desires as physical security and human worth and dignity are threatened, intense emotional reactions are sure to follow. They contribute to the intensity and violence of win-lose conflict.

Real-life win-lose conflicts display these same characteristics

Everyone has been or is now involved in a real-life conflict of some kind. In examining one's own experience, it is interesting to discover the same dynamics and results that were found in the laboratory and field experiments described above.

A typical example from business is the win-lose struggle that occurs when a company is no longer able to sell a highly profitable item at a very favorable price because a competitor is starting to distribute the same item, or one very similar, at a much lower price. What happens? Win-lose tactics are used by all parties. The marketing department insists that the manufacturing department cut its production costs. Manufacturing presses marketing to reduce its distribution costs. Both marketing and manufacturing press research and development to undertake a crash program to come up with a new, superior item for the market that can be sold at a profit. These pressure tactics arouse all the antagonisms and hostilities associated with the win-lose approach to solving problems.

In school systems, win-lose tactics yield similar outcomes. When a high school has a cut in budget, each department typically seeks to have the other departments absorb the cuts. Each strives to win and have other departments lose. Here, as elsewhere, this kind of struggle creates or intensifies hostility and adversely affects the functioning of the total organization.

Widely used methods of conflict resolution are win-lose in character

Bargaining, negotiating, compromising, and similar approaches to the handling of conflict are, essentially, forms of win-lose confrontation. They all start with a relatively clear solution which each party to the conflict prefers and wishes to attain. Each party strives to attain its preferred solution by forcing it on the other party, by outsmarting the opponent. If unable to achieve complete success, each party seeks to attain as much of its preferred solution as possible. A polarized, adversary orientation is maintained at all times. All these various forms of win-lose conflict fail to create the problem-solving orientations and processes which stimulate the search for innovative solutions acceptable to both parties.

Mediation almost always starts with the conflicting parties locked in a win-lose battle. Commonly, the negotiator persuades each party to compromise its position step by step until a position is reached which both parties will accept, although often reluctantly.

The most able mediators appear to go beyond this compromise approach and, at least partially, use the kind of innovative, problem-solving search for solutions acceptable to both parties that we shall discuss at length in subsequent chapters.

Ignoring the conflict, burying it, or withdrawing or running from it are, like win-lose, unsatisfactory ways to deal with conflict. These passive approaches allow conflict to fester under the surface and often to become worse over time.

Reliance on win-lose approach is no longer necessary

In the attempts to resolve present-day conflicts, the win-lose approach is used in a substantial proportion of situations. Wars, whether hot, cold, limited, or total, are the extreme examples. Strikes, lockouts, slowdowns, bargaining, and negotiations in industry are win-lose battles between unions and management. Riots in cities and conflicts involving political parties and candidates both in elections and in legislatures are commonly win-lose in character. A sizable proportion of present-day conflicts in business and government also are of the win-lose type, i.e., conflict between headquarters and field or operating divisions, between research and development and manufacturing and sales, and between line and staff.

The win-lose approach to problem solving is inherent in Systems 1 and 2 and to some extent in System 3. Since most organizations and institutions throughout the world are operating under these systems, it is not surprising that win-lose methods are commonly used.

There is no need to continue this widespread use of the win-lose approach with all its costs and other adverse consequences. The entire mode of interaction used in any conflict situation is learned. The use of win-lose or of other ways of dealing with conflict is a reaction acquired from those around us, i.e., from our culture, through the processes of socialization. Since win-lose and other inadequate methods for coping with conflict are learned, more effective ways, such as those based on System 4T and proposed in this volume, can be learned equally well and, through socialization, can be passed on from person to person and from generation to generation. In this manner System 4T win-win strategies and methods of resolving conflicts can be substituted for the win-lose approach. The win-win methods yield solutions satisfactory to all; each party to the conflict wins something, and the conflict is resolved constructively. There are no continuing, often-suppressed, hostile attitudes.

5

The effectiveness
of System 4T

The basic proposition of this volume, as will be recalled, is that the management of conflict can be improved substantially by replacing the traditional structure and processes of organizations with those based on a more effective social system, namely System 4T. The degree of improvement in conflict management which can be expected from the proposed action depends, of course, on the magnitude of the superiority of the new social system over the one it replaces. This chapter will examine briefly some of the available data dealing with this issue.

In 1969 The University of Michigan's Institute for Social Research undertook a project for the General Motors Corporation. One of the objectives of this project was to test the System 4T theory. Did two assembly plants in the same labor market that differed substantially in productivity, costs, quality, and labor relations display the differences in the human organizational measurements that would be expected from the theory? The results for salaried employees (see fig. 5-1) show that they did. Plant A, the highest-producing assembly plant, has a substantially more favorable profile than does plant B, the lowest-producing, highest-cost plant. The measurements were obtained in October and November, 1969. Tables 5-1 and 5-2 briefly define the human organizational variables based on the items used to measure them. The questionnaire is described fully in Taylor and Bowers (1972).

A second objective of the General Motors–Institute for Social Research project was to test whether the knowledge and skills were available to help the managements of the two plants—and especially the poorer plant—shift closer to the System 4T model and, if these shifts were successful, whether the performance data of the plants would show corresponding improvement.

In October, 1969, the president of General Motors asked the Institute director whether shifting the manager of the high-producing plant to become the plant manager of the poor-producing plant would cause any difficulty in carrying out the objectives of the project. When assured that this shift would

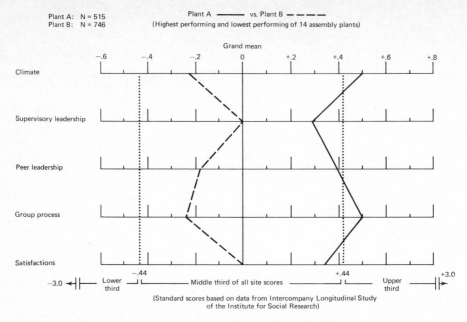

Plant A: N = 515
Plant B: N = 746

Plant A ——————— vs. Plant B — — — — —
(Highest performing and lowest performing of 14 assembly plants)

Grand mean

Climate

Supervisory leadership

Peer leadership

Group process

Satisfactions

−.44   +.44

−3.0 ◄━╂╟─ Lower third ─╜╙──── Middle third of all site scores ────╜╙─ Upper third ─╂╟► +3.0

(Standard scores based on data from Intercompany Longitudinal Study
of the Institute for Social Research)

Figure 5-1 *Human organizational scores for all salaried personnel in November, 1969.*

have advantages rather than disadvantages, the change was made. This high-producing manager was employing the kinds of principles that our organizational theory (System 4T) indicated would yield the best performance. The Institute staff felt that the measurements and organizational model could help this manager more rapidly achieve a sizable improvement in the poor plant after he took it over.

Figure 5-2 shows the kind of management this manager was seen to be providing to the high-producing plant prior to his transfer. These data are based on the perceptions of the top 52 managers in that plant. As the profile for his current (now) behavior shows, he is seen to be a System 4 manager. In addition, he had high performance goals, high technical competence, and scored high on "help with work." Therefore, his scores on all these dimensions showed that he was a System 4T manager.

This man made extremely good use of our survey measurements when he took over as plant manager of the poor plant. The data helped him understand his problems and how best to proceed. He saw to it that the managers and supervisors reporting to him were aided by the survey-feedback organizational improvement process and coaching. He provided the foremen with assistants (utility trainers) to train workers, chase stock, and do similar tasks, thereby freeing the foremen to spend time on the human problems. As Figure 5-3 shows, he made unusually rapid progress in bringing about substantial improvement in the human organization and its productive capability, as

Table 5-1
Items used to measure human
organizational causal variables

SUPERVISORY (MANAGERIAL) LEADERSHIP

- *Support:* Friendly; pays attention to what you are saying; listens to subordinates' problems.

- *Team building:* Encourages subordinates to work as a team; encourages exchange of opinions and ideas.

- *Goal emphasis:* Encourages best efforts; maintains high standards.

- *Help with work:* Shows ways to do a better job; helps subordinates plan, organize, and schedule; offers new ideas, solutions to problems.

ORGANIZATIONAL CLIMATE

- *Communication flow:* Subordinates know what's going on; superiors are receptive; subordinates are given information to do jobs well.

- *Decision-making practices:* Subordinates are involved in setting goals; decisions are made at levels of accurate information; persons affected by decisions are asked for their ideas; know-how of people of all levels is used.

- *Concern for persons:* The organization is interested in the individual's welfare; tries to improve working conditions; organizes work activities sensibly.

- *Influence on department:* From lower-level supervisors and from employees who have no subordinates.

- *Technological adequacy:* Improved methods are quickly adopted; equipment and resources are well managed.

- *Motivation:* Differences and disagreements are accepted and worked through; people in organization work hard for money, promotions, job satisfaction, and to meet high expectations from others and are encouraged to do so by policies, working conditions, and people.

reflected in the measurements of the human organization. From November, 1969, to August, 1970, he had moved the human organization scores for the 750 salaried employees about one-half the distance from the poorest to the best plant.

The data in Figure 5-4 show the pattern that we typically find: improvement in productivity and costs lags in time behind improvement in the human organization. Even though the human organization scores (fig. 5-3) showed a sizable improvement by the end of the 1970 model year (August, 1970), both direct and indirect labor costs continued to *deteriorate* rather than improve. Costs were increasing even though there was an improvement in the human organization. The deterioration in indirect labor costs continued for one more

Table 5-2
Items used to measure human
organizational intervening variables

PEER LEADERSHIP

- *Support:* Friendly; pays attention to what others are saying; listens to others' problems.

- *Goal emphasis:* Encourages best efforts; maintains high standards.

- *Help with work:* Shows ways to do a better job; helps others plan, organize, and schedule; group shares with each other new ideas, solutions to problems.

- *Team building:* Encouragement from each other to work as a team; emphasis on team goal; exchange of opinions and ideas.

GROUP PROCESS

- Planning together; coordinating efforts.

- Making good decisions; solving problems.

- Knowing jobs and how to do them well.

- Sharing information.

- Wanting to meet objectives.

- Having confidence and trust in other members.

- Ability to meet unusual work demands.

SATISFACTION

With other workers, superiors, jobs, this organization compared with others, pay, progress in the organization up to now, chances for getting ahead in the future.

year. Direct labor efficiency showed a sizable improvement in the 1971 model year and continued this trend in the 1972 year. Indirect labor efficiencies, however, did not improve until the 1972 model year when a sizable improvement occurred. Figure 5-5 shows some of the improvement attained by the 1972 model year. The improvement in labor efficiency alone represents a $5 million saving. In addition, there were various other savings, such as a reduction in tool breakage and an improvement in quality. There was also a sizable improvement in employee satisfaction which has been found to be associated with employee health, both physical and mental.

It usually requires substantially more time for a new plant manager to begin to show improvement in productivity and costs after taking over a poor plant than was required by this manager in improving plant B. Two and three years are not uncommon. The survey-feedback organizational improvement process enabled the plant B manager to achieve much more rapid improvement than would have been likely without this resource.

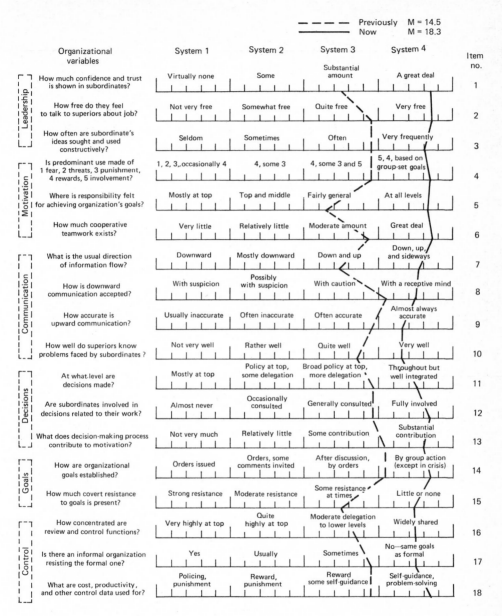

Figure 5-2 *Profile of organizational characteristics of plant A's new manager.*

A related and more intensive improvement effort was made in one part of the plant. This involved the application of a "cross-functional business team" described later in this chapter. This approach was used in one department of

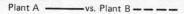

Plant A ———vs. Plant B — — — —

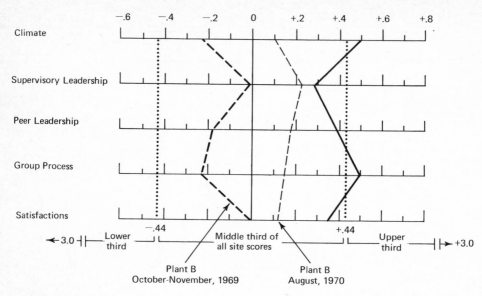

Figure 5-3 Human organization scores for salaried personnel in November, 1969, and August, 1970.

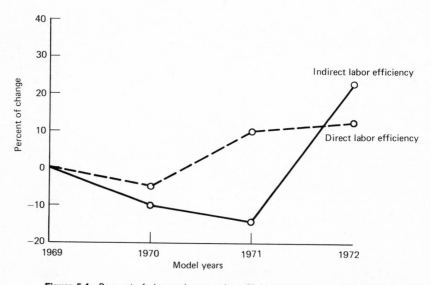

Figure 5-4 Percent of change in operating efficiency at an assembly plant (plant B).

Direct labor efficiency	14% Improvement
Indirect labor efficiency	23% Improvement
Monitored quality index	10% Improvement
Grievances per 100 employees (January–April)	60% Decrease

Figure 5-5   *Plant B performance 1972 vs. 1969.*

PRODUCTIVITY (% OF STANDARD)

1970 Average	115.60
1971 Goal set by group	97
1971 Year to Date	88 (approximately)

COMMITTEEMAN CALLS

1970 Average	75/month
1971 Goal set by group	50/month
February	17
March	20
April	10
May	9

WRITTEN GRIEVANCES

1970 Average	50/month
1971 Goal set by group	17/month
February	1
March	4
April	2
May	3

SCRAP COST/UNIT

1970 Average	4
1971 Goal set by group	2
February	1
March	1
April	½
May	½

Figure 5-6   *Improved management yielded better performance and less conflict.*

about 150 employees with the help of George E. McCullough. As the results in Figure 5-6 show, within one year's time there was a 28 percent increase in productivity, scrap was cut to less than one-fourth of the previous level, and there was a substantial decrease in "committeeman calls" and written grievances. (A "committeeman call" is a demand by a worker that a union representative be present when the supervisor talks to a worker. If the representative is not present, the worker will not listen or talk.) The reduction in committeeman calls and written grievances reflects a substantial reduction in the hostility and conflict that had existed in this department prior to its shift toward System 4T.

These data from the assembly plants confirmed the validity of the System 4T organizational theory. The measurements of the human organizational variables of the two assembly plants differed as expected. The high-producing plant had substantially more favorable human organization scores than did the low-producing plant. Moreover, when organizational improvement efforts in the poor plant yielded better human organization scores, these changes were followed, as the theory predicted, by gains in productivity and other performance variables and by a substantial reduction in hostile conflict.

Using the survey feedback method to improve a sales organization

In September, 1969, a feasibility project was started in one sales region of a nationwide consumer products firm by Charles A. Waters. The region was chosen because it was typical, rather than an exceptionally good or poor performer, in its sales results. The major effort in this pilot project focused on working with the regional sales manager and the personnel reporting to him, and on two of the five sales districts in the region. The survey feedback method was used to help these managers improve performance.

The important human organizational variables, such as leadership and teamwork, were measured in September and remeasured in May. During this period, the immediate subordinates of the regional sales managers saw a substantial improvement, from their point of view, in these human organizational variables. These results are shown in Figure 5-7.

Figure 5-8 presents the data from the district managers and sales staff in the two districts in which an improvement effort was undertaken. Here, again, there is significant improvement in the way these persons saw the situation in May, 1970, compared with September, 1969.

When the measurements of the human organizational variables for the entire region (all five districts) are examined, the data show a small favorable shift. These results for all the personnel in the region are presented in Figure 5-9.

In the spring of 1970, this company had a sales contest for its entire nationwide sales organization. To qualify, a district sales manager had to be above quota on total sales and had to exceed a stated minimum in each of three different product lines. A regional manager, to qualify, had to meet the same

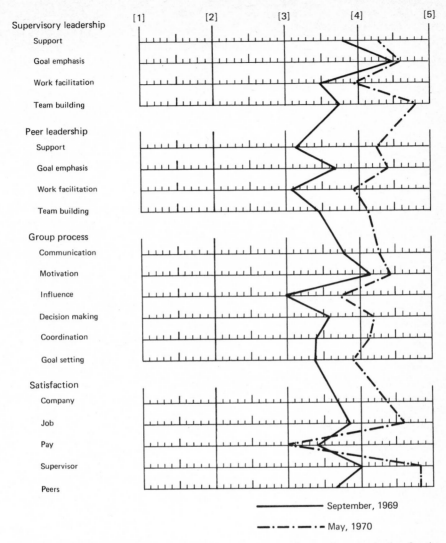

Figure 5-7 *Major indices profile, nationwide consumer products sales organization for the regional manager's immediate work group.*

requirements in his region: to be above quota and to exceed specified requirements in three product lines.

As Table 5-3 shows, the region in which this pilot project was being conducted, region B, surpassed all others. It was the *only* region where sales exceeded quota for the *entire* region and for *every* sales district. It was also the only region in which *every* district exceeded minimum requirements in three product lines. All five district managers in region B qualified for the contest, and, of course, the regional manager did also. Only *one* other district in the

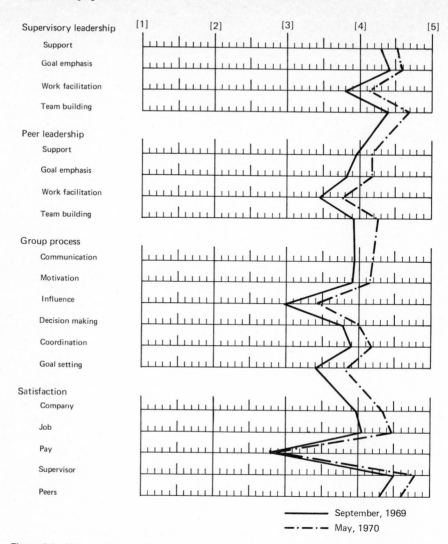

Figure 5-8 *Major indices profile, nationwide consumer products sales organization for the two districts given "intensive" effort.*

entire nation met the contest requirements, namely one district in region A. No region other than region B qualified in the contest.

Prior to September, 1969, when this feasibility project was started, region B's sales performance was close to the company's average. By the spring of 1970, as has just been mentioned, marked improvement in region B's sales performance had occurred. Moreover, this improvement continued. In the early summer of 1970, region B sold more merchandise than a larger region which has a market potential more than 25 percent greater than region B. This is the first time in the history of the company that this has occurred.

An important aspect of the improvement in region B is the increase in cooperation and teamwork at all levels: district manager, sales supervisors, and salespersons. The shift toward System 4T brought less conflict, better cooperation, and better performance.

As the data in Table 5-3 and Figures 5-7 to 5-9 show, impressive improvement was obtained in region B in a relatively short period of time. Moreover, the sales-performance data indicated that this improvement was not only sustained, but continued to grow.

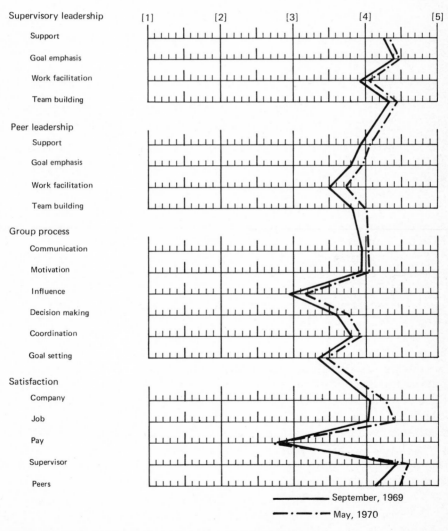

Figure 5-9 *Major indices profile, nationwide consumer products sales organization for the entire region B.*

Table 5-3
Performance in 1970 national sales contest

Region	% of sales to quota	Proportion of districts		
		Whose sales exceeded quota	Which met requirements in three product lines	Which qualified in contest
A	Less than 100%	½	¼	¼
B	More than 100%	all	all	all
C	Less than 100%	0	0	0
D	Less than 100%	0	0	0
E	Less than 100%	0	0	0

Using the "cross-functional business team" to improve performance and reduce conflict

For decades the widespread use of System 2 management has led to excessive application of the principle of functionalization. In most firms, this has resulted in the creation of many functional departments and in splitting the work into small, highly repetitive cycles within these departments. Moreover, those who do the work have had no voice in the way the work is organized. Each job has been developed by staff specialists, and the particular task and the way to do it have been imposed on both the worker and the supervisor.

As research findings show, this traditional and widely used method for establishing the job of each worker has made many of the jobs monotonous and often meaningless and has resulted in low motivation, lack of coordination, low productivity, poor quality, high costs, and unsatisfactory labor relations (Argyris, 1957; Katz, Maccoby, & Morse, 1950; *Work in America,* 1973).

These adverse effects of the excessive application of functionalization have been increased greatly by the conflicts that specialization produces among departments and within departments. When interdependent operations are put under different managers, conflict is likely to result. When there is pressure to achieve high productivity, earnings, and quality and to meet tight delivery schedules, conflict is almost inevitable (Price, 1968). Difficulties in responding to these pressures cause one manager and department to blame others for any performance failure. These conflicts are aggravated when the vertical line organization is entirely functional in character and there is little or no provision in the formal structure for cross-functional linkage and coordination except at the very top of the organization. This form of organization exists where System 2 classical principles of management have been conscientiously applied and is rather common in American business and government.

One approach, mentioned above, to overcoming the adverse effects of excessive functionalism is the "cross-functional business team" developed by McCullough (McCullough, 1975; McCullough & Likert, 1972). These business teams are used at all hierarchical levels in a firm and especially at the lower levels to reduce the inefficiencies caused by conflicts among such functions as engineering, sales, maintenance, production and quality control. The supervisors and nonsupervisory personnel who perform a total task, such as making cushions for an automobile body, are built into a business team. Teams are established with the full involvement of all the personnel affected. For example, if two levels of supervision are involved, the team building usually starts with meetings of the general foremen and supervisors. Every supervisor whose work affects the task of the business team is included in the group whether or not that person reports to the general foreman. The supervisors included will be all those who supervise production, maintenance, quality control, safety, or similar functions. Maintenance workers and their supervisors, for example, usually do not report to the production general supervisor. Even so, the maintenance supervisor would be part of the business team since maintenance must be done promptly and well if cushions, for example, are to be produced efficiently. The general foreman included in the team usually is the one responsible for most of the personnel engaged in that total task, i.e., making cushions.

In the meeting of the general foreman and supervisors, they are informed that the plant management has agreed to the establishment of a business team if the supervisors would like to undertake it. The nature of a business team is described and mention made that its membership necessarily includes all persons whose work is required to get the particular task done. The group members are reminded that they know more about how to do the job than anybody else and that if a business team were established, they would be expected to use their knowledge to organize and conduct the work in the way that seems best to them providing they meet the production requirements.

After the group members have become thoroughly familiar with the business-team concept, they are asked if they would like to try it. If they decide to do so, they are asked to have each supervisor explain the concept to the workers and ask them if they would like to be part of a business team. If the supervisors and workers all agree, the project is launched.

The business team consists of enough personnel from each functional department to do the work required of that function. To help the teams in their problem solving, they are provided with all relevant performance data. Typically, they are given the following information for the larger entity, e.g., plant or department, of which they are a part: (1) the quantity of goods and/or services to be provided, (2) the engineering and quality standards to be met, (3) the promised delivery schedules, and (4) the cost of operations allowable to meet corporate and competitive requirements. With this information at hand, the business team defines its own mission and sets its own goals for quantity, costs, etc., in the light of the requirements of the larger entity. The team is provided regularly with current performance data for its own operation to enable it to see how well it is meeting its goals. Measurements are obtained of the human organizational variables and made available to the teams for goal-setting, diagnoses, and problem-solving purposes. Supervisors and workers in groups engage in problem solving focused on the best way to organize and conduct the work for which they are responsible, including the efficient coordination of their activities with other related units. There is no limitation on the scope of the team's efforts. It can tackle all phases of the problems that affect the productivity and performance for which it is responsible. Jobs can be enlarged, processes altered. Any change that will bring improvement is permitted.

The number of persons involved in a particular application of the business-team method varies widely, from 15 to 20 or a few hundred or more persons. One level of supervision may be involved or two or three levels. The teams virtually always cut across functions, crafts, or other forms of specialized activity. All persons whose efforts directly affect the accomplishment of the goals or missions for which the business teams are responsible are included. The teams are structured to provide a mission-oriented focus for problem solving. They are trained in group problem solving so that they can deal effectively both with the *intellectual* processes of problem solving and with those *emotional and motivational* processes involved in building highly effective, cooperative teams (see chaps. 7–9).

In one company where this business-team approach is being used, four teams have been established in one large plant. Although the general plan for these teams is essentially the same, the activities of each team vary with the specific character of the particular operations. The smallest of the four teams includes 30 persons, the largest almost 300. One of the teams is responsible for shipping; another deals with motorized equipment; a third handles construction; and the fourth is concerned with the maintenance and operation of continuous-process units which produce one class of products.

This fourth team was the first to be established and was launched in April, 1970. The activities of this team can be described briefly to illustrate the work of all four teams. All the employees in this team participate fully in planning and operating their "business." For example, they established the initial business plans listing the goals they wanted to achieve in terms of tangible, measurable, and economically important results. All team members are kept well informed concerning the operations of their business. Team members are encouraged to contribute all that they can toward effective operations. Managers from different functional departments who were members of the top group of the team recognized that coordination among them was poor and could be improved appreciably if they were housed together in the main office rather than at scattered locations in the plant. On their initiative, this change in office arrangements has occurred. As this top group worked on its problems, its members realized that they needed to expand their team to include four additional business functions from two other divisions. This expansion occurred in September, 1970, and resulted in further improvements in both communication and coordination.

Figure 5-10 shows the improvement in the human organization that has occurred from April to October, 1970. The improvement shown in Figure 5-10 is large for a period as short as six months. The improvement is greatest, moreover, in those variables which other studies show have the greatest impact subsequently on teamwork and cooperation and on financial and other performance variables.

Improvement in financial and productivity results followed the improvement in the human organization. For instance, a production increment of 20 percent

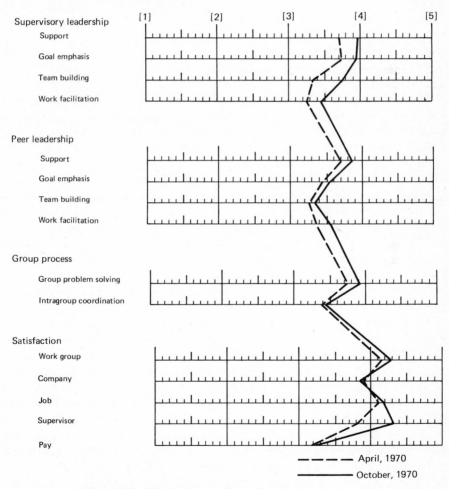

Figure 5-10 *Major indices profile, continuous process plant, pilot-group survey.*

was realized with an operating cost increase of 1 percent; higher production records were set in three of the last four months of the year; in one area, minor maintenance costs are down 40 percent; grievances have dropped to an almost insignificant level. There is also a definite trend toward flexibility of skills with the various crafts working out-of-craft voluntarily—without union or group problems. Techniques for business planning and departmental organization developed by this set of business teams have been adopted plantwide. (See also the example of a cross-functional business team described in chap. 10.)

Weldon: another example of improving performance and reducing conflict

In January, 1962, the Harwood Manufacturing Company, the leading firm in the pajama industry, purchased the Weldon Company, which was second in volume in this industry. The Weldon Company had been unprofitable for several years. These same years, however, had been profitable for the Harwood Manufacturing Company.

After its purchase, the corporate management of the Weldon Company was taken over by Harwood, but the plant manager and the managerial and supervisory staffs in the Weldon plant were retained. A few additional supervisors were appointed subsequently. The Weldon plant had approximately 800 employees.

Starting in 1962, a number of changes were introduced in the management system of the Weldon plant and in the layout and organization of the work. These changes are described in a book by Marrow, Bowers, and Seashore (1967).

Briefly, the major changes involved extensive engineering modifications in the organization of the work, improved maintenance of machinery and equipment, an "earnings development" training program for employees, training of managers and supervisors in the principles and skills required by a system of management well toward System 4T, the use of this system by the plant manager and the manager's encouragement of all the subordinate managers and supervisors to do the same. All these changes were initiated and supported by the new top management of the company.

At the request of Dr. Alfred Marrow, chairman of the board of the Harwood Manufacturing Company, Seashore and Bowers of the Institute for Social Research obtained measurements starting in 1962 of the causal and intervening variables in the Weldon plant. Figure 5-11 shows the substantial changes from 1962 to 1969 in the management system used in the Weldon plant as seen by its supervisors and managers (Seashore & Bowers, 1970). A shift from low System 2 to low System 4 occurred. By 1969, Weldon had improved return on investment by one-third, cut absenteeism in half, reduced employee turnover by 60 percent, and increased employee productivity by nearly 40 percent. Union-management relationships also improved greatly.

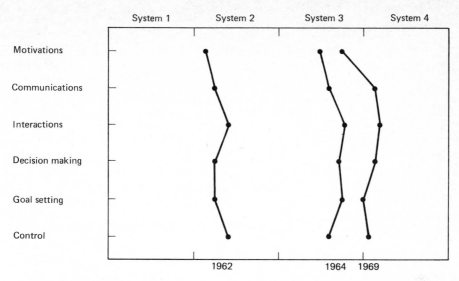

Figure 5-11 *Change in profile of organizational characteristics. (From Seashore & Bowers, 1970.)*

Recent studies confirm greater effectiveness of System 4T

Findings from several other studies, similar to those just reported, have been summarized in previous publications (Likert, 1961, 1967), and so they need not be repeated here. There are, however, several additional studies.

In one, Roberts, Miles, and Blankenship (1968) analyzed the relationship between the management system used by each operating division and that division's performance for six operating divisions of a West Coast firm. The System 1 to 4 score for each division was obtained by responses to five items, such as those in Tables 2-1 and 2-2, of five levels of managers in each division and computing the average score (mean) for the division. Roberts, Miles, and Blankenship (1968) reported:

> Objective performance data for the preceding fiscal period were available for each of the six divisions. The performance data were based on the following criteria: (a) per cent growth in shipments, (b) operating profit as a per cent of sales, (c) warranty expense, (d) return on assets. Rank order standings on each of these dimensions were combined to provide a single, overall performance measure for each division. As can be seen in the list of specific criteria, the overall performance rank for each division reflects several of the most important measures of organizational success, i.e., quantity of output, quality, growth, and profitability. (pp. 406–407)

The relationship in terms of relative rank between the System 1 to 4 score for each division and its performance is shown in Table 5-4. For each variable, a

Table 5-4
Relationship between
management system
(System 1-4)
scores and performance

Division	Rank* on system 1-4	Rank† on performance
A	2	1
B	4	3
C	5	4
D	1	2
E	3	6
F	6	5

* High ranking (1) is more toward System 4, low (6) toward System 1.

† High ranking (1) is highest performance; low ranking (6) is lowest performance.

From Roberts, Miles, & Blankenship, 1968.

rank of (1) is highest and (6) is lowest. Although the relationship between the management-system score and performance is quite marked, as shown in the table (rho = +.61), there is a high probability that the results understate the true relationships. The performance data were for the fiscal period *preceding* the collection of the System 1 to 4 scores. Since the relationship of the management system of a firm to its financial performance is found to be higher when trends over time are taken into consideration, i.e., management system scores obtained at one point in time are related to performance measurements for a *subsequent* period, the data in Table 5-4 very likely show a less marked relationship than actually exists. From the relative ranks shown in Table 5-4, a reasonable prediction would be that division E would show an appreciable improvement in performance subsequent to the time when the management-system scores were obtained.

Comparable results are obtained in other countries

Research in other countries is yielding an increasing body of findings consistent with the general pattern found in the United States. In each nation, there is a range in the management systems used by the enterprises in that nation. In the most highly industrialized nations, the distribution is more toward the System 4 end of the continuum and less toward the System 1 end. In the less industrialized nations, the distribution tends to extend more toward System 1 and less toward System 4. That is, the management systems used, on the average, in more industrialized nations tend to be more complex and sophisticated than those in the less industrialized nations. Regardless, however, of where along the System 1 to 4 continuum the range of a particular nation may fall, the available evidence indicates a comparable pattern from country to country. In each nation:

1. *The higher-producing, more successful enterprises, departments, or offices tend to fall more toward the System 4 end of the range for that nation.*

2. *The lower-producing, less successful organizations have management systems more toward the System 1 end of the range.*

This pattern of findings is illustrated by a study conducted in Yugoslavia to learn whether System 4 is applicable in that country. The following is taken from a paper describing the findings which was published in a modified form by Jerovsek, Mozina, Tannenbaum, and Likert (1970).

> In order to investigate this notion (that System 4 is applicable in Yugoslavia), we selected ten pairs of industrial organizations, each pair containing a high-performing and a low-performing organization. The organizations within each pair were comparable with respect to type of product, technology, amount of capital investment, market conditions, opportunities for credit, degree of modernity and location (rural-urban). The more successful plants were slightly larger (average size 871) than the less successful (average size 751) and the former experienced some growth in manpower while the latter suffered some decline during the past three years. The more successful plants also have a slightly higher proportion of professional personnel than do the less successful.

> Two criteria that define the "end-result variables" were employed in selecting the more successful and less successful plants: (1) net profit, which reflects overall performance including productivity, sales, and costs, and (2) average wages and salaries of all employees, which are related to gross profit. Figure 5-12 shows the levels of the plants on measures of these criteria averaged separately for the more successful and less successful plants. These data come from company records.

Figure 5-13 shows the results obtained in the 10 more successful and the 10 less successful plants. The data for scoring the management system used by each plant were obtained from 10 respondents in each plant including the 5 leading managers and the 5 top officers of the worker's council. The respondents in the more-successful plants did not differ from those in less-successful plants in age, education, seniority, or party membership. Approximately 50 percent of the managers and 35 percent of the leaders of the councils are party members. Each respondent answered the items in Table 5-5. Although Figure 5-13 does not show the results for each plant separately, an analysis of these data reveals that *each* successful plant is closer to the System 4 model in its profile than its less successful counterpart.

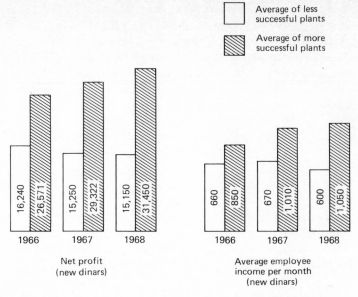

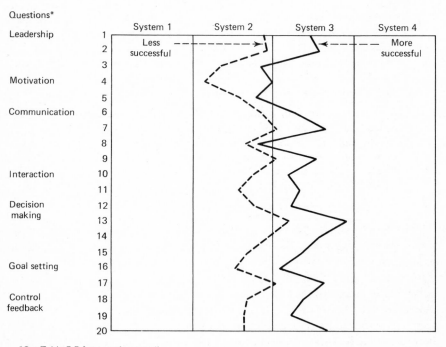

Figure 5-12 *Levels of two end-result variables for the more successful and less successful Yugoslav plants.*

Figure 5-13 *System characteristics of more successful and less successful Yugoslav plants.*

Table 5-5

Profile of organizational characteristics

		System 1	System 2	System 3	System 4
Leadership	1. How much confidence is shown in subordinates?	None	Condescending	Substantial	Complete
	2. How free do they feel to talk to superiors about job?	Not at all	Not very	Rather free	Fully free
	3. Are subordinates' ideas sought and used, if worthy?	Seldom	Sometimes	Usually	Always
Motivation	4. Is predominant use made of (1) fear, (2) threats, (3) punishment, (4) rewards, (5) involvement?	1, 2, 3, occasionally 4	4, some 3	4, some 3 and 5	5, 4, based on group-set goals
	5. Where is responsibility felt for achieving organization's goals?	Mostly at top	Top and middle	Fairly general	At all levels
Communication	6. What is the direction of information flow?	Downward	Mostly downward	Down and up	Down, up, and sideways
	7. How is downward communication accepted?	With suspicion	Possibly with suspicion	With caution	With open mind
	8. How accurate is upward communication?	Often wrong	Censored for boss	Limited accuracy	Accurate
	9. How well do superiors know problems faced by subordinates?	Know little	Some knowledge	Quite well	Very well

Table 5-5

Profile of organizational characteristics (Continued)

	System 1	System 2	System 3	System 4
Interaction				
10. What is the character of interaction?	Little, always with fear and distrust	Little, usually with some condescension	Moderate, often fair amount confidence and trust	Extensive, high degree of confidence and trust
11. How much cooperative teamwork is present?	None	Relatively little	Moderate amount	Very substantial amount throughout organization
Decisions				
12. At what level are decisions formally made?	Mostly at top	Policy at top, some delegation	Broad policy at top, more delegation	Throughout, but well integrated
13. What is the origin of technical and professional knowledge used in decision making?	Top management	Upper and middle	To certain extent throughout	To a great extent throughout
14. Are subordinates involved in decisions related to their work?	Not at all	Occasionally consulted	Generally consulted	Fully involved
15. What does decision-making process contribute to motivation?	Nothing, often weakens it	Relatively little	Some contribution	Substantial contribution
Goals				
16. How are organization goals established?	Orders issued	Orders, some comments invited	After discussion, by orders	Group action (except in crisis)
17. How much covert resistance to goals is present?	Strong resistance	Moderate resistance	Some resistance at times	Little or none

	Highly at top	Relatively high at top	Moderate delegation at lower levels	Quite widely shared
18. How concentrated are review and control functions?	Highly at top	Relatively high at top	Moderate delegation at lower levels	Quite widely shared
19. Is there an informal organization resisting the formal one?	Yes	Usually	Sometimes	No, same goals as formal
20. What are cost, productivity, and other control data used for?	Policing, punishment	Reward and punishment	Reward, some self-guidance	Self-guidance, problem solving

Management systems: More successful versus less successful plants

It is quite clear that the two groups of plants differ in their leadership practices and in the social, psychological, and motivational consequences of these practices as reported by our respondents. As the data in Figure 5-13 show, the more successful compared to the less successful plants are characterized by:

1. Greater confidence by superiors in subordinates

2. More freedom felt by subordinates to talk to their superiors

3. More frequent seeking and use of subordinates' ideas

4. Use of involvement rather than threats

5. Mutual confidence and trust in interactions rather than condescension by superiors and fear by subordinates

6. Greater participation by subordinates in decisions related to their work

7. Productivity, cost, and other accounting data used by departments for self-guidance rather than by top management for punitive purposes

The motivational bases for control (Tannenbaum, 1968) also display a different pattern in the two sets of plants. The more successful plants, to a greater extent than the less successful, are characterized by:

1. Widespread feeling of responsibility for achieving the goals of the organization

2. Mutual expectations that each person will do the job well and help others

3. Cooperative attitudes to achieve goals rather than covert resistance to them and restriction of output

The results of another study involving four Yugoslav organizations provide further evidence that the System 4 theory applies in Yugoslavia (see Kavcic, Rus, & Tannenbaum, 1971).

A study was conducted in Sweden by Nils Elofsson and Alvin Zander. They studied 37 sales districts of a firm. They found that the sales volume of the salespersons in these districts was related to the management system used by their sales managers. The districts of managers whose management is more toward System 4 had appreciably higher sales volume than did the districts of managers who were more toward System 1 in their management. This relationship of the management system of the manager to the sales volume of the district was sufficiently large to account for one-fourth of the variation among districts in the volume of their sales.

Results from Japan

In 1966, 100 middle managers in Tokyo were asked to describe the management system used by the highest-producing firm or department which they knew well. For this purpose, a table comparable to Table 5-5 was used. After completing this task, they were asked to answer the table again to describe the management system of the lowest-producing firm or department which they knew well. They were requested, if possible, to use, for their lowest-producing firm, one from the same general industry as their high-producing firm and preferably of about the same size. Similar data were obtained from another group of 80 middle managers in Fukuoka, Japan.

The results from these two groups of managers were essentially the same. The average (mean) management-system score of their high-producing organizations placed them in the upper-middle part of System 3. The average score for their low-producing organizations was at the border between System 1 and System 2.

Results from other studies in Japan confirm the pattern of findings concerning the management system used by the most successful managers. When measurements are obtained from Japanese managers who achieve high productivity and earnings, the data show that their style of leadership and management is much more like System 4 than is the style of the low-producing managers. Results for a bank in Tokyo are shown in Figure 5-14 and for a Japanese chemical plant in Figure 5-15. These data were obtained by J. Misumi of Kyushu University. (See also Misumi & Seki, 1971; Misumi & Shirakashi, 1966; Misumi & Tasaki, 1965.)

Additional studies in other nations add confirming evidence concerning the superiority of System 4T compared with Systems 1, 2, and 3 (Bose, 1957, 1958a, 1958b; Chowdhry, 1953, 1960; Chowdhry & Pal, 1957; Chowdhry & Trivedi, 1953; Ganguli, 1963; Habibullah, 1967; Lammers, 1967). Since System 4T is found worldwide to be the most productive and effective system, especially in industrialized nations, it appears that System 4T can be used throughout the world to improve the success with which conflicts are resolved.

Superiority of System 4T greater than indicated originally

Data obtained as a consequence of two methodological developments are revealing that System 4T in comparison with other management systems is appreciably more effective than earlier studies indicated. These two methodological developments are: (1) a substantial improvement in the capability of measuring with accuracy where on the 1 to 4 scale a management system falls, and (2) measurement and inclusion of trends over time in the analyses. An example of the latter (2) is the study of assembly plants reported earlier in this chapter.

Trends over time are proving to be highly important in assessing the effectiveness of a management system. A manager with high technical competence and high performance goals who uses System 1 or 2 and puts pressure on the organization for high production and low costs through such procedures as tight budgets, across-the-board budget cuts, personnel ceilings, and tight or

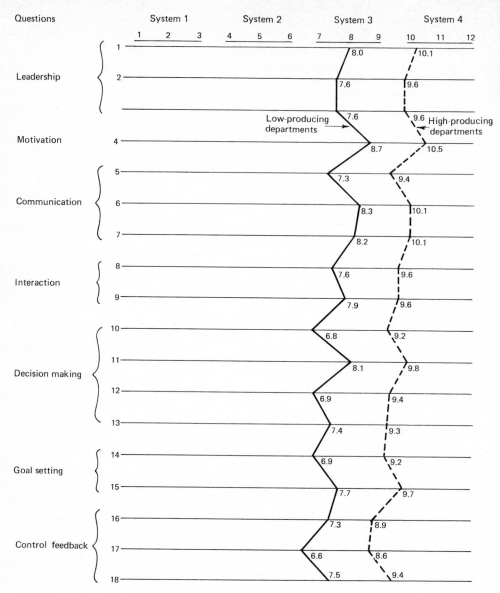

Figure 5-14 Management system of high- and low-producing departments of a bank in Tokyo.

tightened standards can achieve impressive productivity and financial results over the short run. This is true especially if the manager is put in charge of a relatively effective human organization. Studies show, however, that the human organization's productive capability will deteriorate under this kind of manager. As a consequence, over the long run the favorable productivity and earnings usually are not sustained. The profit and loss statements for that short-run period were, of course, spurious since the profits reported were larger than the actual true earnings for that period (Likert, 1973a). The length of time over which these spuriously high earnings can be achieved, i.e., the "short run,"

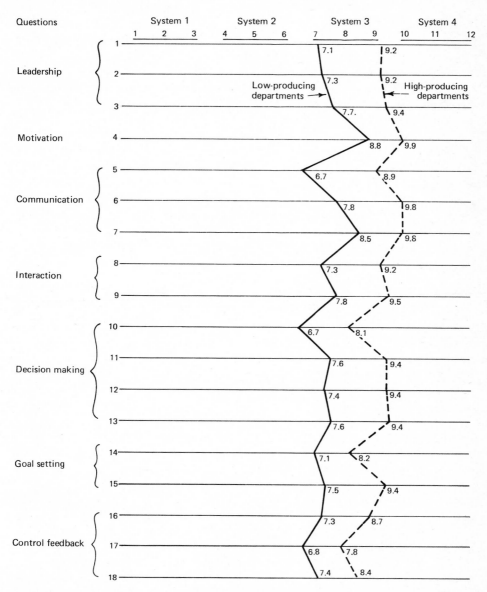

Figure 5-15 *Management system of high- and low-producing departments of a chemical company in Japan.*

varies with the size of the organization. In small organizations, this time span can be one to three years; in medium-sized organizations the range is likely to be about three to five years. In large corporations, the "short run" can be ten years or even longer.

System 4T operations are found commonly to be 20 to 40 percent more productive and profitable than the average firm. In the United States, the average company is about System 2 or 2½. This superiority is as true of sales organizations as it is of plants or entire firms. For example, one System 4T life insurance agency has been selling more than 50 percent of all ordinary[1] life insurance sold within its state. As might be expected from this superior productivity in production and sales, firms and decentralized divisions which have used System 4T for at least a few years tend to dominate their product line. It is not uncommon for them to have as much as 50 to 85 percent of the market for their products. The product quality of these System 4T firms excels as do their capacities to market new products successfully.

Organizations under System 1 or 2 managers tend to be inflexible and hence have difficulty in adapting readily to changes in technology, products, markets, processes, etc. Such organizations are apt to lose out competitively whenever change becomes necessary. System 4T firms tend to be more flexible and adaptable; there is better interdepartmental cooperation and far less irreconcilable conflict. Their union-management relations are far more satisfactory to both the union and the company than are these relations in most firms.

Shifts toward System 4T yield improvement

As would be expected, when a firm shifts from System 2 to System 4T, it experiences substantial improvement in its performance and its capacity to resolve conflicts constructively. Examples discussed at the beginning of this chapter are the assembly plant, continuous-process plant, sales region, and the Weldon Company. In addition, there are a number of projects under way currently in which companies are being aided in shifting their management toward System 4T. These projects are yielding results demonstrating that as this shift takes place, corresponding sizable improvements are occurring in productivity, earnings, and other performance measurements, in employee satisfaction, internal teamwork, and union-management relationships. The management of conflict within these organizations shows similar improvement. Widely different kinds of work, such as research and development, manufacturing, continuous-process plants, sales, and office work, are included in these projects. Personnel at all hierarchical levels from the president to nonsupervisory employees are involved.

---

[1]Ordinary life insurance consists of policies sold to individuals, the amount of the policy being $1,000 or more, and premiums paid quarterly or less often.

System 4T excels on variables important in conflict mangement

The superiority of System 4T is significant for conflict management since such intervening variables as the capacity to communicate, to motivate, to coordinate, and to influence are very important in resolving conflicts constructively. Specific data concerning these intervening variables have been published extensively elsewhere, for example, Bowers and Seashore, 1966; Guest, 1962; Katz and Kahn, 1966; Likert, 1961, 1967; Likert and Bowers, 1969; Marrow, Bowers, & Seashore, 1967; Tannenbaum, 1968; Taylor and Bowers, 1972.

These and other studies show that the closer an organization is to System 4T in character rather than to System 1, the greater is the likelihood that the intervening variables will show the following:

1. *Communication:* The communications in all directions—downward, upward, and laterally—are all appreciably more accurate and adequate and are accomplished without overloading the system. This applies both to the information that members provide one another and to the confidence with which each accepts communications from others as accurate and genuine.

   Perceptions are also more accurate. If any distortions occur, they are readily corrected by the members communicating with each other in a candid, forthright, and supportive manner. Suspicion is replaced by giving others the benefit of the doubt.

2. *Influence:* The capacity to exert influence by every hierarchical level usually is greater. This is especially true for the lower hierarchical levels since subordinates in System 4 organizations, in comparison with subordinates in Systems 1, 2, and 3, have much greater capacity, as research findings show, to influence their superiors through the group problem-solving process (Lawrence & Lorsch, 1967; Likert, 1961, 1967; Tannenbaum, 1968). This capacity at every hierarchical level to exert greater upward influence in a System 4 organization compared with others is supported, moreover, by the more efficient and accurate upward communication.

   The capacity of subordinates to exert greater upward influence does not occur, however, at the expense of their superiors' capacity to exert influence. On the contrary, superiors as well as subordinates at every hierarchical level are able to exert more influence in a System 4T interaction-influence network than they are in other systems. Since all levels generally have more influence, the *total capacity* of the organization to exert influence is appreciably greater, i.e., the size of the influence pie is greater (Cooper & Wood, 1974; Likert, 1961; Tannenbaum, 1968). All members in the organization can exert more influence within the interaction-influence network of which they are members. Reciprocal influence is greater.

3. *Responsiblity:* Each member of the organization feels greater commitment to the organization and its goals and displays greater responsiblity for its success by taking the initiative when action is required to assist the organization to prevent failure and to achieve its objectives.

4. *Motivation:* Influence and responsiblity are, of course, both aspects of motivation. In addition, the members of the organization are more highly motivated in all other ways to achieve the established objectives. There is more confidence and trust among the members of the organization and across departments and across hierarchical levels. Greater commitment to the success of the entire enterprise is present; members strive, consequently, to resolve their differences and disputes for the greater good of the total organization. They have greater loyalty to the entire organization, and there is greater group loyalty among the members of each work group. This greater group loyalty helps create all the positive motivational forces present in highly effective groups (Cartwright & Zander, 1968; Likert, 1961, chap. 11). More favorable and cooperative attitudes are present throughout the organization, i.e., toward the organization as a whole, toward the objectives sought, toward superiors, toward other members, etc. These more favorable attitudes and loyalties reflect the cumulative character of the motivational forces in a System 4T organization. All the motivational forces are additive and oriented toward achieving the organization's goals efficiently. This is in contrast with other management systems where some of the motivational forces oppose achieving the goals. Restriction of output, for example, occurs commonly in System 1 and 2 organizations and may be present to a lesser extent in System 3.

5. *Coordination:* The capacity to achieve highly effective lateral as well as vertical coordination exists because of the better communication, higher motivation, higher levels of reciprocal influence, and also because the organizational structure provides better lateral as well as vertical linkage.

6. *Decision Making:*
   a. As a result of the better communication, problems are detected in their earlier stages and solved promptly with full use of the relevant information and knowledge available within the organization.
   b. Problem solving is done through the multiple overlapping group structure. All groups affected by a decision are involved in making it and can influence the outcome. The decision is made at or near the point in the organization where the most information concerning the problem is available. The groups who will be most involved in implementing the decision are highly motivated to do so since they have been fully involved in making the decision.
   c. Decisions reached by groups are generally better decisions than are those made by individuals, even though persons working alone often can suggest more possible alternative solutions in a given number of hours than can the same person working in a group (Barnlund, 1959; Cartwright & Zander, 1968; Dunnette, Campbell, & Jaastad, 1963; Lorge, Davitz, Fox, & Herrold, 1953; Lorge & Solomon, 1959; Maier, 1950, 1967; Taylor, 1965).
   d. The decisions reached through group problem solving are likely to be carried out well since persons understand the decisions they have helped to reach and are highly motivated to see them implemented.

Two phenomena contribute to the greater effectiveness of System 4T interaction-influence networks and deserve consideration. An understanding of them increases one's insight into the reasons for System 4T's superiority as an effective social system and for the strength of its "social fabric." These phenomena are related organizational processes and are called *peer leadership* and *organizational climate.* The first refers to the leadership functions within the group performed by the subordinate members of that group. The second is concerned with the effect of leadership behavior, especially the behavior of top-level managers, upon the total organization.

Peer leadership

The phenomenon of peer leadership contributes appreciably to the much greater strength and effectiveness of System 4T interaction-influence networks compared with other networks. Bowers and Seashore (1964) state the following concerning peer leadership:

1. Our data sustain the idea that group members do engage in behavior which can be described as leadership, and that in these groups, it appears likely that the total quantity of peer leadership is at least as great as the total quantity of supervisory leadership. The groups varied greatly from one another with respect to the degree and the pattern of emphasis in peer leadership behavior.

2. The four dimensions of leadership developed initially for the description of formal leaders appear to be equally applicable to the description of leadership by group members. These four dimensions are:

   a. Support: Behavior which serves the function of increasing or maintaining the individual member's sense of personal worth and importance in the context of group activity.
   b. Interaction Facilitation: Behavior which serves the function of creating or maintaining a network of interpersonal relationships among members of the group.
   c. Goal Emphasis: Behavior which serves the function of creating, changing, clarifying, or gaining member acceptance of group goals.
   d. Work Facilitation: Behavior which serves to provide effective work methods, facilities, and technology for the accomplishment of group goals.

3. The supervisor's pattern of leadership (i.e., relative degree of emphasis on each of the four dimensions) tends to be replicated in the leadership behavior of his subordinates; that is, the subordinates tend to provide leadership in much the same way as does the formal leader. This correspondence of pattern, however, is not so great as to preclude the possibility that some compensatory leadership by the members is occurring. (pp. 49–50)

The Intercompany Longitudinal Study of the Institute for Social Research (Likert, Bowers, & Norman, 1969) launched a series of investigations in which the same instrument was used to measure the human organization of firms (Taylor & Bowers, 1972). Since the pilot projects for this study were started in

1966, more than 50,000 persons in about 75 plants or divisions in some 25 companies have been surveyed at least once. A number of sites have been surveyed two or more times. Results from these studies confirm the above conclusions concerning the phenomenon of peer leadership as well as adding confirmation to the earlier statements of the superior effectiveness of System 4T (Taylor & Bowers, 1972).

The evidence is substantial and clear that peer leadership is an important phenomenon in every organization and strengthens—or weakens—the operating capacity of their interaction-influence networks. In System 4T organizations, peer leadership strengthens the organization. In Systems 1 or 2, peer leadership often weakens the organization by stimulating behavior oriented toward defeating rather than achieving the goals of the organization. Restriction of output is common.

The leadership behavior of subordinates toward their peers tends to reflect that of the superior on all four causal dimensions. Subordinates also display the same leadership behavior in dealing with their own subordinates. In this manner, the leadership behavior of the superior at the top of the organization is mirrored, and perhaps often magnified, by successively lower levels in the organization.

Organizational climate

The effect of this impact of the leadership behavior at the top and upper levels of an organization upon all levels of that organization is now being referred to as *organizational climate*. Tagiuri and Litwin's (1968) definition of the term is:

> Organizational climate is a relatively enduring quality of the internal environment of an organization that (a) is experienced by its members, (b) influences their behavior, and (c) can be described in terms of the values of a particular set of characteristics (or attributes) of the organization. (p. 27)

In measuring intervening variables in the Intercompany Longitudinal Study, it was discovered that members of an organization have two frames of reference in answering items in a questionnaire. One is the respondent's own immediate work group. The other is the total organization or some other large entity, such as the plant or division. The answers to the same question can be quite different for these two different frames of reference. For example, upward communication within the individuals' own work group can be excellent, as they see it, whereas their view of upward communication for their entire department is that it is poor and highly inaccurate.

Data obtained from items asked concerning the individuals' view of the situation within their work groups are called *work-group intervening measurements*. When the items ask questions concerning the department or the larger organization, the data obtained reflect the state of the variables for that larger organizational entity. The composite state of these organizational variables measures the organizational climate of that larger organizational entity.

Analyses of the extensive data obtained by the Institute for Social Research since 1946 reveal that the organizational climate experienced by a particular work group or by a particular hierarchical level in an organization is determined primarily by the leadership behavior of echelons above it. The behavior of the leaders at the very top echelon exerts by far the greatest influence. The capacity to exert influence on the organizational climate drops sharply by hierarchical level unless some conditioning factor such as geographical distance from top management alters the situation (Samuel, 1970).

As one proceeds down the hierarchy, superiors at each level are found to exert less and less influence on the organizational climate and to be increasingly influenced by the organizational climate in which they are embedded. This climate provides powerful restraints upon the kind of management which they feel free to use. The sizable correlations, e.g., +.5, found in organizations between the management systems used by the higher echelons and those used by lower levels of management reveal the substantial constraint exerted by the organizational climate upon the behavior of superiors at middle and lower levels in an organization. Figure 5-16 illustrates graphically the manner in which organizational climate functions in an organization. The wider lines at lower hierarchical levels depict the progressively greater constraining force of organizational climate.

The effect of a System 1 or 2 organizational climate is to put pressure on the superiors at middle and lower echelons to use System 1 or 2 leadership and methods of conflict management. A superior has to be highly competent and highly courageous in a System 1 or 2 organization to deviate from the established pattern. This same situation exists also in a System 3 organization, but the restraining forces of the climate are less and it is easier for a lower-level superior to move toward System 4.

In System 4T organizations, the effect of the organizational climate is beneficial since it encourages lower echelons to use System 4T styles of leadership and conflict mangement. Moreover, the effect of the organizational climate in System 4 organizations is much less restraining than in other kinds of organizations since lower levels in a System 4 organization have much greater capacity to exert upward influence successfully upon the organizational climate and other variables and decisions than is the case in System 1, 2, or 3 organizations.

Superiority of System 4T
even more marked
in voluntary organizations

There have been far fewer studies made of the leadership style or management system used by organizations which make little or no use of economic motiva-

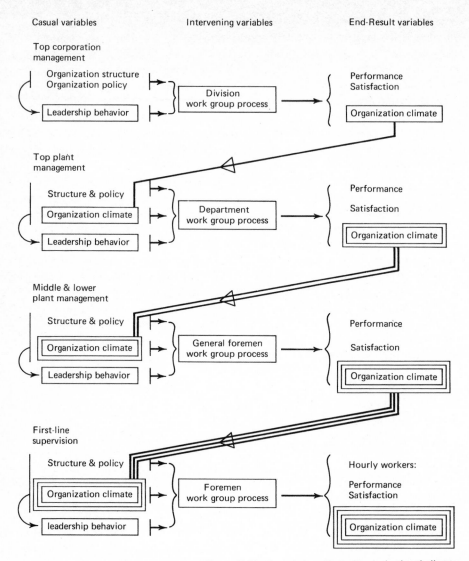

Figure 5-16 *Cumulative effect of organizational climate.*

tion than of those which make extensive use of it. The studies, however, which have been made of these organizations, such as voluntary organizations, show essentially the same patterns of relationships among the causal, intervening, and end-result variables as has been found for organizations which make extensive use of economic motivation. There is one important difference. As a rule, the studies in voluntary organizations reveal much more marked relationships among the variables than is found in organizations which make use of economic motivation. Evidently, Systems 1, 2, and 3, and leadership styles based on them, make much poorer use than does System 4 of the major noneconomic motive sources, such as the desire to achieve and maintain a sense of personal worth. As a consequence, the relationships between leadership behavior, on the one hand, and the intervening and end-result variables, on the other, are appreciably more marked when the masking influence of economic motivation is removed.

Figure 5-17 illustrates the marked relationships found between leader behavior and organizational effectiveness in studies of a voluntary organization. These results are from a study of 104 local leagues representative of all local leagues of the League of Women Voters of the United States (Tannenbaum, 1958).

This appreciably greater capacity of System 4, in comparison with other systems, to make effective use of major noneconomic motive sources makes System 4 especially applicable for improving the resolution of conflicts. Economic motivation, as used typically by Systems 1, 2, and 3, involves buying a person's time and thereby achieving the right to issue orders and compel compliance. This is a form of power *over* others and stimulates the use of the win-lose approach to resolving conflicts. As we have seen, win-lose is an unsatisfactory and ineffective approach to resolving conflicts.

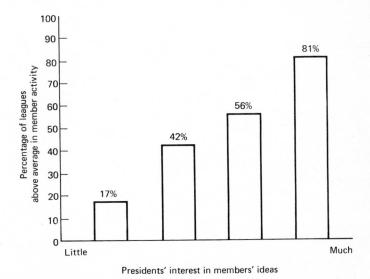

Figure 5-17 *Relation between presidents' interest in members' ideas and member activity, League of Women Voters. (From New Patterns of Management, Fig. 10-9, copyright © 1961 by McGraw-Hill, Inc. Used by permission of McGraw-Hill Book Company. No further reproduction or distribution authorized.)*

*Effective groups contribute
to conflict resolution*

Additional insights into the operating characteristics of a System 4T interaction-influence network are readily obtained by recalling that System 4 relies heavily upon problem solving by highly effective face-to-face work groups. This reliance permits the substantial body of findings from research on the small group to be used to derive additional insights into the operating characteristics of a social system consisting of multiple overlapping groups. This knowledge can be employed also to facilitate the use of System 4T interaction-influence networks to resolve conflicts. An understanding of the dynamics of small groups, consequently, can be of great value. Excellent reports, surveys, and summaries are available of the nature and operating characteristics of small groups (Bales, 1950; Berkowitz, 1965; Cartwright & Zander, 1968; Hare, 1962; Kelley & Thibaut, 1969; Thibaut & Kelley, 1959; Zander, 1971).

Some feeling for the potential contribution of an understanding of group dynamics in resolving conflicts can be obtained also from Cartwright (1951). Since the resolution of conflicts virtually always involves change, the orientation in Cartwright's excellent paper is especially pertinent; the following casts light on the level of the motivational forces which effective groups can create:

> In one series of experiments directed by Lewin, it was found that a method of group decision, in which the group as a whole made a decision to have its members change their behavior, was from two to ten times as effective in producing actual changes as was a lecture presenting exhortation to change (Lewin, 1951). We have yet to learn precisely what produces these differences of effectiveness, but it is clear that by introducing group forces into the situation a whole new level of influence has been achieved. (p. 385)

This capacity of groups to create strong motivational forces even in the absence of economic and similar motivation can be crucial in many conflict situations. High levels of motivation often are necessary if conflicting parties are to struggle through their differences to creative solutions and then implement the decisions reached. Face-to-face groups in a System 4T interaction-influence network can provide this necessary motivation. (The characteristics of highly effective groups are described in Likert, 1961, pp. 166–169.)

Other studies show the substantial power that groups having high group loyalty can exert. For example, Perrucci and Pilisuk (1970) have found in a community of 50,000 that power is exerted by a small group of elite leaders who are linked together by organizational and social ties. These leaders also share common views on community issues. This small group has a "general reputation for power" within the community and is "identified as involved in past community issues of major proportions." The interorganizational ties among these elite leaders create a "resource network which can be mobilized and brought to bear upon particular community issues" (p. 1056).

6

The role of
supportive behavior
in System 4 leadership

Reinhold Niebuhr remarked several years ago at a meeting of the National Commission for UNESCO, "What the world needs is a social fabric so tough that it cannot be torn asunder or punched full of holes by conflicts or disputes."

A tougher, more tightly knit social fabric is needed to withstand the tensions of conflict wherever conflict appears: between nations, between various segments of a nation, and within and between a nation's social institutions.

As we have just seen, the System 4 interaction-influence network is more effective than are the networks of Systems 1, 2, and 3 for providing the tough social fabric that difficult conflicts require. The evidence concerning the superior effectiveness of the System 4 interaction-influence network has come primarily from business. Since System 4 networks have been developed most fully and used most extensively there, an understanding of their basic principles and characteristics and how these differ from the interaction-influence networks of Systems 1, 2, and 3 can best be obtained by examining these networks in business firms. After an understanding of the fundamental principles and essential characteristics of the System 4 interaction-influence network has been acquired, they can be applied readily to any kind of conflict.

Every interaction-influence network consists of a structure and of leadership and interaction processes within that structure. This and the next three chapters will discuss System 4 leadership and interaction processes and their application to any conflict situation. Chapters 10 to 12 are devoted to the structure of a System 4 interaction-influence network.

The effectiveness of an interaction-influence network depends upon the adequacy of its structure and interaction processes. The interactions occurring within a network are profoundly affected by the leadership provided. Leadership, consequently, is of major importance in building and operating highly effective interaction-influence networks.

System 4 leadership differs in important respects from the leadership required by other systems. The focus in this chapter and the next will be on the leadership principles relatively unique to System 4 and essential for building and operating a System 4 interaction-influence network. The emphasis will be on principles of wide applicability rather than on specific techniques or practices for a very practical reason. As our society has industrialized, it has become progressively more complex. This has made the task of leaders in our large, complex business firms, governmental agencies, and other organizations difficult at best. Imagine, however, the complex task leaders would face if every time they assumed a leadership role in a different situation, they had to learn a whole new set of specific ways of behaving in order to be an effective leader. Under such circumstances, a leader's manual in a highly complex industrialized society would have to approach *Webster's Third New International Dictionary* in size to describe fully how leaders should behave in the countless varieties of situations in which leaders and managers must function.

A set of general principles that can be mastered and, when understood well, can be applied in widely different situations with appropriate specific procedures is clearly to be preferred to a huge master volume listing countless "dos and don'ts." Fortunately, as was observed in Chapter 3, substantial research findings now support the view that there are general leadership principles, broadly applicable. One principle discussed there, the most fundamental of all System 4 leadership principles, is the principle of supportive relationships which is stated (Likert, 1961) as follows:

> The leadership and other processes of the organization must be such as to ensure a maximum probability that in all interactions and all relationships with the organization, each member will, in the light of his background, values, and expectations, view the experience as supportive and one which builds and maintains his sense of personal worth and importance. (p. 103)

There is a substantial and growing body of research findings demonstrating that the application of this leadership principle yields favorable attitudes and highly motivated, cooperative behavior and helps an organization achieve its objectives efficiently. These relationships, moreover, are appreciably more evident when performance over time is examined (Guest, 1962; Likert, 1967; Likert & Bowers, 1969; Marrow, Bowers, & Seashore, 1967).

Research in other areas, such as consumer behavior, voting behavior, child and personality development, and mental health, all yield additional findings providing further evidence of the universality and strength of the desire to achieve and maintain a sense of personal worth and importance (e.g., Rogers, 1951).

Applying the principle of supportive relationships

The most important principle for a leader who is seeking to apply System 4 in an organization or in a conflict situation to master is the principle of supportive relationships. This principle embodies two highly important concepts about human behavior: (1) all persons have a strong, inherited desire to achieve and maintain a sense of personal worth and importance;[1] (2) all individuals respond to an experience on the basis of its relation, as they see it, to their own values, goals, traditions, expectations, and skills.

The culturally relative nature of all human reaction and behavior is one of the major findings of cultural anthropology. Studies concerned with the relative influence of heredity and environment upon behavior as well as research on perception, personality, and child development also have added impressive evidence to demonstrate that every individual's perception of an experience and reaction to it is determined by all that he or she has learned from previous experiences. It is in this sense that all behavior is culturally relative.

It is not enough for leaders to believe genuinely that they are reacting in a supportive manner. Leaders often are distressingly insensitive and incorrect in their own perceptions of their behavior and of others' perceptions of their behavior. The principle of supportive relationships is being applied only when the persons with whom the leader is dealing see the leader's behavior as contributing to their sense of personal worth. This second dimension of the principle emphasizes the necessity of the leader's being correctly informed of the other person's perceptions and reactions and of behaving so as to respect them.

Since the particular way of applying the principle of supportive relationships must fit the immediate situation, appropriate leadership behavior varies widely from one situation to another. The unique circumstances, the traditions of the organization or institution, the personality of the leader, and the values, expectations, and skills of those with whom the leader is interacting are all important factors in determining which particular way of behaving in a given situation represents the best way to apply this basic principle. An individual who has a quiet, reserved, or even cold manner should not try suddenly to become a hail-fellow-well-met in order to be seen by associates as warm, friendly, and approachable. Supportive behavior can be displayed in ways consistent with the individual's personality without any sudden strained attempt to change a characteristic mode of behaving.

The personality of an individual can change and does change as organizational or interactional environment is altered and as that individual seeks to improve his or her usual mode of behavior. These changes, however, occur slowly over several years' time. Any attempt at rapid change by leaders usually is futile since it is viewed with distrust and suspicion by those with whom they interact.

---

[1]This desire is the motive source for a variety of needs. Depending upon the socialization that a particular person has experienced, this desire can yield such needs as the need for power, the need for achievement, the need for recognition or status, or the need to be submissive and humble.

A comparison with the
situational or contingency model

Fiedler and others who adhere to the contingency or situational view of leadership would select in each situation a leader whose style of behavior fitted the characteristics of those being led. For example, if the members of an organization or organizational unit had experienced System 2 leadership and expected it, a System 2 leader would be selected for them in an effort to achieve the most effective results. There would be no attempt to move the behavior of leaders and members progressively, at an assimilable rate, to System 4.

As pointed out in Chapter 3, research shows that a System $2\frac{1}{4}$ or $2\frac{1}{2}$ leadership style achieves better results with a System 2 organizational unit than does System 2 leadership. Steady, progressive shifts to System 4 leadership that the unit members can readily assimilate and respond to achieve steadily improving performance.

The use of the contingency model with no attempt to change the leadership and membership interaction style to a more effective model is a static view of organizations. It minimizes the likelihood of improvement beyond that realized by selecting an appropriate leader.

A dynamic view of organizations is much to be preferred. Leaders and members can learn to modify their behavior. Leaders can learn to use leadership behavior that deviates in the direction of System 4 but still is well within the range of the interaction skills, values, and expectations of those with whom they are interacting.

Increasing the accuracy of perceptions

The principle of supportive relationships places a heavy demand upon a leader. To apply it effectively, leaders must be relatively sensitive persons with reasonably accurate insights into the reactions and behavior of others. If not, they would be wise to take steps to help develop this capacity for accurate perception. A particularly effective step in getting an accurate picture of a leader's behavior and of the reactions of others to it is to obtain objective measurements of the causal and intervening variables. These measurements can be quite simple or, for more accurate results, they can be extensive and complex.

One way to measure perceptual errors is to ask leaders to fill out a form such as Table 6-1 so as to describe how they believe those with whom they are interacting see them behaving. Members of these groups would be asked to fill out, anonymously, the same form describing how *they* see their leader behaving. When the leader's answers and the average of the answers of members are compared, there often are appreciable discrepancies revealing errors in perception. This helps the leader to see correctly the values, expectations, and reactions of the others and the extent to which they feel the leader's behavior is supportive and contributes to effective problem solving.

Valuable additional insights can be obtained by discussing the discrepancies

Table 6-1
Profile of leadership behavior (Form LB)

This questionnaire is designed to describe the behavior of the leader in any group engaged in problem solving.

In completing the questionnaire, it is important that you answer each question as thoughtfully and frankly as possible. There are no right or wrong answers.

The answers will be summarized in statistical form so that individuals cannot be identified. To ensure complete confidentiality, please do not write your name anywhere on this questionnaire.

Please indicate your answer to each question by filling in the circle under the choice that best describes your view on that question.

For example, suppose the question were:

	Rarely		Sometimes		Often		Very often	
How often does the sun shine in your town?	①	②	③	④	⑤	⑥	⑦	⑧

If you think that the sun shines often, you would fill in ⑤ or ⑥. You would fill in ⑤ if you feel that the situation is closer to "sometimes" than to "very often." You would fill in ⑥ if you feel that the situation is closer to "very often."

To what extent do you feel that your leader:

	Very little		Some		Considerable		Very great	
1. Is friendly and easy to talk to	①	②	③	④	⑤	⑥	⑦	⑧
2. Listens well to you and others whether she or he agrees or disagrees	①	②	③	④	⑤	⑥	⑦	⑧
3. States your point of view as well or better than you can even though she or he disagrees	①	②	③	④	⑤	⑥	⑦	⑧
4. Encourages you and others to express your ideas fully and frankly	①	②	③	④	⑤	⑥	⑦	⑧
5. Encourages you and others to express your feelings frankly	①	②	③	④	⑤	⑥	⑦	⑧
6. Displays confidence and trust in you and others whether or not she or he agrees	①	②	③	④	⑤	⑥	⑦	⑧

Table 6-1
Profile of leadership behavior (Form LB) **(Continued)**

To what extent do you feel that
your leader:

	Very little		Some		Considerable		Very great	
7. Shares information frankly	①	②	③	④	⑤	⑥	⑦	⑧
8. Expects each member to do her or his very best	①	②	③	④	⑤	⑥	⑦	⑧
9. Expects a high-quality job from herself or himself	①	②	③	④	⑤	⑥	⑦	⑧
10. Thinks what she or he and the group are doing is important	①	②	③	④	⑤	⑥	⑦	⑧
11. Encourages innovative and creative ideas	①	②	③	④	⑤	⑥	⑦	⑧

	Very little		Some		Considerable		Very great	
12. Is willing to take risks	①	②	③	④	⑤	⑥	⑦	⑧
13. Is not defensive when criticized	①	②	③	④	⑤	⑥	⑦	⑧
14. Avoids treating you and others in a condescending manner	①	②	③	④	⑤	⑥	⑦	⑧
15. Avoids pontificating	①	②	③	④	⑤	⑥	⑦	⑧
16. Avoids stating her or his views dogmatically	①	②	③	④	⑤	⑥	⑦	⑧
17. Avoids being impatient with the progress being made by the group	①	②	③	④	⑤	⑥	⑦	⑧

	Very little		Some		Considerable		Very great	
18. Avoids dominating the discussion	①	②	③	④	⑤	⑥	⑦	⑧
19. Encourages group to work through disagreements, not suppress them	①	②	③	④	⑤	⑥	⑦	⑧
20. Uses "we" and "our" rather than "I" or "my"	①	②	③	④	⑤	⑥	⑦	⑧
21. Shows no favorites; treats all members equally	①	②	③	④	⑤	⑥	⑦	⑧
22. Gives credit and recognition generously	①	②	③	④	⑤	⑥	⑦	⑧

Table 6-1
Profile of leadership behavior (Form LB)   (Continued)

To what extent do you feel that
your leader:

	Very little		Some		Considerable		Very great	
23. Accepts more blame than may be warranted for any failure or mistake	①	②	③	④	⑤	⑥	⑦	⑧
24. Avoids imposing a decision upon the group	①	②	③	④	⑤	⑥	⑦	⑧
25. Waits until members of the group have stated their positions before stating hers or his	①	②	③	④	⑤	⑥	⑦	⑧
26. Presents own contribution tentatively or as questions	①	②	③	④	⑤	⑥	⑦	⑧

in scores with the group members. In this discussion, it is useful to try to discover why each major discrepancy in answers occurred.

Tape recorders or videoscopes can be very useful also in collecting material to help a leader and group members listen more attentively and understandingly and in other ways to apply the principle of supportive relationships in a sensitive and insightful manner. Analyzing recorded sessions helps to provide insights as to the causes of successful progress or of difficulty and breakdown. Supportive behavior is readily recognized as are ego-deflating attacks. As a rule, these aspects of leader and member behavior are even more obvious when played back than when experienced in the original situation.

The analysis of data revealing leader behavior and membership reactions needs to be done in a friendly, supportive atmosphere in keeping with the principle of supportive relationships and not in an ego-deflating manner. Supportive discussion by the group of these data and of what can be done to bring about an improvement can be of great value in assisting the leader and the members to improve. Ego-deflating attacks can be disastrous.

The bilateral check

Another step which often helps leaders see a situation as others see it is to apply what Elliott Dunlop Smith (1928) years ago labeled "the bilateral check." Smith suggested that managers or leaders, after viewing a situation from their own standpoint, take a fresh look at it from the point of view of the other relevant persons with whom they are interacting. Carl Rogers (1961) has urged the same empathic behavior in his concept of "becoming the other." Leaders can benefit greatly by developing the habit of consciously looking at every situation from the point of view of the others involved as well as from the leaders' own initial orientation.

As these suggestions indicate, there are many steps leaders can take to help increase the accuracy of their perceptions of how others see the leaders' behavior. But no matter how it is done, the leaders' aim should be to help all those with whom they are interacting to achieve and maintain a sense of personal worth and importance.

Improving the supportive behavior of each member of a group

Although it is especially important that the leader apply the principle of supportive relationships, the effectiveness of a group's interactions and problem solving is improved greatly when *every* member of the group also behaves supportively. Tables 6-1, 6-2, and 6-3 can be used to help each member of a group, as well as its leader, develop the habit of supportive behavior. For this purpose, all members should complete these tables describing both how they feel they are behaving and how they see the other members behaving. The average (mean) score on each item in Table 6-2 should be computed. A profile of these average scores should be plotted. The highest response of any member on each item and the lowest also should be shown. The group then should examine the profile and range in responses, item by item, and ask itself, "Are we behaving in the way that we know is necessary if we are going to solve problems well and resolve conflicts constructively? What changes should we make in our behavior to more successfully do the task we have undertaken?"

If some members of the group are particularly insensitive and show a lack of supportive behavior toward the others, another step can be taken. Every member of the group could be asked to complete a separate short questionnaire based on Table 6-3, namely items 1, 2, 4, 5, 7, 15, 16, and 19, showing their perceptions of the behavior of each member of the group. If there were 10 members, there would be 9 completed short questionnaires for each member showing how the other members saw that person behaving. The average score on each item could be computed for each person and given to that person to show how the other members of the group see that person behaving. This average could then be compared with the score the member had assigned himself or herself to see the extent to which the others' view of that behavior is the same as, or different from, that member's. For some individuals, the differences will be small. Their perception of their behavior is relatively accurate. For others, the differences will be large. The persons whose perceptions are inaccurate should be encouraged and assisted in asking the other members why they see them behaving so differently from the way they believe they are

Table 6-2
Profile of group members' behavior (Form GMB)

This questionnaire is designed to describe the overall behavior of the members of any group engaged in problem solving.

In completing the questionnaire, it is important that you answer each question as thoughtfully and frankly as possible. There are no right or wrong answers.

The answers will be summarized in statistical form so that individuals cannot be identified. To ensure complete confidentiality, please do not write your name anywhere on this questionnaire.

Please indicate your answer to each question by filling in the circle under the choice that best describes your view on that question.

For example, suppose the question were:

	Rarely		Sometimes		Often		Very often	
How often does the sun shine in your town?	①	②	③	④	⑤	⑥	⑦	⑧

If you think that the sun shines often, you would fill in ⑤ or ⑥. You would fill in ⑤ if you feel that the situation is closer to "sometimes" than to "very often." You would fill in ⑥ if you feel that the situation is closer to "very often."

To what extent do you feel that the members of your group:

	Very little		Some		Considerable		Very great	
1. Are friendly and easy to talk to	①	②	③	④	⑤	⑥	⑦	⑧
2. Listen well to you and others whether they agree or disagree	①	②	③	④	⑤	⑥	⑦	⑧
3. State your point of view as well or better than you can even though they disagree	①	②	③	④	⑤	⑥	⑦	⑧
4. Encourage you and others to express ideas fully and frankly	①	②	③	④	⑤	⑥	⑦	⑧
5. Encourage you and others to express feelings frankly	①	②	③	④	⑤	⑥	⑦	⑧
6. Display confidence and trust in you and others whether or not they agree	①	②	③	④	⑤	⑥	⑦	⑧

Table 6-2

To what extent do you feel that
the members of your group:

	Very little		Some		Considerable		Very great	
7. Share information frankly	①	②	③	④	⑤	⑥	⑦	⑧
8. Expect you to do your very best	①	②	③	④	⑤	⑥	⑦	⑧
9. Expect a high-quality job from themselves	①	②	③	④	⑤	⑥	⑦	⑧
10. Think what the group is doing is important	①	②	③	④	⑤	⑥	⑦	⑧
11. Encourage innovative and creative ideas	①	②	③	④	⑤	⑥	⑦	⑧

	Very little		Some		Considerable		Very great	
12. Are willing to take risks	①	②	③	④	⑤	⑥	⑦	⑧
13. Are not defensive when criticized	①	②	③	④	⑤	⑥	⑦	⑧
14. Avoid treating others in a condescending manner	①	②	③	④	⑤	⑥	⑦	⑧
15. Avoid pontificating	①	②	③	④	⑤	⑥	⑦	⑧

	Very little		Some		Considerable		Very great	
16. Avoid stating their views dogmatically	①	②	③	④	⑤	⑥	⑦	⑧
17. Avoid being impatient with the progress being made by the group	①	②	③	④	⑤	⑥	⑦	⑧
18. Avoid dominating the discussion	①	②	③	④	⑤	⑥	⑦	⑧
19. Encourage group to work through disagreements, not suppress them	①	②	③	④	⑤	⑥	⑦	⑧
20. Use "we" and "our" rather than "I" or "my"	①	②	③	④	⑤	⑥	⑦	⑧
21. Show no favorites; treat all members equally	①	②	③	④	⑤	⑥	⑦	⑧
22. Give credit and recognition generously	①	②	③	④	⑤	⑥	⑦	⑧

Table 6-2
Profile of group members' behavior (Form GMB) **(Continued)**

To what extent do you feel that
the members of your group:

23. Accept more blame than
    may be warranted for any
    failure or mistake

    ① ② ③ ④ ⑤ ⑥ ⑦ ⑧

24. Avoid imposing a decision
    upon the group

    ① ② ③ ④ ⑤ ⑥ ⑦ ⑧

acting. Candid, supportive discussion of these differences can help such members see their own behavior more accurately and, in turn, learn to behave more supportively in group problem-solving sessions.

Confidence and trust in others is essential

To behave in ways consistent with the principle of supportive relationships, leaders must have a basic faith in people and a generous attitude toward others. They cannot deal openly and supportively with others unless they have confidence in their abilities, judgment, and integrity, and have trust in them. They must believe that people fundamentally and inherently are decent and trustworthy and will behave that way when given the opportunity and encouragement to do so. This, of course, is the view of others which McGregor (1960) has labeled "Theory Y." When leaders lack confidence and trust in other persons and believe that they are generally deceitful, lazy, and unreliable, the leaders are compelled to use a System 2 (or 1) form of interaction-influence network. This latter view of other persons is McGregor's "Theory X." Leaders must have a high level of confidence and trust in people, otherwise they are violating the principle of supportive relationships.

An important aspect of System 4 interaction-influence networks is that experience in such an organization helps a person progressively acquire confidence and trust in others. In the groups in a System 4 organization, each person encounters friendly, supportive relationships. Communication is open, candid, and unguarded. Confidence and trust permeate interpersonal relationships. As persons experience this environment and are treated with confidence and trust, they gradually learn that the best results are achieved when they treat others in the same way. As a consequence, in a System 4 interaction-influence network, those who move into positions of leadership and management generally have confidence and trust in the other persons with whom they interact, including subordinates, associates, peers, and superiors.

Table 6-3
Profile of own behavior (Form OB)

This questionnaire is designed to enable a member of a group engaged in problem solving to describe his/her own behavior.

In completing the questionnaire, it is important that you answer each question as thoughtfully and frankly as possible. There are no right or wrong answers.

The answers will be summarized in statistical form so that individuals cannot be identified. To ensure complete confidentiality, please do not write your name anywhere on this questionnaire.

Please indicate your answer to each question by filling in the circle under the choice that best describes your view on that question.

For example, suppose the question were:

	Rarely		Sometimes		Often		Very often	
How often does the sun shine in your town?	①	②	③	④	⑤	⑥	⑦	⑧

If you think that the sun shines often, you would fill in ⑤ or ⑥. You would fill in ⑤ if you feel that the situation is closer to "sometimes" than to "very often." You would fill in ⑥ if you feel that the situation is closer to "very often."

To what extent do you feel that you:

	Very little		Some		Considerable		Very great	
1. Are friendly and easy to talk to	①	②	③	④	⑤	⑥	⑦	⑧
2. Listen well to others whether you agree or disagree	①	②	③	④	⑤	⑥	⑦	⑧
3. State the points of view of others as well or better than they can even though you disagree	①	②	③	④	⑤	⑥	⑦	⑧
4. Encourage others to express their ideas fully and frankly	①	②	③	④	⑤	⑥	⑦	⑧
5. Encourage others to express their feelings frankly	①	②	③	④	⑤	⑥	⑦	⑧

Table 6-3
Profile of own behavior (Form OB) **(Continued)**

To what extent do you feel that you:

	Very little		Some		Considerable		Very great	

6. Display confidence and trust in others whether or not you agree ① ② ③ ④ ⑤ ⑥ ⑦ ⑧

7. Share information frankly ① ② ③ ④ ⑤ ⑥ ⑦ ⑧

8. Expect others to do their very best ① ② ③ ④ ⑤ ⑥ ⑦ ⑧

9. Expect a high-quality job from yourself ① ② ③ ④ ⑤ ⑥ ⑦ ⑧

10. Think what you and the group are doing is important ① ② ③ ④ ⑤ ⑥ ⑦ ⑧

11. Encourage innovative and creative ideas ① ② ③ ④ ⑤ ⑥ ⑦ ⑧

    Very little   Some   Considerable   Very great

12. Are willing to take risks ① ② ③ ④ ⑤ ⑥ ⑦ ⑧

13. Are not defensive when criticized ① ② ③ ④ ⑤ ⑥ ⑦ ⑧

14. Avoid treating others in a condescending manner ① ② ③ ④ ⑤ ⑥ ⑦ ⑧

15. Avoid pontificating

    Very little   Some   Considerable   Very great

16. Avoid stating your views dogmatically ① ② ③ ④ ⑤ ⑥ ⑦ ⑧

17. Avoid being impatient with the progress being made by the group ① ② ③ ④ ⑤ ⑥ ⑦ ⑧

18. Avoid dominating the discussion ① ② ③ ④ ⑤ ⑥ ⑦ ⑧

19. Encourage group to work through disagreements, not suppress them ① ② ③ ④ ⑤ ⑥ ⑦ ⑧

Table 6-3

Profile of own behavior (Form OB) (Continued)

To what extent do you feel that you:

	Very little		Some		Considerable		Very great	
20. Use "we" and "our" rather than "I" or "my"	①	②	③	④	⑤	⑥	⑦	⑧
21. Show no favorites; treat all members equally	①	②	③	④	⑤	⑥	⑦	⑧
22. Give credit and recognition generously	①	②	③	④	⑤	⑥	⑦	⑧
23. Accept more blame than may be warranted for any failure or mistake	①	②	③	④	⑤	⑥	⑦	⑧
24. Avoid imposing a decision upon the group	①	②	③	④	⑤	⑥	⑦	⑧

As persons acquire confidence and trust in others, they deal openly and frankly with them. They share information candidly rather than withholding it and do not try to outsmart or outmaneuver anyone. Argyris' findings concerning the importance of "authentic behavior" illustrate this form of supportive behavior (Argyris, 1964).

Greater confidence and trust displayed in highly industrialized nations

Studies in countries which are not highly industrialized indicate that leaders have much less confidence and trust in subordinates than is the case in highly industrialized nations. This is true also of the confidence and trust citizens of these countries have in each other (Almond & Verba, 1963; Loomis, 1970; Loomis & Loomis, 1969; Loomis, Loomis, & Gullahorn, 1966).

The level of confidence and trust among a nation's citizens appears to be related to the nature of its political system. In nonindustrialized nations, the political system is much more toward System 1 than are the political systems of the highly industrialized nations. Nations using political systems that are System 1 in character will display System 1 patterns of relationships among their citizens. Fear and hostility will be widespread, and there will be much jealousy, distrust, and fighting between them. Although no nation has as yet established a System 4 political system, the citizens of those nations that approach it most closely tend to display more friendliness, confidence and trust, and cooperative behavior than do citizens of System 1 nations.

Apparently one of the essential social developments that must occur in an industrializing nation if it is to be successful in its efforts to resolve conflicts constructively and to achieve high levels of industrial output is for its citizens and especially its leaders to develop confidence and trust in others. As it examines its own progress and experience, each of these nations will find that its most successful enterprises are closer to System 4 in their management style than are those that are less successful (Likert, 1969). These observations will create forces in the nation to move the management systems of all enterprises progressively toward System 4. As the management systems of its enterprises move toward System 4, the entire society, including the political system of the nation, will move correspondingly. Every nation that strives to attain a high level of output from its investments in industrial technology will find its leaders and the total society pushed by their experience toward valuing integrity and confidence and trust in others.

There are societies which make extensive use of groups and of behavior in groups but which are not System 4 in character. In these societies, individuals are expected to sacrifice themselves for the group and for the larger society. Little value is placed on individuals. They are weak and have little influence on decisions affecting them. Decisions which control their behavior and fate are made by higher hierarchical levels in the society. This latter form of society is essentially System $1\frac{1}{2}$ or 2 in character and does not attach importance to supportive behavior.

Expecting little from others deflates their sense of personal worth

The initial discussion of the principle of supportive relationships in *New Patterns of Management* (Likert, 1961) appears not to have been sufficiently clear. Some readers misinterpreted the principle and assumed that an appropriate application of the principle occurred when a leader was "nice to persons and kept them happy, never expected them to do much, merely took care of them so that they could live an easy, relaxed life." This, of course, is a gross misunderstanding of the principle. Most persons wish to obtain a sense of accomplishment and self-actualization from useful work or activity. One who is not expected to perform at a high level of competence will assume that others view him or her as weak, incompetent, inferior, and in need of being taken care of. This view is ego-deflating and violates in a fundamental manner the principle of supportive relationships.

A related role of the leader in applying the principle of supportive relation-ships is to help the members of an organization keep firmly in mind the significance of what they and their organization are doing. The leader, person-ally, must see clearly the importance of the organization's mission and the valuable contributions it is making. In all relations to members, the leader should radiate enthusiasm for the importance of the entire organization's activities as well as for the mission of his or her own unit.

High aspirations for the attainment of excellence are an important aspect of the leader's job. Members of the League of Women Voters speak of doing a "League-like job" which means a job of high quality. The conviction that League members are the kind of persons who can be counted on for top-quality performance creates a personal and organizational image that encourages excellence.

If leaders are to help create such an image in an organization, a group, or an individual, they must have expectations of superior accomplishment for themselves as well as for others: "I am the kind of leader who is supportive and sympathetic in my treatment of others"; "Ours is the kind of group that can solve our conflicts successfully." Such attitudes create ego images that will be both a goal and a nudge.

Some leaders provide strong motivation for excellence by expecting "the impossible" from their members and having complete confidence that they will achieve it. This orientation by leaders stimulates not only outstanding performance but the growth and development of the members. One highly successful company has found that this kind of behavior by superiors is one of the most effective procedures for helping subordinates accomplish difficult tasks and, in the process of doing so, acquire increased competence and self-confidence. They found that expecting "the impossible" is seen by subordinates as a vote of confidence in their abilities and is highly effective in helping them grow in their leadership skills. They want to live up to the expectations of a supportive boss. The boss's belief in them makes them willing to undertake with confidence more and more difficult assignments. As they move into more complex situations, the new experiences enlarge their abilities and give them an opportunity to develop additional skills.

Another related application of the principle of supportive relationships is for leaders to be a source of restless dissatisfaction with all that is mediocre, complacent, and inadequate. They should strive for excellence and stimulate others to pursue excellence (Gardner, 1961).

An essential role of leadership, consequently, is to foster creativity and innovativeness and to encourage imaginative, long-range thinking and planning. By such behavior, leaders can stimulate others to establish the same orientation as a pervasive value and help the organization avoid contentment and stagnation. Excellent, creative organizations resolve conflicts better than do those burdened with complacency.

Applying the principle of supportive relationships to conflict management

The principle of supportive relationships is of no value, obviously, to those who wish to use win-lose confrontation or who wish to deal with a conflict by complete domination of their opponents and have the power to do so. But for all conflicts where it is advantageous to resolve existing differences in a way which is fully acceptable to all the parties and to establish cooperative relationships among the parties rather than to continue hostilities, the principle of supportive relationships is fundamental.

When leaders treat supportively those colleagues who agree with them but deal with those with whom they differ in an ego-deflating manner, they are creating a win-lose confrontation and not a System 4 interaction-influence relationship. Leaders must apply the principle of supportive relationships fully to *everyone,* especially to those with whom they differ. To aid themselves in doing so, they should ask themselves two questions:

1. To what extent do those colleagues who agree with my position see me behaving supportively?

2. To what extent do those with whom I differ see me behaving supportively?

Tables 6-1, 6-2, and 6-3 contain items dealing with these two orientations.

The great importance of supportive behavior in contributing to productive problem solving and the constructive resolution of conflicts has been summarized by Walton and McKersie in their excellent volume entitled *A Behavioral Theory of Labor Negotiations* (1965) as follows:

> A supportive and trusting climate facilitates joint problem solving. Defensive and low-trust atmospheres inhibit the process. A supportive climate is marked by encouragement and freedom to behave spontaneously without fear of sanctions. A defensive atmosphere is one in which the parties perceive threat and risks associated with provisional behavior. Why is climate important?

> First, when support is lacking and a person anticipates threat, he behaves defensively, diverting energy from the problem-solving task.

> The person who behaves defensively, even though he also gives some attention to the common task, devotes an appreciable portion of his energy to defending himself. Besides talking about the topic, he thinks about . . . how he may win, dominate, impress, or escape punishment, and/or how he may avoid or mitigate a perceived or an anticipated attack (Gibb, 1961).

> Defensive behavior on the part of this person tends to create similarly defensive postures in others, and the ensuing circular response becomes increasingly destructive of problem solving.

> Second, if trust is lacking, the sender will control information or deliberately miscommunicate. Each participant must have sufficient trust that the other will use the information only for purposes of problem solving and not for some other purpose (such as distributive bargaining). It has been demonstrated that an individual will distort his opinions and the facts available to him in communicating them to a person he distrusts (Mellinger, 1959).

> Third, trust and support lead to more complete and more accurate reception of problem-relevant communications. The more supportive the climate, "the less

the receiver reads into the communication distorted loadings which arise from projections of his own anxieties, motives, and concerns. As defenses are reduced, the receivers become more able to concentrate on the structure, the content, and the cognitive meaning of the message" (Gibb, 1961). Experimental evidence of the biasing effect of competitiveness and defensiveness on comprehension of another person's position is provided by Blake and Mouton (1961).

Fourth, support allows for more experimentation with attitudes and ideas and more testing and retesting of perceptions and opinions. Problem solving produces more thorough and innovative solutions if there is a phase "of stimulation and sharing, during which ideas get kicked around, elaborated, and defended— this is the process of finding new meanings that would not occur to one by oneself" (Stock & Thelen, 1958). As Stock and Thelen point out, "To engage in this process with others requires conditions such that one not only can take the risk of sticking his neck out but will, in fact, be rewarded for so doing . . ." (1958, p. 257).

Fifth, participants who are threatened and who experience anxiety suffer a loss in efficiency in processing the information they receive. They may, as individuals, show a loss in their ability to abstract and in other flexibilities of intellectual functioning (Beier, 1951).

Some caution is required in relating conditions of trust and support to effectiveness in problem solving. We are convinced that some minimum level of trust and support is a precondition to the process—for the reasons enumerated above. However, there is no clear evidence that a completely harmonious context is the one most productive for problem solving. Consider the finding of one experimental study which suggests the positive stimulation value of a degree of competition: When the system of emotional control is constant, groups with a primary valency to *fight* differ from the others in their ability to dig into a problem, to raise issues, and to settle them in one way or another. Their products show the widest range of ideas employed in problem solution, a high level of specificity within a flexible organization, much attention to causation, and a high amount of emotional involvement and commitment to act on their proposed solutions (Glidewell, 1958). (pp. 141–143).

When differences and diversity occur *in a supportive climate,* they contribute substantially to innovative problem solving. Since conflicts often are resolved best by new creative solutions, we will discuss productive problem solving in conflict situations in the next chapter, including the contribution of differences to the process.

7
The role of System 4 leadership in problem solving

System 4 interaction-influence networks are composed of small face-to-face groups linked together by persons who hold overlapping memberships in two or more groups. If the interaction-influence network is to function effectively in resolving conflicts, each of these groups must be skilled in the art of group problem solving. This requires that two quite different but interdependent tasks be performed well by each group:

1. Intellectual problem-solving activities must be performed skillfully.

2. A high level of confidence, trust, loyalty, and candor must be established among the group's members along with loyalty to the group as a whole. This often is called "group building and maintenance" (Benne & Sheats, 1948) and deals with the emotional and interpersonal aspects of the group in contrast to the intellectual, problem-solving processes.

Human beings do not possess the skills to perform these functions at birth; they are learned. Many persons today have had the good fortune to learn the skills required for intellectual problem solving. Far fewer persons have had the opportunity to learn the skills required for group building and maintenance. Even fewer persons have learned to use these two skills simultaneously in a coordinated manner so as to build and maintain a group while solving a problem.

There are two reasons for this. First, our educational institutions have devoted appreciably more effort to teaching intellectual problem-solving skills than to developing skills in group building. Second, the explicit recognition of the knowledge and skills required for group building and maintenance is of more recent origin than that concerned with intellectual problem solving. A substantial proportion of persons, consequently, will need to acquire more knowledge and skill in both aspects of group problem solving and in their coordinated use than they now possess if they are to apply System 4 successfully to resolving conflicts.

This chapter will discuss the role of leadership in both the intellectual aspects of problem solving and the group building and maintenance tasks. Much more attention will be devoted to the latter, however, since it is especially important in applying System 4 to the management of conflict.

Steps involved in intellectual problem solving

The steps involved in intellectual problem solving usually are described about as follows (Dewey, 1910; Maier, 1963; Kepner & Tregoe, 1965[1]):

1. Locate the problem and state it clearly. Be sure the problem as stated is *the real* problem and not a symptom or just a part of the problem.

2. Define the conditions or criteria which a solution *must* meet to be satisfactory. These are the *essential* criteria. List, in addition, the other conditions which it would be desirable for a solution to fulfill, if possible.

3. Search for all reasonably promising solutions and list them. Try to use different frames of reference and ways of looking at the problem in order to develop new and better solutions. Use brainstorming.

4. Obtain all the relevant facts concerning the extent to which each of the proposed solutions will or will not meet the criteria for an acceptable solution—or be likely to do so.

5. Evaluate all the suggested solutions by examining them in terms of the criteria or conditions which a solution must meet (essentials) and also those which are considered desirable (desirables).

6. Select the solution which best meets the criteria. In this process, eliminate first all the suggested solutions which do not meet the essential conditions. Then eliminate, progressively, those solutions which meet the desirable conditions least satisfactorily.

7. Check the solution finally selected against the problem as stated to be sure that the solution really solves the problem. Check also to be sure the solution does not produce adverse side effects.

The steps described above for intellectual problem solving and decision making are discussed fully elsewhere and need not be elaborated here. Two particularly good descriptions are Maier's *Problem-Solving Discussions and Conferences* (1963) and the chapter on decision making in Kepner and Tregoe's *The Rational Manager* (1965). Maier's book is especially relevant since he considers both the intellectual processes and the group building and maintenance functions. Other publications of Maier's also are very useful, as subsequent references to them will indicate.

---

[1]Kepner and Tregoe call this process "decision making" (pp. 48–50). Maier uses "problem solving" and "decision making" synonymously. This use is followed here, also. Either label may be used depending upon the reader's preference or the term that best fits a particular situation.

Effective group problem solving requires effective groups

In addition to its strictly intellectual activity, the emotional and motivational factors present in every group are of great importance in group problem solving.

A group in which there is conflict and distrust, i.e., a group in which there is need for group building, usually will perform the intellectual problem-solving processes poorly. When there are divisive forces in the group, when the group loyalty is low, and when the group lacks interaction skills, the problem-solving processes of the group are adversely affected. Under these conditions, some members of the group are apt to have interests and purposes which they do not openly reveal to the others in the group. These are commonly called "hidden agenda." The goals they really seek, the objections they actually feel to proposed solutions, their true reasons for favoring or opposing solutions are never stated. As each of their openly expressed objections is disposed of by the group, they shift to others. Full, honest disclosure of their reasons for preferring or opposing solutions never occurs, and, consequently, productive problem solving is never done on the real problems. Hostility, win-lose battles, interpersonal friction, lack of confidence and trust among group members soon bog down any effort to deal productively with a problem.

The powerful emotional, motivational, and interactional phenomena of a group profoundly affect both its determination to do group tasks well and its capacity for productive problem solving. These phenomena, consequently, determine the productivity of its intellectual efforts. Successful problem solving requires a high level of group loyalty and cooperative attitudes and behavior (Bradford, Gibb, & Benne, 1964).

Zand (1972) has conducted an important experiment demonstrating the influence that trust has on problem solving. He used groups of upper middle-managers from all functions and product division of a large, international electronics company. There were no subordinates, superiors, or peers from the same department or division in any group. The experiment was designed as a learning event embedded in a four week in-residence management training program. None of those who participated in the experiment either as subjects or observers had any prior knowledge about the experiment. Each group of subjects or of observers consisted of eight persons. As Zand (1972) states:

> ***Problem.*** The central problems involved (1) developing a strategy to increase short-term profits without undermining long-term growth of a medium-sized electronics company with very low return on investment, outdated manufacturing facilities, whose labor force had been cut 25 percent and whose top management personnel had been changed and reorganized two years before, and (2) obtaining commitment to implement such a program despite strong managerial disappointment because expectations of immediate investment for expansion and modernization would not be met. The situation, a variation of one described by Maier et al. (1959), involved four executive roles: president

and vice presidents for marketing, manufacturing, and personnel. Subjects were randomly assigned to the roles.

Procedure. All subjects and observers were given a written description of the production, marketing, financial, and personnel difficulties of the company.

In the presence of the observers, subjects were told they were to conduct a meeting lasting thirty minutes in the president's office to make appropriate management decisions. Ostensibly, they were to demonstrate their decision-making competence to their fellow managers, the observers.

Each subject was then given an additional written statement with factual and attitudinal information relevant to his function. He had no knowledge of the role information given to other subjects. The subjects privately read and absorbed this problem information for twenty-five minutes so there would be minimal need to refer to it during the meeting.

Treatments. Subjects were randomly assigned to one of two group conditions: an entering mental set toward high or low trust.

The factual data about production, marketing, finance, and so on was identical in both conditions, and all vice presidents were led to expect that the president would announce approval of a long-studied plant expansion.

In both conditions the president's statement told him that on the preceding day, he had received an ultimatum from the board of directors demanding an increase in profits within one year or else he would be forced to resign. Furthermore, he was told that expansion was not feasible because it would reduce short-term profits, take more than a year to build and start up a new plant, and the board was not likely to approve the financing, so as a first step toward increasing profits, he would have to announce his decision against expansion. The vice presidents had no knowledge of the president's dilemma when they started their thirty-minute problem-solving meeting.

Induction of conditions of trust. The induction of the two levels of trust was accomplished by operating on the following entering beliefs of subjects: (1) the task competence of others, (2) norms on introducing information and new ideas, (3) norms on attempts to influence managers outside of one's primary responsibility, (4) likelihood that others would abuse trusting behavior, and (5) competitiveness or collaborativeness for rewards.

In a high-trust group, a manager's entering mental set toward trust was shaped by the following paragraph, which followed the factual information in the role statement:

> You have learned from your experiences during the past two years that you can trust the other members of top management. You and the other top managers openly express your differences and your feelings of encouragement or of disappointment. You and the others share all relevant information and freely explore ideas and feelings that may be in or out of your defined responsibility. The result has been a high level of give and take and mutual confidence in each other's support and ability.

Subjects in low-trust groups had a similar paragraph in their role information, but worded to induce a decrease in trust.

The reward system was operated on by information placed only in the president's statement. In the high-trust condition, the president was led to see his relation to his vice presidents as collaborative. His role statement said that "although the Board's decision considered you specifically, since you appointed the current top management team it is likely that the Board will go outside for a successor and possibly other vice presidents."

In the low-trust condition the president was led to see his relation to his vice presidents as potentially competitive. His role statement said that since the board's ultimatum pertained to him, it was possible that they might appoint one of the vice presidents as his successor. The vice presidents in both conditions were given no information about whether their relation to the president was potentially competitive or collaborative.

All subjects were told that "whenever information is incomplete, introduce whatever facts and experiences seem reasonable under the circumstances."

Observers. In addition to reading the written general description of the company's problems, before observing the problem-solving meeting, the observers were told of the vice presidents' factual basis for seeking and expecting to get final approval for plant expansion and that the president had received a one-year ultimatum from the board the preceding day, but they were given no information about the attitudinal parts of the statements.

Measures. After thirty minutes, group discussion was stopped and each subject and observer completed a questionnaire with eight or nine items. The respondent was to indicate whether in his group, or the group he observed, there was "much" or "little" of the property described in each item.

The items were: (1) trust, (2) openness about feelings, (3) clarification of the group's basic problems and goals, (4) search for alternative courses of action, (5) mutual influence on outcomes, (6) satisfaction with the meeting, (7) motivation to implement decisions, (8) closeness as a management team as a result of the meeting. The subjects' questionnaire had a ninth item: "As a result of this meeting would you give little or much serious consideration to a position with another company?" The written statement could only suggest to each subject an entering mental set toward high or low trust. By the end of the meeting each subject's level of trust would depend on the extent to which his entering beliefs were confirmed by the behavior of the other managers.

RESULTS

High-trust groups. In the high-trust groups the president consistently disclosed voluntarily the board's demand for better short-term performance. These teams, after initial frustration with the disapproval of immediate expansion, dealt with the short-range plans to increase profitability and then began to design long-range plans for modernization and expansion that they would present to the board.

Short-range plans emerging from the discussion among the vice presidents included straightforward proposals to review the product line, to identify and promote sales of high-profit items, and to cut back output of low-profit items. Their more creative proposals, flowing from substantial changes in their perceptions, included, for example, leasing space in a nearby vacant plant, rearranging work flow, selectively modernizing equipment that would provide greatest cost benefits and require minimal capital, subcontracting standard components, and rapidly converting two new products from research to production. In one group the managers agreed to invest their personal savings to help finance modernization, to show the board their strong commitment to the company's future.

Low-trust groups. In low-trust groups, the vice presidents had difficulty understanding the basis for the president's decision against expansion and his desire for short-range profits. In several groups they asked him if there were reasons behind his decision other than those he had disclosed, but he steadfastly refused to reveal information about the board's demands. As a result the vice presidents in low-trust groups could not sense how close the company might be to reorganization and possibly dissolution. They spent most of the meeting disagreeing with the president by repeating their basic arguments for immediate expansion. Finally, after prolonged frustration, the president would impose directives on the group. Usually he would demand review of the product line to eliminate low-profit items. If there was any creativity it came from the president, who was desperately seeking a solution in spite of the resistance of his vice presidents. Occasionally, the president would propose that it might be possible to lease space in a nearby vacant plant, but his idea would be discarded as unworkable by the belligerent vice presidents. In several groups the president threatened to dismiss a vice president.

Conversation among subjects of the low-trust groups after they had answered the questionnaire, showed the high defensiveness and antagonism they had induced in each other. For example, half the vice presidents said that they were so discouraged they had started to think of looking for another job in the middle of the meeting, and several said they hoped the president's plane would be hijacked or crash. The president usually retorted that he had decided to dismiss them before the next meeting.

Discussion. One might contend that the managers were attempting to follow rigidly the attitude toward trust suggested in their briefing, but in the debriefing interviews, the managers said that after their meeting had started, their level of trust varied in response to the behavior of the other managers. In low-trust groups, for example, about half of the vice presidents said that by the end of the meeting they found themselves trusting one or another vice president more than they expected to and trusting the president much less than when they had started.

An unanticipated incident illustrates how difficult it may be for one person acting alone to break the reinforcement pattern even though he has formal power. In one low-trust group, in an effort to behave with trust toward his vice presidents, the president early in the meeting disclosed that the board wanted better profit performance in one year or else might ask for his resignation, but this attempt to show trust did not alter the emergence of low-trust behavior among the vice presidents. Indeed, in interviews after the meeting, the vice presidents said they interpreted the president's statement as a means of shifting blame to the board for his decision not to approve expansion, so that instead of increasing their trust, his behavior confirmed their mistrust. Also, they interpreted the president's comment that he might be forced to resign as evidence that the board did not trust him, so they should not either. Two vice presidents in this group said that by the middle of the meeting they were thinking about how they might hasten the president's resignation. It seems that behaving with high trust towards others who are not trusting will not necessarily induce trust, and if one does so it is wise to limit one's increase in vulnerability.

Another illustration of the difficulty of interrupting the spiral reinforcement pattern occurred in a high-trust group, in which the president did not reveal the board's demand for short-term profits. The vice presidents said that the president seemed troubled, and asked him if he was explaining all the reasons behind his decision not to expand. In the debriefing interviews, after they learned about the president's predicament, one vice president turned to the president and said, "Why didn't you tell us? We could have done so much more to help you and ourselves." The group's level of trust had remained high, but the creativity and comprehensiveness of its solutions had suffered in comparison with other high trust groups.

The data also indicate that patterns of low-trust and high-trust group behavior are recognizable by untrained observers.

Finally, this study revealed that theory and research on group forces have had only a minor impact on the thinking of managers. The managers in this study were among the best educated and the most sophisticated to be found in corporate organizations. After completing the questionnaires, but without any information about the trust model, they were brought together and asked for their explanation of what had happened in the two groups. They consistently responded that the outcomes were the result of the personalities of the men (who had been randomly assigned to the different roles) or the president's style (which they interpreted as autocratic or democratic) or the time he stated his decision not to expand (early or late in the meeting). The possibility that a shared level of trust, that is, a group force or a belief held by several or all members of a group, could constitute a social reality which could significantly affect problem-solving effectiveness was not mentioned.

CONCLUSIONS

It appears that when a group works on a problem, there are two concerns: one is the problem itself, the second is how the members relate to each other to work on the problem. Apparently in low-trust groups, interpersonal relationships interfere with and distort perceptions of the problem. Energy and creativity are diverted from finding comprehensive, realistic solutions, and members use the problem as an instrument to minimize their vulnerability. In contrast, in high-trust groups there is less socially generated uncertainty and problems are solved more effectively.

This study also offers qualitative support for the spiral-reinforcement model. It suggests that mutual trust or mistrust, among members of a group, are likely to be reinforced, unless there is marked or prolonged disconfirming behavior. (pp. 234–238)

Zand's experiment demonstrates the important contribution that trust makes to the capacity of a group to solve problems well. Although a high level of trust among its members is necessary for a group to be productive in its problem solving, it often is difficult to move a group from a low level of trust to a high level. As the experiment showed, the tendency for low levels of trust to spiral downwards is not easily broken and reversed. Even when leaders or group members display high trust in a low-trust situation, there is a tendency for the downward spiral to continue. Showing high trust in a low-trust atmosphere is not an effective causal variable to start an upward-trust spiral, at least not in the short run.

The causal variable that can be used to shift a low-trust climate to a high-trust level is the principle of supportive relationships. The display of sincere supportive behavior toward persons who initially hold an orientation of distrust can gradually bring them to hold a more friendly and more trusting view toward those who display the supportive behavior (Likert, 1967, app. 1).

System 4 principles help build effective groups

Leaders can help to build and maintain their groups as effective, cooperative, problem-solving units by skillfully applying the principle of supportive relationships and other relevant System 4 principles at every step throughout the entire intellectual problem-solving process. If these System 4 principles are applied skillfully by the leaders and members in the interactions which occur during intellectual problem solving, the cooperative attitudes and behavior among the group members will be increased or maintained at a high level. Friendliness, confidence and trust, attraction to the group, and similar reactions will grow in response to the supportive treatment each member experiences from leader and colleagues.[2] On the other hand, if these principles are violated and members have ego-deflating experiences, the loyalty of members toward each other and toward the total group will deteriorate. Friendliness, trust, and cooperation will be low; hostility and distrust will prevail.

---

[2]For a further discussion of the nature of highly effective groups, see Chapter 11 in *New Patterns of Management* (Likert, 1961).

It is highly important, consequently, in building and operating a System 4 structure, for both the leader and group members to apply continuously and fully the principle of supportive relationships and the other relevant principles of System 4 while making full use of the most effective and sophisticated procedures for intellectual problem solving (Kahn, 1953; Likert, 1953; Zander, 1953).

Diversity contributes to
creativity but augments conflict

The capacity of a group to develop new, innovative solutions to difficult problems is especially important in resolving conflicts constructively. Where disagreements or conflicts exist, there typically is no readily available solution seen by all parties as acceptable. A new, innovative, integrative solution which will meet the needs and desires of *all* interested parties must be found. Unless this is done successfully and an integrative solution is developed, the likelihood is great that the disagreement will continue as a win-lose struggle or deteriorate into one.

Creativity in group problem solving in these situations is highly desirable. A major factor which contributes materially to the capacity of a group to find innovative, creative solutions is diversity among the members of the group in background, experience, and points of view (Pelz & Andrews, 1966).

Pelz (1967) calls the stimulation to creative thinking which comes from diversity the "dither effect" and has summarized findings concerning its importance:

> Another way in which a man's colleagues can provide challenge is through questioning his ideas. An apt label was borrowed by Warren Weaver (1959) from British colleagues who built into antiaircraft computing devices a "small eccentric or vibrating member which kept the whole mechanism in a constant state of minor but rapid vibration. This they called the 'dither.' . . . We need a certain amount of dither in our mental mechanisms. We need to have our ideas jostled about a bit so that we do not become intellectually sluggish."

> A scientist's colleagues may jostle his ideas if they and he approach a problem differently. To test this hypothesis, we measured similarity or dissimilarity between the scientist and his colleagues in several ways. One method was subjective—the respondent's perception of how his own technical strategy resembled that of his co-workers. Other measures were objective, in the sense that we examined the approaches reported by the respondent and by each of his colleagues and numerically scored the similarity among them.

> How much dither or disagreement is healthy? In our data the answer depended on the kind of dither. One objective measure concerned the source of motivation—whether one's superior, the technical literature, or some other source. Scientists who responded to the same sources were somewhat more effective—perhaps because they had similar interests.

On three other measures we found the opposite to be true. Scientists and engineers did somewhat better when they saw themselves as different from colleagues in technical strategy, and when, as scored objectively, they differed from colleagues in style of approach (when, for example, the individual stressed the abstract, his colleagues the concrete) or differed in career orientation.

How to reconcile this paradox? In some preliminary data obtained by Evan (1965) for industrial R & D groups, the teams he found most effective reported personal harmony or liking among members, but intellectual conflict. Colleagues who report the same sources of motivation as the scientist's own probably provide personal harmony and support—a form of security. When they argue about technical strategy or approach, they provide dither or challenge. (pp. 163–164)

When creative thinking is particularly important, the leader can actively encourage steps which contribute to it. Oftentimes examining the present frames of reference and then using other possible orientations opens up whole new areas of possible solutions. Shifting the points of view in the search for new solutions can greatly increase the probability of finding a really creative solution which will meet much more adequately the essential conditions than will any solution suggested prior to taking these fresh points of view.

The potential value of examining the frame of reference which a group is using in its search for solutions is illustrated by the experience of a professor at New York University in teaching the principles of problem solving to engineering students. He asked the class: "Think of the numbers 2, 4, 6, and 8, and tell me the next two numbers."

The class members rapidly responded, "10 and 12." He then said, "Think of the numbers 1, 2, 4, 8, and tell me the next two numbers." The members of the class again responded promptly with, "16 and 32." The professor than said, "Think of the numbers 14, 34, 42, 72, 96, 110, and tell me the next two numbers."

This problem was posed to many classes of junior and senior engineering students who prided themselves on their mathematical prowess. Even though each of these classes worked several weeks on the problem, no student ever solved it. After finally giving up, each class was asked, "What assumptions are you using in your search for a solution?" After very little discussion, the class members all recognized that they were assuming that the problem they were working on was a mathematical number series.

The professor then explained, "The problem is not a number series. Another assumption or frame of reference is needed because the next two numbers are 116 and 125. These numbers are the express station stops on the 7th Avenue Subway."

Although the students who had labored hard seeking to solve the problem as a number series were ready to strangle the professor at this point, they were likely to remember, from that moment on, the necessity of examining the frame of reference being used in the search for a solution to a problem.

Both the leader and members of a group should always strive to be as innovative in their search for alternative frames of reference in working on a problem as they are in seeking a novel solution within a particular frame of reference.

A dramatic illustration of an innovative approach to a conflict was the invitation by the People's Republic of China to the United States table tennis team to visit China and the well-publicized, friendly treatment the team received. In seeking to resolve difficult conflicts, highly imaginative, creative solutions are likely to be required.

Using differences creatively

Diversity increases the amount of conflict since the group has to cope with greater differences among its members than otherwise would be the case. Consequently, when a group seeks to be innovative in its problem solving, diversity may be either a serious liability or a great resource, depending upon whether the diversity immobilizes the group in win-lose conflict or stimulates highly creative thinking.

The leadership of a group plays a major role in determining whether diversity is used to stimulate productive problem solving or whether it causes the group to be immobilized in a win-lose struggle. As Maier (1967) has demonstrated:

> Acceptance of a solution also increases as the leader sees disagreement as idea-producing rather than as a source of difficulty or trouble (Maier & Hoffman, 1965). Leaders who see some of their participants as troublemakers obtain few innovative solutions and gain less acceptance of decisions made than leaders who see disagreeing members as persons with ideas. (p. 244)

Members who hold a minority viewpoint clearly contribute to the capacity of a group to develop innovative solutions. The minority members, however, need to experience supportive reactions from the other members if a group is to benefit from their differing outlook and their capacity through the "dither effect" to help the group do unorthodox and creative thinking. This, as Maier points out, is not likely to occur unless the leader encourages it. He continues:

> The leader can upgrade the quality of a decision because his position permits him to protect the person with a minority view and increase his opportunity to influence the majority position. This protection is a constructive factor because a minority viewpoint influences only when facts favor it (Maier, 1950, 1952; Maier & Solem, 1952).
>
> The leader also plays a constructive role insofar as he can facilitate communications and thereby reduce misunderstanding (Maier, 1952; Solem, 1965). The leader has an adverse effect on the end product when he suppresses minority views by holding a contrary position and when he uses his office to promote his

> own views (Maier & Hoffman, 1960b, 1962; Maier & Solem, 1952). In many problem-solving discussions, the untrained leader plays a dominant role in influencing the outcome, and when he is more resistant to changing his views than are the other participants, the quality of the outcome tends to be lowered. This negative leader-influence was demonstrated by experiments in which untrained leaders were asked to obtain a second solution to a problem after they had obtained their first one (Maier and Hoffman, 1960a). It was found that the second solution tended to be superior to the first. Since the dominant individual had influenced the first solution, he had won his point and therefore ceased to dominate the subsequent discussion which led to the second solution. (p. 244)

Maier suggests that these findings can be applied profitably by having a group go through the complete problem-solving process to seek a second solution after achieving their first. In particularly difficult conflict situations, this strategy of developing a second acceptable solution is likely to increase the likelihood of finding a truly innovative solution more acceptable to all parties.

Maier's research findings and conclusions clearly point to the importance of the leader's supportive role in the group.

Valuing differences contributes to innovative solutions and group harmony

The capacity of a group in conflict to develop an innovative solution acceptable to all is influenced substantially by the behavior of the group members as well as that of the leader. The extent to which each member of the group listens attentively and reacts supportively to each of the other members, especially to the most deviant, greatly affects the group's capacity to do creative problem solving. To facilitate this supportive behavior by the members of a group, the leader can encourage the group to set about deliberately to create a climate where a positive value is placed on diversity, dissent, and differences. Here again, the leader's role is crucial in assisting the group to recognize the usefulness of diversity and dissent and to encourage the group to establish it as a cherished value.

The leader should help the group keep this value clearly before it, particularly at those points in the problem-solving process where the stimulation arising from differences will contribute most to achieving a creative solution. For example, when the group is working on the problem-solving step of listing the conditions that a satisfactory solution must meet, the leader should encourage the group and the members should encourage each other to list fully *all* these conditions, both essential and desirable. The essential conditions will vary from member to member and are likely to be quite different for members who hold conflicting points of view. At this step, the leader should foster in the group an eagerness to have *each member, no matter how deviant,* state fully the conditions which that member feels are essential. The members will be much more likely to believe that others wish to know their views if the group explores their "essential conditions" sympathetically and understandingly. This feeling will be reinforced as the group earnestly strives in the subsequent steps to find a solution which meets these requirements. This supportive behavior toward deviants fosters cooperative relationships among the group members. It contributes appreciably to resolving conflicts amicably.

To obtain the full benefit from diversity, it is necessary that the differences among the group members be explored at each step in the problem-solving process. Attention must be focused on one step at a time. The *subsequent step should not be started* until the step the group is working on is executed well.

The untrained leader and the untrained group usually are unaware both of the value of diversity and dissent and of the role of supportive relationships in enabling them to develop innovative and excellent solutions. As a consequence, they not only fail to make use of their deviant members but typically behave in ways which force these members to leave the group (Festinger, 1950). By behavior which ignores or depreciates the comments and contributions of those members with diverse points of view and by hostile remarks and behavior, the group makes the deviants feel rejected and alienated and motivates them to give up group membership. Schachter (1951) has shown that the more a member's communications differ from the rest of the group, the greater are the forces created by the group to encourage that member to leave (Cartwright & Zander, 1968).

Shepard designed an experiment to show both the contribution and the vulnerability of the deviant who differs from the group. He set up a number of small groups. Some groups contained a deviant member; others did not. The groups with a deviant member came up with richer, better, more elegant solutions than did the groups without a deviant. But when each group was asked to reduce its membership by one person, the deviant always was the person thrown out. Even though the deviant made a major contribution to the work of the group, the challenge of their views made the members uncomfortable and they were glad to see the deviant go. Skilled leadership is needed to help provide a supportive atmosphere for the dissidents so that they will be kept in the group and so that their ideas will be used to enrich the group's thinking.

Supportive listening

When a group makes the desirability of diversity a positive value, it is simultaneously establishing another pervasive value, namely the need to listen supportively.

Listening attentively at every stage of the problem-solving process is an important way to apply the principle of supportive relationships in aiding those holding deviant views to express themselves. Leaders can create an atmosphere of attentive, supportive listening by their behavior, by what they respond to favorably, and by what they are seen as valuing. In all interactions in the group and at every step in problem solving, each member should be encouraged to listen to the other members in a supportive and encouraging manner. Each member's manner of listening should convey the feeling to the speakers that whatever that speaker says is of great interest and importance. It should not necessarily convey that the listener agrees with the speaker. It should convey the view that the listener values the speaker as a person, values that person's ideas, and, consequently, is eager to hear his or her point of view and to understand it.

This attentive listening should occur when members are endeavoring to define clearly and accurately the particular problem being dealt with. It should occur as members state all those conditions which they feel a solution should meet, both those which they feel are essential and those which they view as desirable. This same attentive, encouraging listening is needed during the search for solutions and the development of innovative alternatives. It is required during all the interactions involved in evaluating alternative solutions and selecting the one which is best. It can vary from such passive acts as not interrupting, to asking questions to improve one's understanding of what is being said, to strong, positive, supportive responses to the other's statements. One particularly effective way of demonstrating supportive listening is to restate the other person's position and his or her reasons for holding it more clearly and strongly than that person has done.

Training in supportive listening

A procedure to help train persons to listen supportively, particularly in a conflict situation, was stated first by Carl Rogers (1951) and developed and applied by Mann (private communication to authors):

> Real communication is very hard to achieve. We tend to judge, to evaluate, to approve or disapprove before we really understand what the other person is saying—before we understand the frame of reference from which he is talking. This tendency of most humans to react first by forming an evaluation of what has just been said, and to evaluate it from one's own point of view is a major barrier to mutual interpersonal communication.

> Progress toward understanding can be made when this evaluative tendency is avoided—when we listen with understanding—and when we are actively listening to what is being said. What does this mean? It means to see the expressed idea and attitudes from the other person's point of view, to sense how it feels to him, to achieve his frame of reference in regard to the thing he is talking about.

> This sounds simple, but it is not.

> To test the quality of your understanding, try the following. If you see two people talking past each other, if you find yourself in an argument with your friend, with your wife, or within a small group, just stop the discussion for a moment, and for an experiment, institute this rule of Carl Rogers: "Each person

can speak up for himself only *after* he has first restated the ideas and feelings of the previous speaker accurately—and to that speaker's satisfaction."

This would mean that before presenting your own point of view, it would be necessary for you really to achieve the other speaker's frame of reference—to understand his thoughts and feelings so well that you could summarize them for him. This is a very effective process for improving communications and relationships with others. It is much more difficult to do behaviorally than you would suspect.

What will happen if you try to do this during an argument?

You will find that your own next comments will have to be drastically revised. You will find the emotion going out of the discussion, the differences being reduced. There is a decrease in defensiveness, in exaggerated statements, in evaluative and critical behavior. Attitudes become more positive and problem-solving. The differences which remain are of a rational and understandable sort—or are real differences in basic values.

What are the risks? The obstacles? What are the difficulties that keep this bit of knowledge from being utilized?

Try this and you risk being influenced by the other person. You might see it his way—have to change your position. There is the risk of change. In this sense, listening can be dangerous—and courage is required. . . .

Another difficulty stems from our notions as to what is proper to ask a person to do in a discussion. It seems quite within good taste to ask a person to restate how he sees the situation. But to ask him to restate the other man's position is not consistent with our common sense ways of handling differences. The one who would change the pattern—try to break out of the vicious circle of increasingly greater misunderstanding—must have enough confidence in himself to be able to propose something different. He will have to have an appreciation of how to go from dealing with misunderstandings to handling conflict and using differences—of how differences can be used to find more elegant solutions to problems. Equally useful will be an awareness that thesis, antithesis, and synthesis is a potential outcome from a developmental discussion of differences. Discussions in which one person loses and the other wins seldom solve anything permanently. When a person senses a win-lose situation developing, it should be interpreted as a clue to the need for a new approach, a search for alternate solutions, to be sure that there is not another answer to the problem.

The greatest difficulty of all, of course, is to learn to use the rule when you yourself are in an increasingly heated verbal exchange. Not to be dependent on a third person to intervene when you create or are a party to a growing misunderstanding is real evidence of understanding the approach proposed here. The full value of this rule is available to us only when each of us can note that we are getting increasingly irritated, angry, and unable to communicate effectively—when we can use these signals to identify the situation in which we are personally involved and even trapped in which the rule might be employed—*if* we could retrieve the rule from our memory and *if* we could behaviorally use it in an effective manner.

Mann and his colleagues, in training sessions, laboratories, and day-to-day on-the-job situations, have helped many persons learn to use this powerful rule to facilitate supportive listening. The capacity to deal with conflicts constructively in business, education, government, hospitals, and elsewhere is much improved by its use.

8

Integrative goals and consensus in problem solving

The research on conflict and decision making clearly indicates the great importance of integrative goals, common values, and mutual interests in facilitating the constructive resolution of conflict (Blake et al., 1964; Maier, 1963; Sherif, 1962). These goals reflect more deep-seated, more overriding, more fundamental wants than those which either party would be able to obtain by "winning." For example, citizens and leaders of the United States and the U.S.S.R. share the goal of wishing to stay alive, of not being annihilated in a nuclear holocaust. It is hoped that this mutual goal will motivate both nations to keep the peace.

"Common values," "mutual interests," or "superordinate goals" are terms used by different writers to describe the powerful forces compelling conflicting parties to seek the "integrative solution" urged by Mary Parker Follett (Fox & Urwick, 1973). Following her lead, we have selected "integrative goals" as the most satisfactory term for our purposes. Integrative goals which express the deep-seated needs and desires of the conflicting parties will bring them to the conference table when all else fails and will keep them hard at work seeking to find or create mutually acceptable solutions. In the presence of integrative goals, conflicting groups attempt to solve the problem in terms of the best interests of all rather than in terms of the parochial goals of a few.

When individuals feel indifferent toward an organization or institution and do not see the relationship between their well-being and its success, they have little motivation to strive to reach agreement to serve its objectives. If the conflict between units is strong and becomes structured into a win-lose struggle, they may well seek to have their unit win even though it may seriously damage or even destroy the entire organization. When individuals are deeply committed to the objectives of an organization, they are not willing to sacrifice its well-being for the benefit of one of its parts. Stagner (1956) found, for example, that union members were loyal to their union, but they also were loyal to the company. They felt that they needed the union to protect their interests but that the company had to succeed if they were to have interests to protect.

The task of leadership to make integrative goals operationally effective in helping to resolve a particular conflict varies with the extent to which these goals are clearly present and accepted or must be developed from potential sources. In some conflicts, these integrative goals are clearly present and accepted by everyone. The role of the leader in such conflicts is to see that the influence of shared goals is used fully. In other situations, the integrative goals may exist but may not yet have been explicitly recognized. In still others, nothing more is present than the potential for creating goals. Leadership is responsible for seeing that the integrative goals that are potentially or implicitly present become explicitly and fully recognized and accepted.

This task of leadership varies, of course, from one conflict situation to another and also is affected by the character of the integrative goals. Integrative goals, for example, can derive from basic human motive sources, such as the desire for physical security and survival. They also can be based on the situational requirements (i.e., the hard facts of life). Common problems can be a source of integrative goals. Regardless of their source or character, leadership has an extremely important role to play in any conflict in helping to make all potentially integrative goals as clear and operationally effective as possible.

In field experiments in a boy's camp, Sherif (1962) demonstrated the great power of integrative goals in resolving conflicts (Sherif uses the term "superordinate goals"). He found that: "When groups in a state of friction come into contact under conditions embodying superordinate goals, they tend to cooperate toward the common goal" (p. 11). In one experiment with two groups of boys, the superordinate or integrative goals included preparing for an outing much desired by all, overcoming a threatened water shortage, and repairing a truck. Both of the latter two provided resources greatly needed by both groups. These integrative goals required greater efforts than either of the conflicting groups could provide by itself. These goals brought about highly effective cooperation in a situation in which there had been bitter hostility and conflict between the two groups (Sherif et al., 1961).

An example of excellent leadership in making explicit an integrative goal and of using it in decision making is the following (*National Civic Review,* October, 1959):

> "I dislike contentiousness," our (National Municipal League) former president, Lawson Purdy, used to say. "It doesn't accomplish anything; it only tightens snarls."

> But then in 1916 he faced an official commission organized to consider regulating the heights and bulks of buildings in New York City. The real estate fraternity was hostile to governmental interference with any man's right to build what he pleased on his own plot. Socialism! Ruination! It was well represented on the commission. Contention was waiting to explode. Purdy, the city's esteemed tax gatherer, looked around the lion's den, waited for the right moment and

obtained quiet attention. "Let's all agree," he said, "to propose no regulations that do not enhance the values of the properties affected."

"*Enhance* values? Do you mean it?" "Yes," said Purdy. "It will, for instance, enhance residential neighborhood values to protect them from ruinous invasions by filling stations or shops. . . . Let's begin that way and see if we don't get somewhere on that principle!"

Down the table faces changed. Fiery speeches, constitutional doubts, conservative scorn faded out unspoken. Well, they'd try it. The talk turned creative and amiable. Within the hour, constructive work began. Eventually as their interest grew in their task, members did diverge where necessary from Purdy's proposed standard. The outcome was the first zoning ordinance in America, pioneer of a practice that is now all but universal in our cities, profoundly stabilizing the tax bases and reducing the hazards of home ownership. An era started by one wise phrase! (p. 452)

Serious problems faced by both parties to a conflict can become integrative goals. The Scanlon Plan, for example, came into being as a result of such integrative goals. As Clinton Golden[1] describes it:

It was my good fortune to have known and worked with Joe Scanlon for twenty years prior to his untimely death a little more than a year ago. He was one of the millions who suffered cruelly as a result of the depression of the Thirties. He did not become embittered as a result of these trying experiences. Indeed, while unemployed and without enough food and fuel for his family, he took the leadership among the workers in his community in securing unused land, in borrowing tractors and other equipment, in literally begging seed and fertilizer so that he and his fellow workers could raise food and get wood for fuel to meet their basic needs.

Perhaps it was out of these experiences in cooperative effort to assure simple survival that he first became aware of the capacity of people to work together. As the depression lifted and he was able to get back to work in the local mill, the friendships created in the common struggle for survival encouraged a continuation of cooperative endeavor.

Even before the Steel Worker's Organizing Committee was formed in 1936, and the organizing campaign was launched, a local union had been formed among the employees of the company he worked for. Wages were low, employment was uncertain, and competition for a share in the limited market was keen.

The company had but recently emerged from bankruptcy, equipment was obsolete, and costs were high. Then came the union demands for higher wages and improved conditions of employment to compound the difficulties of management. If the demands were granted, it would threaten the survival of the company.

---

[1]Reprinted from *The Scanlon Plan,* edited by F. G. Lesieur, by permission of The M.I.T. Press, Cambridge, Massachusetts, © 1958.

Joe took the leadership again in this period of adversity. He induced the president of the company to come with a committee of the union employees to the Pittsburgh office of the International Union to seek advice and help if possible. It was at this point my acquaintance with him began.

I have told the story of subsequent events so many times I am reluctant to repeat it. Suffice it to say that I suggested that the group return to the mill and arrange to interview every employee in an effort to enlist his aid and familiarity with work processes in eliminating waste, improving efficiency, reducing cost, and improving the quality of the products in order to keep assured of the survival of the company.

My advice was accepted; they returned to the mill and under Joe's leadership and with the full cooperation of management, set about in a most thorough and systematic manner to do just what I had suggested.

The local union did not immediately press requests for higher wages and other improvements. Within a few months, as a result of the sustained cooperative efforts of the workers and management, costs were reduced noticeably, and the quality of products improved. Even with its obsolete equipment, the company survived and was able to grant the wage increases and improved conditions of employment already granted by their more prosperous competitors.

The employees were rightfully proud of their part in this effort to assure the survival of the company and so to preserve their jobs. Management was equally proud of the dramatic but practical result of the teamwork. Thus was the foundation laid for building what has since come to be known as the Scanlon Plan.

Unless hostilities are so deeply ingrained as to preclude any cooperation, leaders can help conflicting parties recognize that their common problems can be integrative goals by having them examine the benefits both parties would experience if these problems were solved.

A company which needs to merchandise new products attractive to customers in order to survive is another example. If the company fails, there will be no jobs. The explicit recognition of this situational requirement can establish a strong integrative goal among the production, sales, and research and development departments of the firm. This will facilitate cooperative group problem solving focused on how to improve cooperation among the departments and on how to accelerate the successful development, production, and marketing of new products.

As this example indicates, situational requirements often can be powerful integrative goals. Not all situational requirements, however, are integrative goals. For example, time or budgetary limitations set boundaries within which a solution must fall to be acceptable. These serve as constraints and usually do not provide strong motivational forces in the parties to a conflict to find a mutually acceptable solution.

A leader can help a group recognize which situational requirements can become powerful integrative goals by having the group list all these requirements and select from among the total list those situational requirements which are integrative in character. This process usually will result in the discovery of several important integrative goals.

Basic human needs often are important integrative goals. Since their presence in a particular conflict situation may go unrecognized, the leader plays a crucial role in helping a group state them explicitly. All human beings, for example, seek to achieve and maintain a sense of personal worth and importance but do not ordinarily think in these terms. This is equally true of many of the motives or needs derived from the sense of personal worth and importance, including such needs as those for achievement, self-fulfillment, recognition, and self-actualization.

Many persons who recognize the existence of their own basic needs do not mention them because of the "of course" phenomenon. They feel that "of course" everyone recognizes the existence of these needs, and hence there is no point in mentioning them. By means of questions and even direct statements, the leader can help the conflicting parties recognize that they hold *in common* many of these basic human wants which will be satisfied more fully if their differences can be resolved.

Integrative goals can be used in a bitter conflict to mitigate the adverse effect of hostile attitudes on problem solving. When hostile attitudes are both pervasive and intense, they create strong forces in the persons holding them. These forces influence the behavior of those persons at every step in the problem-solving process. It is difficult to behave supportively toward persons for whom one feels a strong hostility. It is equally difficult to accept at face value their statements concerning the essential conditions that a solution must meet to be acceptable. Prejudices and hostile attitudes often seriously limit creativity in the search for new solutions.

Recording and analyzing the problem-solving process of the conflicting parties as they seek an innovative, mutually acceptable solution is a useful device in assisting them to recognize clearly the adverse influence of their hostile attitudes and the need to reduce the hostility by bringing into play the integrative goals. Tape recorders or videoscopes can be used to record the problem-solving behavior. In addition to the analysis of these tapes, each person can examine his or her own behavior by listening to the tapes and learning how well that person has been able to be objective and productive in the various steps of the problem-solving process. When recording equipment is not readily available, observers can be used to help the group be objective and productive in its problem solving.

The need for consensus

If win-lose confrontation is used in resolving a conflict, the winning party, whether a nation, organization, or an individual, imposes its preferred solution on the other. Victory brings elation for the winner. Defeat brings feelings of rejection, failure, and impotence and is accompanied by bitterness and hostile attitudes. The losing party may be forced to accept the solution imposed on it, but it will continue the conflict, at least subversively, and sooner or later seek to achieve an outcome more acceptable to it.

Win-lose always means that the solution fails to give one party the minimum it needs for the solution to be acceptable. If all parties are to accept the outcome of a dispute willingly, the conditions that each feels are essential for a satisfactory solution must be met. Each party must win, at least to that extent. To bring this about, the conflict must be resolved with a win-win approach rather than a win-lose.

The use of consensus is essential at each step in the decision-making process and especially in the selection of the final agreement if the solution is to be win-win. Consensus, in Quaker terms, is "the sense of the meeting," a willing acceptance of the group's conclusions. The process of arriving at consensus is a free and open exchange of ideas which continues until agreement has been reached. This process assures that each individual's concerns are heard and understood and that a sincere attempt has been made to take them into consideration in the search for and the formulation of a conclusion. This conclusion may not reflect the exact wishes of each member, but since it does not violate the deep concerns of anyone, it can be agreed upon by all.

Consensus, then, is a cooperative effort to find a sound solution acceptable to everyone rather than a competitive struggle in which an unacceptable solution is forced on the losers. With consensus as the pattern of interaction, members need not fear being outsmarted or outmaneuvered. They can be frank, candid, and authentic in their interactions at all steps in the decision-making process. Win-win problem solving is being used increasingly in corporations, governmental agencies, and other organizations. The top committees or work groups of several of America's most successful corporations habitually use win-win problem solving and reach decisions with consensus.

In the League of Women Voters, a highly effective voluntary organization, most decisions are made by members of the various local Leagues in small groups by consensus. The national program also is developed in this way with suggestions going back and forth from local and state Leagues to the National Board and back and between local Leagues and between state Leagues. The resulting proposed national program is then presented to the representatives from all the local and state Leagues in the country at a national convention, held every two years. Changes may be made from the floor in the wording of items and sometimes a proposed item is rejected and another substituted, but since there has been thorough preliminary discussion and substantial agreement prior to the convention, radical changes at the convention are the exception rather than the rule. Although the final determination of the program is made by this large body using parliamentary procedures and majority rule, its use has a minimum of the win-lose consequences that often accompany such procedures. The prior give and take of ideas throughout the membership, the substantial agreement reached by consensus before the convention opens, and the conviction by the members of the value of using consensus whenever possible all contribute to a problem-solving attitude and not to a win-lose confrontation. Of great importance, too, is the membership's dedication to a common cause. The League's superordinate, integrative goals override differences about specifics.

Since the parliamentary procedure and *Robert's Rules of Order* are widely used today in dealing with conflict, their capacity to achieve consensus and win-win solutions deserve to be examined. As a rule, parliamentary procedures structure an interaction into a win-lose relationship. The rigidity of a formal motion with changes possible only by amendment makes the orderly problem-solving steps required for the search and discovery of a mutually acceptable solution difficult if not impossible. The parliamentary struggle is a confrontation between alternative solutions already formulated. Arguing from a fixed position rules out the possibility of innovative ideas generated by the systematic search for them in a free and open manner. Ruses such as tabling the motion in an attempt to defeat an opposing position or the maneuvering of countermotions and amendments are devices that can transform a group of well-intentioned and intelligent persons into warring camps. In the heat of argument, bruising statements may be made which never are entirely forgotten or forgiven. Parliamentary procedures typically yield a win-lose rather than a win-win outcome.

Achieving consensus

The material in this and the preceding chapters on problem solving proposes many principles and procedures for facilitating the achievement of consensus. Evidence confirming the effectiveness of these principles and procedures is reported by Guetzkow and Gyr (1954). Their paper was a part of a larger project concerned with problem-solving conferences (Marquis, Guetzkow, & Heyns, 1951). The groups studied ranged in size from 5 to 20 persons and were called together to make policy and staff decisions. Only one session of each group was observed and analyzed.

The main headings in the material quoted below from Guetzkow and Gyr (1954) are taken from their summary of their findings. Under the headings are quotations from their paper which amplify the summary statement:

> Study of the conflict itself revealed it not as a single characteristic, but rather consisting of two relatively unrelated traits. "Substantive conflict" is associated with intellectual opposition among participants, deriving from the content of the agenda. "Affective conflict" is tension generated by emotional clashes aroused during the interpersonal struggle involved in solving the group's agenda problems.
>
> Certain conditions existing within the conference in either type of conflict are associated with the conference ending in high consensus.

A. Conditions associated with High Consensus in Groups in either Substantive or Affective Conflict.

(i) When there is little expression of personal, self-oriented needs.

(ii) When whatever self-needs are expressed tend to be satisfied during the course of the meeting.

It is found that the expression of many self-oriented or personal needs by the conference participants is detrimental to the reaching of consensus. This is true under high as well as under low conflict conditions. The self- or ego-oriented needs of a participant express themselves in many ways in the social interaction which constitutes a conference. Some persons express such needs by verbally arguing with others; some need to dominate the scene. Expression of these needs in a conference, either in an overt fashion or in more subtle, hidden ways, does not promote consensus. With reference to the expression of ego-needs it is interesting to note that when self-needs are satisfied through rewarding personal interrelations within the conference itself, there is a significant tendency for the group to achieve consensus, especially when intense conflict prevails.

(iii) When there is a generally pleasant atmosphere and the participants recognized the need for unified action.

(iv) When the group's problem-solving activity is understandable, orderly, and focused on one issue at a time.

Those meetings in which discussion is orderly in its treatment of topics, and without backward references to previously discussed issues, tended to end in more consensus, despite large amounts of substantive or affective conflict. When participants discussed but one issue at a time, instead of simultaneously dabbling in two or three, it was more possible for the group to reach consensus. The ability of the members to understand what each said led to agreement. When participants knew the vocabulary the others were using, when they talked on a common conceptual level, then high conflict tended to end in consensus.

B. Conditions associated with High Consensus in Groups in Substantive Conflict. (These conditions do not hold for groups in affective conflict.)

(i) When facts are available and used.

Comparison of the high consensus and low consensus groups reveals that facts resolve substantive conflict. Those groups that have more expertize available and that utilize this knowledge are those whose substantive conflict ends in more consensus. The utilization of expertize does not significantly influence affective conflict, however, except in low conflict groups.

These results are made more understandable by analyzing the behaviour of the leader. Chairmen of groups in high substantive conflict which ended in consensus did three times as much seeking for information of an objective factual nature from members of their groups as did chairmen in groups which did not end in consensus.

(ii) When chairman, through much solution-proposing, aids the group in penetrating its agenda-problems.

(iii) When the participants feel warm and friendly toward each other in a personal way.

When the members of the group seem to like each other personally, substantive conflict tends to be more easily resolved. The attractions of the participants towards each other on the basis of personal characteristics, help to achieve consensus. This friendliness permeates their problem-solving activities. The participants are warm and supportive of each other and encourage the full expression of personal opinions, without restrictions. (pp. 378–382)

Samuel (1971, p. 36) found a sizable relationship ($r = +.74$) between managerial support scores and consensus when consensus was measured both by the "distance" between the views among the members of a group and the extent of agreement. He also found that supportive behavior among the members of a group, i.e., peer support, showed a marked relationship to his two measures of consensus ($r = +.69$).

These findings show that the probability of resolving substantive conflicts by consensus is enhanced substantially by the orderly group problem solving undertaken in a supportive atmosphere described at length in this and preceding chapters on leadership and problem solving. This research demonstrates again the importance of the principle of supportive relationships in contributing to the successful management of conflict.

Pragmatic consensus: Agreeing to cooperate

In some situations where a conflict is extremely bitter and of long duration and where attitudes between the parties are very hostile, it is unrealistic to expect that consensus will be reached in the early efforts to resolve the conflict by problem solving. Even though the initial efforts focus on those aspects of the conflict which can be most easily resolved, it still may be impossible to achieve full consensus. When this occurs, it may be possible to reach a useful form of working relationships which we will call "pragmatic consensus." Pragmatic consensus is a willingness to give a particular solution a trial run. It represents an agreement to try out a solution for a period of time even though some members of the group still have reservations concerning it. The solution on trial may deal with only a part of the problem, but, even so, the willingness to agree to try a part often represents an important step toward ultimately achieving a solution to the total conflict.

A leader should seek to use pragmatic consensus when a group is unable to reach full consensus. When the reluctant persons agree to "go along" with a trial run of the proposed course of action, it is extremely important that the effort be accompanied by special attention to their expressed interests and concerns. The principle of supportive relationships needs to be applied fully in these attempts since its use will increase greatly the likelihood of success.

Every successful use of pragmatic consensus in dealing with some aspect of a major conflict yields more favorable attitudes and greater confidence and trust among the parties to the conflict and strengthens the interaction-influence network between them. This improvement in the interaction-influence network makes it more capable of dealing successfully with the more serious aspects of the conflict. The likelihood of reaching full consensus in dealing with them is increased.

The backup, recycling technique

When it is impossible to reach full consensus or even some simple form of pragmatic consensus, it is advantageous for the leader to use the "backup, recycling technique." The group starts over and repeats all the steps in the problem-solving process. In essence the group says, "Since we have not reached consensus, we must not have done the problem solving well. Let's try again." The group starts by reexamining the statement of the problem to be sure that it is considering the real problem and that the problem is stated well and clearly. It would be well to examine the conditions that were originally thought to be essential to see if any of these conditions can be classified as desirable but not essential. Two steps, in particular, need intensive effort when trying to do a better job the second time. These are (1) searching for both additional and stronger integrative goals and relevant situational requirements, and (2) seeking to create or discover an innovative solution which will meet all of the essential conditions and, consequently, be acceptable to all.

When the conflict is intense and bitter, it may be necessary for the group to use the backup, recycling technique more than once. This technique is likely to be most effective when the parties to the conflict recognize that the well-being of all will suffer serious consequences if a constructive solution is not reached.

Action without consensus

At times, a problem will be so difficult or the hostilities will be so great that even with able leadership and the use of the backup, recycling procedure, the group is unable to reach consensus on a final solution within the time available for its deliberation. When this occurs, the leader may face situational requirements which necessitate that something be done by a given time and be compelled to take action.

There are several courses open. If the group is a unit in a hierarchical organization, the leader can select the solution that best meets the essential conditions and that is least detrimental to any of these conditions. Another alternative, which may be less damaging to the group, is for the leader to suggest that, since they have not reached consensus and yet action must be taken, they proceed with the solution favored by the persons who have the major responsibility for implementing the decisions since it is up to them to make it work. This procedure usually meets with a favorable response providing that the solution does not seriously violate any of the conditions felt to be essential by the group or some of its members.

When consensus is not reached and a solution which does not meet all the essential conditions stated by the group is put into effect by hierarchical pressure, some members of the group will be displeased. When this occurs, the attitudes of the members toward each other tend to become less favorable. The same will be true of the loyalty of members to the group and of the confidence and trust which the members have in each other and in the leader. These developments are apt to result in a general deterioration in the problem-solving and performance capability of the group. Leaders can permit this to occur occasionally, but not often. The loyalty and cohesiveness of groups need to be rebuilt and sustained by successful problem solving, or leaders will find that they and their groups have overdrawn their goodwill bank account.

The failure to reach consensus is much more serious when the group is a unit in an interorganizational linkage structure between two organizations in conflict. In this situation, leaders can make little use of hierarchical authority. They must rely on the skillful use of situational requirements, common values, and integrative goals, and the sensitive and skillful use of the principle of supportive relationships. One procedure for arriving at a course of action is to encourage the group to review its problem-solving activity, step by step, and to ask each member whether that member feels that the rest of the group understands his or her position, needs, goals, and point of view. If members feel that they are understood, the leader may be able to obtain action by suggesting that, since everyone has been heard fully and with empathetic understanding, the group should adopt for action, on a pragmatic consensus basis, that solution which appears to meet the essential conditions best. This procedure is likely to result in action when the group recognizes the existence of compelling situational requirements and strong common values and integrative goals.

Industrial relations experience supports the use of consensus

Many leaders in industrial relations recognize the superiority of consensus over win-lose procedures. In his presidential address to the Industrial Relations Research Association, Dunlop (1960) emphasized the substantial advantages achieved from the greater use of consensus.

> The theme of the preceding three sections [of this paper] has been that our national industrial relations system suffers from seeking solutions to problems in

terms of legislation and litigation, formal arbitration and public pronounce-
ments. This malady afflicts alike national governmental policy, the labor federation, and the confederation level of management. The common difficulty in its
essence is a failure to develop a consensus within government, the labor movement, or management. The consequence is resort to partisan legislation and
litigation and the ascendency of the politicians in national industrial relations
policy. An alternative policy is reliance, to a greater degree, upon the development of consensus.

Greater reliance upon consensus is particularly appropriate since the range of
industrial relations problems has become increasingly technical, and uniform
rules across wide reaches of the economy are impractical in many cases. Moreover, in our society, rules and policies which have been formulated by those
directly affected are likely to receive greater respect and compliance than when
imposed by fiat. The rapidly changing circumstances of technology and markets
require greater reliance on consensus since those most directly affected are more
sensitive to such change, and adaptation can be more gradual than that imposed
belatedly from without. Consensus develops habits of mind which encourage
continuing adaptation to new circumstances.

The method of consensus is admittedly difficult to apply; it is so much easier
simply to pass another law, or issue another decision or another resolution. The
achievement of consensus is often a frustrating process since it must triumph
over inertia, suspicion, and the warpath. It is slow to build. But it is clearly the
most satisfying and enduring solution to problems. It always has significant by-
products in improved understanding in many other spheres than those related
to the consensus. . . .

An industrial society requires a considerably greater measure of consensus on
industrial relations problems than we have. The present course is set toward an
unending sequence of legislative regulation, litigation, and political pronouncement. The community has a right to expect more from organized labor, confederation levels of management, and governmental agencies. Indeed, a shift in the
method of national policy-making in the industrial relations area is required if
labor and management are to make their potential contributions to the larger
problems facing the community. The place to begin is to resolve that the method
of consensus will be used internally in reaching decisions within the federation
and confederation levels of management and in the formulation and administration of governmental policies. This is the fundamental challenge—in my view—
of the next four to ten years in industrial relations in the United States. (pp. 14–
15)

Consensus does not mean complacency

Employing consensus does not mean that the group is to settle into sweet,
complacent unanimity. If it does, the leader is failing in his role. There should
be full recognition of genuine differences, and the problem solving should be

done in an atmosphere of "no nonsense." The existing differences should be used to stimulate the search for innovative solutions. Moreover, if the disagreements are significant and important to the group members, they, themselves, will help maintain the "no-nonsense" orientation. Complacent unanimity will occur only when the problems are inconsequential, the disagreements of no significance, or the leadership incompetent and the problem solving done poorly.

Consensus does not mean leveling to mediocrity

A criticism of consensus voiced by some is that it leads to mediocre decisions since the decision must always represent the average of the views held by the problem-solving group. This criticism is based on the assumption that each person's opinion carries equal weight in arriving at a consensual decision. Nothing is farther from reality in a group skilled in problem solving. The influence exercised by each person reflects the group's estimate of the significance of that person's contribution. Those persons who customarily make the more important contributions tend to be the more influential. This is true concerning both the process of decision making and the content of the decision being dealt with. On highly technical problems, the persons best informed on that problem tend to be more influential. In discussing the concept of consensus, the chief executive officer of a large corporation said, "Although we use consensus in our top finance and and operating committees, this does not mean each member of a committee exercises the same amount of influence from decision to decision. Those who do their 'homework' well, who come fully informed and fully prepared to discuss all aspects of the problem are the influential members."

Decisions reached by consensus are distinctly different from those reached by voting, particularly when each person's vote carries equal weight.

Farris (1969) has found that, among engineers and scientists, those who exert more influence on decisions are those persons who have demonstrated that they are better performers. Those who accomplish more exert more influence than do others on decisions related to their area of competence.

When consensus is used, each member of the group has the opportunity to exert influence on the decision. The magnitude of this influence depends upon such variables as the level of the member's technical knowledge related to the problem, the member's knowledge of the problem and the situation, the importance of the issue to the member, how strongly the member feels about it, how well the member knows and adheres to the group problem-solving process, how much the member contributes to building group loyalty, how innovative-minded the member is, the member's competence, judgment, and strengths as demonstrated in previous decision making, and the member's sincerity, integrity, and supportive treatment of others.

System 4 leadership is <u>not</u> "permissive"

The principle of supportive relationships which emphasizes the importance of aiding each person to achieve and maintain a sense of personal worth had led some persons to conclude that leaders should be "permissive," i.e., exert no influence, but let each member of the group go his or her own independent way. This is a serious misinterpretation. In a System 4 interaction-influence network, leaders first must see that a multiple overlapping structure is built whereby each person can exert significant influence upon decisions and, in turn, be *influenced by the system.* There is a *reciprocal* relationship in a System 4 social system: each person can influence the system and each accepts influence from it. This is basically different from being subjected to relatively little influence which would be the case if the leadership were permissive. *System 4 is participative, not permissive. Permissiveness is a characteristic of System 0 and is laissez faire.*

Freedom may not be motivating

Some persons hold the view that freeing an individual from influence by managers, or even by peers, will bring substantial improvement in performance. This view holds that each person knows exactly what to do and how to do it, can and will provide his or her own direction, will be more highly motivated, and will accomplish more if freed from the influence of the organization. Experience as well as quantitative research shows that this is not the case. Over the centuries, artists and scholars who experience long periods of isolation have been less productive than those who were members of "schools" and "colleges." Extensive research shows that persons who are entirely or substantially on their own and do not experience the stimulation from structured interaction with others tend to be less motivated and less productive than persons who are an integral part of a highly effective interaction-influence network. Persons in a System 4 interaction-influence network are much more highly motivated and productive than persons in a System 0, laissez-faire organization (Likert, 1961; Pelz, 1957; Pelz & Andrews, 1966; White & Lippitt, 1960).

This same confusion exists concerning self-actualization. This motive, like all the others which derive their strength from the desire to achieve and maintain a sense of personal worth and importance, is powerful. But the values one embraces, the goals one sets in terms of which self-actualization is sought, and the level of motivation to achieve these goals are all determined by the individual's social environment. The isolated person derives far less motivation from self-actualization than does the person who is an integral part of a System 4 interaction-influence network.

Any attempt to create highly motivated behavior in a conflict situation by relying on permissive leadership or self-actualization isolated from an effective interaction-influence network will yield highly disappointing results. Permissive leadership which frees persons from all constraints is likely to yield irresponsible behavior and to fail to achieve the coordinated, motivated behavior that membership in an effective interaction-influence network attains. Permissive leadership is ineffective in resolving conflicts.

9

Deemphasizing status and depersonalizing problem solving

Status can have serious adverse effects upon a group's capacity to resolve disagreements effectively. Persons at upper levels in a hierarchy express themselves much more freely than do those in lower levels (Bass & Wurster, 1953a, 1953b). To take full advantage of the contribution that diversity can make to creative problem solving in a conflict situation, all members of the group need to feel that they are expected to express their ideas fully. Hierarchical status acts as a strong deterrent on the willingness of group members to speak up.

Persons in leadership positions commonly are unaware of the impact of their status on the discussions and interactions in the problem-solving process. In a System 1 to 3 interaction-influence network, leaders often strive to maintain and exploit status. When this happens, members of each group learn that it is best for them to listen only to the leader. They say "yes" to the leader's solution without exploring other possibilities. There is no search for better, more creative solutions.

When members see their leader striving for status, they in turn compete for status; this pits subordinates against subordinates and creates hostile relationships. Confidence and trust, favorable attitudes toward other group members, loyalty to the group, candid communication, innovative and efficient problem solving, and efforts to minimize conflict all are appreciably poorer in groups where the leader seeks to use the power of status.

In an experimental setting, Alvin Zander (1953, p. 22) conducted an exercise with approximately 1,200 business managers to help them understand the behavior of a group toward two latecomers, one with extremely high prestige in the business world and another with very little status. In discussing the exercise, Robert L. Kahn (1953) made the following observations:

> One important point is the tremendous effect of what we might call status labels, the signs of position in a hierarchical organization. Remember that Dr. Zander did not tell us how to treat the newcomers to our experimental groups; he told us

only that one was the head of a large company and the other a bookkeeper. How differently many of us behaved toward these people, not because of their abilities or potential contributions, but because of their differential prestige, power, and position.

Another lesson to be drawn from this experience is that such treatment of people has enormous significance for their productivity. In this experiment, productivity can be thought of in terms of how much each person contributed to the discussion and to the constructive solution of the problem before the group. The reports of some of the "rejected" members show that they felt angry and frustrated, unable and unwilling to make their best contribution to the group goal. Whatever their contribution might have been was lost to the group. The new members of high status, who were accepted, gave a different report. They were relatively secure and highly motivated to participate in solving the problem before the group. By their own report and that of their colleagues, they were not only better satisfied but also much more productive.

A third point to be gained from this experimental experience has to do with the power that a group has over the behavior of its members. We have seen an example of that power in what was really a very brief and artificially contrived situation. If a group can have this much power over behavior and feelings in a laboratory setup, is it hard to believe in the ability of a natural group, or a work group in a plant, to stimulate or restrict production? Is it hard to believe that this kind of group power can be stronger than incentive plans and stronger than the formal communications on which management sometimes puts so much reliance?

Lastly, perhaps one of the most important principles derivable from the experiment is the reality of what we might call interpersonal forces, the influences that emanate from one person to another within a group.

These are forces that can be observed—or at least their effects can be observed. They can be felt (some of our tests give evidence of that), and they can be measured. Furthermore, these are forces that can work for an organization or immobilize it. Unfortunately, there are many organizations which, if not immobilized, are drastically impeded just because these kinds of forces are working against the organizational goals. To sum it up, the notion of psychological forces is not merely something invented by psychologists in their spare hours at the university. Such forces have reality. They determine human behavior, and they are present all the time, willy-nilly, in every group which exists. The issue is not whether these forces will continue, not whether they are important. The issue is simply whether we will understand them and use our understanding to maximize human satisfactions and accomplishments, or whether we will be ignorant of them and suffer the results. (pp. 27–28)

An example of deemphasizing status

In an unpublished study of a firm operating nationwide, The University of Michigan's Institute for Social Research found that managers in the first level (lowest) and second level in a particular region were doing an extraordinarily good job of developing their subordinates into highly effective work groups. These groups had substantially higher group loyalty; more favorable attitudes toward the manager, the company, and their work; higher performance goals; and higher productivity and lower costs than comparable units doing similar work in other parts of the company.

When the regional vice-president was asked what he was doing that might account for these findings, he replied that in his efforts to develop managers he followed a few major principles. One of his most important principles was deemphasizing status. He said that members of a group will talk freely in the presence of their managers and pass along their knowledge of problems and their ideas and suggestions only if status is deemphasized. He felt that this flow of information from group members and the use of their experience and ideas was essential if the best solutions were to be reached and the best performance obtained. He was convinced that unless a major effort is made to deemphasize status, the information flow and the interactions essential for success will not occur. One of his methods was to refrain from presiding at meetings of his subordinates. Instead, he arranged to have someone on the same hierarchical level as the others preside. He also tried to give people experience in taking an active part in meetings in order to make it easier for them to speak out when they had something that ought to be said in a meeting. He described the following as an illustration of his procedure:

> Every month there is a dinner and evening meeting which includes all of the managers who report to me and also all of the managers who, in turn, report to them. Our first and second level managers who are doing a good job of building highly effective work groups report to the lower echelon of managers in this dinner and evening meeting. In these dinner meetings, I use every opportunity to give people experience in running meetings and taking an active part in them. For example, each month I go over the list of eighty or so managers who are coming to the dinner meeting and pick one of them who has never presided at a meeting and who, as a rule, says nothing in our evening meetings. These persons are almost always managers who report to the men directly under me. Well in advance of the meeting, I call the manager I have picked and ask him to preside. Almost invariably, he replies that he has never presided at a meeting and that he does not know how to do it and he tries to beg off. I tell him that the job will not be difficult and that we can work together in preparing the agenda and the plans for the meeting. I go on to assure him that I am confident he can do it. With some reluctance he usually agrees to preside.

> It is interesting and encouraging to watch what an experience like this does to help a manager develop confidence in his ability to express himself in a group meeting. Two months ago we persuaded one of our older managers to preside. He was very reluctant to do it and quite apprehensive. He worked over the agenda carefully and gave a lot of thought to the meeting. When the meeting started, his opening remarks were, "Fellows, I have never presided at a meeting before. I feel very uncomfortable and unsure of myself. Tom (the Regional Vice

President) assures me that I'll have no problem, but I know that I'll make mistakes and, if I do, I just hope you will bear with me and help me out. Bill, the story you told me last Friday is just right for introducing our first speaker. Will you get up and tell it?" Everyone laughed appreciatively. He used this same procedure throughout the meeting, which he conducted in an apprehensive, but sincere manner. His presiding was a real success. The group enjoyed it greatly and let him know he had done well.

His success in running that dinner meeting gave him sufficient confidence to enable him to participate for the first time in the next month's business meeting. Until then he had never said a word at any of our meetings. Last month, he spoke up three times. He is beginning to feel comfortable in the meetings and is now giving us the benefit of his ideas. I could tell you of several other managers just like this fellow. All of them were fearful of speaking up in a meeting. Give them this kind of experience in presiding or in other ways put them in the spotlight in a successful way before the group and every one of them begins to feel sufficiently important and sure of himself to become an active participant in meetings. In this way, we get the benefit of the information these managers possess and the insights they have.

In addition to arranging for others to help perform leadership functions, a leader can do the following to deemphasize status:

1.. Avoid displaying authority and status by never showing impatience with the progress being made by the group, particularly on difficult problems.

2. Accept more blame than may be warranted for any failure or mistake.

3. Be generous in giving credit to others and especially to members of the group for successful results.

4. Share with the group all relevant information.

5. Be humble in the group's problem-solving discussions; e.g.:

    a. Encourage the group members to express their thoughts prior to stating your views.

    b. State your contributions tentatively, or better still, state them in the form of questions; or

    c. Ask questions to explore the general content area of your ideas; your ideas may emerge in an improved form.

    d. Be careful not to impose a decision upon the group or to dominate its discussions, especially when presiding.

6. Encourage the group to evaluate solutions proposed by you with a more critical eye than they turn upon solutions proposed by others.

The steps a leader takes in deemphasizing status will vary to fit the particular situation. There is no one best way.

Depersonalize decision making

Another application of the principle of supportive relationships should occur at every step in the decision-making process. This is the "depersonalizing" of differences and removing the identification of anyone's ego from that person's contribution. This "de-egoizing" of the decision-making process is necessary at every step as, for example, in stating the problem, listing the essential and desirable conditions which a satisfactory solution must meet, suggesting possible alternative solutions, contributing relevant facts, and evaluating solutions.

The leader should see that all contributions are accepted and treated as coming from the group as a whole and are not identified with any one person. Care should be taken so that one statement of the problem is not referred to as "Mary's" and another as "Bill's." All contributions at every stage in the problem-solving process should be treated as "ours": "One of *our* proposed solutions is A; another is B." *In all situations involving actual or potential differences or conflict among the members of the group, procedures should be used to separate the ego of each member, i.e., the member's sense of personal worth, from the member's contribution.* Under these circumstances, persons do not cling to a point "to save face" since their points have been carefully separated from their egos.

In this way, ego forces do not stimulate conflict among members. Instead, each member's desire to achieve and maintain a sense of personal worth is harnessed to the efforts of the entire group at each stage and to its final decisions and goals. The strong motivational forces created by the desire for a sense of personal worth are used to stimulate creative problem solving, to gain understanding and acceptance of the group's decisions, and to secure commitment to implement these decisions. The powerful motivation from ego forces is not wasted in win-lose battles within the group.

Use situational requirements to depersonalize decision making

The cold, hard facts of life frequently impose clear boundaries within which a decision obviously must fall to be sound and acceptable. These boundaries are readily recognized by all members of a group and all parties to a conflict. These facts of life are the *situational requirements* that cannot be ignored in decision making. They consist of such constraints as economic conditions, including costs and resources, the limitations imposed by geography and time, and the relevant perceptual and motivational variables.

The explicit recognition and use of the situational requirements in a conflict situation can contribute materially to creative problem solving by helping to depersonalize the process. Listing them should be recognized as an important, specific step in group problem solving. Usually this step should be taken just after the conditions for an acceptable solution have been stated.

The use of the situational requirements facilitates productive problem solving by making the group clearly aware of all conditions that impose objective constraints on possible courses of action and that, at the same time, create demands that must be fulfilled. Situational requirements contribute also to reaching consensus in decisions by providing an impersonal framework for achieving agreement. This was pointed to years ago by Mary Parker Follett (Fox & Urwick, 1973):

> My solution is to depersonalize the giving of orders, to unite all concerned in a study of the situation, to discover the law of the situation and obey that. Until we do this I do not think we shall have the most successful business administration. This is what does take place, what has to take place, when there is a question between two men in positions of equal authority. The head of the sales department does not give orders to the head of the production department, or vice versa. Each studies the market and the final decision is made as the market demands. This is, ideally, what should take place between foremen and rank and file, between any head and his subordinates. One *person* should not give orders to another *person,* but both should agree to take their orders from the situation. If orders are simply part of the situation, the question of someone giving and someone receiving does not come up. Both accept the orders given by the situation; employers accept the orders given by the situation. . . .
>
> Our job is not how to get people to obey orders, but how to devise methods by which we can best *discover* the order integral to a particular situation. When that is found, the employee can issue it to the employer, as well as employer to employee. This often happens easily and naturally. My cook or my stenographer points out the law of the situation, and I, if I recognize it as such, accept it, even although it may reverse some "order" I have given.
>
> If those in supervisory positions should depersonalize orders, then there would be no overbearing authority on the one hand, nor on the other that dangerous *laissez-aller* which comes from the fear of exercising authority. Of course, we should exercise authority, but always the authority of the situation. (p. 58)

In addition to the "law of the situation," Mary Parker Follett also spoke of the "authority of facts." Objective data can contribute greatly to productive problem solving and to the resolution of disagreement. Resistance and resentment are aroused whenever other persons, whether superiors, peers, or parties to a conflict, try to impose their particular solutions on others (Brehm, 1966). Most persons and groups, however, are quite prepared to accept *facts* and be guided by them in their search for a solution to a problem.

To depersonalize decision making have relevant facts available

An especially important responsibility of leadership, therefore, is to see that all relevant facts are available and used well. Since objective problem solving is facilitated by facts, the greater the total amount of relevant facts available, the better will be the decision and the easier it will be to reach consensus even in situations where there is marked conflict. In addition to the situational requirements, many other facts can be obtained in most situations with reasonable effort.

The constructive use of facts in depersonalizing decisions in situations where marked differences exist is illustrated by the experience of the War Finance Division of the U.S. Treasury Department in its effort to sell Series E bonds to as many people as possible during World War II. This example also shows the important role of the leader in seeing that the relevant facts are obtained and used productively in decision making.

T. W. Gamble became national director of the War Finance Division after the First War Bond Drive. Prior to this he had been chairman of the Oregon State War Bond Committee. Under his leadership, Oregon had made an outstanding record. Only Hawaii and Alaska, both of which had been bombed by Japan, could compare with Oregon on a per capita basis.

From his experience, Gamble knew many of the important steps to be taken to assure the success of a war bond drive. He had found it particularly important to have as many potential bond buyers as possible asked personally to increase their purchase of bonds. In planning the Second War Bond Drive, Gamble urged the head of every state War Bond Committee to mobilize a large number of volunteers to solicit all potential buyers and ask them to buy. Everyone recognized that recruiting and training of these volunteers was a tremendous task. Gamble nevertheless was convinced that it was necessary if a high level of sales of the Series E bonds was to be achieved. In spite of his outstanding record and his persuasiveness, he was unable to convince many of the state chairpersons that the substantial task of recruiting a large number of volunteers to solicit potential buyers was necessary.

The typical reply was about as follows: "Mr. Gamble, personal solicitation may be necessary in Oregon in order to achieve a high level of sales, but in this state that is not the case. We don't need to go to all that trouble here. If we put on an intensive campaign through the mass media and with mass meetings, we will achieve and surpass our quota."

Although Gamble's persuasive abilities failed to move state chairpersons who resisted using personal solicitation, he was successful when he marshaled the authority of facts. He arranged with the Division of Program Surveys of the Department of Agriculture (the staff of which later became the Survey Research Center of the University of Michigan) to conduct a national survey of the results of the Second War Bond Drive. A major purpose of the study was to learn what kinds of people did or did not increase their buying of war bonds during the campaign and why this was the case. Immediately after the Second War Bond Drive, about 1,800 persons were interviewed to appraise the drive and particularly to discover how to improve the third drive. The most important findings, as Gamble expected, concerned the effect of personal solicitation.

Since it was felt that personal solicitation might be a crucial variable affecting bond buying, the study was designed so that each respondent was specifically asked whether during the drive he or she had been asked personally to buy war bonds. At another point in the interview, these persons were asked how many bonds they had bought during the period of the drive and how many bonds they had been buying prior to the drive and would ordinarily buy.

When respondents were asked why they increased their buying of war bonds during the drive, most of them gave a patriotic reason. They would say, for example, that the government needed the money to buy war equipment. Only a small proportion answered that they bought because they were asked to buy. Yet when the data were analyzed, this reason was found to be of greatest importance. Of all gainfully employed people, 25 percent reported that they had been asked personally to buy war bonds. When these people were grouped together, it was found that 47 percent of this group bought more bonds during the Second War Bond Drive than they had been buying. Among the three-fourths of gainfully employed persons who had not been asked to buy, however, only 12 percent had bought more than usual.

This relationship between bond buying and solicitation held for every income group, for every occupational group, and for every geographical region. No matter how the data were grouped, it was found that among those who were asked to buy, there were about 35 percentage points more buyers than among those who were not asked to buy.

Gamble then arranged a series of regional meetings attended by the state chairpersons, the members of the state committees, and the members of the state staffs. The purpose of the meeting was to discuss the initial plans and promotional material for the Third War Bond Drive and to plan for the activities at the state and local levels.

After a brief introductory statement, Gamble had a member of the research organization which had conducted the study present a rather full summary of the major findings. The findings of the powerful influence of personal solicitation loomed large in the presentation because this variable had been found to be particularly effective in influencing buying behavior. In addition to the regional meetings, a short report of the findings was published and placed in the hands of every member of every state, county, and local War Bond Committee.

Although Gamble made frequent reference to the research findings, he did not press state committees to make greater use of personal solicitation in the Third than in the Second War Bond Drive. He relied on the authority of facts.

The power of this approach is demonstrated by the results. In the survey following the Third War Bond Drive it was found that personal solicitation in the Third Drive had been doubled: 50 percent of all gainfully employed persons were solicited. In this drive, 59 percent of those who were personally solicited bought more bonds than usual. Among those who were not personally asked to buy, only 18 percent bought additional bonds.

The major purpose of the War Bond Drives was, of course, sales of bonds to individuals. This one finding on the importance of personal solicitation and its application in the Third War Bond Drive helped materially to increase the sale of Series E bonds and the total sale of all bonds to individuals. The doubling of personal solicitation in the Third Drive over the Second was a major factor in almost doubling the amount of Series E bonds that were sold. In the Second Drive, 1.5 billion dollars of Series E bonds were sold; 2.5 billion dollars of bonds were sold in the Third. Throughout all the Bond Drives, there was a close relationship between the amount of solicitation and the total amount of bonds sold to individuals. Moreover, under the continuing impact of the authority of facts, the total level of solicitation increased until two out of every three potential buyers were asked to buy, and of those who were asked to buy, approximately 64 percent bought more bonds than they had been buying. This level of solicitation was reached by the Fifth War Bond Drive (Cartwright, 1947, 1949).

The War Bond Drive example illustrates the important contribution which objective data can make in helping persons who hold different points of view to reach agreement. A common body of facts replaced a variety of experiences and convictions. This increased the likelihood that all the different persons involved would arrive at that solution most adequately supported by facts.

Treat perceptions and attitudes as facts in depersonalizing decision making

People act on the basis of what they perceive the situation to be, whether the perceptions are accurate or grossly inaccurate. Since behavior is based on perceptions, the existence of each of them is a fact to be considered. Similarly, the frustrations, attitudes, loyalty, and hostilities felt by each member and the information and misinformation possessed by each are facts as is their evaluation of the merits and desirability of each particular course of action under consideration.

Depersonalize the gathering of facts

The leader should see that facts, including relevant situational requirements, are obtained in such a manner that every person involved in the problem solving will recognize them as accurate and accept them. In a controversy, the probability of facts being accepted by all persons regardless of their points of view can be increased appreciably by ensuring that:

1. The methods used are recognized by all persons as being fully objective or as objective as the situation permits.

2. The persons collecting the data range about as widely in viewpoint as do those involved in the conflict.

3. Full opportunity is provided for any person who wishes to do so to check fully on the methods used and the results obtained.

4. All needed assistance is given to anyone who wishes, independently, to obtain data to check on any or all the reported facts.

The contribution of objective facts to the successful resolution of conflicts, especially when used with group problem solving, can be shown schematically:

1. *"Go-my-own-way" approach to resolving a conflict.* In this case, each party to the conflict goes through the entire problem-solving process independently of the other, including collecting the facts and stating the situational requirements.

My facts	Analyzed and interpreted in terms of *MY* experience	Yield	*My* solution which *I* think is good and to which I am committed
Your facts	Analyzed and interpreted in terms of *YOUR* experience	Yield	*Your* solution which *YOU* think is good and to which you are committed

If the two persons above have to agree on a common solution, their only choice is to reconcile their independent solutions in a win-lose confrontation unless the two solutions happen to be identical. If each person thinks his or her solution is the only acceptable one, two courses of action are open:

a. Conflict: Each person seeks to force his or her solution on the other.

   Motivational consequences: The person who wins will be highly motivated to make the solution work. The person who loses will be motivated to hold back and, if it is at all possible, to sabotage the activity, at least partially, to show that the solution was a poor one.

b. Compromise: Each person modifies his or her solution as little as possible and seeks through bargaining to force the other to make the greater change. Each gives up some aspects of his or her own preferred solution.

   Motivational consequences: Since each person has given up some aspects of his or her preferred solution, the final solution usually is seen as being inadequate in some respects. Neither person feels the solution meets his or her needs fully, and both are inclined to carry it out half-heartedly.

2. *Coordinated fact-gathering approach.* In this case the two persons or parties jointly collect the facts and state the situational requirements.

| Same facts | Analyzed and interpreted by each person separately in terms of his or her experience | Yield several solutions, depending on number of persons and range of previous experience. But because of use of same facts, solutions are likely to be less diverse than in process 1 above | One solution achieved by conflict or compromise and with corresponding motivational consequences as stated in process 1. But conflict and compromise apt to be less bitter than in process 1 because solutions are less diverse due to same facts |

3. *Approach based on coordinated fact gathering coupled with group decision process, i.e., win-win problem solving.*

| Same facts | Analyzed and interpreted by group in terms of experience which is shared in the discussion process. This leads to less diverse experience being focused on decision-making processes | Wide variety of decisions examined but narrowed to one solution | Yield a single solution reached by consensus accepted by all as their solution | Excellent solution, with each person highly motivated to carry it out well |

As the above schematic diagram indicates, when the two conflicting parties carry out each step in the problem-solving process jointly, the probability that they will reach a solution acceptable to both parties is much greater. An important responsibility of leadership, consequently, is to facilitate in every way possible the full involvement of all parties to a controversy in every step of the decision-making process.

Use third party interventions to help depersonalize interaction

Schmidt and Tannenbaum (1960) discuss what a manager can do to help turn differences into creative problem solving. As they point out, these procedures can be used by a third party who has the advantage of a more detached viewpoint.

1. A third party can welcome the existence of differences and stress their value in suggesting a greater variety of possible solutions to the conflict.

2. A third party can listen with understanding rather than evaluation. Conflicting parties all too often fail to listen to each other. Each party is too busy making its own point and trying to impose its views on others. By listening and comprehending, the third party can contribute to the conflicting parties' understanding of each other's position. The third party's actions also can serve as a pattern which the conflicting parties may follow.

3. By listening carefully to the discussion, a third party can clarify the nature of the issue and make evident whether it is based on different perceptions of facts, methods, values, or goals. Disputants themselves often depart from the original issue by chasing a tangential point or by transposing the issue. The third party, by being more detached, can perform a welcome function by helping the disputants develop a common understanding of the issue and by repeatedly bringing them back to it.

4. The third party can recognize and accept such feelings as fear, jealousy, anger, or anxiety without judgment. By accepting such feelings, the third party can make it possible for the conflicting parties to face their true feelings and to analyze the impact of these feelings on the disagreement.

5. The third party can suggest procedures and ground rules for resolving the differences. The particular techniques will depend on whether the disagreement is over facts, methods, goals, or values.

6. The third party can help maintain relationships between the disputing parties. Disputes tend to disrupt ongoing relationships. If a conflict is to be transformed into a problem-solving situation, someone must perform the functions of encouraging, supporting, reducing tension, and expressing common feelings which, in the heat of battle, may be neglected. If the disputing parties themselves do not provide these functions, the third party can provide encouragement to see that they are undertaken.

Depersonalize by solving generalized problem before tackling specific case

It usually is much easier to engage in productive problem solving and reach consensus on general policy issues than it is on a specific problem since most persons are less likely to hold or to jump to a fixed "position" on a policy question than on a specific case. Moreover, the integrative goals (chap. 8), relevant situational requirements, and essential conditions usually are more readily stated and accepted by all in solving problems of general policy than is possible with specific issues. When dealing with a difficult, emotion-laden issue, the discussion of the specific problem should be postponed, if possible, until after the problem has been stated and resolved in its generalized form by means of creative problem solving.

Whenever a specific case is tackled first, the interaction almost inevitably is thrown into a win-lose confrontation. All members immediately see the solution which serves best their own or their unit's well-being and, consequently, press to have that solution accepted. If, however, the general problem and underlying issues are solved first, they become guidelines and criteria. Once these guidelines are available, their use usually makes it much easier to solve the specific issue in a constructive rather than in a win-lose manner.

Seeking and stating underlying policy issues is not easy. Imaginative, competent leadership contributes greatly to a group's capacity to do this task well. This same skillful leadership is required also in helping the group to keep its problem-solving efforts focused on achieving an integrative solution to the generalized problem which is acceptable to all and serves the interests of all.

Allocating scarce resources

An example may help to illustrate the value of solving the generalized problem prior to tackling the specific case. One of the difficult problems of a large college in a major university is the task of allocating scarce resources among its various departments. There are limitations as to the allocation of the number of full professorships, the number of students who can be admitted, space for additional offices, funds for next year's operating budgets or for salary increases. Several years ago, in an effort to cope with these problems more constructively and with less adverse consequences, the dean of a college tried to use group problem solving to allocate budgets and resources for the next fiscal year among the college's departments. The heads of departments had no experience in group problem solving, and each of them saw a department head's role, not as a linking pin (see chap. 10) but as a representative to fight for and protect the interests of that department. This view of a department head's role was held also by most of the members of each department. As a consequence, in the group meetings with the dean, each "representative" pressed for solutions beneficial to that particular department, regardless of the consequences which these solutions would have upon the college as a whole. The win-lose confrontations and battles created so much hostility and cleavages within the college that the attempt to use group problem solving to deal with the allocation of scarce resources was given up. The unhappy experience with the group approach convinced most of those involved that it was an ineffective way to deal with such problems.

A few years after this unsuccessful and painful attempt, the dean had a series of experiences which clarified the difference between the role of a representative and that of a linking pin. He became convinced that an essential responsibility of a dean was to see that the problems worked on were at the dean's level, namely college-wide and not problems at the department level. He realized that in tackling every problem in meetings with the heads of departments the focus had to be on finding a solution that would serve the best interests of the *entire* college and not the narrower interests of a particular department or two (See chap. 10 for a fuller discussion).

Using this new insight as a guide, the dean concluded that the way to launch group problem solving in his college was to start first with problems of concern to all departments and to the college generally, such as: What are our objectives concerning teaching and research? What interrelations do we wish to establish between teaching and research? What are our plans concerning growth, and how should such plans be financed? The dean and the heads of departments dealt successfully with these general policy questions and, as they did so, their cohesiveness as a group increased and so did their capacity to engage successfully in group problem solving.

This enabled the dean to put on the agenda problems that were somewhat less general in character. For example, they dealt with such questions as: What general principles of compensation and salary administration do we wish to use? What implications do these principles have for our situation? What do we want our compensation system to accomplish? On what basis shall salary increases be granted? Must individuals rely on the pressure of outside offers to force increases or is there a better way? How can compensation be used so as to contribute most to assisting the college to accomplish its objectives? The solutions reached became policy guidelines for such issues as compensation, size of graduate and undergraduate enrollment, and budget and space allocations.

The dean next brought to the group the tough problem of departmental budget allocations for salary increases for the following year. The group tackled this problem by applying its new skills in creative problem solving. The group members also drew upon the confidence and trust they had established among themselves. The group recognized the relevance and value of previous decisions reached concerning the goals of the college and the principles they wished to have applied to faculty compensation. The heads of departments decided, consequently, to have these major policy decisions summarized with a focus on salary administration since it was agreed that these policies would be used by all departments as general guides in reaching decisions for salary increases.

In response to a proposal that each department should receive an amount for salary increases equal to approximately 6 percent of its faculty salary budget for the current year, the head of the largest department objected. He stated that a new, small department, which the members of the group had agreed was important to the college and should grow, ought to receive an appreciably larger sum than an amount equal to the flat percentage figure for it. He pointed out that the salary levels in this new field were unusually high and that greater increases than average were going to be necessary to hold the excellent person- nel they now had and to attract others to the department. After some discus- sion, this was agreed to by the group as being in the best interest of the entire college. The action on this problem led a different chairman to remind the group that another department, not his own, had for many years had an unusually low salary level because of the previous department chairman who prided himself on his ability to recruit able faculty at low salaries. Further discussion of the salary levels of this department led to a decision that this department, too, should be allocated a larger sum for salary increases than the flat percentage figure would yield.

Another decision reached by the group was that, for the first time in the college's history, the heads of departments as a group would review the salary recommendations of every department. The review would be overall in charac- ter to assure reasonable equity across departments, but each department head would have full information on the salaries of every department. Open, candid exchange of information concerning salaries was replacing secrecy and distrust.

A significant development occurred during this work on salary increases. One of the department heads observed that there was another orientation from which their problem could be viewed. Instead of trying to develop a satisfactory way of dividing a small pie, it might be possible to enlarge its size so that each department would get a bigger piece. The group considered this view of the problem briefly but long enough to convince themselves that there were several possible steps for increasing the sums available for salaries and salary increases. They decided that this was an important approach to the problem and appointed a small committee to do preparatory work. This committee met with the president of the university and the vice-president for university relations and discussed what department heads and department members could do to help obtain more funds. They also examined the various ways for the faculty of the college to meet with citizen groups throughout the state to develop under- standing and support for teaching and research. They found that much could be done and that when shared among many faculty members the work would not be burdensome for any one person.

The dean and heads of departments are now working with the president in a pilot project to test the amount of increased financial support which can be generated. Although everyone recognizes that this is a long-range project and the full payoff is not likely to come for several years, the initial results are highly promising.

A case from business

Sometimes persons, for reasons of their own, want to worsen a conflict rather than to help resolve it constructively. This occurred in a company created by consolidating several smaller, more specialized firms. This consolidation was forced through by the principal stockholder. The president of one of the smaller companies was made president of the new firm. Presidents of some of the other smaller companies became vice-presidents in the new firm.

The new president sought to build the 10 senior officers who reported to him into a cohesive, highly effective team. His efforts, however, were resisted by some of the persons who were former presidents of the smaller companies. This was especially true of Mr. A, a senior vice-president, recognized by all as a very able person possessing great technical competence in his particular field. He was resentful, however, of being passed over for the top job. The new president faced the problem, consequently, of building an effective managerial team with some members accepting the new arrangements, some displaying mild to moderate resistance, and one, Mr. A, strongly opposed to the effort and out to prove himself a better man than the president.

Mr. A sought to defeat the president's efforts by pursuing two different strategies, neither of which involved clear-cut insubordination. One strategy was to bring to the meetings of the president's management team complex problems in the field of Mr. A's technical speciality and for which he had functional responsibility. Typically, they were problems which should have been resolved at echelons below the top managerial team but which were prevented from resolution there by Mr. A. Moreover, when he presented each problem to the top management team, he usually stated them in such a way as to cause the group to split into win-lose factions.

The other strategy Mr. A followed was to bring to the top managerial team a specific, but controversial, recommendation in the area of his recognized competence and request its approval. Often these recommendations involved allocations of scarce resources. This solution-minded behavior by Mr. A also succeeded in splitting the top managerial team into win-lose factions.

As long as the president permitted Mr. A to pursue his two strategies, the top management team was divided. Over time, their win-lose battles widened their differences and prevented the president from making any progress in building the top group into a cohesive, effective, managerial team.

The president was distressed by his failure and studied the situation carefully with the aid of a consultant. Meetings of the group were observed, and tape recordings were made of the sessions. Analyses of these data helped the president to gain insights into Mr. A's disruptive behavior.

The president decided that he should use group problem solving to deal with the situation and asked his top managerial team, with the aid of the consultant, to analyze their meetings and especially their decision-making processes. When this was done over several weeks, it became evident to the group that many of the problems on which they had become deadlocked or badly split were recommendations Mr. A had submitted for approval. As they examined these problems, the group became aware that substantial agreement would have been possible had they looked at the underlying policy questions prior to trying to reach a decision concerning the specific recommendation. The group decided, consequently, that if anyone proposed a specific recommendation to the group for action, they would set this recommendation aside until they had looked first at and resolved the underlying policy issues.

A second conclusion emerging from the group's analysis of its decision making was that they often dealt with problems that should have been resolved at lower echelons. They established, therefore, policy guidelines to prevent this from happening in the future.

These two decisions, based on the group's insights from analyzing their own experience, effectively prevented Mr. A from pursuing his two disruptive strategies. As these two group decisions took effect, the interactions in the group moved slowly from win-lose to constructive problem solving. Even more slowly, the group began to develop into an effective managerial team.

As this case from business and the previous example from higher education illustrate, general problems tend to be less emotionally charged and dominated by self-interest than are specific cases. Focusing on general problems makes it easier to reach consensus and, in the process, to build group loyalty and skill in problem solving. In turn, the decisions on these general problems provide the group with criteria and policy guidelines for solving specific problems. With agreed-upon criteria and guidelines to use in approaching and dealing with specific cases, and with increased group loyalty and problem-solving skills, it is much easier for the group to avoid win-lose confrontation and to deal with specific cases by consensual problem solving.

Progressive success strengthens problem-solving capability

Solving general problems prior to tackling difficult specific problems not only decreases the adverse influence of forces arising from personal interest but has the advantage also of building on group success. In any group, and especially in a newly created group, which has to deal with difficult problems involving strong and marked differences or disagreements among the group members, it often is sound strategy for the leader to have the group tackle some of the easier problems first. Success contributes to group strength and problem-solving capabilities. When a group resolves a problem successfully, it develops pride in its problem-solving capabilities, the attitudes become more favorable among the members, the loyalty to the group by its members increases, and the group acquires additional skill in problem solving. These developments strengthen the group's problem-solving capacity and increase the likelihood that difficult conflicts will be resolved successfully.

Failure by the group to reach consensus on a problem of importance to it has the opposite effect since irreconcilable disagreements continue. Pride in the group and loyalty to it decrease with failure in problem solving. These developments, in turn, weaken the group and decrease its ability to solve conflicts successfully.

Favorable attitudes and pride in its problem-solving capabilities are valuable assets to a group when it tackles any difficult problem involving marked disagreements among its members. A group with high group loyalty is much more likely to apply the principle of supportive relationships in its problem solving and more likely to recognize and to be motivated by common values and integrative goals than is a group lacking these attitudes. These values and goals, plus the group's own desire not to be split into win-lose factions, increase the group's effort, commitment, and capability for finding a constructive solution to its problems and disagreements.

A leader, consequently, needs to help a group begin by selecting problems with little or no built-in hostility and those which the group can be reasonably certain of solving successfully. As the group succeeds and gains both problem-solving skills and increased group strength and loyalty, its ability to solve more and more difficult problems increases. Sensitive pacing by the leader is a crucial ingredient of success. The leader should gear the problems to the group's internal strength and problem-solving capability.

Take adequate time for each problem-solving step

When a group rushes through some or all the steps to the solution phase, it is not likely to find an innovative solution that all members are really happy with. Those for whom the accepted solution has some unsatisfactory aspects are likely to feel resentful because in their view the group has pushed on them a solution that has deficiencies. This causes the original cleavages to persist. The initial disagreements among the members are apt to continue on the same lines and usually become intensified. To prevent this, the leader should encourage the group to take adequate, but not excessive, time for each step. This assures that each step is done well by the group and greatly increases the probability that the group will develop an innovative solution satisfactory to all concerned and that the group will emerge with greater cohesiveness.

Jumping to the solution is likely to increase the probability that the "valence" phenomenon will occur. This is described by Maier (1967):

> When leaderless groups (made up of three or four persons) engage in problem solving, they propose a variety of solutions. Each solution may receive both critical and supportive comments, as well as descriptive and explorative comments from other participants. If the number of negative and positive comments for each solution are algebraically summed, each may be given a *valence index* (Hoffman & Maier, 1964). The first solution that receives a positive valence value of 15 tends to be adopted to the satisfaction of all participants about 85% of the time, regardless of its quality. Higher quality solutions introduced after the critical value for one of the solutions has been reached have little chance of achieving real consideration. Once some degree of consensus is reached, the jelling process seems to proceed rather rapidly.

The critical valence value of 15 appears not to be greatly altered by the nature of the problem or the exact size of the group. Rather, it seems to designate a turning point between the idea-getting process and the decision-making process (idea evaluation). A solution's valence index is not a measure of the number of persons supporting the solution, since a vocal minority can build up a solution's valence by actively pushing it. In this sense, valence becomes an influence in addition to social pressure in determining an outcome.

Since a solution's valence is independent of its objective quality, this group factor becomes an important liability in group problem solving, even when the value of a decision depends upon objective criteria (facts and logic). It becomes a means whereby skilled manipulators can have more influence over the group process than their proportion of membership deserves. (p. 241)

Maier (1967) summarizes the importance of the leader in aiding the group to take adequate time on each step as follows:

When the discussion leader aids in the separation of the several aspects of the problem-solving process and delays the solution-mindedness of the group (Maier, 1958, 1963; Maier & Solem, 1962), both solution quality and acceptance improve; when he hinders or fails to facilitate the isolation of these varied processes, he risks a deterioration in the group process (Solem, 1965). His skill thus determines whether a discussion drifts toward conflicting interests or whether mutual interests ["Mutual interests" and "integrative goals" are synonyms (see chap. 8).] are located. Cooperative problem solving can occur only after the mutual interests have been established and it is surprising how often they can be found when the discussion leader makes this his task (Maier, 1952, 1963; Maier & Hayes, 1962). (p. 243)

Avert win-lose struggles by avoiding solution-mindedness

In the early stages of building problem-solving groups to deal with difficult, conflict-ridden issues, it is highly important for the leader to help the group avoid being solution-minded. When a group comes to grips with a problem in business, government, universities, and other organizations, its members typically are solution-minded in their orientation and behavior unless they are highly skilled in group problem solving.

Observations and recording of meetings at every hierarchical level in business organizations reveal the prevalence of solution-minded behavior in dealing with problems. In the board of directors of one firm, for example, officers with conflicting personal goals regularly came to the board meetings with proposals or recommendations to be approved rather than problems to be solved. Whenever a proposal was presented for approval, the interaction in the board was immediately structured into a win-lose battle. The officer presenting the proposal and others who felt they would benefit fought for it. Those who felt they would be adversely affected struggled vigorously to have it defeated.

The same kinds of win-lose battles occur also at departmental and lower levels in firms. The production department commonly makes recommendations favorable to it but apt to have adverse consequences for sales. The sales department is likely to do the same and so is the research and development department.

Even sophisticated managers who often engage in problem solving, such as directors of research and development departments, display solution-minded behavior, jumping immediately from one problem to a solution (Havelock & Mann, 1968).

A form of solution-mindedness is seen in the "unnegotiable" demands by students and by blacks and other minority groups. It also is seen in the dogmatic pronouncement of government representatives, of heads of business, industry, and labor, and of university presidents.

When arbitrary positions are taken on opposite sides of the same issue, the result is a win-lose confrontation precluding problem solving. For instance, an "unnegotiable" demand by students for barring ROTC units from a college campus met by an announcement from the college president that under no circumstances will the ROTC be denied a place, establishes two irreconcilable positions. Black demands for admitting a percentage of black students equal to the number of blacks in the population, without regard to the students' preparation and the established academic standards, will result in a deadlock if met with a pronouncement that present educational admission standards for all students will be maintained or with a ruling that no fixed percentages for admission will be applied to any race, religion, or other groups.

Status and other dimensions of personal worth and importance always are present in such win-lose battles and provide strong motivation to hold a position and win. A college president's reputation, if not his job, may depend on how well he stands up to attack. He cannot retreat without losing face and effectiveness. The students, convinced of the righteousness of their cause, cannot retreat from their unnegotiable demands without losing self-respect and the loyalty of their group.

Avoid solution-mindedness
but do not dawdle

Although it is highly important for the leader to encourage the group to take adequate time for each step to avoid solution-mindedness, it is equally important that the group be helped not to waste time. Dawdling on unimportant points and continuing on topics after the group has reached consensus is inefficient, results in boredom, and creates frustration.

The leader may help the group save time and facilitate its work by the use of subcommittees to prepare material for the group's consideration. If subcommittees are used, their creation and appointment must have the group's full and wholehearted approval so that the work of the subcommittees will not be rejected by the group without genuine consideration. Groups tend to reject the work of unauthorized subcommittees.

In addition, members should work as individuals when individual effort can be more productive per unit of time than can group effort. Available evidence indicates, for example, that quite generally persons working alone can list more possible alternatives in a given period of time than when they tackle this step as a group. [See, e.g., the summary by Kelley and Thibaut of the research of Taylor, Dunnette, Lorge, and others in Lindzey and Aronson (1969).] Other kinds of activities in which members often are more productive when working as individuals rather than in a group include the collecting of relevant facts and information, the reducing to writing of tentative expressions of consensus, and the preparation of draft statements to be used as "chopping blocks" in efforts to reach consensus.

Substantial time will be saved by having decisions made at appropriate levels and by the relevant groups in the interaction-influence network. In an effort to build a System 4 organization or to use System 4 in resolving conflicts, some persons mistakenly assume that everyone should take part in every decision. This is an erroneous interpretation of System 4. There is no need for everyone in all groups to sit in on every decision made by the organization. This would be extremely wasteful. Through the linkage provided by the System 4 multiple overlapping groups, each person is able to exert substantial influence on decisions without a personal appearance in every decision-making session. In fact, in a System 4 organization, each person is able to exert appreciably more influence through the linkages provided than if that person were physically present every time a decision is made. This requires, however, that there be a structure consisting of linked groups. This is the topic of the next chapter.

Improving group problem-solving skills

A leader and a group can use feedback to help them make rapid progress in developing their capacity to solve problems well while simultaneously building their effectiveness as a group. Reading the principles proposed in this and other chapters usually does not lead to their rapid internalization and ready use. Practice is required with periodic assessment of how well the principles are being applied, followed by further practice focused on improving the weak spots revealed by the evaluation.

A questionnaire designed for this purpose is shown in Table 9-1. At the end of the problem-solving sessions, the members of the group can fill out the questionnaire. The average scores, along with the highest score and lowest score checked on each item by any person, should be tabulated and reported to

Table 9-1
Profile of group problem solving (Form GP)

This questionnaire is designed to enable each member to describe the group's problem-solving behavior.

In completing the questionnaire, it is important that you answer each question as thoughtfully and frankly as possible. There are no right or wrong answers.

The answers will be summarized in statistical form so that individuals cannot be identified. To ensure complete confidentiality, please do not write your name anywhere on this questionnaire.

Please indicate your answer to each question by filling in the circle under the choice that best describes your view on that question.

For example, suppose the question were:

	Rarely		Sometimes		Often		Very often	
How often does the sun shine in your town?	①	②	③	④	⑤	⑥	⑦	⑧

If you think that the sun shines often, you would fill in ⑤ or ⑥. You would fill in ⑤ if you feel that the situation is closer to "sometimes" than to "very often." You would fill in ⑥ if you feel that the situation is closer to "very often."

In our problem solving, to what extent are we:

	Very little		Some		Considerable		Very great	
1. Selecting problems that we can do something about	①	②	③	④	⑤	⑥	⑦	⑧
2. Making sure that we are discussing the real problem	①	②	③	④	⑤	⑥	⑦	⑧
3. Stating the problem clearly	①	②	③	④	⑤	⑥	⑦	⑧
4. Searching for and stating situational requirements	①	②	③	④	⑤	⑥	⑦	⑧
5. Avoiding solution-mindedness	①	②	③	④	⑤	⑥	⑦	⑧

	Very little		Some		Considerable		Very great	
6. Searching for and using integrative goals	①	②	③	④	⑤	⑥	⑦	⑧
7. Realistically facing hard facts rather than just being nice to each other	①	②	③	④	⑤	⑥	⑦	⑧

Table 9-1
Profile of group problem solving (Form GP)   (Continued)

In our problem solving, to what
extent are we:

	Very little		Some		Considerable		Very great	
8. Using "win-win," not "win-lose" procedures	①	②	③	④	⑤	⑥	⑦	⑧
9. Depersonalizing problem solving, e.g., by not identifying contributions with persons	①	②	③	④	⑤	⑥	⑦	⑧
10. Building group cohesiveness prior to tackling hard problems, e.g., tackling easy problems first	①	②	③	④	⑤	⑥	⑦	⑧
11. Candidly dealing with "hidden agenda"	①	②	③	④	⑤	⑥	⑦	⑧

	Very little		Some		Considerable		Very great	
12. Applying the principle of supportive relationships, e.g., listening supportively	①	②	③	④	⑤	⑥	⑦	⑧
13. Encouraging members who hold differing points of view to express themselves freely and fully	①	②	③	④	⑤	⑥	⑦	⑧
14. Deemphasizing status	①	②	③	④	⑤	⑥	⑦	⑧
15. Using consensus	①	②	③	④	⑤	⑥	⑦	⑧
16. Using the authority of facts rather than the authority of persons	①	②	③	④	⑤	⑥	⑦	⑧

	Very little		Some		Considerable		Very great	
17. Taking each problem-solving step in sequence	①	②	③	④	⑤	⑥	⑦	⑧
18. Taking adequate time for each problem-solving step	①	②	③	④	⑤	⑥	⑦	⑧
19. Not wasting time by dawdling	①	②	③	④	⑤	⑥	⑦	⑧
20. Solving general problem before tackling specific cases	①	②	③	④	⑤	⑥	⑦	⑧
21. Defining conditions that a solution must meet to be acceptable	①	②	③	④	⑤	⑥	⑦	⑧

Table 9-1
Profile of group problem solving (Form GP) **(Continued)**

In our problem solving, to what extent are we:

	Very little		Some		Considerable		Very great	
22. Evaluating all suggested conditions as to whether they are merely desirable or are essential	①	②	③	④	⑤	⑥	⑦	⑧
23. Separating the discovery and listing of alternative solutions from their evaluation	①	②	③	④	⑤	⑥	⑦	⑧
24. Searching innovatively for all reasonably promising solutions and listing them	①	②	③	④	⑤	⑥	⑦	⑧
25. Seeking innovative solutions by using different frames of reference and through brainstorming	①	②	③	④	⑤	⑥	⑦	⑧
26. Obtaining facts to check whether the proposed solutions meet the conditions for acceptability	①	②	③	④	⑤	⑥	⑦	⑧

	Very little		Some		Considerable		Very great	
27. Selecting the solutions that best meet the conditions for acceptability	①	②	③	④	⑤	⑥	⑦	⑧
28. Using backup and recycling technique when group cannot reach consensus	①	②	③	④	⑤	⑥	⑦	⑧
29. Checking the solution against the problem as stated to be sure that it really solves the problem	①	②	③	④	⑤	⑥	⑦	⑧
30. Rechecking the solution for undesirable side effects	①	②	③	④	⑤	⑥	⑦	⑧
31. Specifying how, by whom, and when action is to be taken	①	②	③	④	⑤	⑥	⑦	⑧
32. Establishing review procedures to be sure agreed-upon action will be taken	①	②	③	④	⑤	⑥	⑦	⑧

the group. If the group is to meet again soon, the report can be given at the next meeting. If the group is not likely to meet again soon, the results should be reported and discussed before the meeting ends. If there are large discrepancies in the scores, the persons who differ in their perceptions can tell why they saw the behavior as they did. Often important insights into the group's problem-solving behavior are elicited by this procedure. The group should look at the average score on each item and consider how well the group has performed and whether it wishes to strive for further improvement. If so, members may wish to refer to the sections in this volume or other materials that discuss the particular item and the effective ways of applying the relevant principle.

10

The structure of the System 4 interaction-influence network: Linked multiple overlapping groups

If an interaction-influence network is to be effective in resolving conflict successfully, it must have an adequate structure as well as System 4 leadership, interaction, and problem-solving processes. If either structure or process is deficient, the problem-solving and conflict-resolving capacity of the network will be adversely affected. We will describe the nature of System 4 structure in this and the next two chapters.

The structure of the interaction-influence network in System 4 organizations consists of cohesive work groups with high performance goals linked together by persons who hold overlapping memberships in two or more groups. The interaction-influence networks of Systems 1, 2, and 3 are essentially person-to-person. In Systems 1 and 2, the interactions, influence, and motivation processes, problem solving, and conflict resolving take place on a person-to-person basis. The superior deals with the subordinates individually and makes the final decision. In System 3, the interaction is largely person-to-person, although the superior may convene the subordinates to get their views but not to make group decisions. The superior makes the decision after the discussion.

In System 4, the face-to-face group plays a major role in interactions. These work groups can vary in size from two persons to several. Job problems and other work-related problems are solved typically in work group problem-solving meetings and generally by consensus. This System 4 pattern has been derived from the behavior of the highest-producing managers in American business as discovered from extensive research. It is supported also by many studies which show that the communication, influence, motivation, and conflict-resolving processes are done best in organizations which are composed of small face-to-face groups using consensus (Cartwright & Zander, 1968; Likert, 1961, 1967; Maier, 1963, 1967; Tannenbaum, 1968).

The System 4 overlapping-group structure is shown in Figure 10-1. It can be drawn also in another manner (fig. 10-2). Each enclosed area in Figure 10-1 or 10-2 represents a work group with a superior and with subordinate members.

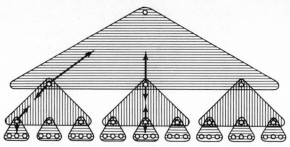

(The arrows indicate the linking-pin function)

Figure 10-1 *The overlapping-group form of organization. Work groups vary in size as circumstances require, although they are shown here as consisting of four persons. The arrows indicate the linking-pin function.*

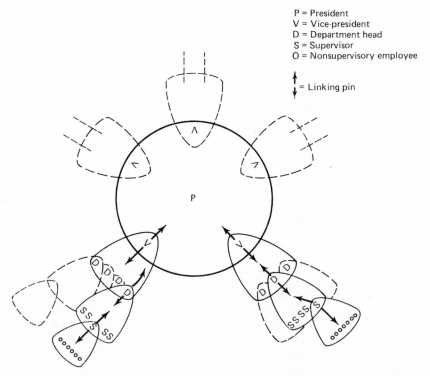

P = President
V = Vice-president
D = Department head
S = Supervisor
O = Nonsupervisory employee

= Linking pin

Figure 10-2 *The multiple-overlapping-group form of System 4 interaction-influence network.*

Thus, in Figure 10-2, the president, *P,* and the vice-presidents, *V,* comprise one work group. Each vice-president and the department heads, *D,* reporting to him constitute another group, and so on throughout the organization. In each case, the superiors serve as linking pins between their subordinate work groups and the ones in which they, in turn, are subordinates. The president, alone or with other senior officers, links the center work group (shown in Figure 10-2) to the board of directors of the organization.

The work groups in a System 4 organization usually are larger in the lower, or more peripheral, parts of an organization and smaller at the upper or more central parts. The peripheral groups in some situations can be as large as 30 or more, as, for example, when all members of the group are doing the same task and the task is relatively simple. Groups dealing with difficult operating, policy, or coordinating problems usually function better when they are much smaller, for example, 5 to 10 persons.

It is rarely desirable for work groups to exceed 35 or 40 in number. Sometimes in efforts to decentralize, a firm or a governmental agency may have as many as 50 or more persons doing different tasks report to a single person (Warwick et al., 1975). This gives freedom to the subordinates, but it results, usually, in a lack of coordination among them, especially if they are doing or supervising different kinds of work. Such situations are apt to take on many of the characteristics of System 0.

Alternate forms of linking

There has not been sufficient research on the role of the linking pin and how this linkage can best be performed to state positively and unequivocally how it should be undertaken in widely different kinds of conflict situations. In addition to single linking pins (fig. 10-1 and fig. 10-2), there are at least three additional ways in which multiple linking can be performed when there are particularly difficult linking problems to be handled.

One approach is to include more than two hierarchical levels in the group problem-solving meetings. Thus the subordinates of a subordinate can be included, and, if desirable, so can a superior's superior. In one plant of a large corporation, this plan appears to be working well. Emanuel Kay, at the time a member of the personnel research staff of the firm, stated the following in a letter to one of the authors:

> I have been impressed by the use of group problem-solving by one of our more successful managers. This manager holds quarterly "skip-level" meetings; i.e., he meets periodically with a subordinate manager and the work group who reports to that subordinate manager, to review goals and progress in achieving them and to solve problems. As you might expect, the subordinates are "up" for this meeting, and attach considerable importance to it. There is no question in my mind that the "skip-level" and group approach produced motivation far superior to that which the average superior can create in a man-to-man situation alone.

The second way in which multiple linking can be done to handle particularly difficult problems is to have two, or even more, members of a work group serve as linking pins rather than just one. This form of overlap will be particularly valuable when the problems being tackled by the groups involve serious conflict.

When there are marked differences of opinion strongly held between two groups or two departments, a single person linking the two groups has a very difficult job of seeing that each group has the same facts, is aware of the same situational requirements,[1] understands fully the points of view and thinking of the other group, and is kept abreast of the decision-making progress of the other group. Studies have shown that it is hard for one person in a group to retain his or her opinion if all the other members of the group are unanimous in holding a different view. If one other person in such a group, however, begins to support the lone dissenter's position, the research shows that the capacity to maintain his or her point of view and present it persuasively is greatly increased (Asch, 1951; Cruthchfield, 1955; Foundation for Research on Human Behavior, 1958). Where there are differences strongly held and accompanied by deep-seated feelings, it is difficult for a single individual to express himself or herself so clearly that misunderstanding cannot occur. In such situations, it usually will be advantageous to have the linking between groups performed by at least two persons rather than a single linking person.

Findings from a program of research being conducted by Claude Flaucheux and Serge Moscovici indicate, however, that a single person who *persistently maintains* a position in the face of solid opposition from the rest of the group can influence others in the group to shift to that position. This influence by a single dissident member is probably more effective when relevant situational requirements can be cited as persuasive evidence to support that position. These findings are very important concerning the role of the linking pin and the capacity of a problem-solving group to reach innovative solutions (Moscovici, Lage, & Naffrechoux, 1969).

It is significant that many corporations are using multiple linking pins between their top-management echelon and their boards of directors. It is not uncommon for some and often several members of top management to be members of the board.

It may be desirable to use a third modification of multiple group linkage when the linking among work groups involves particularly complex, technical matters. In such situations, the member in the work group who has the highest level of technical competence in the relevant field can be designated to serve as the linking pin if that person happens to be other than the head of the work group. This may be the most effective linking, for example, in dealing with the

---

[1]Situational requirements are those hard, objective realities, such as deadlines and minimum financial conditions, which provide guidelines and constraints for the decision-making processes.

problems which involve coordinating activities among technical staffs, such as research and engineering. This kind of linking is likely to be particularly useful when lateral linkage is involved.

The role of the linking pin in coordinating problem solving

An essential function of a linking pin is to provide an information flow and to establish reciprocal influence between the two groups of which he or she is a member. This is an especially important role when the two groups are engaged in problem solving on the same or on a related problem. The linking pin should function as a channel between the two groups so that they both have before them the same statement of the problem and the same facts, knowledge of situational requirements, awareness of differences and conflicts, and other relevant information. It also is part of the linking pin's responsibility to see that the pacing in the problem solving of the two groups is coordinated, especially on difficult problems where there are strong feelings and substantial differences in point of view. By not letting one group run too far ahead of the other in the problem solving, the linking pin keeps one group from confronting the other with its final decision. Such confrontation causes the second group to feel that it is having a decision forced upon it whether it likes the decision or not. Keeping each group at about the same stage in the problem-solving process and keeping both of them well informed of the problem-solving work of the other, as, for example, conditions which an acceptable solution must meet, possible alternate solutions, etc., will increase greatly the probability that the two groups will reach essentially the same decision, or mutually compatible decisions.

In the problem-solving process, particularly in a difficult conflict situation, if one of the groups begins to arrive at a decision that the other group(s) for good reasons cannot accept or adapt to, it is the job of the linking pin to take the action needed to prevent this from occurring. This can be done by calling attention to the situational requirements that one group feels are important but which the others are ignoring. It might involve pointing out additional conditions that a solution must meet to be acceptable but which have been overlooked by the first group. It could involve the linking pin's aiding either or both groups to do an even better job of performing the essential steps of effective problem solving and to keep from becoming "solution minded." (See table 10-1.)

In an effectively functioning System 4 organization, there are strong motivational forces, including loyalties and commitments to the overall organization and its goals, that can be mobilized in each group to avoid decisions incompatible with those reached by other groups. It is the responsibility of the linking pins to mobilize these motivational forces and to focus them on constructive, cooperative problem solving.

Table 10-1
Problem-solving steps in seeking consensus
when two or more levels of persons are involved

A. Top coordinating group (CG) states the problem and prepares a short illustrative list of essential conditions.

B. Head of each subordinate group (SG) takes problem and illustrative list to his or her work group. The group:

1. Prepares lists of its essential and desirable conditions.

2. Brainstorms, trying to find a few solutions that meet all essential conditions and most of the desirable conditions.

3. Does not select one preferred solution, i.e., does not become solution-minded.

C. Coordinating group meets again to:

1. Hear, from the head of each SG, that group's list of essential and desirable conditions.

2. Prepare master lists of essential and desirable conditions by consolidating the lists from all the groups.

3. Hear, from the head of each work group, the results of the search by his or her group for an acceptable solution, namely, those solutions felt to meet all the essential conditions.

4. Test these proposed solutions against the master lists of essential conditions.

a. If only one of the solutions satisfactorily meets the essential conditions, select it and state why.

b. If more than one solution meets the essential conditions, array all these solutions in a preferred order and state why they are in this order.

c. If no solution meets the essential conditions, the CG should brainstorm to see if it can find an innovative solution that meets the essential conditions. If the CG succeeds, it selects the acceptable solution (as in the above) and states why. If it does not succeed, it concludes that more brainstorming by all is required.

D. Subordinate groups meet again to hear from their heads the results of the CG's work.

1. If only one solution has been found by the CG to meet all conditions, this is reported by each head to his or her group and its concurrence is sought. If the subordinate groups generally agree, the CG states that solution as the final one. If one or more subordinate groups strongly disagree, the previous step is repeated with each group examining the reason for the disagreement. If necessary, the previous steps are repeated.

Table 10-1
Problem-solving steps in seeking consensus
when two or more levels of persons are involved   (Continued)

2. If two or more solutions have been found to meet the essential conditions, each head reports the preferred order of the solutions to his or her group, and the group's reaction is obtained. The CG examines these reactions of the subordinate groups and selects the solution preferred by most and informs the groups. This solution stands unless strongly challenged, which is unlikely.

3. If no solution has been found that meets the essential conditions, the CG, through the head of each group, asks the subordinate groups to do more brainstorming to find such a solution. If this fails to yield a solution that meets the essential conditions, the CG, through the group heads, asks each subordinate group to select the two or three solutions that come closest to meeting the essential conditions. Based on these preferences of the subordinate groups, the CG selects the solution most preferred, reports this choice, through the group heads, and seeks its acceptance.

Representatives are <u>not</u> linking pins and fail to perform the linking role

It is essential to differentiate clearly between the role of the linking pin and the traditional concept of representation. Strictly speaking, a representative in our form of democracy is expected to perform in an essentially unilateral manner. That person must press for action that will benefit those he or she represents. Although the action sought and the win-lose battles fought may be costly to *all* the parties to the conflict, including the representative's own party, this usually does not alter the behavior.

Linking pins are <u>not</u> representatives

The System 4 linking pin is *not* a representative from *either* of the groups of which the person is a member. The task is multidirectional. The aim is to achieve coordinated problem solving within and between these groups. The task includes helping both groups to state and to solve problems with the focus on what is best for the larger, or superordinate, organization, entity, or society. In this effort, the objective is to have the problem solving create a solution that all parties to the conflict willingly accept as satisfactory.

If a linking pin behaves as a "representative" from either of the groups of which that person is a member, the interaction processes will be pushed from a System 4 problem-solving effort seeking to develop a new solution acceptable to all to a win-lose confrontation. *It is absolutely essential, if the System 4 approach to resolving conflicts is to be used, that the linking pins never become representatives.*

Representation without responsibility versus linking with responsibility

There is another fundamental distinction between representatives and linking pins. In a legislative body, whether a university senate, a board of directors, a state legislature, or the Congress, representatives are expected to obtain action benefiting those they represent and to see that the action is carried out; but if the tide goes against them, they feel little responsibility for influencing constituents to accept and help implement the decisions reached by the deliberative body where they serve as representatives.

Lack of responsibility is a common occurrence in today's conflicts. For example, the student or faculty representatives on a committee in a large university press vigorously and unilaterally for action that they and their colleagues wish. Even though they are successful, they feel little or no responsibility to urge and motivate their faculty colleagues, or the vast student body, to live by the decisions and make them effective. In fact, they may be the first to take potshots at the decision. This unidirectional nature of the representative role is *clearly representation without responsibility.* In situation after situation "representatives" today are aggravating rather than ameliorating major conflicts. This is true in school systems, universities, business firms, labor unions, inner cities, legislative bodies, and international organizations.

The situation is fundamentally different when linking pins are used. The focus is not on winning at any cost but on reaching solutions acceptable to all and making them operationally effective. This orientation brings with it a continuing responsibility. Since a solution is no better than its implementation, linking pins have the continuous obligation to use the interaction-influence processes involved in the linkage to create the goals and motivate the behavior required to implement fully the decisions reached.

The advantages of linking pins

Some of the characteristics of linking pins and advantages in using them can be listed:

1. A linking pin exerts influence in two or more directions.

2. A linking pin is psychologically closer to each group than any other member of one group is close to the other group.

3. A linking pin is an accepted member of both the linked groups; hence, that person is more acceptable to each group than is an outsider and has more influence.

4. A linking pin can communicate effectively with each group of which that person is a member since:

   a. The person knows the vocabulary and jargon of each group, and, as Triandis (1959a & b) has shown, the greater the vocabulary similarity between people the better they like each other;

    b. The person knows the norms, values, needs, and goals of each group and can express ideas and communications in ways which respect and embrace them. This facilitates the acceptance of the ideas (Hovland, Harvey, & Sherif, 1957);

    c. The person understands both groups as a consequence of knowing their vocabulary and values.

5. A linking pin plays an essential role in coordinating problem solving between the two or more groups of which that person is a member and enables the different groups to reach compatible solutions to the problems dealt with.

6. A linking pin creates reciprocal responsibility to implement the decisions reached jointly.

Lateral linkage

When functionalization was first introduced in business, governmental agencies, and other organizations, substantial improvement in productivity and reduction in costs resulted. It became a basic principle of organization and has been universally applied. Along with the gains that functionalization brought, however, came an increase in the amount and intensity of conflict in these organizations. Today, fights between maintenance, quality control, and production are commonplace as are the conflicts between the manufacturing and marketing departments. These inefficient and costly consequences of the conflicts that accompany functionalization in firms or governmental agencies using System 1, 2 or 3 management are unnecessary. They can be eliminated or materially reduced by the addition of lateral linkages, making the network of lateral and vertical linkages provided by System 4 a part of the formal organizational structure.

Linking pins are as essential in lateral linkages as in the vertical structure of any medium-sized or large organization or institution, especially one dealing with problems involving complex technology. This is true of large institutions, such as business firms, governmental agencies, medical centers and hospitals, and school systems. Linking pins also are required to provide the interaction-influence network between conflicting institutions, such as a company and a labor union, or between two nations. The principles concerning linking pins are applicable to all these different institutional and interinstitutional relationships.

Cross-functional teams are a form of lateral linkage to reduce conflict and improve performance. McCullough (1975) describes several business teams. The structure of one, a shipping and docking operation, will be used as an example of new lateral linkage. As McCullough reports:[2]

> Operating personnel serviced the pipelines and hoses and monitored the actual loading together with the ships' crews. Maintenance personnel connected the

hoses and maintained the docks facilities. The docks operation was centrally directed from the chief operator's dock house where communications equipment and records were maintained. Each loading station had a booth which served as a communications point and shelter for the monitoring operator. The maintenance and monitoring crews each had separate lunchroom facilities which served as waiting rooms between assignments at a loading station when a ship or barge required servicing. The custom was for the monitoring operators to align the pipe routes by proper valving according to a supervisory plan, lay out flexible hoses, and act as dock hands for mooring vessels. Then the connecting crew would connect the hoses dock-side and ship-side. Next the operator and the ship's personnel would signal for pumping to commence. Several connection and pumping operations would be required for loading large vessels. After the operator signalled the completion of loading, the connecting crew would disconnect the hoses and the operator would cast off the vessel and store the flexible hoses.

It was evident that a more efficient operation would merge the operating and connecting crews but the union contract and refinery tradition discouraged, if not forbade, this. It proved practical, however, to make several structural changes designed to move the docks personnel to a more integrated, challenging and effective organization:

1. The services department manager and the maintenance department manager agreed that the docks supervisor would supervise all personnel. He continued to report to the services department manager but was also responsible for the maintenance activities and personnel at the docks.

2. A bright new lunchroom—waiting room was built, large enough for both operating and maintenance crews and located adjacent to the chief operator's station. This required all personnel to relax together and share all communications and to get acquainted.

3. The old maintenance lunchroom was converted to office space for the first-line maintenance and operating supervisors thus making them available to their hourly personnel on the day shift. The hourly personnel would move around them as they rotated their shifts. These supervisors were responsible for the day to day guidance, counseling and administration of the docks personnel.

4. The docks supervisor undertook a planned comprehensive program of instructing all personnel in the operation of the docking facilities including the planning, economics, hazards, relationships with other organizations and such other topics as would enable all personnel to be knowledgeable of the total enterprise.

5. Together with business information system personnel, the docks supervisor developed a game simulating the complete commercial operation of the docking facilities. This was used effectively as an information sharing technique: real operations data such as the comparison of plan to execution, the use of materials and supplies, the delivery of crudes and products across the

docks and facilities maintenance, enabled all personnel to understand what it took to operate the facilities at a profit.

6. The scheduling of overtime was assigned to the chief operator who was to consult with the leader of connecting crew in his determination of overtime requirements.

7. The first-line or day supervisors undertook to relate their guidance, counseling, and instructions to the economic and operating data so that the men would understand that they were, in effect, "receiving their instructions from the situation." Further the day supervisors were urged to minimize instructions to the crews that would stress their maintenance or operating department backgrounds or traditional duties. (pp. 243–244)

Figure 10-3 shows the organizational structure of the shipping and docks operation before the reorganization, and Figure 10-4 shows the structure after the business team was established.

Cross-functional teams can be particularly effective in reducing conflicts and improving performance when they are set up so that their mission is clear and their objectives, subobjectives, and tasks are carefully stated. Their mission should deal with a total task to be accomplished, such as building cushions or loading barges and ships. When the tasks, themselves, are clear, they alone provide all the direction needed to the personnel. Mary Parker Follett's "Law of the Situation" makes orders from supervisors unnecessary and reduces conflict (Fox & Urwick, 1973).

If a cross-functional business team is to work well, coordinated direction must be established at the top of the team. In the case of the shipping and docks business team, the services department manager and the maintenance manager agreed that the docks supervisor would supervise all personnel. He continued to report to the services department manager but was also responsible for the maintenance activities and personnel. This required cooperation from both these managers, especially the maintenance manager. In creating cross-functional teams, the necessary cooperation is often facilitated by encouragement from the top executive of the plant or the organizational entity involved.

As long as this cooperation and support is maintained, the cross-functional team usually works well in substantially reducing conflict and improving performance (McCullough, 1975; see also the cushion room data in chap. 5.) If the top support and the managerial cooperation is no longer present because of a change in managerial personnel or for some other reason, the cross-functional team is likely to cease functioning as such, and the operation will revert to its former state of greater conflict and poorer performance. A cross-functional team must have continuing, adequate support and cooperation from the levels above it if it is to perform effectively.

As a rule, it is not difficult to maintain these conditions for the effective performance of cross-functional teams over a short-run period. Over the longer run, however, this usually is not the case. Changes in managerial

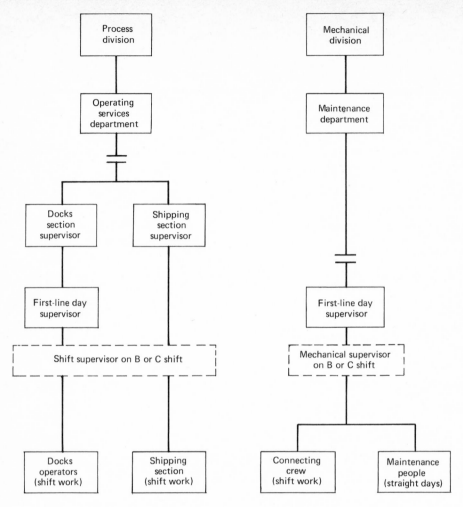

Figure 10-3 *Shipping and docks before the reorganization.* (Courtesy of Robert S. Toronto.)

personnel are inevitable and are apt to disrupt the required managerial support and cooperation. It is necessary, consequently, to make changes in the organizational structure and the interaction processes. The changes in structure require adding cross-functional teams in the hierarchical levels above the lower-level teams. The interaction processes need to shift to System 4 leadership and win-win problem solving. These changes in structure and interaction processes create a matrix form of organization capable of resolving conflict and of achieving cooperation and high levels of performance. This form of organizational structure is discussed in Chapter 11.

Sometimes attempts are made to achieve cooperative lateral relationships by

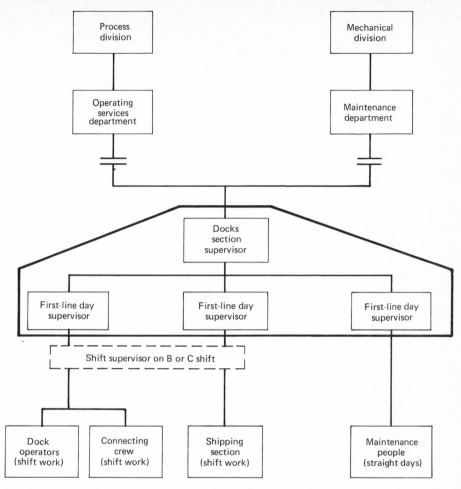

Figure 10-4 *Shipping and docks after the reorganization. The heavy black line encompasses the current shipping cross-functional team.* (Courtesy of Robert S. Toronto.)

providing training in interaction skills but not making any changes in the organizational structure. Improvements achieved by this approach are likely to be short-lived since the existing structure without cross-functional ties tends continuously to produce breakdowns in communication and to heighten distrust, misunderstandings, and conflict. Changes in both structure and interactional patterns are needed for any enduring improvement.

A matrix organization is appreciably more complex than a vertical line organization both in its structure and its interactional processes. The general characteristics and performance capabilities of a System 4 matrix organization are described briefly in the next chapter.

Achieving decisions best for the entire organization

In this discussion, for purposes of brevity, System 2 alone will be used although the points made are equally applicable to System 1 and often to System 3. Problems handled in a System 2, person-to-person interaction pattern are typically problems of subordinates and their units. Often many of these problems are those initiated by the lower echelon. When a subordinate (e.g., *d* in fig. 10-5) presents a problem to a superior, the subordinate states the problem and tries to have it solved from the standpoint of what is best for the subordinate and the subordinate unit. He or she presses for a decision which facilitates effective performance by that unit, even though the decision may increase conflict, handicap other units, and be costly to the total organization. If, for example, *d* heads a production operation, *d* may seek approval for a product change which simplifies the manufacturing operation and thereby reduces *d*'s costs. Supervisor *d* may seek this action even though the product is less acceptable to consumers and hence harder and more expensive for the marketing department to sell and less profitable to the firm.

In this situation, the superior (*D* in fig. 10-5) is handicapped in any attempt to deal with the problem from a broader point of view by the orientation constantly maintained by the subordinate. The superior also is at a disadvantage because the superior often does not possess all the facts, information, and technical knowledge which the subordinates (*b, c, e,* and *f* in fig. 10-5) have and which are necessary in order to arrive at a solution satisfactory, or at least not detrimental, to the other units affected by the solution (i.e., units under *b, c, e,* and *f* in fig. 10-5). There, consequently, are forces present in the decision-making processes of System 2 which cause problems to be stated in terms of what is best for a particular subordinate unit and, in turn, to be solved within this framework. This situation is aggravated by distortion in communication. The motivational forces present cause each subordinate to provide the chief

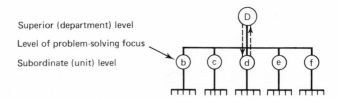

Figure 10-5 *Problem-solving focus in System 2 person-to-person (D-to-d) model of interaction and decision making. With System 2, person-to-person decision-making problems, especially those raised by subordinates, tend to be stated, examined, and solved from the point of view of the subordinate level; i.e., they serve the interest of the smaller organizational entity at the expense of the well-being of the total organization.*

with operating information or technical knowledge likely to lead to a decision favorable to that subordinate and to withhold all information, regardless of its importance to the total organization, which might lead to a decision unfavorable to that subordinate.

The chief, himself, often contributes to the focus on the interests of the subordinate unit at the expense of the larger organization. For example, a chief may ask a subordinate to prepare a memorandum presenting the subordinate's recommendations for handling a particular problem. The subordinate is likely to look at the problem from the standpoint of what is best for the subordinate's unit and not what is best for the entire department. Moreover, the subordinate may not be familiar with every dimension of the problem, particularly those dimensions that affect units other than the subordinate's. The subordinate's memorandum, consequently, will recommend action favorable for the subordinate's unit but all too often likely to have costly results for the entire department. The better the memorandum and the more persuasive the case made by the subordinate, the greater will be the likelihood that the superior will act without being fully aware of the negative consequences to the organization as a whole.

The situation is no better if the superior recognizes that other units will be affected by the decision and asks the head of each such unit for a memorandum stating his or her recommendations. The superior then has several conflicting memoranda each looking at the problem and recommending an action in terms of what is best for a particular subordinate unit. The superior at this time usually does not use creative problem solving to develop a new solution which meets the requirements of all the subordinate units but instead proceeds to select the final solution from among those proposed by the different subordinates. Generally, such a solution serves the interest of one or a few subordinates and their units, at the expense of the others and the entire firm. Consequently, with System 2 problem solving by the superior, subordinate is likely to be pitted against subordinate, win-lose battles are intensified, and the firm suffers. Innovative problem solving focused on serving the best interests of the entire organization does not occur.

System 4 prevents parochial problem solving

The nature of the decision-making process in a System 4 organization assures that each problem is stated and solved with a broader orientation. Any problem raised for consideration tends to be a problem at the level of the superior and tends to deal with the needs and requirements of that level (department head R in fig. 10-6). If a unit head (e.g., r in fig. 10-6) states a problem for consideration solely from the standpoint of that unit, one of two developments occurs: (1) the

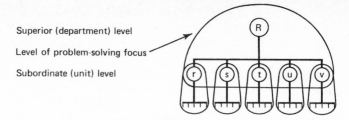

Superior (department) level

Level of problem-solving focus

Subordinate (unit) level

Figure 10-6 *Problem-solving focus in System 4 group model of decision making. With System 4, problems that affect the subordinate (unit) level only are referred to that level for decision. Problems that affect more than one unit are stated as departmentwide problems and solved in terms of what is best for the entire department rather than serving the interests of a particular subordinate unit.*

superior R, or others in the work group, point out that if the problem deals only with the subordinate unit, the unit itself should handle it and not raise it for consideration by the superior unit; or (2) the problem is restated by the superior R, or other group members, so that it deals with matters of concern to other units as well as to the one which raised it; i.e., the problem is redefined so as to be of departmentwide concern. In solving this departmental problem, the heads of the various units (*r, s, t, u,* and *v*) are careful to see that all the situational requirements and particularly those affecting their own units are stated fully. They also take pains to see that the head of each subordinate unit adds to the list of essential conditions those of especial importance to the work of that unit. The solution which emerges from such group decision making, consequently, is one which is deemed best for the *entire* department and for all its units. It is not a decision which meets the requirements of one particular unit and benefits it (e.g., the unit of *r* in fig. 10-6), while handicapping the other units (those under *s, t, u,* and *v*).

This difference between System 2 and System 4 occurs *at every hierarchical level* in the organization. There is, therefore, a multiplying effect of the tendency of System 2 organizations to state problems and to solve them in terms of what is best for the subordinate level, and in System 4 organizations to deal with and solve problems in terms of what is best for the superior level. As a consequence, the decisions and actions which emerge when System 4 is used are much more likely than in Systems 1, 2, and 3 to be those that are *best for the entire organization.*

In System 4, the decisions are reached through group problem solving. Problems are formulated and solved from the standpoint of the best interests of the entire organization. Group problem solving does not pit subordinates against each other in win-lose battles; it builds cooperative behavior and decreases conflict.

The top group is not
an executive committee

In establishing the proposed multiple-overlapping-group structure, it is well to keep in mind that the top group should not reach a final decision on matters affecting other groups until all the linked groups have been fully involved in the decision-making process and have reached essentially the same conclusion. The top group in a System 4 structure is not an executive committee making decisions for lower levels. Its role is to coordinate the decision making of all groups affected to assure the full involvement and participation of these groups. An example will illustrate the problems created when the top group acts as an executive committee.

In trying to strengthen the role of the grade level chairperson, a principal of an elementary school called a meeting of grade level chairpersons to deal with a problem. There had been a teachers' strike which, among other things, delayed sending out the third-quarter report to parents. It was within a month of the end of school and the fourth-quarter reports were due to be sent soon. Should the teachers send the third-quarter reports, which had been prepared by some teachers but not by others, to the parents now?

After discussion, all the grade level chairpersons but one felt that the report should not be sent. The dissenting grade level chairperson finally went along reluctantly with the provision that a letter be sent to parents telling them why they would not receive a third-quarter report and offering conferences with any parents who wished them. She also asked to see the letter before it was sent, fearing that if not carefully worded there would be an avalanche of parental requests. The principal agreed to do this and to send the letter to all grade level chairpersons for their comments before it was sent.

The grade level chairpersons then met with the teachers in their grades and told them of the decision. Some of the teachers thought the decision unwise and objected. The principal then sent a note to all the grade level chairpersons asking if they wished to meet to "rediscuss" the matter. Most of them said, "No." The principal was left with dissatisfied teachers and at least one unhappy grade level chairperson. He did not know what went wrong.

The principal had forgotten that everyone affected by a decision should have a voice in making that decision. The teachers' relationships to parents was affected, and yet the teachers had not been involved in the decision. They had been informed of a decision made by the next higher level. Although the principal thought he was using the grade level chairpersons as linking pins, in fact he was using them as an executive committee.

If two of the System 4 principles had been followed: that everyone affected by a decision should have a voice in making it and that a group should make only those decisions which affect it and no one else, the procedure would have been quite different. The principal would have presented the problem to the grade level chairpersons and asked them not for a solution but to take the problem to the teachers in their grade to get the teachers' ideas as to what conditions a solution should meet to be satisfactory. Examples of such conditions are: parents should get from the school the information they want about their children; parents should not be given the impression that the teachers were lazy and did not want to bother to send the reports; and teachers should not waste their time preparing reports that may not be wanted and may not be used. The principal also would have asked the grade level chairpersons to have their groups suggest one or more innovative solutions that they felt would meet all the essential conditions that any of the teachers would be likely to propose. Each of these innovative solutions would be suggested tentatively as an alternative and would not be presented by any one group as *the* solution. The grade level chairpersons, as linking pins, would meet again with the principal and would list all the conditions that the different grade groups had developed in their meetings. The conditions viewed as essential would be listed separately from those considered as only desirable. The principal and grade level chairpersons would then proceed with the problem-solving steps and arrive at a solution that would meet all of the conditions felt to be essential. The grade level chairpersons would report back to their teachers telling them of the solution reached, making sure that it was acceptable to all.

As the discussion in this chapter indicates, the organizational structure of an organization using a science-based theory, like System 4, is appreciably more complex than is the usual vertical structure of Systems 1, 2, and 3 and requires greater learning and skills to operate it well. It is not a line or a line-staff form of organization; it is a complex network system with an elaborate, interlaced, organizational structure. It provides powerful resources for horizontal as well as vertical coordination. This complex network, through its alternate linkages, provides, as we have seen, better communication, substantially greater capacity to deal with differences and to resolve conflicts by group decision making, and better coordination than can the organizational patterns of Systems 1, 2, or 3. System 4 yields a more flexible organization in which individuals at all hierarchical levels are motivated to exercise more initiative in dealing constructively with conflicts and in bringing about improvement and change. It also gives them the means for doing so.

Studies show that the more effective the groups which perform the linking function are, the more tightly knit and better coordinated the total organization proves to be, and the more effective is its interaction-influence network and its capacity to resolve conflicts constructively. Highly effective groups add strength and flexibility to the organizational structure and greatly enhance its performance capabilities. As long as the number of groups performing this multiple linking function is not excessive, the greater their number, the greater will be the capacity of the organization to coordinate its activities and to resolve conflicts successfully. These additional linkages act as strong fibers binding the organization together and strengthening its social fabric (Tannenbaum, 1968).

The formal and informal organization are identical in System 4

In spite of the complexity of the System 4 organizational structure, it is more functional and usually less complicated than the combination of the formal and informal networks which exist in System 1, 2, or 3 organizations. The informal networks in Systems 1, 2, and 3 are often covert, and parts of them sometimes are engaged in efforts to prevent the organization from accomplishing its objectives. This negative behavior is greatest in System 1 organizations and least in System 3. In contrast, there is nothing secret about the System 4 network, and one part does not seek to defeat the efforts of other parts. Full information is readily available, and every unit in the structure seeks to engage in activities which aid the organization to achieve its objectives.

Chapter 11 describes the characteristics of the structure when System 4 principles are applied to business organizations. Although this discussion is focused on business, the structures proposed are directly applicable to governmental and other agencies that face the same problems. Chapter 12 discusses the nature of the structures of school organizations when System 4 principles are applied. Chapter 13 deals with the structure of large universities, and Chapter 14, with the structure of cities when System 4 principles are applied.

11

System 4 structure applied to conflicts in industrial organizations[1]

A science-based theory of organization, such as System 4, offers modern society new resources to cope with the conflicts created by complex organizational problems. It provides formal solutions to organizational difficulties which cannot be solved within the framework and concepts of traditional organizational theory. At present these problems often are handled by means of informal solutions at variance with the formal organizational theory of the enterprise. Coordination characterized by cooperation rather than by conflict will be discussed as an example of the capacity of System 4 to provide better formal solutions than can System 2 to the difficult problems of organizing and managing a highly complex, technologically based, modern enterprise—a business firm, a medical center, a governmental agency, a large university.

Virtually every large enterprise faces, in more or less serious form, the problem of whether to organize on a functional basis or on a product or geographical basis or to try some compromise solution. The requirements of both specialization and low unit costs achieved by large-scale operations (economy of scale) press for a functional form of organization. But it is not easy for a large, highly functionalized organization to achieve effective coordination. New products emerging from research, for example, do not move from research to development to manufacturing to marketing with the speed and coordination required to capitalize on the large demand for a new and useful product. Interdepartmental conflict all too often causes costly delays.

Unfortunately, major trends are aggravating this already serious problem of how to achieve coordination in a highly functionalized organization. New knowledge and methodologies have been created at a rapidly accelerating rate as the national expenditures for research and development increased. Because of the limits of human capacity, more, not less, functionalization is required to

---

[1]This chapter used some material from Chap. 10 of *The Human Organization* (Likert,1967).

make effective use of these new resources. Increases in functionalization, in turn, increase conflict and make effective coordination both more necessary and more difficult.

The greater volume of research findings contributes in another way to these trends. To use the new findings from research (R&D) effectively, many different kinds of changes are required, such as changes in products, technologies, markets, and organizational structure. But the readiness and willingness to change are virtually never the same among the different members and parts of the organization; thus every change involves stresses, differences, conflicts (Kahn, Wolfe, Quinn, Snoek, & Rosenthal, 1964). When conflicts occur among operating personnel from such departments as R&D, engineering, production, and sales, members of each department take the conflict up their hierarchical line to get the problem solved in ways satisfactory to them. At each level the conflict between departments is almost always a win-lose battle. The appeals usually go to the top of the organization since it is only at that point that the departments come together under a single superior. The department which has the greatest influence with the chief executive wins. The other departments lose. Effective ways of resolving these differences constructively and with reasonable rapidity must be found if the changes are to occur smoothly and with a minimum of delay, thus enabling the new products to be marketed at a time when they are most profitable to a firm.

The difficulties created by a functional form of organization have caused many companies to turn to a product form of organization, or a regional form. Decentralization on a product basis has been used widely to meet the problems created by functionalization. But as decentralization solves some problems, it produces others. With decentralization, some of the gains of specialization are lost; economies of scale are often sacrificed, and new problems of coordination are created. For example, a company producing industrial goods with six different sales organizations representing its different decentralized divisions must provide coordination of the efforts of those sales departments so that purchasing agents are not irritated by excessive calls.

Decentralization is becoming, moreover, an inadequate solution as technologies become more complex and as ever more extensive functionalization becomes necessary. Decentralization, furthermore, does not eliminate differences among staff or among departments; it merely changes the relationship of who differs with whom about what.

Large governmental agencies as well as business enterprises are suffering from this failure to solve the complex problems of coordination and the accompanying conflicts caused by extensive functionalization. This results in inefficient performance, higher costs, and poorer service than need be. Moreover, those federal agencies that are spending substantial sums on research are experiencing the same conflicts and difficulties as is industry in getting the new knowledge applied efficiently. As a consequence, those federal agencies are not realizing a prompt and full return on their substantial research expenditures in the physical and biological sciences and cannot do so until they can solve this organizational problem.

Similarly, large hospitals and medical centers are encountering increasingly difficult problems as medical technology becomes more complex and function-alization more extensive. System 2 works no better in hospitals than it does in industry, and since most hospitals have administrative systems falling at about System 2 or 2½, they have problems with conflict and poor coordination. The consequences are at least as serious in hospitals as in business because of the importance of good coordination for achieving low-cost excellent patient care. This is borne out by studies of hospital administration which consistently show that good coordination is an especially important factor affecting the cost and quality of patient care (Georgopoulos & Mann, 1962; Georgopoulos & Matejko, 1967).

An important step toward improving coordination, namely the creation of patient-care teams, now is being undertaken by some medical centers. These teams consist of doctors, nurses, and supporting personnel. Each team depends upon many other departments to provide it with the services it needs at a particular time.

In trying to provide each patient with the services and care his or her particular case requires, the patient-care team often is in conflict with the vertical (functional) line departments, such as radiology, nursing, physical therapy, and dietetics. The vertical line departments may have policies or instructions contrary to the conditions that the team finds necessary for excel-lent patient care. Thus, a patient-care floor team may develop plans and procedures for the care of a particular patient requiring services from the team member that the head of that vertical line department has decided is contrary to established policy. Or it may be that a patient-care team needs a specific service at a particular time—a portable chest x-ray, for example—that the department refuses to provide either because it feels that there are other priorities or that the service is inappropriate.

When a conflict occurs between a patient-care floor team and one or more line departments, the line department is likely to settle the controversy with a decision favorable to its position, since the formal authority lies with the vertical line. The conflict will be suppressed and the patient-care team defeated. When a patient-care team encounters this situation, it has no formal channels to use in seeking a solution except to appeal upward through one or more vertical (departmental) lines. The patient-care team, however, is in a weak position since the vertical departmental lines are powerful. Moreover, the procedures and practices of medical centers reinforce control by the line organization since evaluation, pay increases, promotion (hire-and-fire authority) are executed through it.

The extent to which the present administrative system of medical centers handicaps such developments as patient-care teams and fails to meet present-day requirements is not recognized because the system works far better than its inherent character should permit. Its good performance is due to a very powerful influence that permeates all hospitals: a great, overriding concern for the survival and health of patients. This motivating force causes persons to ignore frustrations and strive to do their best in spite of difficulties. Highly motivated, ingenious persons today use informal processes to obtain decisions that they cannot get through the formal structure.

If the patient-care teams created by a medical center are to survive and succeed, however, they must have far better decision-making procedures than are provided by informal channels. When these teams are first created, the initial enthusiasm enables the patient-care floor teams to achieve many of their objectives for a period of time in spite of frustrations caused by an inadequate administrative system. Nevertheless, constant conflict and adverse decisions wear the new teams down, and their potential contribution to improving patient care and costs often are not made. In fact, the basic characteristics of most administrative systems provides a hostile environment for their development and, sooner or later, they are rejected as foreign bodies. They cannot survive when grafted to an incompatible host.

To assure the survival and success of the patient-care floor teams, medical centers need an administrative system that will enable both the patient-care teams and the vertical line departments to exert constructive influence on decisions. Creative problem solving rather than win-lose confrontation must be employed. Solutions reached should be fully satisfactory to both the vertical line departments and the horizontally linked patient-care teams.

Attempts to find a creative and satisfactory solution to conflict, poor coordination, and poor performance in industry, government, and hospitals have been seriously restrained by the limitations imposed by the currently accepted, formal organization theories upon which Systems 1, 2, and 3 are based. As we shall see, as long as a company, university, hospital, governmental agency, etc., is bound by these traditional theories, it is unlikely to solve this important management problem and reduce the extensive conflicts that now exist.

The requirements of a satisfactory long-range solution

Although the cross-functional business team described in earlier chapters can be effective over the short run, there is need for a long-range solution if their effectiveness is to continue. This requires both extensive functionalization and the mechanism for resolving differences and achieving efficient coordination on a product or geographical basis. As mentioned in Chapter 10, this necessitates effective coordination laterally (horizontally) as well as vertically. To meet these requirements, an organization needs to have two or more channels of decision making and coordination, with at least one occurring via the vertical, functional lines and the other via the horizontal, product (or geographic) line. Many persons in such an organization will have two or more superiors.

This organization needs to have decision-making and influence processes sufficiently effective to reach first-rate decisions and to achieve highly motivated, coordinated behavior directed toward efficiently attaining the organization's goals. These decision-making and influence processes must be able to achieve coordination in spite of initial and often substantial conflict coming through two or more channels or lines.

At least four conditions must be met by an organization if it is to achieve satisfactory coordination when there is extensive functionalization:

1. It must provide high levels of cooperative behavior between superiors and subordinates and especially among peers. Favorable attitudes and confidence and trust are needed among its members.

2. It must have the organizational structure and the interaction skills required to solve differences and conflicts and to attain creative solutions.

3. It must possess the capacity to create the motivation needed for excellent performance without the hire-and-fire authority of the traditional line organization.

4. Its decision-making processes and superior-subordinate relationships must be such as to enable persons to perform their jobs well and without hazard when they have two or more superiors.

These four conditions are not and cannot be met by a System 1, 2, or 3 organization operating on the basis of currently accepted organizational theory. This is not to say that the highest-producing managers are not operating within System 2 and System 3 companies in such a way as to provide these conditions. They are. But, as we have reported elsewhere (Likert, 1961, 1967), these high-producing managers are deviating in fundamental ways from the formal theory upon which their company's organizational structure and standard operating procedures are based.

The inadequacies of Systems 1, 2, and 3

The formal oranization theory underlying Systems 1 to 3 fails to meet these four conditions in that: (1) the theory specifies that a person can have only one boss; (2) it calls for managerial procedures and behavior that, on the average, tend to produce competition and conflict between subordinates (peers) accompanied all too often by resentment or apathy; and (3) it fails to make full use of those motivational forces that must be employed if cooperative attitudes and effective coordination are to be achieved.

The view that a person can have only one superior and should be given orders by that superior and no one else is based on hire-and-fire authority (White, 1963, pp. 36–41). Hire-and-fire authority and such related concepts as direction and control and the view that a person can have only one boss stem from the underlying motivational assumption of classical management theory. This theory is essentially System 2 in character and relies primarily on the economic needs of humans. The basic motivational assumption of Systems 1 and 2 is that when an organization buys a person's time it obtains control over that individual's behavior. When this assumption first was made, it probably was valid. Lack of income often meant in those days lack of food and shelter and even, perhaps, loss of life. But today this assumption is totally inadequate as a basis for organizational theory.

As many studies have demonstrated, supervision based on economic needs and reliance on coercive, *have-to* motivation produces apathy or hostility in the subordinate toward the superior and toward the organization and its objectives.[2] It also stimulates competition and conflict among subordinates who, as peers, strive for recognition and reward from their boss and often "knife" each other in order to get more for themselves. When an organization relies primarily on economic needs, it fails to use adequately those basic, human, motive sources capable of developing the kinds of cooperative relationships needed to operate productively and with a minimum of conflict the highly complex, highly functionalized organizations required by modern industrial technologies.

Fortunately, as research shows, the highest-producing managers in American business and government are, on the average, bound neither by the inadequate motivational assumption of Systems 1 and 2 nor by the systems themselves. (For some summaries of this research, see Katz & Kahn, 1966; Likert, 1961, 1967; Marrow et al., 1967; Myers, 1970; Taylor & Bowers, 1972.) They do not reject motivation based on economic needs. They seek to use it more fully than present wage-and-salary plans by providing economic rewards for behavior which clearly helps the organization achieve its objectives. They seek to avoid giving economic rewards for behavior which fails to serve the company's objectives or which defeats their attainment. For example, they avoid using salary plans which generously reward managers for liquidating a firm's assets, particularly its human assets. In addition to making more effective use of economic needs, these managers strive to use fully those noneconomic motives that yield cooperative attitudes and behavior.

Meeting the conditions
for effective coordination

Let us examine the nature of the solutions suggested by System 4 and how well they help resolve conflict by starting first with the situation in which an

---

[2]Argyris, 1957; Katz & Kahn, 1966; March & Simon, 1958; Mathewson, 1931; Roethlisberger & Dickson, 1939; White & Lippitt, 1960; Whyte, 1955.

individual is responsible, for all practical purposes, to two superiors. How would the operation work as a formal system if that person were a member of both a functional work group and a product, or cross-functional, work group? These two work groups each consist of a superior to whom all subordinates under that particular superior report. Figure 11-1 shows these two work groups and the overlapping members, *M-1c,* who reports to two superiors. One work group is functional-line (e.g., marketing) work group, and its superior is *M-1.* The other work group is the product, or cross-functional, work group with its superior, *A-1.*

If both these work groups have high group loyalty and are using group decision making well (See chaps. 6–9), subordinates in each work group would be able to exercise significant amounts of upward and lateral influence (Cartwright & Zander, 1968; Likert, 1961, chaps. 8, 9, 11, 12; Tannenbaum, 1968). (If these groups are not performing in this way, the superiors of these work groups and, in turn, their own superiors, as we shall see, have some training and organization building to do.) This would mean, of course, that the individual we are considering (*M-1c*), who is the subordinate under two superiors, can exert upward influence via group decision-making processes in both work groups. As a consequence, when one superior (e.g., product, cross-functional superior, *A-1*) and the work group reporting to that superior approach decisions about *M-1c*'s work or assignment which are incompatible or in conflict with the points of view held or decisions being arrived at by the other superior (marketing-department superior, *M-1*) and that superior's work group, the individual who is in both work groups is obligated to bring such information to the attention of both work groups. This information is relevant data to be used by each work group in its decision making. Even though the chief of one or the other groups may be reluctant to consider such information, the group members are likely to want to do so. They, themselves, are likely to be members of other cross-functional work groups and recognize that they, too, sooner or later, may find themselves caught in a developing conflict between the two or more work groups of which they are subordinate members. They will wish, consequently, to resolve this conflict constructively and thereby help to create a well-established process and precedent for handling such differences.

Under System 4, both work groups shown in Figure 11-1 will be expected to

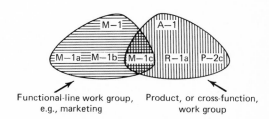

Functional-line work group,   Product, or cross-function,
e.g., marketing   work group

Figure 11-1 *Example of subordinate serving as linking pin for horizontal coordination.*

engage in group decision making in order to resolve the differences. The decision-making processes should strive to create an innovative solution that satisfactorily meets the requirements and opportunities presented by the situations faced by both groups. The focus should not be, as is often the case with System 2 person-to-person decision making, on obtaining a decision favorable to a particular work group or its department, regardless of how costly it is for the rest of the organization. The primary objective of the decision making of the two work groups should be to discover a solution which will serve the best interests of the entire organization.

Whenever the members of one or both of the two groups display inability to use group decision making sufficiently well to reach agreement in terms of the best interests of all concerned, the higher-level work groups must provide further training in group processes. This training of the subordinate work groups in group problem solving and related processes should enable all work groups to recognize from their own experience that everyone in the organization benefits when the decision making is focused on discovering the best solutions for the entire organization and that almost everyone suffers when the decision-making processes break down into a bargaining, or win-lose, battle.

If the individual (M-$1c$) were in a System 2 organization and caught in a developing conflict between two superiors, the situation could be resolved only by getting one or both of these superiors to change their decisions and their expectations regarding the subordinate's behavior. The individual's sole recourse in an attempt to change the conflicting demands would be person-to-person, separate interaction with each superior. Often the requested change would be seen by the particular superior as implying a criticism of that superior or as taking sides with the other superior. Neither criticism nor taking sides is warmly received. In this System 2 situation, the subordinate's attempts to change the decisions of one or both of the two superiors would not be likely to succeed, and the subordinate would be left in jeopardy, unable to satisfy the conflicting demands. It is for this reason that a cardinal principle of System 2 is that a person can have only one boss.

System 4, as we have seen, handles this problem by providing the resource of group rather than person-to-person interaction. With System 4, the individual caught between conflicting demands initiates discussion of the problem in the relevant work groups. Discussion takes place in a much more impersonal way than is possible when the subordinate raises the question individually with each of the two superiors.

There is impressive evidence to show that, in comparison with person-to-person interaction, a work group using effective group decision making with its superior can give the superior substantially more valuable information even though it involves possible criticism. It also can present a strong case for a course of action other than the one the superior initially prefers. In group decision making, individual members of the group can "toss the ball" back and forth among themselves and through such group processes communicate safely to the chief important information which no single individual dares communicate in a person-to-person session.

This kind of group decision making requires two broadly different kinds of skills. Group members need skill in leadership and in membership interaction processes in order to build and maintain a group efficient both in solving problems and in coping with conflict and differences. Skill also is required in the intellectual processes of problem solving. This was discussed in Chapters 6 to 9.

When both of the groups of which $M\text{-}1c$ is a member use group problem solving, $M\text{-}1c$ and the other members of each group are able to communicate to each supervisor the trend in the other group's thinking and the factors affecting their thinking. These communications can be used to lead the two groups to compatible decisions so that $M\text{-}1c$ is not caught with conflicting orders from two supervisors.

When an individual has two superiors, one must be designated to take the initiative on personnel functions, such as salary review and recommendations. In the System 4 model, decisions are reached through consensus, and recommendations or action reflect the combined judgment of the superiors involved. Therefore, it is immaterial which superior is given the responsibility for initiating any necessary actions and for seeing that the decisions or recommendations are implemented. It is merely necessary that one superior be given this assignment.

Applying System 4 to coordination across functions

If a large organization, such as a firm, hospital, governmental agency, or university, were to seek to handle differences more constructively and to achieve better coordination by shifting to System 4, what would be its structure and how would it operate?

The same basic concepts and principles are applicable to achieving effective coordination, regardless of the purpose and activities of the organization. It makes no difference whether the large organization is a business firm, medical center, university, governmental agency, international organization, or some other kind of institution.

The structure required would consist of multiple overlapping groups (figs. 10-1 and 10-2) linked by linking pins. The vertical line would consist of such groups and so would the horizontal line or lateral linkage. In very complex organizations, there also might be need for linkages through a third or even a fourth dimension. Groups at the middle and higher level of the organization would consist usually of about 5 to 10 persons. Those at the very bottom would generally be larger, e.g., 25 to 30 persons and sometimes even more.

The leadership, problem solving, and interaction processes that would occur in this structure are discussed in Chapters 6 to 9.

This statement of the general nature of a System 4 multiple-overlapping-group structure gives one the impression that the structure is relatively simple. Unfortunately, this is not the case. Both the structure called for by System 4 and its method of operating are more complex than System 1, 2, or 3. This is to be expected since System 4 is a more socially evolved and complex system than its predecessors. As a consequence, the discussion of the structure for achieving effective cross-functional coordination and the related organization charts are not simple and easy to read. To use this information requires careful study. Readers who are faced with the immediate application of these organizational principles and concepts may wish to take the time to study them carefully. They are discussed fully in Chapter 10 of *The Human Organization* (Likert, 1967), including alternate forms of cross-functional linkage.

The self-correcting
capacity of System 4
interaction-influence networks

In addition to the linkages occurring through the line organization (figs. 10-1 and 10-2) and those performed via lateral linkages, there is , in most organizations, a variety of other committees or groups. Some are permanent committees; others are ad hoc groups or task forces. These groups include such committees as those concerned with safety, salary administration, and the use of computers. All these groups, if they are performing well as groups, strengthen the linkage of the total organization. They do this in two important ways. First, they provide alternate channels through which communication and influence can flow and through which productive problem solving can occur. These alternate channels can be particularly helpful when there are unusually difficult problems or conflicts to solve. The alternate channels can help develop innovative, acceptable solutions especially when the primary linking groups bog down and are unable to find a mutually acceptable solution.

Second, along with the cross-functional, lateral-linkage groups they provide an efficient means for promptly detecting any breakdown in the interaction-influence network of a System 4 organization or in the linking structure between organizations engaged in conflict. If, for example, a work group in the vertical line fails to perform its linking and problem-solving functions effectively, these linkage groups would recognize that this condition existed through information provided by their linking pins which tie to the failing group. The linkage group which is aware that the vertical group is failing can call attention to this organizational breakdown through other effective vertical lines to which it also is linked. These alternate vertical channels, however, should *not* undertake to perform the linking, interacting, and problem-solving role of the deficient linking unit. To do so would weaken the overall organization. The information should be used by the appropriate superior work groups to diagnose weaknesses and to plan to take such corrective steps as coaching, training, and organization building. Whenever information is flowing through channels other than the normal ones, it suggests that there is a deficiency in the normal channel which needs to be examined and that steps must be taken to improve the problem solving in the work group or groups where the deficiency exists. In case of a serious breakdown in crucial linking, the information that the breakdown exists and needs to be dealt with is likely to flow through several alternate channels to the appropriate superior work group for problem solving and action focused on organizational building and correction.

This capacity for information to flow to the relevant work group or groups calling attention to the failure of a subordinate linking work group to perform its designated functions effectively is one of the strengths of the System 4 interaction-influence network in comparison with the structure of the other systems. In a System 2 organization, the usual way that higher levels discover that linking pins or subordinate groups are failing to perform their functions well is when the end-result data, such as production, costs, and earnings, or the level of unresolved conflicts, reveal this fact. Since end-result data are *after-the-fact* data, the breakdown goes undetected long after it should have been corrected. With the alternate communication channels of the System 4 interaction-influence network, any deficiency can be discovered in its early stages and corrected long before it manifests itself in costly breakdowns in the organization's performance and its conflict management. System 4 makes valuable lead-time data available to recognize and correct organizational weaknesses when the conflicts or problems are still minor.

Present trends support the theory

There is growing evidence that attempts to resolve conflicts and to improve coordination in highly functionalized organizations by employing the solutions called for by System 4 are yielding successful results. There are examples from business indicating that the general approach suggested here is now being used at least partially in a variety of situations and is contributing to effective decision making and coordination. In most of these situations, the approach is not being used on a companywide basis as a formal system of organization but has been developed by able managers as solutions to specific problems. In many cases, the particular solution is an informal organizational process and often is viewed apologetically as a violation of accepted principles of management. Nevertheless, since the solution seems to work, its use is continued. In some instances, the idea represented by the solution spreads to other parts of the company but usually not as an accepted, generalized, and formal principle of management.

An example of these developments is found in a company in which one major division tried to improve coordination in order to speed up the manufacturing and marketing of new products. This was done by appointing cross-functional product committees. The committees consisted of one person each from development, manufacturing, and sales. Several of these committees performed group decision-making processes well, and when they did so, the division found that the committees significantly reduced the amount of time required for a new product idea to move from the development stage through manufacturing to successful marketing. This put the company ahead of competition in getting new products on the market at a time when they were highly profitable.

The company tried to extend this committee plan of operation to another division by ordering the second division to establish comparable product committees with members from development, manufacturing, and sales. The members of these committees lacked training in group decision making, and the order to use the cross-functional committees created neither the motivation to try to use them well nor the skill to do so. The members attended the meetings but came as "representatives" from their departments. They engaged in win-lose tactics and were ineffective in speeding up the process of marketing new products profitably. These committees were a dismal failure.

A study of the factors affecting the successful use of research in Scottish electronics companies (Burns & Stalker, 1961; Croome, 1959) yielded results similar to the above example. Most of the companies were small. In several of them, because of a cooperative, informal atmosphere encouraged by the president, an informal structure emerged for handling problems of coordination. This structure included persons from research, production, sales, and, in some companies, the president. By means of this informal structure and use of group decision-making processes, planning for each phase was started in these companies in ample time for the operation to proceed smoothly from one phase to the next. The product design fitted the manufacturing capabilities of the company. Marketing plans and efforts were started early enough to sell the product as soon as it became available. These informal activities enabled new products to be marketed in time to be profitable and made the investment pay off handsomely.

In other Scottish electronics companies, however, a different pattern was used. The president adhered to the System 2 organization and dealt with the heads of research, production, and sales on a person-to-person basis. The president maintained tight control and prevented the development and use of informal channels for dealing with these problems. When decisions were made in the formal, System 2 manner, the head of each successive operation tended to criticize the work done at preceding steps and to point out why the operation would not work as planned. All the friction which occurs when peers compete and belittle the work of the others to gain the superior's favor was present. This friction caused serious delays in getting new products marketed and often resulted in their being unprofitable. Companies which adhered to this "proper" use of System 2 found that their investments in research and new products were financially disastrous.

The experience of these Scottish electronics firms indicates that the use of an informal, cross-functional, group structure facilitated lateral coordination and thereby made R&D profitable. This was the case even though this informal structure violated the formal, organizational principles of these firms.

Another illustration comes from a company whose technology is extremely complex. This company has been using project teams to help achieve coordination. The establishment of project teams, however, does not assure the skillful use of group processes. The head of one team, for example, was not sure that the subordinates could be trusted to tackle a difficult problem as a group. That person feared they might recommend a solution which would be easy for them, but which would work so poorly that the chief would be in difficulty with managers above him. As a consequence, the chief asked each of the four subordinates individually to prepare a report telling how that person felt the problem should be solved. The problem involved the work of all four subordinates since their activities were interdependent. In accordance with the instructions, each subordinate worked alone and did not discuss the problem with the others. Each prepared a report which handled well the aspects of the problem important to that subordinate and that section but which did not take into consideration the situations or needs of the other three sections. The chief then had four reports with four different solutions and had the problem of selecting among them or combining them in some way.

At this point, the work group became involved in a training activity aimed at improving their group interaction skills. This resulted in much more candid interaction among the group members ("leveling") and led the chief to observe in a group meeting that he now had the tough problem of deciding what the solution to the problem should be. He had four separate and conflicting recommendations, since each report had been prepared from the vantage point of that particular subordinate. He concluded it would have been better had he asked the four subordinates to tackle the problem as a group and come up with a single solution. His subordinates agreed and observed that by his instructions to them the chief had made impenetrable the 4-inch office wall separating one subordinate from another.

The chief and his four subordinates then did a "backup" in decision making. They did not try to select from among the four solutions already at hand. Instead they started decision making on the problem from the very beginning and went through all the steps of productive group decision making in sequence (See chap. 7). This included listing all the requirements which a satisfactory solution must fulfill and an innovative search for acceptable choices. As a consequence, they came up with a better solution than any of those recommended by the subordinates working alone. This successful use of group processes led progressively, with additional training and coaching, to its general use by this work group. The chief can now cite impressive evidence for the effectiveness of this procedure. It has gained valuable time on contracts by reducing the period required for the successful accomplishment of important missions; it has resulted also in substantial budgetary saving, as well as sizable bonuses for the corporation for completing projects ahead of contract dates.

These examples illustrate what appears to be a growing trend. It is significant that this trend is consistent with and supports the System 4 approach to managing conflict and achieving effective coordination.

12
System 4 structure applied to conflicts in schools

In this chapter, we shall discuss ways of managing conflict in schools and improving educational performance by providing an adequate interaction-influence structure. Schools were selected as an example because they are plagued by a wide variety of conflicts and their structures have serious deficiencies for coping with them.

School officials are keenly aware of the magnitude and seriousness of conflict in schools. Many feel the need of greater skill in managing it. Bailey (1970) says: "As with other public executives, his [the high school principal's] prime task is conflict management and he knows it. To our survey question, 'Should there be more in-service training about conflict management for topside administrators?' 90 percent agreed, eight percent were neutral and only two percent disagreed" (p. 50). Teacher strikes, student demonstrations and disruptions, struggles of neighborhood groups or boards with the central boards of education, conflicts over desegration and busing, differences within the school system and with parents about teaching methods and curriculum content and emphasis, conflicts encountered in introducing new curriculum, differences concerning the disciplining of students, and differences about the financing of buildings and of operating budgets are but a few of the conflicts that our school systems must handle.

The intensity of many of these conflicts is increased by the feeling of students and teachers that they are involved much less in decisions affecting them than they feel they should be and have the right to be. Frustration over being inadequately involved in decisions affecting them would be great even if their major concerns dealt only with academic life and problems. Their frustrations, however, are much more broadly based. Threats to the environment, eroding of civil rights, distrust of government, unequal employment opportunities, inadequate housing are some of the problems greatly needing solution but receiving insufficient or inept attention. The belief that the people of our country are unable to make their voices heard and influence decisions that will make or break the nation is causing students and teachers to press vigorously and, at times, irrationally for actions that they feel are necessary.

In discussing disruption in urban public secondary schools, Bailey says:[1]

> It would come as no surprise to any big city principal to be told that a huge backlog of emotional freight produced by some very rough social conflicts in our time is being dumped on his school. Black students coming to school with the heady message of black power or white students coming to school with a *"never"* button would only be two symbols of the inexorable process by which public schools are being sucked into the important social quarrels of the day. This intergenerational gap . . . adds fuel to this fire as well. The impatience level among adolescents runs high. As is the case in many universities, students want the school to be a stronger social force for goals they consider correct and necessary. Students, naturally, are politicized by the media, by local community leadership, and indeed by the more political teachers at the school.
>
> If politicized students are deeply dissatisfied and urging action, they will probably create some kind of scene right at the school for the very simple reason that that is where they are. It is commonplace to note that adolescents have very little leverage on the wider society's politics, so they strike where they are and where they do have leverage. The management of these very important social conflicts within a school is probably the toughest problem administrators have. (p. 32)

The widespread unionization of teachers has not been accompanied by the development of an adequate structure for communication, interaction, and problem solving between teachers and their unions on the one hand and school administrators and boards of education on the other. As a consequence, teachers' strikes are increasing in number, duration, and bitterness. The strikes, themselves, are intensifying conflict since they cause teachers and their unions to develop more hostile and bitter feelings toward the school administration and the board of education. Strikes also often increase hostilities among teachers. Unless all the schools are closed and no teacher is encouraged or permitted to go to work, bitter attitudes, even hatreds, develop. Even though only a small minority may report for work, teachers who have been friends for many years suddenly find themselves on opposite sides of the conflict and, as the strike continues and economic pressures mount, their treatment of each other becomes vitriolic. The hurt feelings and disillusionment about the character and sensitivity of their longtime friends will last for years to the detriment of the persons and of the educational process.

The interaction-influence networks of our schools all too often are proving to be incapable of dealing constructively even with the internal school problems and conflicts, not to mention the conflicts impinging from the outside. Moreover, the present decision-making structure of the schools requires patterns of interaction that often aggravate conflict rather than resolving it constructively.

Faculty meetings, for example, almost always employ parliamentary procedures that force a System 2 win-lose confrontation. The systematic, orderly problem solving that small groups can use does not and cannot occur in large

---

[1]S. K. Bailey. *Disruption in urban public secondary schools.* Washington, D.C.: National Association of Secondary School Principals, 1970.

meetings. When controversial issues are discussed, it is distressing to observe the extraordinary capacity of *Robert's Rules of Order* to turn the interaction among sincere, intelligent persons into bitter, emotional, win-lose confrontation. Meetings of 50, 100, or more faculty members are completely unable to engage in innovative, creative problem solving when dealing with a difficult emotion-laden problem. Motions and countermotions split the meeting into factions. Each faction seeks by one parlimentary maneuver or another to have its preferred solution win. Creative problem solving does not occur (See chaps. 7–9). Many persons who vote for a motion feel little or no commitment to it. They often vote for it halfheartedly as the best of the available alternatives but with a feeling that none is really satisfactory. Feeling that the final choice is not going to deal adequately with the problem and feeling little commitment to it, these persons all too often accept little responsibility for implementing the decision or even abiding by it. The dissenters reject the decision and are prepared to sabotage it actively or passively.

These procedures are just as ineffective with students as they are with faculty. Student government typically consists of highly unrepresentative "representatives." The members usually are elected by a small proportion of the students. Their deliberative bodies employ the usual parliamentary procedures with the usual unsatisfactory results.

In an effort to increase student participation in school matters, some schools and school districts are appointing student representatives to major boards or committees. The objective is desirable, but the mechanism is faulty. These student representatives usually are selected by the student government, unrepresentative in itself. The great majority of students have little continuing opportunity to be heard by their representatives, nor are they able to exert influence upon them or be influenced by them. Most students feel little responsibility, consequently, to abide by or to help implement any decision made by these bodies.

The structure for real interaction and influence does not exist. To cope effectively with their problems, schools and school systems must have a structure that facilitates creative problem solving and gives each person, student, teacher, and administrator an adequate opportunity to be heard and to exert influence on all decisions affecting them. As we have seen in Chapter 10, the structure needed consists of small groups linked together by persons who hold overlapping memberships and serve as linking pins. This structure seldom exists in student government. It rarely is present to link principals, department heads, and teachers or to link students with teachers and administrators. It often is absent at upper organizational levels to link schools with the district.

A System 4 structure for elementary schools

The appropriate interaction-influence structure for any school or school system must be tailored to fit the culture, traditions, size, and needs of that particular institution. The examples that follow illustrate one way of applying System 4 principles to create such structures. Other ways which may be more appropriate to a specific school can be developed by that school. Experience with a new structure, moreover, will yield new insights likely to suggest further possible improvements in the structure that will make it even more effective.

We will start discussing the simplest structure, that of a small elementary school with 1 principal, no more than 12 teachers, 1 counselor, and 3 or 4 nonprofessionals. The small size of such a school requires only two overlapping groups: one consisting of the principal, all the teachers, and the counselor; another consisting of the principal and the nonprofessional staff (fig. 12-1). Although this structure sometimes may make the first group slightly larger than is desirable for constructive problem solving, it seems preferable to introducing another layer—grade level chairpersons—between the principal and the teachers. These two problem-solving groups would be responsible for dealing with the problems of the school.

A possible structure for the organization of the professional staff of large elementary schools is shown in Figure 12-2. It is illustrative and not intended to be complete. There are likely to be, for example, more grade level chairpersons than shown, and there also may be more subject matter specialists. If the school has grades K–8, it, of course, will have more grade level chairpersons than if it is K–6.

The top group in the structure would consist of the principal, the assistant or vice-principal, the head librarian, the head counselor, and the grade level chairpersons. Subject matter specialists also would be included in this top group if persons other than the grade level chairpersons are designated to perform this role. The next level would consist of librarians, counselors, and groups of teachers. Each group of teachers would be linked to the top group by both a grade level chairperson and a subject matter specialist. The number of grade level chairpersons would depend upon the number of grades. Ideally, each group should have at least 4 or 5 teachers and no group should be larger than 10 or 12. The number of subject matter specialists would depend upon the number of academic areas covered by the school's curriculum.

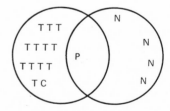

Figure 12-1 *Structure for small elementary schools (P = principal, T = teachers, C = counselors, and N = professionals).*

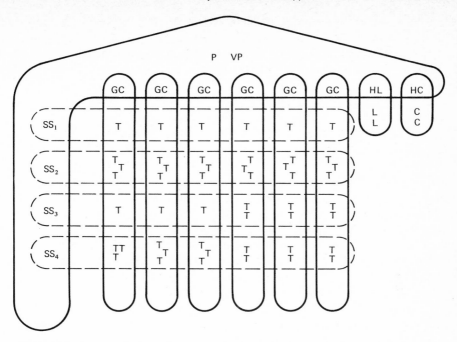

Figure 12-2 *Structure for large elementary schools: academic organization (P = principal, VP = vice-principal, GC = grade level chairpersons, T = teachers; SS = subject matter specialists; HL = head librarian, L = library assistants, HC = head counselors, and C = counselors).*

The grade level chairpersons might be appointed by the principal from a slate selected by the teachers in that grade, or the teachers might select from a slate proposed by the principal, or some other way. Regardless of the specific procedure used, the chairpersons selected should be acceptable to both the principal and the department members. The same procedure should be used in selecting subject matter specialists.

The term of office of the grade level chairpersons should be long enough for each chairperson to build the department into a well-knit unit that solves problems efficiently and constructively. This person also needs to become an effective linking member of the top group. Unless the group of teachers from a grade is small and its members know each other well, it is likely to take a year for a chairperson to build the department into a cohesive, highly effective problem-solving group.[2] As a consequence, it may be desirable to have the grade level chairpersons and subject matter specialists serve for a term of about three years with the possibility of being selected to serve a second term.

---

[2]A description of the nature and operating characteristics of highly effective groups can be found in Chap. 11 of *New Patterns of Management* (Likert, 1961).

A matrix form of organizational structure

The coordination of teaching activities by subject matter fields can be handled in either of two ways. One plan adds persons to handle the additional set of roles. The other plan adds additional roles to persons who already are performing a linking function. If the first plan is followed, one group of teachers performs the role of grade level chairpersons while another group of teachers serves as subject matter specialists. This is the plan shown in Figure 12-2. This plan increases the number of persons in the top group. If the second plan is followed, the same group of teachers performs both tasks. It serves both as grade level chairpersons and as subject matter specialists. This plan increases the load on the persons performing the two roles. The relative advantage of each plan and the operating characteristics of each are discussed at greater length in Chapter 10 of *The Human Organization* (Likert, 1967).

Either of these plans or a modification of them can be used depending upon which best suits the requirements of a particular school or school system. The important point is that provision needs to be made for the two kinds of linking and coordinating functions shown in Figure 12-2.

Figure 12-2 shows the coordination by grade level as the vertical linkage line and coordination by subject matter as the lateral linkage line. Each linking line is of equal importance, so that the figure could be shown equally well if rotated 90 degrees. This matrix form of organization is necessary if a school is to handle simultaneously and well the problems and conflicts related to grade levels and those arising from subject matter areas. The usual form of organization does not treat both grade level and subject matter problems with equal emphasis and priority. One or the other is established as *the* line organization. The problem solving for the school is done through this line organization and with a primary focus on its interests. If the basic organization is by grade level, the subject matter problems receive lower priority. Conversely, if the line organization is by subject matter, the problems related to grade level are treated as of secondary importance. The matrix form of organization requires the System 4 style of leadership and System 4 group problem solving throughout the organization, i.e., by both the grade level line of linkage and the subject matter line of linkage.

In addition to the structure shown in Figure 12-2, there are likely to be several committees of the faculty, some standing, and some ad hoc. Innovative procedures, such as team teaching, also may require committees or groups of faculty members to coordinate and perhaps carry out the activity. These committees will provide additional structure and, if they perform well, the addition will strengthen the interaction-influence network of the school. Often the chairpersons of these committees will be grade level chairpersons or subject matter specialists and, consequently, members of the top group of the school. When one of these committees is dealing actively with matters of general interest to the faculty, the chairperson should meet regularly with the top-level group if he or she is not already a member of the group. The chairpersons of less active committees would meet with the top level group only when there are matters that need to be brought to their attention.

All teachers who assume additional work, such as heads of departments or grade levels, of course, would be relieved of enough other duties to have adequate time for their leadership and linking roles or would receive additional compensation for the extra work they perform.

A structure corresponding to Figure 12-2 is needed for the nonprofessional group. The top group would consist of the principal, the vice-principal, the cafeteria manager, the head custodian, the clerical supervisor, and persons with similar supervisory positions. Each of these persons would link his or her group to the top nonprofessional work group; i.e., the cafeteria manager would be a linking pin between the top nonprofessional group and the cafeteria workers. It is just as important, of course, for the nonprofessional staff as it is for the professional staff to use System 4 leadership and problem-solving processes in each group: both the top group and those groups linked to the top.

Problems of an academic nature should be dealt with through the academic structure. Nonacademic problems should be handled through the nonacademic. Problems affecting both groups should be dealt with by the two top work groups meeting as a single group.

This suggested structure for an elementary school is one way to apply the principles of System 4 organizational structure stated in Chapter 10. Each school and school system should apply the principles in ways that fit its own particular size and requirements. As a consequence, a particular elementary school may have a structure such as shown in Figure 12-2, or it may make use of the principles in some other appropriate manner. This observation, of course, applies equally to the discussion of other suggested structures in the rest of this chapter. In each case, the organization should apply the principles of System 4 structure in ways that fit its own unique traditions and characteristics.

The structure for senior high schools

A proposed structure for the academic personnel in large senior high schools with a dozen or more subject matter departments and additional staff, such as librarians, counselors, grade chairpersons, and registrar, is shown in Figure 12-3. To keep the chart simple, only some of the grade level chairpersons, heads of departments, and teachers in these departments are shown.

If these groups are to be efficient and productive, they must be relatively small in size. A group including all the heads of departments, the head librarian, head counselor and registrar, the principal and vice-principals would be much too large for effective problem solving and coordinating. The addition of a hierarchical level consisting of the vice-principals reduces both the top group and the groups of department heads to manageable proportions.

There are two advantages to this structure. First, the vice-principals would

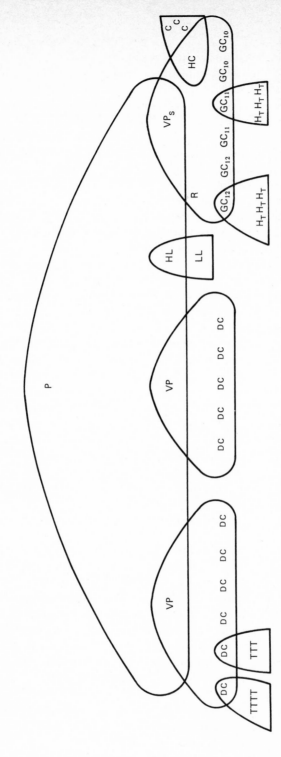

Figure 12-3 Structure for large senior high school (P = principal, VP = vice-principal, DC = department chairperson, T = teachers, HC = head counselor, C = counselors, HL = head librarian, L = librarian, R = registrar, VPS = vice-principal for student affairs, GC_{12} = grade chairpersons—12 grades, and H_T = homeroom teachers). Note that GC and H_h as teachers, are also members of the departments.

become trained in providing effective leadership to their problem-solving groups and in serving as linking pins. Second, in the absence of the principal, one or more of the vice-principals could handle any problem that might arise, guided by the policies and objectives that their top group had established.

The top group would consist, as shown, of the principal, the three vice-principals, and the head librarian. Two of the vice-principals would each link a group of about six or so department chairpersons to the top group. It may be desirable to have departments with related interests, such as mathematics and science, linked by the same vice-principal.

The vice-principal in charge of student affairs would link the grade level chairpersons and the head counselor to the top group. The grade level chairpersons would be the linking pins between the homeroom teachers and the vice-principal for student affairs, as shown in Figure 12-3. In high schools that do not have homeroom teachers, those performing the linking role can be teachers of any required subjects, such as English or social studies. The role of the grade level chairperson, or others who serve as linkages to the top group, is discussed below. They are part of the structure that links the student government to the teachers and administration.

In an effort to keep Figure 12-3 from being too complex, the matrix nature of the structure is not shown. Nevertheless, the structure for high schools, like that for elementary schools, is a matrix form of organization. The teachers who are shown as linked to the grade level chairpersons are also members of departments. Hence, there is the dual linkage characteristic of matrix organizations. As mentioned previously, this matrix form of organization can be very effective if System 4 leadership skills and group problem solving are used by both the linking lines: through heads of departments and through grade level chairpersons. The structure will not function well unless group problem solving is used effectively.

The heads of departments and the grade level chairpersons should serve a term of office and be selected in the manner described for elementary schools. They also should receive extra compensation or a lighter teaching load as mentioned previously.

Principals and heads of departments who are accustomed to dealing directly with each other may feel that the proposed additional hierarchical level creates too much of a gap, that the principal will be too far removed from the department heads and their problems. One way that the principal can keep in touch with the department heads and their thinking and concerns is by sitting in regularly, perhaps at every second or third session, at the meetings of the department heads and a vice-principal. In these meetings, the principal should make clear the purpose of attending and be careful not to usurp the role of the vice-principal who is chairperson of the group. The principal also can make clear to all heads of departments that it is perfectly appropriate for any one of them to come to the principal any time they wish to discuss any question or problem of concern to them. The vice-principals must understand this as well. When the head of a department goes to the principal, the principal should listen carefully and sympathetically. If the problem is purely personal, the principal, of course, should be as helpful as possible. If the problem is other than personal, the principal should take no action without involving the relevant vice-principal and the other persons or groups that will be affected by any decision.

In addition to the structure for academic matters shown in Figure 12-3, there is need for a similar structure linking nonacademic services to the top group. If feasible, each of the vice principals should take turns in providing this linkage. Sharing the load for linking the nonacademic services to the top group would enable each of the vice-principals to have substantial time for involvement in the administration of academic matters which, of course, is likely to be their primary interest.

From time to time, there may be questions and problems that are of concern to all the nonacademic personnel. To deal constructively with these matters, there should be periodic meetings of the heads of all the nonacademic functions, e.g., custodial, cafeteria, and office, with the principal and relevant vice-principals.

The structure for small high schools

Small high schools with 10 or less departments and only one vice-principal are not likely to need the additional level of vice-principals shown in Figure 12-3. The top group of not more than 10 department heads, 1 vice-principal, a head librarian, a head counselor, and the principal would not be too large for efficient group problem solving to take place. This structure is shown in Figure 12-4.

The structure for intermediate or junior high schools

For easy reference, schools at this level: middle, intermediate, or junior high schools will be called intermediate schools. They vary in the number of grade levels included, which contributes to variations in size.

Intermediate schools, as a rule, have fewer departments than do high schools. Consequently, even large intermediate schools could use the structure proposed for small high schools (fig. 12-4). The top group of the intermediate school would consist of the principal, vice-principal, eight or so department chairpersons, the head librarian, and the head counselor. The vice-principal would link the grade level chairpersons to the top group. When each grade has more than a dozen homeroom teachers, it usually will be desirable to have two grade level chairpersons for each grade. (See fig. 12-3.) This will keep the number of homeroom teachers linked by a grade level chairperson to not more than 12.

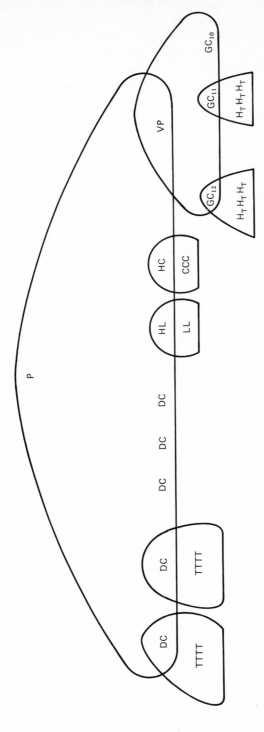

Figure 12-4 Structure for small high school (P = principal, VP = vice-principal, DC = department chairpersons, T = teachers, HC = head counselor, C = counselors, HL = head librarian, L = librarians, GC₁₂ = grade chairpersons—12 grades, and Hₜ = homeroom teachers). Note that GC and Hₕ as teachers, are also members of departments.

In small intermediate schools, i.e., those with 12 or less homeroom teachers to a grade and with 8 or fewer departments, the grade level chairpersons could be members of the top group. This would make the top group rather large, about 15 persons, but would do away with the linkage of the grade level chairpersons to the top through the vice-principal. If the principal finds that the top group performs productively with as many as 15 persons, this structure can be used. If 15 proves too large a group for constructive problem solving, it can be reduced in size by using the structure shown in Figure 12-4. Regardless of size, intermediate schools should employ the same general principles and procedures as those described above, for example, in the selection of grade level chairpersons.

The structure for the nonacademic staffs of intermediate schools, of course, should be essentially the same as that described previously for elementary schools.

Student government

The proposed structure for student government would have the same objective as that for the faculty and administration: to provide a structure that will enable all persons to influence decisions affecting them and, in turn, be motivated to implement, in a responsible manner, the decisions reached. The proposed structure for student government, consequently, would apply the same basic concepts of System 4 interaction-influence networks as that described above for teachers and administrators and would do so in essentially the same manner. Through this structure, all students would have an adequate opportunity to participate in decisions affecting them and to be heard on matters of concern to them. This structure, moreover, would facilitate the constructive resolution of conflicts among students, and between them and their teachers and the school administration. As emphasized previously, this proposed structure is only one way to apply System 4 principles. The structure for student government used in any particular situation should, of course, fit the unique requirements and traditions of that situation.

The proposed student-government structure would consist of multiple overlapping, face-to-face, problem-solving groups, each small enough for effective and creative decision making, i.e., not more than 25 persons. These groups would be organized by grade level.

A senior high school with approximately 1,000 students in the 10th grade, 900 students in the 11th grade, and 800 students in the 12th grade can be used as an illustration of a possible structure of student government. Clustering the students into groups of 20 or 25 would be done by homerooms in schools that have them. In schools that lack homerooms, required courses such as social studies or English could be used. The most appropriate grouping will vary from school to school. It would be desirable if these groups had been established for some time and had been meeting regularly for purposes other than student-government activities. Each group would select its own leader who also would link the group to the group at the next higher level in the student-government organization.

The groups at the next-higher level preferably should be no larger than 15 to 20 persons because of the more complex problem solving they would need to do in coordinating the views and decisions of the groups at the first level. With about 800 to 1,000 students to a grade and with about 25 students in each group at the first level, there would be in each grade about 35 to 40 first-level groups, each with its own student leaders. If these 35 or 40 leaders are divided into two groups, each of the second-level groups would contain about 15 or 20 persons, which is the desired size.

Each of these second-level groups would select from among its members its own chairperson and vice-chairperson. They would become members of the top group (third level) and would link their second-level group to the top. (See fig. 12-5.) There, consequently, would be four students from each grade in the top group: a chairperson and vice-chairperson from each of the two second-level groups for that grade.

The 12 students in the top group, 4 from each of the 3 classes, would select from among their members a president and a vice-president of that top group. These persons would become the president and vice-president of student government and be recognized by all the students as such.

When a leader of a first-level group is selected as chairperson or vice-chairperson of a second-level group as well, that leader would be expected to serve, ordinarily, as chairperson of each of the two groups and be a linking pin between the two groups. This dual role is undesirable in itself and is likely to be an overload. To avoid this, whenever a first-level chairperson is moved upward to be the head or vice-head of a second-level group, the chair that person filled as a first-level leader should be viewed as vacated. The group that has lost its leader in this manner should fill the vacancy by selecting another person to that position who would link that group to the second-level group. This same replacement procedure should be used to lighten the load on the persons selected as president and vice-president. They should be replaced as linking pins between the second and third levels by the selection of another person to serve as linkage between these two groups. The other persons, as they move up, should be replaced by members from their lower groups.

The many committees required to carry out the various student activities would be appointed by the president of the student government with the approval of the top-level, coordinating group. To facilitate effective coordination, each committee, as a rule, would include in its membership a person from the top-level group.

The top group for the government of each class or grade would be the two chairpersons and two vice-chairpersons of the second-level groups for that grade. These top groups are encircled with dashes in Figure 12-5 and are marked "class government." Each top group of four would select one of their number to be the president of that class. An alternate procedure would be to

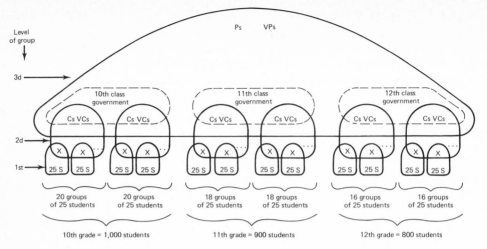

Figure 12-5 *Multiple-overlapping-group structure for student government (Ps = student president, VPs = student vice-president, Cs = student chairpersons, VCs = student vice-chairpersons, X = student leaders of first-level group, and S = student members).*

have all the leaders of the first-level groups select one of the four members of the top group as president of that class.

Matters of concern to only one grade would be dealt with by this class-government structure. In acting on questions of general interest to their classmates, the top group for each grade would see that everyone was involved in the decision making by means of the linkage structure. The decision making should move back and forth between levels until a decision acceptable to all is reached. As was mentioned previously, the top groups, whether acting for a class or for the entire student body, should never behave as an executive committee.

Linking student government to faculty and administration

Between the student government of a school and its faculty and administration, there must be an interaction-influence network through which communication flows readily and by means of which plans are established, decisions made, and conflicts resolved. It must be an effective mechanism for students to exert influence on decisions of concern to them.

The structure for the faculty and administration that can link easily to the student-government structure at the individual student level would be the homeroom teachers, as shown in Figure 12-3. In schools where there are no homeroom teachers, the grouping would be on a basis appropriate to the operation of that school, such as English or social studies classes, as was mentioned previously. In a high school the size of our example (about 2,700 students), each grade would be likely to have about 30 homeroom teachers. This is too large to function well as a problem-solving group. It should be split into 2 groups of 15 each. Each group of 15 would have a chairperson who also would serve as its linkage to the next-higher administrative level. (See fig. 12-3.) Consequently, in a large high school, two teacher grade level chairpersons would be needed for each grade. In a small high school with 15 or less homeroom teachers per grade, only one grade chairperson would be required for each grade.

The higher administrative level would consist of all the teacher grade level chairpersons and the vice-principal for student affairs. The vice-principal would be head of this group. The vice-principal also would be a member of the school's top-level group and link the homeroom structure to the top adminis-tration of the high school (fig. 12-3). When particularly difficult problems involving student relationships to the faculty and administration are being worked on by the top group, the head counselor could be asked also to meet with the top group. This would provide two linking pins between the top level and the grade chairperson group, thus strengthening that linkage.

Cross-linkages at each grade level between faculty and students would be achieved by regular meetings of the two teacher grade level chairpersons for that grade and the two student chairpersons and the two student vice-chairper-sons of that grade. (See Fig. 12-6.) These cross-linkage groups at each grade level would handle the coordination problems of concern only to their grade. Figure 12-6, like the other figures, shows only part of the personnel involved. Enough is shown to make the structure clear, but many students, homeroom teachers, and others are omitted from the figure.

Cross-linkage for dealing with schoolwide matters would be provided by regular meetings of the principal, the vice-principals, the head counselor, and the 14 students in the top level of the student organization. The principal, vice-principal for student affairs, and the student-government president and vice-president also might meet regularly as a small, top coordinating structure.

Since the first-level student groups are likely to be homerooms, social studies or English classes, or some similar grouping, the teacher ordinarily present in those rooms or classes should become an operating member of the group. This teacher would become a linking pin between the first-level student groups and the corresponding level of the teacher-administration structure. He or she also should provide coaching and training to the students in the leadership, prob-lem-solving, linking-pin and interaction processes of System 4. (See chaps. 6–10.) These processes are somewhat more complex and require more learning than the more traditional parliamentary procedures such as *Robert's Rules of Order,* but they, too, can be taught and learned. If a System 4 model of student government is to work well, students need to become skilled in these System 4 processes. Students will find these skills useful in their school and home life

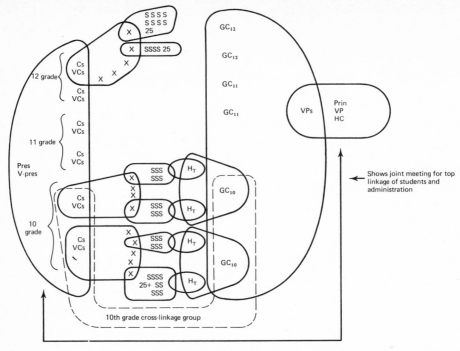

Figure 12-6 *Cross-linkage structure: students to faculty and administration (H_T = homeroom teacher, GC = grade chairperson, Cs = student chairperson, VCs = student vice-chairperson, X = student leader of first-level group, S = students, Prin = principal, VP = vice-principal, VPs = vice-principal for student affairs, HC = head counselor, Pres = president of student government, and V-Pres = student vice-president).*

now. They will find them even more useful, subsequently, in enabling them to perform effectively in business, governmental, voluntary, and other kinds of organizations and in their work, community, and family life.

The opportunity that this interaction-influence network offers should be used also by English, social studies, and other teachers to teach valuable interaction skills. For example, such communication skills as expressing oneself clearly and succinctly and listening carefully and with understanding should be taught. Similarly, students should acquire the capacity to behave in an emotionally mature manner in discussing a problem. They need to learn to make their points in a supportive, friendly manner and with a sense of humor rather than with aggressive hostility (See chaps. 6–9).

There may be times when the students will want to meet without the teacher. When this occurs and the students ask the teacher not to be present, their wishes should be graciously respected. It is hoped this will occur rarely as it is likely to be a symptom of a breakdown in trust. As a rule, the proposed interaction-influence network, when used with System 4 win-win problem solving, should function sufficiently well that trust is built and maintained.

When it breaks down, the causes should be sought and constructive remedial action undertaken promptly.

The linking structure above the school

The nature of the linking structure above the level of the individual school will vary depending upon many factors. These include the total school population, the total number of schools, the composition of the school district—whether it consists of only elementary schools or only high schools or a combination—and whether local or miniboards are used in addition to a central school board.

Regardless of the nature and size of the particular school district, it should have a structure that represents a sound application of the principles and concepts stated in Chapter 10. Since it is scarcely feasible to discuss each of the great variety of structures needed to fit the tremendous variations in school districts, the structure for one fairly large district will be used as an example. This district has 5 senior high schools (grades 10–12), 10 intermediate schools (grades 7–9), and 40 elementary schools (K–6).

If the principles of Chapter 10 are to be applied to this district, the superintendent obviously needs a layer of linking structure between the superintendent and the 55 schools in his district. A "Complex" is one of the alternate forms of multiple-overlapping-group structure that can be used. Since the Complex form of structure offers many advantages, it will be used in the following discussion.

A Complex consists of a senior high school, the intermediate schools that feed students to it, and the grade schools whose graduates go to the intermediate schools. The principal of each school in the Complex would serve as the linking pin between that school and the total Complex. (See fig. 12-7.) If we use as an example a Complex consisting of 1 senior high, 2 intermediate schools, and 8 elementary schools, the linking group would include these 11 persons. The principal of the senior high school would serve also as the head of the Complex. The principal usually would be assisted by a Complex coordinator

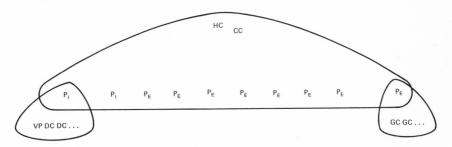

Figure 12-7 *Structure of a Complex (HC = head of Complex—principal of high school, CC = Complex coordinator, P_I = principal—intermediate school, P_E = principal—elementary school, VP = vice-principal, DC = department chairperson, and GC = grade chairperson).*

who would be a curriculum specialist on the staff of the district superintendent. When the high school is large, it may be necessary to give the principal an additional part-time vice-principal to free enough of the principal's time to devote to the administration of the Complex.

Problems of concern to all the schools in the Complex would be the topic for the regular meetings of this group. The agenda might include instructional, budget, personnel, student, community support, and similar issues. The Complex form of organization, with its neighborhood base, facilitates planning and operating the kinds of schools that will serve best the students who live in that particular geographical area. In addition, the Complex form of organization is especially well suited to undertaking efforts to improve neighborhood understanding and support of the school system. This support can be built by working with parents' groups and other neighborhood organizations and, in some situations, by establishing neighborhood advisory groups or boards.

Problems of concern only to the intermediate schools or to the elementary schools would be handled in group problem-solving sessions with the Complex administrator or coordinator, the principals, and probably the vice-principals of those particular schools. If the problems being dealt with by these groups affected the entire district, they would, of course, go up for involvement in the problem solving through linking pins to the highest level affected. This would assure that all persons affected had an opportunity to influence the decisions reached and that those decisions met the needs and best interests of all affected by them.

The structure above the complex

Each senior high school principal, as head of a Complex, would serve as the linking pin between that Complex and the district level (fig. 12-8). Since in our

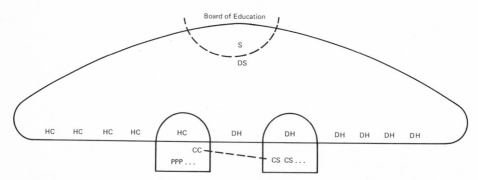

Figure 12-8 *Structure of a school district (S = superintendent, DS = deputy superintendent, HC = head of Complex, DH = department head—assistant superintendent, CC = Complex coordinator, P = principal, and CS = curriculum specialist).*

example there are five high schools, the five heads of Complexes would be members of the district-level group. This group also would include the superintendent, deputy superintendent, and the assistant superintendents or department heads who are in charge of the major functional areas such as curriculum, personnel, budget and finance, student affairs, research and planning, building and grounds, and community relations.

Figure 12-8, like the previous figures, is incomplete and shows only some of the persons in the structure. For example, there may be more department heads than are shown in the figure. Moreover, Figure 12-8 shows only part of the personnel under one of the department heads and none under the others. The dotted line between *CS* and *CC* shows that a curriculum specialist *(CS)* is serving each Complex as a Complex coordinator *(CC)*. Since this coordinator's role may not require full time, the coordinator also would perform curriculum specialist's activities.

There are many other relationships not shown in Figure 12-8. For example, each curriculum specialist has a staff relationship to personnel in the schools, such as department chairpersons or subject matter specialists who are in that particular specialist's field. Ordinarily, this staff relationship between the central staff and the school personnel is viewed as advisory and is shown in the organization charts by a dotted rather than solid line. With the System 4 matrix structure, both relationships—that between the principal and the heads of departments and that between curriculum specialists and department chairpersons—are viewed as lines of influence and shown as solid lines. Conflict between the two lines in setting objectives and reaching decisions is avoided or resolved by using group problem solving in both linkages. In using this structure, each curriculum specialist would meet in group problem-solving sessions with the relevant personnel. The frequency and number of these meetings would depend on the magnitude of the problems currently being worked on. The number of persons in these group meetings should be small enough so that the group is capable of doing constructive problem solving.

Let us use the curriculum specialist for social studies as an example. In working on the social studies curriculum in the high schools, this curriculum specialist would meet with the social studies department chairpersons from the five high schools. The curriculum specialist would meet regularly, e.g., once a month, with this group of five department heads and build them into a creative, effective problem-solving group. When working intensively on a problem, the meetings of this social studies curriculum group, of course, would be more frequent. In a similar manner, this curriculum specialist would meet with the social studies department chairpersons in the 10 intermediate schools.

The head of each social studies department should keep the principal informed of developments in these curriculum meetings. The department head also should be sure that the decisions reached by the social studies curriculum group are compatible with the policies and decisions of both the department head's department and school. When incompatibilities begin to develop, the department head, as the linking pin, should initiate problem solving to achieve and maintain consistency in the decisions and policies of the groups affected.

The situation is different for the 40 elementary schools in the district, and a more elaborate structure would be required. In each Complex, the subject matter specialists in a particular field, e.g., social studies, should be organized as a problem-solving group. They should be assisted in creating these groups by the curriculum coordinator for that Complex. Each group should select a head who would serve as a linking pin, linking his or her Complex group to the districtwide coordinating group for his subject matter field (see fig. 12-9). Each curriculum specialist would meet regularly, perhaps monthly, with the district-wide coordinating group in the curriculum specialist's subject matter field to work on the curricular problems in the elementary schools of the district. The two levels of groups would be used in problem solving and reaching decisions concerning the curriculum in their subject matter field for the elementary schools.

Other department heads should work with the schools in a manner similar to that described for the curriculum specialists. For example, consider the problem of establishing a new or modified personnel policy for elementary school teachers. The director of personnel for the district or a deputy should meet with elementary school principals of each Complex in problem-solving sessions. The Complex coordinator usually would sit in on these meetings, and if a major

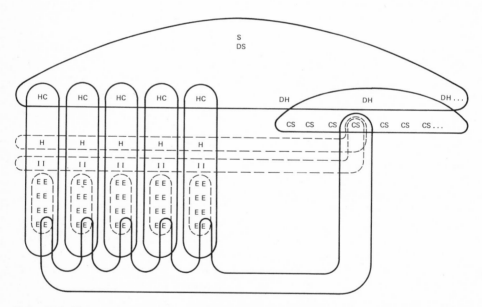

Figure 12-9 Linkage of curriculum specialist to schools (S = superintendent, DS = deputy superintendent, DH = department head, CS = curriculum specialist, HC = head of Complex, H = department chairperson in high school, I = department chairperson in intermediate school, and E = subject matter specialist in elementary school).

policy change were likely to emerge, the head of the Complex might also be present at each meeting. Again, each Complex would select an elementary school principal to serve as a linking-pin member of a districtwide coordinating group. In these coordinating districtwide group meetings, each Complex coordinator usually would be present in addition to the linking pins from each Complex. The heads of the Complexes also might join the meetings when the discussion involves a major policy. The principal of each elementary school would serve, of course, as a linking pin to the grade-level chairpersons to involve them, and through them, the teachers, in any decision affecting the personnel policies concerning teachers. The director of personnel would be responsible for initiating and coordinating the problem solving by the top district group concerning the change in personnel policy for elementary teachers.

If a breakdown occurs in the effective functioning of the proposed structure, the top group shown in Figure 12-9 needs to analyze the causes of the breakdown and to undertake the training and organizational development needed for the structure to be used as intended.

The superintendent of the district in our example faces the same problem of structure as does the principal of a large high school. There are 55 schools in the district. This is far too large a group to engage in productive problem solving. A level between the superintendent and the 55 principals is needed. This level would consist of the heads of the five Complexes. To keep in close contact with the principals, the superintendent should sit in on every second or third meeting of the Complex, being careful not to take over the meeting. This would give him or her the chance to come to know each principal reasonably well. Moreover, as the Complex heads develop effective problem-solving groups in their Complexes, some of the group cohesiveness and goodwill engendered would rub off on the superintendent when that person sits with the groups. The superintendent also could encourage all principals to feel free to come to the superintendent whenever they wish to do so. The superintendent, however, needs to abide by the same general guidelines as were suggested for principals in relation to teachers. The superintendent should listen to problems and act on personal problems; on matters that involve the decisions of others, e.g., complex heads, the superintendent would see that the problem was placed on the proper agenda and all persons and groups who should be involved in the decision would be included.

Functional supervision

High school principals often have had little or no experience in elementary schools. They usually have been vice-principals, heads of departments, coaches, or teachers in high schools. When a high school principal, without elementary school experience, heads a Complex, the elementary school principals in the Complex may feel that the principal lacks the experience to understand their problems. If a superintendent senses this to be the situation, a deputy superintendent can be designated to be responsible for elementary schools to assure that the needs of the elementary schools are understood and acted upon constructively. This deputy superintendent would meet regularly with the eight elementary school principals in each Complex. This arrangement would be a further extension of the matrix structure since each elementary school principal would be linked to the top group of the district both by the head of the Complex and by this deputy superintendent for elementary schools. Here, as elsewhere, System 4 group problem solving should be used to assure that the matrix structure will work well.

If this plan of functional organization is used for the elementary schools, the deputy superintendent should meet regularly also with the 10 intermediate school principals to give them comparable additional linkage to the top group. This additional linkage would not be needed for the high school principals since they, as heads of their Complexes, meet regularly with the superintendent.

The board of education and neighborhood advisory boards

With the increasing interest of neighborhood groups in their schools and in the quality of education being provided to their children, there has come a demand for neighborhood school boards to help provide guidance for the schools in their neighborhoods. If they function properly, these neighborhood or "miniboards" can increase citizen understanding and support of the schools and also help the schools to be more responsive to the goals and aspirations of parents. Many of the attempts to set up these boards, however, have yielded quite unsatisfactory results. Often conflict, bitterness, and sometimes actual disruption of school programs have stemmed from them. Experience appears to indicate that where miniboards do not work well, there is no effective interaction-influence network linking them to the central board.

An important advantage of the Complex form of organization is that its geographical character makes it readily possible to establish a neighborhood school board, or miniboard, in each Complex. In the district that we are using as an example, there would be five miniboards, one for each of the five Complexes.

These miniboards should be advisory to the central board and not have final decision-making authority. Members of the miniboards should live in the neighborhoods served by the Complex and should be both influential in the community and genuinely interested in education. Their terms of office should be long enough to provide continuity: three years, perhaps, with the option of a second, but not a third, term. The terms should be staggered so that there are experienced members on the miniboards at all times.

If miniboards are to be constructive, the principles of structure proposed in

Chapter 10 must be applied. It is absolutely essential that there be an effective multiple-overlapping-group linkage between each miniboard and the central board. There are many alternative ways for doing this. For example, if in a district where there were no more than six miniboards, the head of each could become ex officio members of the central board. This would provide coordinating linkage to the central board. If legal barriers prevent this ex officio linkage, the heads of the miniboards could be invited to sit with the central board and participate in its discussions on an informal basis. If there were more than six miniboards, another level would be required so that the central board would not become too large for effective problem solving.

Linkages through more than one channel help assure that cooperative, constructive problem solving will occur even when one of the channels fails to work well. A second channel of linkage between the miniboards and the central board could occur through the members of the community-relations staff of the district who would provide the staff services to each miniboard. The head of the Complex could appropriately be an ex officio member of each miniboard. The Complex coordinator also could meet regularly with the miniboard as a nonvoting member. In this way, two other channels of linkage would be present. One channel would be through the heads of the Complexes to the top administrative group and the superintendent and through the superintendent to the central board. The other channel would be through the Complex coordinators who would provide a linkage via their department head to the top group and, again, through the superintendent to the central board.

Research in schools supports the proposed structure

The structure proposed in this chapter deviates in several places from that of most schools and school systems. This is to be expected. Research data show that, on the average, schools are about System 2½ in their administration and closer to System 2 than to System 4 in their structure.

A rapidly growing body of research findings, largely doctoral dissertations, shows that System 4 yields better results in schools than do Systems 1, 2, or 3. (*Note:* Bernhardt, 1972; Byrnes, 1973; Carr, 1971; Cullers et al., 1973; Feitler and Blumberg, 1971; Ferris, 1965; Gibson, 1974; Gilbert, 1972; Haynes, 1972; Lepkowski, 1970; Riedel, 1974; Thompson, 1971; Throop, 1972; Wagstaff, 1970.)

Evidence also is becoming available that supports the importance of the face-to-face work group in schools, as elsewhere, as the key building block of organizations. For example, there is a marked relationship between the way teachers view the leadership behavior of their department heads and their perceptions of the leadership behavior of their principals. Teachers' views of their department heads also influence their reaction toward their schools and their own behavior. This is reflected, for example, in teachers' absence. Findings for high schools and intermediate schools show that the more teachers see their department chairpersons as using supportive, System 4 leadership and having high education performance goals, the lower is the teacher absence rate. The leadership behavior of the department heads was measured by asking teachers the extent to which they saw their department chairpersons as:

- friendly and supportive

- displaying confidence and trust in teachers

- being easy to talk to about work-related matters

- seeking and using teachers' ideas

- giving teachers useful information

- knowing the problems teachers face

- interested in teachers' success

- helping teachers with their problems

The teachers whose department heads scored high (greater extent) on these questions were absent significantly less often than were teachers in departments whose department heads scored low (see fig. 12-10). The rank order correlation (rho) by departments is $-.56$. The relationship is negative since the higher the leadership scores are the lower is the absence.

Teachers who see the educational performance goals of their department heads as high or very high are much less likely to be absent than are teachers who feel that their department heads have average or low goals (fig. 12-10). This rank order correlation (rho) by departments is $-.69$.

System 4 is being demonstrated through research to be as effective in schools and school systems as it is in business in achieving excellent performance, low costs, and the constructive resolution of conflict. These research results support the validity of the general principles of System 4 organizational structure presented in Chapter 10 and the proposed application of these principles in the structures described in this chapter.

Keep an eye on organizational structure

It is essential that an organization take a hard and continuing look at its structure to make sure that it is adequate for its current situation. Is there a multiple-overlapping-group structure present at every point where a person, small group, or department needs to interact and cooperate with another person, group, or department? Wherever such structure is missing, there is likely to be a failure in communication, understanding, and coordination. These breakdowns often result in conflicts that are not easily resolved since there is no mechanism for doing so. When there are problems and conflict, it is assumed, many times, that training in interpersonal and human-relations skills

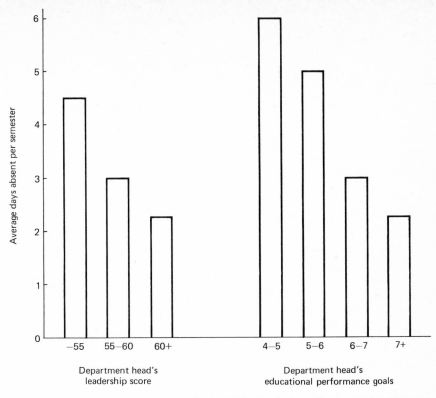

Figure 12-10 *Two factors affecting teachers' absence.*

will correct the difficulty. Unfortunately, when the cause of the breakdown is deficient structure, no amount of training in interpersonal skills will correct the problem. Superintendents of schools cannot engage in productive problem solving with groups of 50 or more principals no matter how skilled the principal is in interpersonal relationships. Enduring improvement will occur only when the real cause, the deficient structure, is corrected.

Sound structure is not enough

Important and necessary as sound structure is, structure alone is not the whole answer. The best structure in the world is no better than the leadership, interaction, and problem-solving processes used by the members of that organization. Moreover, if an organization is to operate at a high level of effectiveness, it is necessary that every group in the organization use System 4 leadership, interaction, and problem-solving skills well. Since groups higher in an organization exert more influence than do groups that are lower, it is particularly important that the top group use System 4 processes skillfully.

13

System 4 structure applied to conflicts in universities

In Chapter 10, we examined the general concepts of the structure of a System 4 interaction-influence network. In this chapter, we will suggest their application to a specific conflict situation—conflict in universities. Although universities are the illustrations, the following discussion is relevant for every kind of major conflict—among nations, between races, between unions and management, in firms, and the like.

Studies, observations, and newspaper reports of conflicts in our universities reveal that prior to sit-ins and other disruptions of various degrees of violence, and even subsequent to them, there was a scarcity of effective face-to-face communications and problem-solving channels between students, faculty, and administration, and, equally serious, within these groups. There was little or no effective interaction-influence network through which a reasonable proportion of disaffected students could make clear to the rest of the university community and its leaders the problems, injustices, and deprivations they felt and what action they believed the university should take. This lack of an effective interaction-influence network also prevented students who disapproved of violent tactics from making their feelings known. It restricted faculty and other members of the university community from making their concerns and problems understood. Little effective face-to-face interaction structure existed (1) for communicating feelings and perceptions, (2) for problem solving to seek and develop satisfactory ways of correcting the unsatisfactory conditions, and (3) for implementing the decisions reached. Few effective mechanisms or channels were available for accelerating acceptable action. Under these circumstances, strong feelings of injustice, deprivation, discouragement, and hostility continued and grew.

These deficiencies in the interaction-influence networks of universities would be no more serious today than they were a decade ago were it not that much more complex and difficult demands are being placed upon them. Many students and faculty members are keenly aware that their right to be involved in decisions affecting them is recognized and accepted by our society. They also are aware that colleges and universities do not provide fully for the realization of this right. This is illustrated by the following communication which appeared in the "Letters to the Editor" page of the student newspaper of a large university:

> We invoke a basic tenet of democratic life, namely that rules, or laws, or "standards" designed to provide for the minimal functioning of a community, shall be made and approved by those affected by them. Therefore, such rules which apply solely to students ought to be made solely by students and such rules which apply to broader segments of the University community ought to be made by a composition of those segments.

Student frustration over being inadequately involved in decisions affecting them would be great even if their major concerns dealt only with academic life and problems, including the steeply rising costs of higher education. Their frustrations, however, are much more broadly based. Pollution and other threats to the environment, corruption in high places, lack of proper regard for civil rights, and inadequate housing are some of the problems they feel must be solved. They think that universities are contributing to society's failure to solve these problems by neglecting to provide appropriate leadership. "Irrelevant" curricula and instruction are, to them, further evidence of the universities' lack of concern.

All these forces cause some students to press vigorously and, at times, irrationally for the action they feel necessary. The interaction-influence networks of our universities all too often have proved to be incapable of dealing constructively with student demands, particularly when vigorously supported by even a minority of faculty members. Major changes obviously are needed in the interaction-influence networks of universities if they are to deal successfully with their serious problems.

Problem solving by the faculty

The existing interaction-influence network of most large universities consists of an administrative structure including the president, vice-president, deans, and department chairpersons. In addition, there is usually a university senate consisting of all faculty or all tenured faculty. This senate is likely to have an executive committee or some similar body.

There generally are several faculty committees both standing and ad hoc to deal with particular problems. These committees vary in effectiveness, but usually they use problem-solving procedures well. Their decisions are generally sound, and the solutions often are innovative. But these committees do not make the final decisions; that function is reserved for the total faculty, either of a particular department, college, or the entire university.

Faculty meetings in universities, like those in public schools, employ parliamentary procedures which structure the meeting into a System 2 win-lose confrontation. The systematic, orderly problem solving done in the small committees does not and cannot occur in the large faculty meeting using *Robert's Rules of Order.* Committee decisions, both those which are innovative and those which are more traditional, come before faculty meetings as reports with recommended actions. After the motion has been made and seconded to accept the report and approve these actions, the win-lose battle typically begins.

With rare exceptions, the more creative and innovative a committee's recommendation is on an academic or a broad societal problem and the more the solution represents an important step forward, the greater is the likelihood that it will be defeated in the win-lose confrontation in faculty meetings. The explanation for this phenomenon is our tendency to resist any change that we have not been involved in planning. The more creative and innovative the solution, the greater the change required; the greater the change, the greater the resistance. Often if the proposed action is an innovative change, a sizable proportion of faculty members reject the decision and are prepared to sabotage it actively or passively. Even persons who vote for a motion feel little or no responsibility for implementing the decision or even abiding by it if the motion is carried.

Student governments are equally unrepresentative and inadequate

The situation is equally unsatisfactory so far as students are concerned. Student governments consist typically of "representatives" elected by undergraduates, graduates, and students in the professional schools. Only a small proportion of the student body votes so that the student government almost always is highly unrepresentative. The deliberative bodies of the student government employ the usual parliamentary procedures, and these decision-making processes work no better for students than for faculty. Moreover, these procedures are just as ineffective with students as with faculty in creating commitment to the decisions reached and a felt responsibility to implement them.

Applying System 4 to the interaction-influence network of universities

The existing interaction-influence networks of large universities, and even of moderate-sized colleges, and their decision-making processes typically are conflict aggravating rather than conflict resolving. Their structures lack the small groups joined together by linking pins and linking groups necessary for creative problem solving and for the development of innovative and acceptable solutions to conflict (chaps. 7–9). These deficiencies make dealing with conflict on academic matters difficult enough, but when universities are compelled to handle highly emotional problems arising from major issues in the larger society, these flaws make the successful resolution of such conflicts next to impossible.

The interaction-influence network of System 4 offers an alternative. It provides a structure and interaction process with a much greater capability for the constructive resolution of conflict. In the following pages, an application of the principles of the System 4 interaction-influence network to the structure of universities will be suggested. The structure of a large department, an entire college, and a whole university faculty will be examined. This will be followed by a consideration of an application of System 4 interaction-influence network principles to the structure of student government and briefly to nonacademic staffs. Finally, the network required for interaction among these various sectors of the university will be considered. Again, it is important to keep in mind that, although the university is used as an example, the basic concepts apply to all conflict situations.

The faculty of most large departments is divided into various fields of specialization with a "subdepartmental" chairperson for each field. In a System 4 interaction-influence network, these subchairpersons would serve as linking pins to link their units to the total department. Figure 13-1 shows the structure of a large department—a psychology department, for example—with such overlapping groups. Each of the specialized groups would consist of all the faculty teaching that subject. In psychology, examples of these specialized groups or fields would include experimental psychology, social psychology, mathematical psychology, and clinical psychology. The top departmental committee would consist of the departmental chairperson, assistant chairperson, and the chairperson of each of the specialized units.

In addition to each of these units, the department should have, as most now have, work groups which cut across fields of specialization to perform essential lateral linkages for the department. One such group, shown in Figure 13-1, deals with the problems of undergraduate instruction. The chairperson of the group is the assistant head of the department. Another work group providing lateral linkage, shown in Figure 13-1, is the committee on graduate instruction for the department. In this case, the chairperson of this work group is the subdepartmental chairperson of the specialized field B unit. This subdepartmental chairperson is serving in two different roles: (1) as head of the specialized field B work group and (2) as head of a cross-specialty work group dealing with problems of graduate instruction. In both roles, that person serves as a linking pin. In the latter case, he or she links the graduate-committee faculty work group to the top work group of the department. This dual role is described more fully in Chapters 10 and 11 discussing cross-function linkages.

There would be need, of course, for other cross-specialty work groups, both continuing and ad hoc, such as the library committee and the building space

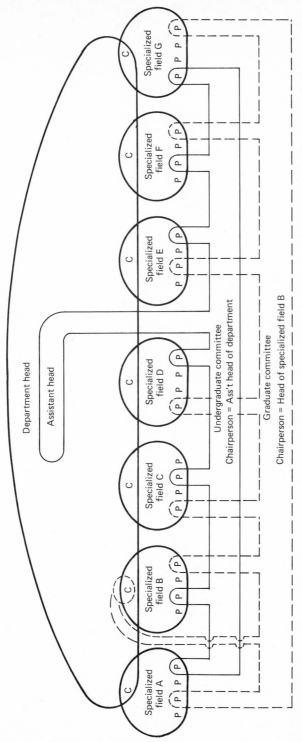

Figure 13-1 Proposed organizational chart, department of psychology (C = heads of subdepartmental specialized fields and P = faculty members of subdepartmental specialized fields).

committee. Each of these should be organized so as to apply appropriately the System 4 principles discussed in Chapters 10 and 11. All these cross-specialty work groups would contribute to the unique capability of the System 4 interaction-influence network to provide efficient lateral coordination for the entire department. They would help strengthen communications within the department and the awareness by its members that they can and do influence important policy and operating decisions. These work groups also would help to increase the identification of department members with the department as a whole.

These cross-specialty work groups would make another valuable contribution in large departments. The contacts and relationships created would facilitate interaction among their members not only on the particular cross-specialty tasks of the committee but also on substantive issues and problems of their discipline. In a supportive System 4 atmosphere, this intellectual interaction on substantive problems among specialists from differing areas within a discipline would contribute to their creativity and intellectual vigor. This is the kind of stimulation which Pelz and Andrews (1966) refer to as "dither." They have found that "dither" contributes to creative research.

The proposed System 4 interaction-influence network for the large department would provide it with the multiple-overlapping-group structure required for innovative problem solving in small groups. Creating the structure required for creative, constructive problem solving does not automatically assure, however, that such processes will be substituted for win-lose confrontations. It will be necessary for the head of the department, subheads, and faculty members to be thoroughly proficient both in innovative group problem solving and in knowing how to substitute this process for win-lose struggles. They need to apply fully the leadership and problem-solving processes discussed in Chapters 6–9.

A suggested interaction-influence network for a large college

The college of literature, science, and the arts of a large university typically includes both undergraduate and graduate instruction. It usually embraces all the sciences, humanities, and languages and generally is the largest college in the university. The same System 4 interaction-influence network principles could be applied to the college as were suggested in the above discussion for a large department. The departments would be the equivalent of the "specialized fields," and the dean of the college would be equivalent to the head of a department.

If the college were very large and had more than 12 departments (it could have easily as many as 25 or more), it would be desirable to add a second level of work groups. The structure would be as shown in Figure 13-2. To keep the structure simple, Figure 13-2 shows only four persons in some departments

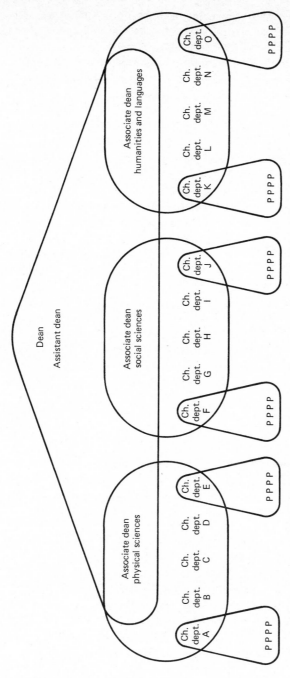

Figure 13-2 *Proposed organizational structure for college of literature, science, and the arts at department-head level and above. Only parts of the departments are shown, and none of the lateral linkage is shown (Ch = chairperson of department, e.g., department A, and P = faculty members of department).*

and omits all the personnel of most departments. Moreover, it does not show any of the committees or groups providing lateral linkage. The top work group would include the dean, an assistant dean for such functional responsibilities as budgets, and two or three associate deans. Each associate dean would head a work group consisting of heads of departments in related disciplines. There might be, for example, an associate dean for the physical and biological sciences, one for the social sciences, and one for the humanities and languages.

Again, there would be many appropriate committees, both standing and ad hoc, providing problem-solving work groups to handle the many tasks and problems of the college, such as those concerned with admissions, language and other requirements, honors programs, and curricular matters. These work groups would provide essential lateral linkages to the structure and would strengthen its overall interaction-influence network capabilities. They also would facilitate substantive interdisciplinary interaction across departments.

The structure of each department would be as suggested above and shown in Figure 13-1. If a department were so small that it did not require subdepartments, it would, of course, have only one level of organization instead of the two shown in Figure 13-1.

In universities which have more than one college of liberal arts, such as one for the physical sciences, one for the social sciences, etc., the same System 4 principles would be applied. The structure of each of these colleges, in most instances, would be similar to the structure shown in Figure 13-2 under an associate dean.

The top structure for a large university

The interaction-influence network for the entire university would be a further extension upward of the kind of structure shown in Figures 13-1 and 13-2. An example of an appropriate structure is shown in Figure 13-3. Again, only portions of the structure are indicated. For example, the associate deans in the medical school and the college of engineering are not shown; most heads of departments are omitted; and no members of the departments appear. The channels of vertical linkage are shown by the multiple-overlapping-group structure with solid lines around the work groups.

There would be, of course, many more work groups than appear in Figure 13-3 which would provide lateral, or diagonal, linkages to handle problems of lateral coordination. The two examples of groups which perform lateral linkage are illustrated in Figure 13-3 by dotted lines. One involves the vice-president for research and the deans of colleges in which research is an important activity. Dean I in Figure 13-3 is dean of the graduate school; dean III is dean of the college of literature, science, and the arts; and dean V is dean of the college of engineering. This work group would be concerned with such problems as establishing universitywide policies and procedures for research activities. Simi-

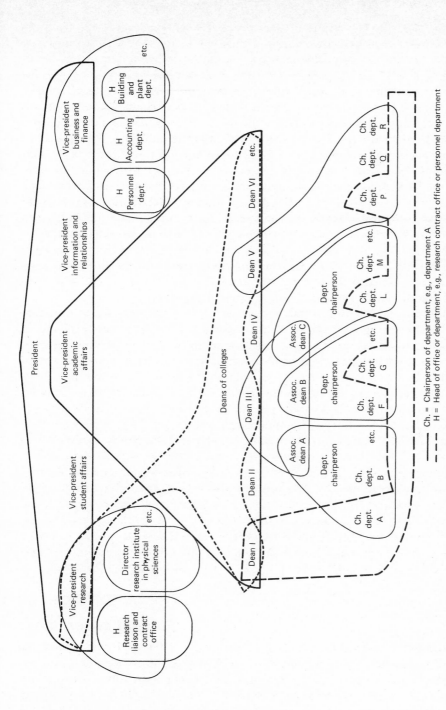

Figure 13-3 *Proposed organizational structure for university at college level and above. Solid lines enclose vertical linking groups; dotted lines enclose groups providing lateral linkage (Ch = chairperson of department, e.g., department A, and H = head of office or department, e.g., research contract or personnel department).*

Ch. = Chairperson of department, e.g., department A

H = Head of office or department, e.g., research contract office or personnel department lar overlapping-work-group structures for lateral coordination would be established between each vice-president and those other persons with whom he or she must deal to handle problems involving lateral coordination.

Another level of lateral-linkage structure is shown in Figure 13-3. This is the work group consisting of dean I and the heads of departments for departments *A, G, L, P,* etc. In this case, dean I is the dean of the graduate school. Typically in large universities this dean has no faculty. The faculties for both graduate and undergraduate instruction are in the relevant colleges. The heads of departments included in this lateral-linkage work group would be those of large departments engaged in substantial amounts of graduate instruction. In addition to the lateral-linkage group shown in Figure 13-3, the graduate dean, dean I, probably would have other similar groups linking small departments or those which have comparable kinds of problems as, for example, those in the biological sciences. For some purposes, dean I might wish to have, also, lateral-linking groups composed of some of the associate deans in the different colleges. Lateral-linkage structures under the chairpersonship of the graduate dean would be concerned with such agenda items as establishing policies related to graduate admission, instruction, and degree requirements.

Lateral-linkage groups, although they strengthen the interaction-influence and problem-solving capabilities of an organization, greatly increase its complexity. For instance, in the example just mentioned, two deans would be involved with each department head in administrative and policy decisions on matters related to graduate instruction. These two deans would be the college dean and the dean of the graduate school. This complex structure handles difficult problems of coordination well so long as the usual vertical-line work groups (e.g., dean V [college of engineering] and his department chairpersons) and the lateral-linkage group (dean I and the department heads linked to dean I shown in fig. 13-3) *both use group problem solving in dealing with their problems.* If either group uses System 2 win-lose confrontation or sends persons to the other group as instructed delegates, the problem solving will break down and coordination will collapse. As long as all the groups involved do problem solving reasonably well, the organization will be able to handle conflicts constructively across vertical lines. When any of the groups fail to carry out problem-solving processes reasonably well, there is an organizational building task to be performed by persons responsible for the effective functioning of that group.

Student government

The proposed structure for student government would apply the same basic concepts of System 4 interaction-influence networks and in a similar manner. This is required to give all students a continuous opportunity to influence decisions affecting them. The structure would consist of multiple-overlapping, face-to-face, problem-solving groups, each small enough for effective decision making, i.e., not more than about 25 to 35 persons.

The organization of these face-to-face groups could be based on the location of student living or on the field of each student's major. For example, in the first two undergraduate years, if the housing arrangements make it possible, the groups could consist of students who live in adjacent units. This grouping would be like the block groups suggested in the next chapter in the discussion of the interaction-influence structure for cities. Each of these groups of 25 to 35 students would be linked to other groups by the chairperson who would be a member also of a second-level group of approximately 20 persons and who would perform the linking-pin role. The chairpersons of these second-level groups would, in turn, be members of a smaller third-level group consisting of about 15 persons. The size of these third-level groups would be determined by the total number of first- and second-year students linked in this manner. Each group at each of the different levels would, of course, elect its own chairperson.

A similar multiple-overlapping-group structure would be used for juniors and seniors but would be based on their field of major. Here, again, first-level groups would not be larger than 25 to 35 persons. The first-level groups would be linked by second- and third-level groups. As a rule, the groups at each higher level would be somewhat smaller than the groups at lower levels.

A corresponding plan of student organization, based on the student's field of specialization, would be used for graduate and professional students.

The head of the third-level groups of each of these three structures (i.e., the freshman-sophomore, the junior-senior, and the graduate-professional) would be members of a top, fourth-level, group. To facilitate coordination at this top level and to decrease the load on any one person, two or even three persons from each of the third-level groups could be members of the top-level group, i.e., the head and one or two other persons. This structure is shown in Figure 13-4. The proposed structure for juniors and seniors and for graduate students is more complex than that for freshmen and sophomores since it provides cross-linkages at every level.

For communication and problem solving by students on matters not involving faculty, there would be cross-linkage groups between the undergraduate majors and the graduate students at both the subdepartment and department levels. This cross-linkage structure at these levels is shown schematically in Figure 13-4. Included also is the cross-linkage structure at the college level.

There also is need for lateral linkages between faculty and students. An example of lateral cross-linking at two levels is shown in Figure 13-5. This is a truncated chart which shows the structure for graduate students in a large department, in this case the same psychology department used in Figure 13-1. The left-hand portion of the chart shows the structure for the departmental faculty and is the same as the comparable part of Figure 13-1. The right-hand portion of Figure 13-5 shows a truncated section of the structure for graduate students at the department and subdepartment (specialized) levels. Down the middle of Figure 13-5 are the cross-linking groups at the subdepartment and department levels.

Figure 13-5 does not show the subdepartment and department structure for

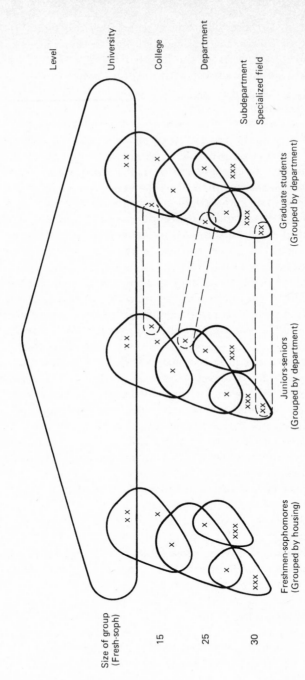

Figure 13-4 Proposed vertical organizational structure for student government. Dotted lines show cross-linkage at each level.

Specialized area faculty-student committee

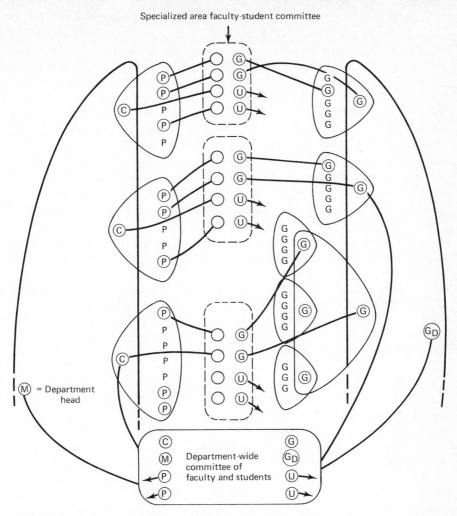

Figure 13-5 *Proposed department organization structure: faculty and graduate students [truncated diagram; C = chairpersons of subdepartmental specialized fields, P = faculty members, G_D = head of departmental graduate-student structure, G = graduate-student linking pin, and U = undergraduate-student (majors) linking pin.]*

juniors and seniors who are majors in that department. This structure would be identical to the structure shown for graduate students and would be linked, as shown in Figure 13-5, to the cross-linkage groups in the middle of the figure. The *U*'s shown in Figure 13-5 are the undergraduate majors who serve as linking pins between the groups of junior and senior majors and the cross-linkage groups at the subdepartment and the department levels.

The same pattern of cross-linkage which exists at the department and subdepartment levels would be replicated at the associate dean level. The linkages at that level would show the same relationships to Figure 13-2 as Figure 13-5 has to Figure 13-1. If, for example, six departments were involved, one possible cross-linkage group would include one undergraduate, one graduate, and two faculty members from each department. This would be a larger group than is usually desirable for efficient problem solving. A smaller cross-linkage group could be created by having the six undergraduates select three of their members for membership in the smaller group, having the graduate students do the same, and having one faculty member from each department a member of that group. If a still smaller cross-linkage group is preferred, the procedure just suggested could be followed to yield a group of the desired size.

At the college level, the same plan of creating cross-linkage groups could be applied. Both the vertical linkage and the horizontal cross-linkage should be done by linking pins who are members of groups of a size appropriate for the needed functions.

At the university level, there would be, as shown in Figure 13-4, a cross-linkage group tying together the three student structures. This top structure for student government, of course, would have many committees and groups each dealing with different problems. The membership of these universitywide groups usually would include persons from all three major student structures and would thereby provide lateral linkages to help achieve universitywide coordination in problem solving. These lateral-linkage groups would strengthen the interaction-influence network of student government.

There also would be, at the university level, the cross-linkage group linking the student and the faculty-administration structures. Four persons would serve as linking pins from the top student structure. Four other members would be linking persons from the universitywide level of the faculty-administration structure.

This top-level cross-linkage structure would create, of course, the numerous ad hoc and standing groups required to deal with the large number of varied problems which every university faces. All these groups at the university level, as well as at lower levels, would provide additional channels of communication and influence which would greatly strengthen the coordination and problem-solving processes of the university.

In creating a plan for cross-linkage at every level in the university, it is not necessary that each of the different interests, e.g., undergraduate students, graduate and professional students, faculty and administration, have equal numbers of linking pins in each group because decision making in each group in a System 4 interaction-influence network is by consensus (chap. 8). However, during the early stages before skill in creative problem solving has been developed and when fear and distrust still prevail, it may be wise to ease tensions and diminish defensive behavior by having a fairly equal balance in the numbers of linking pins in each group who tie to the different sectors of the university. This will make the acquisition of skill in creative problem solving easier and more rapid.

Structure of the nonacademic staff

To enable a System 4 interaction-influence network to be used throughout a university, it would be necessary for the nonacademic staff to be organized and managed in a System 4 manner. The structure for this staff would consist, like the other parts of the university, of multiple overlapping groups, and the same System 4 principles would be used. In organization and operation, the nonacademic departments would apply the principles and procedures discussed in Chapters 6 to 11. Most of the concepts about structure for business organizations discussed in Chapter 11 would be applicable to the nonacademic part of a large university.

There are many places in a large university where efficient coordination is essential between the nonacademic staffs and the academic units. Wherever this cooperation and coordination is needed, an appropriate cross-function linkage should be established. Principles and procedures for establishing cross-function linkages are discussed more fully in Chapter 10 of this volume and at much greater length in Chapter 10 of *The Human Organization* (Likert, 1967).

The total structure proposed for linking all parts of a large university would provide a highly effective interaction-influence network that could resolve problems and achieve cooperative coordination at every point in the university where problems arise and need to be resolved. This interaction-influence network would provide valuable lead time in dealing with problems since it would make each problem visible at an early stage when feelings concerning it are less strong and when creative problem solving to resolve it is much more easily done. Too often, today, problems reach the crisis stage before their existence is recognized and action is taken to solve them.

The interaction-influence networks proposed above for each of the different parts of a large university and for linking these parts together is, of course, only one of many possible structures representing an appropriate application of System 4 principles. Experience with this suggested plan or other appropriate plans would show which works best for a particular kind of university or situation. *Each university should apply the System 4 principles in ways which best fit its own particular circumstances and traditions.*

The capacity to mold one's environment

Attempts in recent years to increase the influence of faculty and students often have had disappointing results. Students have been added to committees, and students and faculty have been added to governing boards, but the structure and decision-making processes of large universities has remained at about a System 2 or 2½ model. Crucial decisions are made in relatively large groups, such as senates or assemblies of 50 to 100 or more persons, where interactions are controlled by *Robert's Rules of Order*. Win-lose confrontation rather than innovative problem solving is the pattern. Members serve as "representatives," not as linking pins, and often strive for influence without responsibility.

The proposed System 4 structure for large universities will provide substantially greater opportunities than now exist for individuals, students, or faculty to exert constructive influence on decisions affecting them. This capacity of the System 4 interaction-influence network to give each person a much greater opportunity for exerting influence occurs because of the linked-group structure and the decision-making processes used. The proposed structure would employ decision making by consensus in all its group problem solving. This would be the case with both the vertical and lateral-linkage groups shown in the figures or discussed previously. When decision making is done in this manner, an individual with an important contribution to make can do so if he or she persists (Moscovici, 1969).

The proposed System 4 structure, consequently, used even with moderate problem-solving and interaction skills, can enable any member or group of members of any of the various components to exert significant influence on decisions, providing, of course, that the action being urged can be supported by sound evidence and proves not seriously incompatible with the needs and desires of most of the other members of the university community. All persons would be able to exert significant influence on the environment in which they live and help to shape it so that it meets the major needs that they and their peers seek to satisfy.

Devoting the effort to a System 4 interaction-influence network

Many persons will question whether the members of a university community would be willing to devote the time to build and use a System 4 structure to improve the problem-solving capabilities of the institution. Two factors are likely to affect the decision: (1) the time and effort required to build and operate a System 4 interaction-influence network in contrast to the time and effort demanded by the existing structure, and (2) the number and seriousness of the problems to be resolved.

Faculty members would need to consider the time they now spend in informal meetings with others in their fields of specialty: the luncheon meetings, the departmental and subdepartmental meetings, and the general faculty meetings. They may well discover that they would spend no more time and perhaps less if a more efficient structure such as the overlapping-group network of System 4 were used.

Similarly deans, vice-presidents, and other administrators might find that the System 4 interaction-influence network would require about the same amount of time as the existing structure, but it would be appreciably more effective in resolving conflicts and yielding efficient administration.

The proposed System 4 structure for student government and student-faculty-administration interaction would take more time than most students now devote. But if students wish to have an influence on decisions affecting their tuition and fees, the curriculum, discipline rules and their administration, and similar matters, they will have to devote more time to student-faculty-administration meetings than is now the case. Among the structures that might be used, the System 4 model would enable every student, not just a vocal few, to be heard and to exert influence. It would yield decisions acceptable to a larger proportion of the students while being satisfactory also to the faculty and administration.

When conflicts become more numerous and bitter among students, faculty, and administration, and especially when the failure to resolve them constructively results in costly consequences, such as violence, the component parts of the university are likely to more willingly take the time to build and use a System 4 structure. The likelihood, consequently, of a university's using a System 4 interaction-influence network is increased by the extent to which the major parts of the university experience painful outcomes from the inability to deal constructively with problems and conflicts.

Coupling responsibility with influence

The present structure and decision-making processes of such organizations as firms, school systems, and universities do not create widespread motivation to accept responsibility for the consequences of decisions nor a commitment to implement them. Many persons who are now striving for more influence do not wish to accept more responsibility. Influence without responsibility, as we observed previously, leads to irresponsible behavior, which no organization can afford.

In a System 4 organization, the bulk of the decision making is done in small, face-to-face groups with the decisions coordinated by linking pins. Extensive research and experience show that decisions reached in such groups create high commitment to each decision among the members of the decision-making group and high motivation to implement those decisions (Cartwright & Zander, 1968; Maier, 1952). As influence is exerted, there is a corresponding degree of felt responsibility. When an organization uses a System 4 interaction-influence network, this coupling of responsibility with influence occurs among its members. Persons in every component of the organization, as, for example, managers, workers, students, teachers, administrators feel this heightened responsibility. Each person is motivated to help implement in a responsible and dependable manner the decisions reached.

14

System 4 structure applied to conflicts in cities

The problems of our inner cities are serious and complex, and the interaction mechanisms to deal with them are inadequate. The kind of interaction-influence network required to provide the most effective communication, problem solving, and action resources is, however, extremely hard to build and put into operation.

Let us take Detroit as an example and describe some of the possible ways in which the basic principles of a System 4 interaction-influence network might be applied if there is motivation to do so. The interaction-influence structure proposed is the kind required to deal with such problems and relationships as those between black and white populations, or between affluent and deprived groups.

A direct application of the interaction-influence network of System 4 would suggest that there be created a formal, effectively functioning, social structure linking all, or virtually all, residents of Detroit or greater Detroit. This should be a multiple-overlapping-group structure similar to that proposed for schools and universities and like those in the business firms, plants, or divisions which use System 4 management.

Many different applications are possible. We will suggest one: a geographical form. A structure based on geography would be supplemented, of course, by all the other linkages which now exist or which might be created. In this respect, the structure would be comparable to the line organization of a firm which is supplemented by cross-function, lateral-linkage groups. The geographically based structure would start with groups of approximately 25 to 35 persons each, who live in adjacent housing units. Insofar as the housing from which a group comes is black, white, other, or integrated, the group itself would reflect this fact in its composition. Each group would select a leader. This person would serve also as the linking pin between this first-level group and the next coordinating level. The basis for this structure already exists in parts of Detroit in the form of "block clubs." Other cities, too, such as New York's West-Side, have block clubs. They appear to serve useful purposes.

At the next (second) level there would be groups of approximately 20 persons, each of whom is the leader of his or her neighborhood group. Each of these groups of 20 leaders would come from adjacent neighborhood groups. Again, each of these groups would select its own leader who usually would perform the normal leadership functions within the group. These elected leaders also would perform the linking function, linking their second-level group to the third level.

This same form of organization would occur at the third level. Here, again, the leaders of each group would serve as linking pins tying their group to the fourth-level group. In a similar manner, the fourth would be tied to the fifth level. At the fourth and fifth levels, the groups would be somewhat smaller, say 15 at the fourth and 12 at the fifth level. These smaller groups at the higher levels would be desirable because of the increasingly complex issues being dealt with and the larger and larger number of persons whose interests and needs are being worked on in the problem-solving activities via the linking process.

Figure 14-1 shows a portion of the organizational structure for this proposed plan of action and the approximate number of persons involved directly or via linking at each level. To keep the figure simple, Figure 14-1 shows only some of the members of the groups at each level. The omitted members and the other omitted groups, however, can be visualized readily at each level. Figure 14-1 can be drawn also in the form of concentric groups with the fifth group in the center. This form of chart appears in Chapter 10, Figure 10-2.

Only one person is shown as performing the linking-pin role for each group. When the problems being dealt with involve strong feelings and widely different points of view, it may be advantageous, as was mentioned previously, to have two members of each group, rather than only one, serve as linking pins between their group and the coordinating group at the next level. A second person from a group can help greatly when a member is endeavoring to express clearly and adequately a point of view important to his or her own group but not understood or accepted by the members of the other group. If the operating experience and the applied research dealing with the proposed structure were to indicate the need for two persons or other modified forms of linking, these should be introduced. Such a development, of course, would increase either the size of the linking groups or their number at a particular level or both. This, in turn, might make it necessary to have six rather than five levels in order to include in the interaction-influence network virtually all adult persons living in a big city like Detroit.

As was mentioned, the first level would consist of groups of people living in the same block or apartment house. The second level would consist of neighborhood groups. The third and higher levels would coordinate larger geographical areas of Detroit. Each level, consequently, *would have the membership needed to speak for the people of its own locality, to enable them to express their views, and to decide on any action that they feel is needed.* Insofar as these block

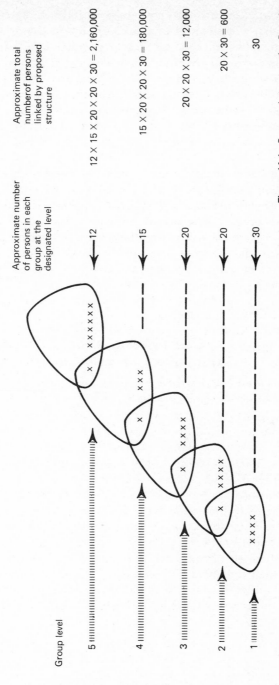

Group level

Approximate number of persons in each group at the designated level

12

15

20

20

30

Approximate total number of persons linked by proposed structure

$12 \times 15 \times 20 \times 20 \times 30 = 2{,}160{,}000$

$15 \times 20 \times 20 \times 30 = 180{,}000$

$20 \times 20 \times 30 = 12{,}000$

$20 \times 30 = 600$

30

Figure 14-1 *Proposed structure for Detroit.*

groups, neighborhood groups, or larger regions have the financial and other resources required to implement any decision which they reach and which affects only them, they can take the action decided upon. If they lack the resources, the other groups which link to the group or groups controlling the needed resources would have to be involved. Similarly, any decision affecting other groups than those who had participated in making it, either directly or via a linking structure, should not be implemented until all affected had voiced their views in the decision via the linking structure. Decisions for the city as a whole would be made by the top level which links the decision making for the entire city.

If the same problem were found to exist in several different blocks or neighborhoods which are not geographically adjacent, effective communication and problem solving would be facilitated by creating a lateral-linkage group. This group would consist of one or more persons from each block or neighborhood where the problem existed linking that group to the lateral-linkage group formed to deal with the problem. If the problem were especially difficult and emotion-laden, two or even three persons from each group would serve as linking pins.

Use existing structures to supplement and strengthen the geographic structure

The proposed neighborhood structure and lateral structures would supplement many of the present organizational ties that now link one sector of Detroit to another. These existing institutions include labor unions, political parties, religious institutions, trade and professional associations, and voluntary organizations such as the League of Women Voters.[1]

To cope with serious problems, however, many more linkages are needed both to tie together the black and white sectors of Detroit as well as to strengthen the linkages within each sector. All the existing organizational structures within each sector and between them need to be continued, but they must be strengthened or supplemented at every point where there is a gap in the interaction-influence network. These existing organizations need to be used fully since their channels of communication and influence and the confidence and trust among their members would both supplement the proposed structure and greatly strengthen it. They provide many different channels through which communications can flow easily and without distortion. This increases the likelihood that information would be accurate, that serious problems would be

---

[1]Studies show that about 60 percent of the residents of Detroit belong to one or more such groups ("*A Social Profile of Detroit: 1952,* a report of the Detroit Area Study of The University of Michigan," Ann Arbor, 1952).

recognized in their early stages, and that constructive decision making would be initiated promptly and focused sharply on the resolution of these problems. Alternative channels of interaction, especially in emotionally charged situations, increase the likelihood of finding a linkage where the prospects are particularly favorable for creative problem solving leading to a satisfactory solution. Such a linkage is one where the confidence and trust levels are relatively high, where communication can be candid, and where the capacity to exert influence is high.

Maintain balance in the strength among parts of the interaction-influence networks

The capacity of an interaction-influence network to deal constructively with serious conflicts is limited by the strength of its weakest linkage. Under stress, any interaction-influence network structure is likely to fail at this weak linkage, its most vulnerable point.

In most urban areas, such as Detroit, the interaction-influence networks *within* both the black community and the white community are seriously deficient. Each of these sectors is not linked internally by a strong and effective interaction-influence network. Each is fractionated or splintered into subsectors. Usually communication between these subsectors is poor, and there is little if any structure for communication and joint problem solving.

Given these conditions, any strengthening of the interaction-influence network *between* the black and white communities would be likely to worsen the relationships among subsectors within each. For example, suppose that a major effort were undertaken to strengthen the interaction-influence network linking the white and black sectors and that the effort were to succeed. If an attempt were made to use this strengthened interaction-influence network to deal with a difficult conflict, the probabilities are that it would work well and that an innovative solution to the conflict would be likely to emerge. But the probabilities are also high that some parts of the black sector or the white sector or both would reject all or parts of this innovative solution. This would occur because of the poor linkage *within* the black or white sectors or both. This poor linkage could be due to a lack of linking pins and linking groups or because of a weak and poorly developed network. All those persons who were *not* involved via an adequate linking structure in arriving at the final solution would be apt to reject the solution reached. They also would feel increased hostility toward those persons in their sector who, as they see it, are endeavoring to impose the solution on them.

This kind of breakdown in the interaction-influence networks *within* the black and white communities would prevent the interaction-influence network *between* the two communities from performing effectively in resolving conflicts.

It is essential, consequently, in building interaction-influence networks to deal with conflicts, to develop highly effective interaction-influence networks *within* each party to the conflict as well as *between* the parties.

Use training to make
proposed structures effective

Adequate training of group members would be required if the proposed neighborhood and other structures are to perform as intended. This training would be particularly important for members of groups at the third, fourth, and fifth levels since each of these groups would be struggling with the many difficult, complex problems passed to them from lower levels. In addition, an important part of the responsibilities of the third, fourth, and fifth levels is to help build the structure under them into a highly effective decision-making and action system (i.e., a strong interaction-influence network). They would be engaged in plans and efforts to help build strong and effective groups at the first and second levels, including the coaching and training of the leaders at these levels.

Fortunately, Detroit, like other urban areas, has large resources of trained personnel in the training departments of business, religious, and governmental agencies. These persons could be used to train group leaders at the third, fourth, and fifth levels. They also could train other persons, such as teachers in neighborhood schools, who could, in turn, train first- and second-level leaders. The training and experience possessed by members of existing organizations would, of course, contribute also to the effective functioning of the proposed neighborhood organization. In turn, the training given to the leaders and members of the neighborhood groups would assist existing organizations to perform better.

At all levels above the first, i.e., at the block, neighborhood, regional, and entire metropolitan area levels, special groups or committees would need to be established, usually with about equal numbers of blacks and whites, to cope with particular problems of a geographical nature or such functional problems as employment, housing, and education. These groups working on designated problems are more likely to establish better decision-making processes and to solve their problems successfully if coaching is available to them when they wish it. Chapters 6 to 9 describe the leadership and problem-solving processes available and suggest how this coaching and training can be done.

The proposed interaction-influence network, in addition to yielding creative solutions, would provide another valuable outcome. Creative problem solving at every level, especially for the inner city and even for the entire metropolitan area, is very likely to reveal that some of the most serious problems require far greater financial and other resources than are now available. The interaction processes would inform and educate citizens concerning each problem and its solution, thereby *mobilizing substantial political support* for the action needed on each solution by local, state, and federal bodies. Moreover, part of the problem solving could be devoted to how best to mobilize this political action to obtain the needed resources.

Strengthening existing interaction-influence networks in cities

Building a System 4 interaction-influence network which includes all, or virtually all, adults in a large city is obviously a tremendous task. Unless a city is faced with very serious conflicts and problems, there is little likelihood of a willingness to devote the effort required to build such an interaction-influence network. Knowledge of the general character of potential System 4 interaction-influence networks for a metropolitan area, nevertheless, can be of great value.

As mentioned previously, every city has many groups and organizations providing to some extent an interaction-influence network linking, at least partially, the citizens of that city. This existing interaction-influence network, inadequate as it may be at present, can be strengthened, often with relatively little work. Efforts to strengthen this existing interaction-influence network are most efficient, however, when there is a clear target toward which to aim. The System 4 model provides this target. Any group of citizens can use this strategy to strengthen the capacity of the interaction-influence network of their city to resolve serious problems and conflicts.

This strategy often can be an important place to start in efforts to resolve a conflict in other kinds of situations as well. In conflicts such as those occurring within universities, firms, school systems, and hospitals, between unions and management, and among nations, the interaction-influence structure characteristically displays serious gaps when compared with the System 4 model. If efforts to correct these deficiencies in the interaction-influence structure were among the first activities undertaken in dealing with a conflict, progress in solving it usually would proceed faster and more smoothly than is now the case.

15

Power, influence, and motivation in conflict management

Power is viewed as the capacity to influence behavior. This chapter uses a relatively simple conceptual model of power to examine the motivational forces that different management and social systems can create for resolving conflict.

In win-lose approaches to resolving conflict, each party to the dispute seeks to force acceptance of its preferred solution upon the other. To attain its ends, each party often tries to mobilize and use some form of power which the opposing party perceives as having harmful effects for it. Strikes, work stoppages, lockouts or layoffs, firings, worker sabotage, and burning and looting in central cities are illustrations. The use of this kind of power creates resentful, fearful, and unfavorable attitudes in the injured party. It is negative power (P−).

In win-win approaches to resolving conflict, each party to the dispute tries to understand the viewpoints and needs of the other, is willing to go more than half way in meeting those needs, and tries to use its power and influence to resolve the conflict in ways that will be beneficial rather than damaging to either party. The use of this kind of power creates favorable attitudes. It is positive power (P+).

Some kinds of power can evoke either favorable or unfavorable attitudes depending on how the power is used. Economic power is an example. When used in a sensitive and supportive manner, this power can be positive power. When used in ego-deflating or threatening ways, this power can be negative power.

The capacity of one party to influence the other party in a win-lose conflict depends upon the magnitude of the motivational forces that can be mobilized. Whenever the first party uses P−, the magnitude of the motivational forces which the first party has available to influence the second party is reduced by the degree of the unfavorableness of the attitudes. The unfavorable attitudes operate via feedback loops to decrease the amount of motivational forces which the first party can marshal.

Exactly the opposite, of course, occurs when P+ is used. With P+ the attitudes via feedback loops reinforce the amount of motivational forces available.

French and Raven's bases of social power

Useful insights are obtained when the bases of social power proposed by French and Raven (Cartwright, 1959) are analyzed by means of P+ and P−. French and Raven (Cartwright & Zander, 1968) state that "there are undoubtedly many possible bases of power which may be distinguished. We shall here define five which seem especially common and important. These five bases of O's[1] power are: (a) reward power, based on R's perception that O has the ability to mediate rewards for him; (b) coercive power, based on R's perception that O has the ability to mediate punishments for him; (c) legitimate power, based on the perception by R that O has a legitimate right to prescribe behavior for him; (d) referent power, based on R's identification with O; (e) expert power, based on the perception that O has some special knowledge or expertness" (pp. 262–63).

French and Raven's discussion of "reward power" reveals that their definition of reward power is limited to the use of P+ only. They do not include in reward power any rewards which are given in a condescending, manipulating, or other ego-deflating manner. Their definition states: "The utilization of actual rewards—by O (the rewarder) will tend over time to increase the attraction of R (the person receiving the reward) toward O and therefore the referent power of O over R" (Cartwright & Zander, 1968, p. 263). If their definition were to be broadened to include rewards which are ego deflating, then reward power, in addition to being P+, would be P− to the extent it is ego deflating.

Coercive power is, of course, P−.

Legitimate power usually will be P+ since, by French and Raven's definition, it involves power "which stems from internalized values in R [the person or target being influenced] which dictate that O [the person exercising the power] has a legitimate right to influence R and that R has an obligation to accept this influence" (Cartwright and Zander, 1968, p. 265). French and Raven point out, however, that the target of influence (R) may not always accept as legitimate the attempt of O to exert influence. In such situations, the attempt to use legitimate power would likely be viewed by the target of the influence attempt as ego deflating and hence be P− in character.

Legitimate power, consequently, usually will involve the use of P+, but at times it can be P− in character. The latter is especially apt to occur in situations in which values are changing; what the influencer sees as legitimate and P+ in

---

[1]French and Raven use O to refer to the person who exercises the power and P to refer to the person upon whom the power is exerted. R is used here instead of P to avoid confusion with P+ and P−.

character, the target of influence rejects as no longer being legitimate, and hence the power is P− in character. The target's rejection of the influence attempt as not being legitimate is apt to be accompanied by strong negative feelings since any change in values is likely to have been accompanied by appreciable conflict and emotional involvement. The role of women as political candidates for high office or as leaders in prestigious professions, or the role of university students in policy decisions concerning their education, are examples of changing values which are differentially influencing the perceptions of what is legitimate.

Concerning expert power, French and Raven (Cartwright & Zander, 1968) observe: "The strength of the expert power of O/R [i.e., of the influencer over the target] varies with the extent of the knowledge or perception which R attributes to O within a given area (p. 267)." As long as the target (R) seeks the influence of the influencer (O) because of the latter's greater knowledge, the power is clearly P+ in character. If, however, the influencer attempts to superimpose the influencer's expertise on the target in order to exert influence, then the influence effort is likely to be resented and the power will be P−.

Referent power is sometimes called *attraction power*. French and Raven state: "It has been demonstrated that the power which we designate as referent power is especially great when R [the target] is attracted to O [the person exerting the influence] . . . the greater the attraction, the greater the identification, and, consequently, the greater the referent power" (p. 267). Since referent power relies on attraction and identification, it clearly is P+ in character.

In addition to these five bases of social power, Raven (1965; Collins & Raven, 1969) has proposed a sixth: informational power. Raven points out that informational power is independent of the source. "It is the content of the communication that is important, not the nature of the influencing agent (p. 166)." Usually informational power will be P+ in character, but when the information is imposed in an ego-deflating manner, it, of course, would be P−.

The bases of power described by French and Raven display a significant pattern. Each source of power, typically, is stated in terms of person-to-person interaction. Referent power conceptually includes the possibility of group interaction but is not so stated. When the basis of power is restricted to person-to-person interaction, no use is made of a source of substantial power, namely, that created by group decision making.

Although expert power can exert substantial influence, Lewin demonstrated in a series of brilliant experiments that forces can be created by group decision which exert much greater influence. As Cartwright (1951) states in his paper, quoted in Chapter 5, when "the group as a whole made a decision to have its members change their behavior, [this] was from two to ten times as effective in producing actual change as was a lecture presenting exhortation to change" (p. 385). The lectures in these experiments were given by recognized experts and sought to make the maximum use of expert power. But as Cartwright (1951) observes, "It is clear that by introducing group forces into the situation, a whole new level of influence has been achieved" (p. 385).

This "whole new level of influence" makes use of another kind of power quite different from P+ and P−. It derives its strength from the desire to achieve and maintain a sense of personal worth and importance. This motive source creates forces which cause an individual (1) to seek membership in groups whose values are consistent with his or her own and (2) to strive to be valued by such groups. The latter, (2), in turn, creates strong motivational forces within individuals to engage in behavior directed toward achieving the goals of the group which they, as members, have helped establish, since the group values this behavior. This kind of motivational power is based on group problem solving and goal setting and will be called *group power*. Since the behavior involved is accompanied by favorable attitudes, it is + in character, and hence it will be called *positive group power,* GP+.

With GP+, each person can influence the other because they are members of the same group. The capacity of each person to influence the other may not be of identical magnitude, but it is nevertheless substantial. This kind of power is reciprocal or mutual in character. It is reciprocal in the sense that it gives each person the means of influencing the other. It is mutual in that both parties can make use of it, although not necessarily to the same extent.

The findings from the research on control and influence help clarify the nature of positive group power, GP+. Georgopoulos, Seashore, and Tannenbaum, using anonymous paper-and-pencil questionnaires, asked the following question of nonsupervisory employees in a large service organization which operates nationally (Georgopoulos & Tannenbaum, 1957, cited in Likert, 1961):

> "In general, how much say or influence do you feel each of the following groups has on what goes on in your department?" The choices were, "Little or no influence," "Some," "Quite a bit," "A great deal of influence," "A very great deal of influence," and the question was asked with regard to: "Higher management of company," "The top management in your plant (city)," "Your department manager," "The men in your department." (p. 131)

These questions were asked of the personnel in 31 geographically separated departments varying in size from 15 to over 50 employees. Essentially the same operations are performed in each department and with essentially the same kinds of equipment. Extensive and excellent productivity and cost figures are available continuously.

The results from the above questions were computed separately for each department. They were then combined for the 10 departments (one-third of all) which were highest in productivity. Corresponding computations were made for the one-third of all departments which were lowest in productivity. These data are shown by the solid lines in Figure 15-1.

The broken lines in Figure 15-1 reflect the amount of influence which the employees want each of the different hierarchical levels to exercise. These data were obtained by asking the above question in the same ways as described but with the words *"should have"* substituted for *"has."*

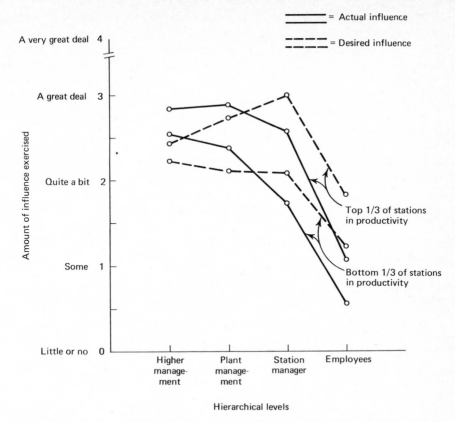

Figure 15-1 *Relation of station productivity to average amount of influence actually exercised by various hierarchical levels and to average amount of desired influence (as seen by nonsupervisory employees).*

The same questions asked of the employees also were asked of the department managers, and the same general pattern of results was obtained. The differences were, however, somewhat less.

An examination of the data shown by the solid lines in Figure 15-1 reveals some very important results. The employees in the top one-third of the departments in productivity see *all* levels in the hierarchy exercising *more* influence as to what goes on in their departments than do the employees in the departments low in productivity. The differences are greatest at the level of the department manager and at the level of the employees themselves.

These data raise serious questions about widely prevalent concepts. The prevailing assumptions are that in a company or plant or among nations there is only so much influence (or authority or sovereignty) which can be exercised. Consequently, the view is widely held that if subordinates are permitted to exercise more influence as to what goes on in an organization the superiors have correspondingly less, or if one nation gains influence, the others have less.

The pie, so to speak, is thought to be just so big; and if some are given more, others must have less.

The data in Figure 15-1 show that this is an erroneous concept. The employees in the more-productive departments see *both themselves and their managers* as having more influence than do employees in the low-producing departments. The "influence pie" is actually seen as being bigger in the high-performing departments than in the low. The results from the analysis of data obtained from these managers show that the managers themselves share this same point of view.

Evidently the managers in the high-producing departments achieve the capacity to exercise more influence on the activity of their departments than do the managers in the low-producing departments. They do this by using a different kind of management system from the system used by the low-producing managers. This better management system, System 4T, while giving the high-producing managers more influence also gives their employees more influence. These managers achieve more capacity to exercise influence by creating a situation in which greater amounts of influence are exerted. But as part of this process, they also *share* more influence with their employees. The high-performing, System 4 managers actually have increased the size of the "influence pie" by means of the leadership processes which they use. They listen more to their employees, are more interested in their ideas, have more confidence and trust in them, accept more influence from them, and make more use of group problem solving. In turn, their employees accept more influence and have greater group loyalty, more favorable attitudes, and greater capacity to influence each other than do the low-producing departments. GP+ is present to a much greater extent in the departments with System 4T managers than in the other departments. Other studies confirm these findings (Cooper & Wood, 1974; Tannenbaum, 1968).

Ecological control

Cartwright and Zander (1968) have added another source of influence: ecological control. As will be recognized from the following description by them, ecological control is an application of the authority of the situation or situational requirements:

> The methods of influence considered thus far involve some direct interaction between O and R. In one way or another O acts directly on R in order to bring about a desired change in R, whether by administering rewards and punishments, by persuasion, or by exploiting R's readiness to be influenced by O. But there is another, more indirect, method of influence. This method relies on the fact that the beliefs, attitudes, values, and behavior of a person are determined in large measure by his immediate social and physical environment. It is possible, then, for a person O who wants to bring about a particular change in R to do so

by taking actions that have effects not directly on R but upon his environment. If O has the ability to control critical aspects of R's environment, we say that O has *ecological control* over R. When O attempts to influence R by means of ecological control, he takes some action which he believes will modify R's social or physical environment in such a way that the new environment will bring about the desired change in R. Since this method of influence can be used without the knowledge or consent of those affected, it is sometimes labeled as "manipulation."

Influence by ecological control can be observed in virtually every kind of social setting. The teacher exerts such influence in forming work groups, designing projects, and making seating assignments. If, for example, she wants to curb a pupil's whispering in class, she may assign him a seat where he is surrounded by well-behaved and orderly children. Parents use their ability to control the environments of their children in a variety of ways in order to shape their interests and values. The manager of a research department who wishes to heighten the creativity of his scientists may periodically reorganize his research teams in the hopes that each scientist, by being exposed to a variety of viewpoints, will consider a broader range of approaches in working on any particular problem. And a therapist in charge of groups of disturbed children may use findings—such as those reported by Gump and Sutton-Smith that different types of games activate different psychodynamic processes in the participants—to design a therapeutic program of recreational activities.

Research in group dynamics has made it clear that many of the beliefs, attitudes, values, and behaviors of an individual are fundamentally shaped by the groups he belongs to. Cartwright, in a discussion of the implications of this research for those who want to bring about change in individuals, has made the following observation (Cartwright, 1951, p. 387):

> To change the behavior of individuals it may be necessary to change the standards of the group, its style of leadership, its emotional atmosphere, or its stratification into cliques and hierarchies. Even though the goal may be to change the behavior of *individuals,* the target of change becomes the group.

We see, then, that anyone who can significantly affect the critical properties of groups has ecological control over its members. And if he has a correct understanding of how these properties determine the states of a particular member R, he can use his ecological control to bring about desired changes in R. (p. 222)

Varieties of social power

We are now in a position to enlarge our conceptual model concerning the motivational forces being used as sources of social power. P+ and P− can be viewed as forms of *direct* power. P+ is *direct reinforced power* since the favorable attitudes accompanying the use of the power strengthens the motivational forces present.

P−, on the other hand, is *direct diminished power* since the unfavorable attitudes established when it is used create antagonistic forces which decrease the strength of the available motivation. If direct diminished power is to continue to exert a force upon the target of change (R), two conditions are necessary:

1. Observability, the person seeking to exert influence (O) must be able to know whether the target of change (R) is conforming.

2. R is unable to leave the field of O's influence; i.e., R cannot escape.

In addition to these forms of direct power there are also forms of *indirect power*. Ecological control is an indirect method of influence achieved by changing the physical or social environment of the target of change (R). In the examples cited in the discussion of ecological control, two different kinds of indirect power are used: *indirect hierarchical power* and *indirect group power*.

Indirect hierarchical power involves the use by the person exerting influence of existing social environments or of social environments which the person creates and which are largely controlled by that person. When a teacher seeks to curb a pupil's whispering by placing the pupil among a group of well-behaved youngsters, the teacher is making use of an existing social environment. A research manager who seeks to stimulate creativity in a research team by reorganizing it so that the scientists are exposed to different points of view is making use of a social environment which the manager has created for this purpose. In both instances indirect hierarchical power is being used.

Indirect hierarchical power, like direct power, can be either + or −. When indirect hierarchical power functions in such a way that it is reinforced by favorable attitudes, it is positive indirect power, IP+. When it is diminished by unfavorable attitudes, it is negative indirect power, IP−. The latter is likely to occur when the target of influence views the experience as ego deflating.

When the attempt to exert power on individuals is done by producing changes in the group of which they are members, indirect group power is being used. This occurs when the target of change is the group as is mentioned in the quotation from Cartwright above.

When the group is the target of change, indirect hierarchical power may at times be used to change the group. When this occurs, the power, of course, can be + or − in character. On the other hand, when the attempt to change the group involves group problem solving and uses the kind of System 4 leadership described in previous chapters, the motivational forces created are accompanied by favorable attitudes. This kind of group power, whether it is indirect or not, is, consequently, always positive, GP+.

Group power, GP+, differs in the following fundamental respects from indirect hierarchical power, both reinforced, IP+, and diminished, IP−:

1. IP+ and IP− rely on hierarchical authority. Generally those persons seeking to use IP+ or IP− prefer more rather than less authority.

2. GP+, on the other hand, avoids the use of authority and seeks to minimize the influence of status (see, e.g., "Deemphasizing Status" in Chapter 9).

3. With IP+ and IP− the person seeking to exert influence does not permit himself or herself to be influenced. The teacher does not expose himself or herself to change when the disobedient child is placed among well-behaved children.

4. With GP+, there is a mutual desire to exert and experience reciprocal influence. There is no avoidance of being exposed to influence. Instead of an influencer (O) seeking to exert power over the target of change (R), there are many O's and many R's exerting mutual influence on one another through group problem solving. O's are influencing other O's as well as R's, and R's are influencing both O's and other R's.

5. GP+ creates relatively strong favorable attitudes among all the persons involved.

6. With IP+, the attitudes are favorable but usually less so than with GP+. With IP−, the attitudes are, of course, unfavorable.

7. GP+ can, and usually does, exert appreciably more motivational power than IP+ or IP−. Each person is *both* a source of influence and a recipient of influence, although the relative amounts of each usually vary from person to person. This reciprocal influence is achieved by means of group decisions which Lewin has shown are 2 to 10 times more effective in producing changes in behavior than is expert power (Cartwright, 1951).

The preceding material provides a framework for analyzing the comparative advantages of System 4, in comparison with other systems, for mobilizing positive, cooperative motivational forces in a conflict situation. The capacity of a system to mobilize high levels of cooperative motivation determines the extent to which that social system can resolve conflicts constructively.

An increase in GP+ benefits all

Group power reinforced by favorable attitudes, GP+, differs in an extremely important manner from the two kinds of direct power, reinforced direct (P+) and diminished direct (P−), as far as their capacity to resolve conflicts is concerned. *An increase in GP+ does not benefit one party at the expense of the others.* Any increase in GP+ in the bridging interaction-influence network between conflicting parties, or within any linking group, benefits all parties to the conflict. Neither party need fear any increase in strength of GP+ as a threat to it.

This, however, is not the case with P+ and P−. In a particular disagreement or conflict, each party, typically, has given amounts of P+ and P−. At times, there are steps which a party can take to increase the amounts of P+ or P− which it has at its disposal, such as steps to obtain allies or to increase its liquid economic strength by means of loans. Any increase in P+ or P− by one party changes the balance of power and is a real threat to the other party or parties as long as win-lose confrontation is the method for resolving the conflict. Such an increase strengthens one party's position in its conflict with the other and puts the latter in a relatively weaker position.

The party whose position is weakened is likely to do all that it can to prevent the other party from increasing the amount of P+ and P− at its disposal and is distressed if any increase occurs. In contrast, since all parties in a conflict benefit from any increase in GP+, regardless of who initiates the increase, all of them as a rule are willing to cooperate in enlarging its magnitude. *The steps involved in increasing GP+ can become, in many conflict situations, the beginning of cooperative win-win problem solving leading to the development of a mutually acceptable solution.*

There is another important respect in which the reinforced power created by group problem solving, GP+, differs from the direct power reinforced by favorable attitudes, P+, and the direct power diminished by unfavorable attitudinal feedback, P−. Usually there are practical limits in any conflict situation on the extent to which either party can increase the amount of P+ or P− which it has at its disposal. This generally is the case unless allies are obtained who have additional amounts of P+ or P− and make this power available to the conflicting parties. The situation is entirely different, however, for GP+. In a conflict situation, the magnitude of GP+ becomes steadily greater as a System 4 interaction-influence network is built and as it is made more synergistic. This increase in the strength of GP+ in any conflict situation can be very sizable and can make available powerful motivational forces oriented to resolving the conflict constructively. Either party, or both parties, can take steps to increase substantially the magnitude of this power. As a rule, the *stronger party has a much greater opportunity for taking the initiative in increasing GP+*. The stronger party also is much more able than is the weaker party to determine the extent to which GP+ is used in contrast to P− or P+.

With indirect hierarchical power, both IP+ and IP−, the situation varies concerning the extent to which the amount of power is fixed or can be increased. When the authority figure seeks to apply IP by making use of an existing social environment, e.g., the teacher placing the whisperer among well-behaved pupils, little or no increase in power occurs. Effective use is made of the potential power offered by the existing social environments, but there is no change in the level of this potential power.

On the other hand, when the authority figure seeks to increase the amount of IP by altering the social environment or creating a new one, either of two events can happen:

1. The authority figure can use direct hierarchical authority to create the social environment sought. This usually involves his or her using P+ or P−, and the person's behavior is essentially System 1, 2, or 3 in character. In this process, the authority figure is not exposed to any influence to change and does not change.

2. The authority figure can start interacting with the group to achieve the desired changes in the social environment, such as the changes suggested above by Cartwright—"change the standards of the group, its leadership, its emotional atmosphere or its stratification into cliques and hierarchies."

As this interaction progresses, if the authority figure continues to use System 1 or 2 leadership, the situation will be essentially the same as 1 above. If, however, in response to the interactions the authority figure shifts to System 4 leadership, the situation becomes entirely different. As soon as this occurs, the authority figure is exposed to influence by the group and is likely to change as that person seeks to change the group. In this interaction, the authority figure is creating essentially a System 4 interaction-influence network and increasingly making it more synergistic.

For all practical purposes, the person has shifted from seeking to use IP and a win-lose strategy to actually using GP+ and a win-win approach. Under these conditions, the influence being exerted is likely to become increasingly GP+ in nature and to display the properties of GP+. Important among these properties is the capacity to increase substantially the amount of power being exerted as the network becomes more and more a System 4T interaction-influence network.

Cooperation versus competition

Cooperation and competition can be used to illustrate the use of P+, P−, and GP+ in evaluating alternate strategies for resolving conflict. Deutsch (Cartwright & Zander, 1968) summarizes his research findings by stating that:

> Greater group or organizational productivity may be expected when the members or subunits are cooperative [P+] rather than competitive [P−] in their interrelationships. The communication of ideas, coordination of efforts, friendliness, and pride in one's group which are basic to group harmony and effectiveness appear to be disrupted when members see themselves to be competing for mutually exclusive goals [P−]. Further, there is some indication that competitiveness [P−] produces greater personal insecurity through expectations of hostility from others than does cooperation. (p. 482)

Cartwright and Zander (1968) observe that "subsequent research [to Deutsch's], conducted in a variety of settings by Thomas (1957), Raven and Eachus (1963), Myers (1962), Julian, Bishop, and Fiedler (1966), and Crombag (1966), lends additional support . . ." (p. 414) to Deutsch's theory and conclusions.

In an important and excellent book on resolving conflict, Deutsch (1973) discusses fully cooperation and competition and their outcomes as well as other aspects of coping constructively with conflict.

A study of the management and performance of the sales offices of a large company which operates nationally provides additional evidence concerning the relative effectiveness of cooperation in comparison with competition (Likert, 1967):

> Another widespread practice among sales managers is to seek to reinforce the motivational forces from the economic needs by adding to them those forces which status and recognition can create. Contests and similar competitive proce-

dures are used in an attempt to capitalize on each salesman's drive for a sense of personal worth. The data from these 40 sales offices, as well as results from other studies (Seashore, 1963), demonstrate that this use of the drive can and often does yield high levels of motivation and quite good sales productivity but does not yield the highest levels of motivation or sales performance. There are serious "side effects" from this use of one of man's most powerful drives which are costly to the organization in its efforts to realize its objectives.

These adverse side effects are the motivational forces created among the salesmen in an office to engage in behavior which will help only themselves and to avoid helping those with whom they are competing. Forces are created, for example, against sharing new information with the other salesmen, against telling them of better appeals, better answers to objections, better sales strategies, new markets, etc. These motivational forces also act to restrain each salesman in other ways. If he sees one of his office mates wasting time with "busy work," he is delighted. He does *not* encourage him to get out and make the calls that yield sales. Similarly, neither he nor his fellow worker feels any motivation to help the other on a tough sales problem or to ask for help. Competitive procedures pit salesman against salesman and reward each economically and with status for keeping what he knows to himself.

Although these negative forces arising from competition often may have their full impact tempered, because most members of an organization like to receive warm, friendly, supportive reactions from their colleagues, this tempering is not sufficient to yield the high levels of cooperative motivation which can be attained from making a more sophisticated use of the drive for a sense of personal worth.

The findings . . . show that the most successful sales managers are discovering and demonstrating that the drive for a sense of personal worth and importance when used to create competitive motivational forces yields productivity and sales performance appreciably short of the best. The best performance, lowest costs, and the highest levels of earnings and of employee satisfaction occur when the drive for a sense of personal worth is used to create strong motivational forces to *cooperate* rather than *compete* with one's peers and colleagues. The use of this motive in ways which yield cooperative rather than competitive relationships appears to yield stronger motivational forces oriented toward achieving the organization's objectives and is accompanied by positive rather than negative side effects. Subordinates aid each other and share leadership tasks rather than putting immediate self-interest ahead of long-range self-interest and organizational success.

The strong motivational forces created by competition can be used without incurring its negative consequences when the enterprise operates under a System 4 model. For example, the individual can compete with his own past record or with "par for the course." Even better, the entire sales office can compete with its own past record and with current goals the group has set for itself. (pp. 74–75)

The behavior of the leader (superior) in any situation plays a crucial role in whether cooperation or competition becomes the prevailing pattern. The more the leader displays team-building leadership behavior, the greater is the likelihood that cooperation rather than competition will be present. Peer leadership also plays a role. Supportive and team-building behavior by the leader stimulates the members of the group (peers) to display these same kinds of leadership behavior to one another. Member (peer) leadership behavior can contribute significantly to whether cooperation or competition is the usual mode of interaction (Bowers & Seashore, 1966; Taylor & Bowers, 1972).

Large-scale field studies as well as experimental studies in laboratories show the same findings: Cooperation achieves better results than does competition since it creates greater total, coordinated, motivational forces. These forces are derived primarily from the desire to achieve and maintain a sense of personal worth and importance. Although competition is often a powerful way to harness the desire to achieve and maintain a sense of personal worth and importance, it makes much less effective use of this strong motive source than does cooperation. Competition pits one person against another and encourages behavior which benefits one person at the expense of the other. Competition makes use of P+ and P− and tends to create unfriendly and even hostile attitudes. Those who lose out often develop resentful attitudes toward the winner since losing is ego deflating just as winning is ego inflating. Competition, in contrast with cooperation, does not make use of group decision making and the 2 to 10 times greater motivational forces which group decision making creates.

Cooperation makes full use of the motivational forces which group decision making can create. It makes extensive use of GP+ along with P+ and hence benefits from favorable attitudes. Cooperation is a more socially evolved and effective way to harness the desire to achieve and maintain a sense of personal worth and importance than is competition. Cooperation usually involves more complex forms of interaction than does competition and requires more learning and more skill on the part of those who seek to use it.

Consistent with the differences between competition and cooperation are the differences that exist between a System 2 and a System 4 interaction-influence network. A fundamental change in the nature of the motivational forces and power used by the interaction-influence network of an organization occurs as it shifts from the System 1 to 3, to the System 4 model. This shift is related to the change from a person-to-person interaction pattern to one which makes extensive use of group problem solving. Interaction-influence networks based on Systems 1, 2, and 3 do not make use of group decision making and consequently do not use GP+. System 4T interaction-influence networks make full use of the power (GP+) which group decision making can create, the "two to ten times" greater motivational forces for change demonstrated by Lewin. System 4, in contrast with Systems 1, 2, and 3, makes use of this "whole new level of influence" which, as Cartwright (1951) pointed out, is attained "by introducing group forces into the situation" (p. 385).

This difference between the motivational forces used by System 4, on the one hand, and Systems 1, 2, and 3, on the other, can be stated in another manner. Only System 4 uses GP+; the other systems do not. GP+ involves joint power *with* others. P+, P−, IP+, and IP− are all power *over* others. IP+, as suggested above, can shift to GP+ in character. This takes place when the interaction shifts from a hierarchical person-to-person pattern to a group problem-solving pattern. When this occurs, there is a corresponding shift from "power over" to joint "power with." *In conflict situations, the shift from using power over others (win-lose) to using joint power with others (win-win) represents an extremely fundamental change in the strategy of resolving conflicts and usually mobilizes an appreciably higher level of motivation along with cooperative behavior.* The probability of resolving a conflict constructively is greatly increased when this shift is made. The stronger party, as a rule, is in a better position to initiate this shift since the stronger party usually plays a crucial role in determining whether the conflict is resolved by a System 1, 2, 3, or 4 interaction-influence network.

Societies based on Systems 1 or 2 create desire for power over others

The socialization processes in organizations or societies which are System 1 or 2 in character appear to develop in their members higher levels of need for power than do System 4 societies. In such societies, the need for power is a major channel through which the inherited motive source of the desire to achieve and maintain a sense of personal worth and importance exerts its motivational force. Progressively, as a society patterns itself after the System 4 concepts, the socialization process changes from creating the need for power *over* others as the more important value to creating the need for achievement *with* others as the more important. In System 4 societies, the need for achievement thereby becomes a more important channel than the need for power through which the basic inherited motive source of a desire for personal worth influences behavior. A limited but growing body of research findings demonstrates these relationships (Loomis, 1960; Misumi, 1973).

Table 15-1 shows the form of power customarily used in conflicts by social institutions based on Systems 1, 2, 3, and 4 and reveals the important role group power, GP+, plays in the System 4 approach to resolving conflicts. Items 1 and 2 in Table 2-1 are also relevant. Items in Table 15-1 also indicate for each system some of the consequences of the kinds of power used by that system. In addition to the items in Table 15-1, the outcomes for each system of the approach used in resolving conflict are indicated by the items in Table 2-3. It is well to examine Table 2-3 along with Table 15-1 in appraising the capacity of social institutions based on each of the different systems to resolve conflicts constructively.

Table 15-1 can be used in any specific situation along with Table 2-3 to measure the forms of power being used and some of the consequences of their use. In using Table 15-1 in this manner, the same instructions should be used as were proposed for Table 2-3.

Any social system, strategy for resolving conflict, or interaction-influence network can be analyzed by means of P+, P−, IP+, IP−, and GP+ as to the

Table 15-1

Form of power used to resolve a conflict and resulting consequences

Item no.	System 1	System 2	System 3	System 4
1. What kinds of power are being used to resolve this conflict?	Largely or entirely P− and IP−	P−, P+, IP−, and IP+	A little P− and IP−; much P+ and IP+	GP+ with some P+ and IP+
2. How is this conflict being resolved?	Solution imposed; conflict suppressed; usually by ruthless power	Solution imposed; conflict generally suppressed by authority; ruthless power curtailed by checks and balances	Some solutions imposed; some suppression by authority; checks and balances commonly used; mutually acceptable solution achieved at times by consultation during problem solving	Mutually acceptable solutions achieved by cooperative group problem solving
3. Is win-lose or win-win problem solving used?	Virtually always win-lose	Largely win-lose; very little win-win	Some win-lose and some win-win	Virtually always win-win

Table 15-1

Form of power used to resolve a conflict and resulting consequences (Continued)

Item no.	System 1	System 2	System 3	System 4
4. To what extent are the following used:				
A. Integrative goals?	Virtually never	Occasionally	Sometimes to often	Virtually always
B. Mutual interests?	Virtually never	Occasionally	Sometimes to often	Virtually always
C. Situational requirements and the authority of facts?	Virtually never	Occasionally	Sometimes to often	Virtually always
D. Principle of supportive relationships?	Virtually never	Occasionally	Sometimes to often	Virtually always
5. To what extent is status deemphasized	Virtually never	Occasionally	Sometimes to often	Virtually always
6. To what extent is problem solving depersonalized?	Virtually never	Occasionally	Sometimes to often	Virtually always

7. To what extent does the method for coping with this conflict heighten or lessen differences in values and goals?

Heightens differences in values and goals	Usually heightens; sometimes lessens	Sometimes heightens; more often lessens	Establishes integrative goals; builds common values

8. What effect does the method for coping with this conflict have on:

A. Communication?

Worsens communication	Usually worsens	Sometimes worsens, sometimes improves	Improves communication

B. Confidence and trust?

Decreases confidence and trust	Often decreases; sometimes increases	Sometimes decreases; more often increases	Increases confidence and trust

9. To what extent do the conflicting parties seek to exert influence only or are they willing to be influenced as well?

Seek strongly to exert influence only; resist vigorously any attempt by others to influence them	Primarily seek to exert influence; moderately resist being influenced by others	Willing to accept some influence from others while seeking to influence others	Desire to be influenced as well as to influence

extent to which it is relatively primitive or highly evolved. The greater the extent to which an interaction-influence network or strategy for dealing with conflict relies on P− and IP−, the more it is likely to be primitive, undeveloped, and unable to resolve the conflict constructively. Networks and strategies, such as win-lose, which rely heavily on negative power are likely to continue and intensify the hostilities and the conflict even though the defeated party may withdraw or "go underground" for a period of time. Conversely, the greater the extent to which an interaction-influence network used in a conflict is win-win and relies on GP+, the more socially evolved it is and the more effective it is likely to be. Primitive societies and ways of dealing with conflict rely heavily on power over others, such as P− and IP− with some use of P+ and IP+. Highly developed societies and ways of resolving conflict are relying increasingly on power with others in the form of GP+.

The soundness, adequacy, and sophistication of the attempts to resolve the most serious, bitter, long-standing, present-day conflicts can be analyzed in this manner. When this is done, one is distressed by the extent to which humanity is attempting to resolve these extremely costly, complex conflicts by primitive and ineffective interaction-influence networks relying on equally inadequate and primitive forms of social power. Further evidence of the inadequacy and primitive character of present-day attempts to resolve serious major conflicts becomes evident when they are scored by means of Tables 15-1 and 2-3.

This and the preceding chapters have proposed that conflicts can be resolved appreciably more successfully than at present by using more socially evolved and effective motivational power and interaction-influence networks. What evidence is there which lends support to this view? The next chapter examines some examples of the limited findings now available.

16
Two studies supporting the System 4 approach to managing conflict

Extensive research findings from Walton and his colleagues, reported in this chapter, provide data concerning the capacity of the System 4T model to resolve conflicts constructively.

Walton has published a general theory dealing with conflict in lateral (horizontal) and interorganizational relationships (Walton, 1966). The following statement of key concepts of the theory appear in Walton, Dutton, and Fitch (1966):

> Walton distinguishes two opposite types of relationships, and refers to them as "distributive" and "integrative." [See Table 16-1.] The theory which underlies these constructs is concerned with lateral relationships in which the parties are required to enter into a joint decision-making process. Three components of such relationships are considered: (1) information exchange in the joint decision process; (2) the structure of interunit interactions and decision making; and (3) attitudes toward the other unit. The theory consists of a set of propositions about how the modal process utilized by the participants for making joint decisions (i.e., bargaining versus problem solving) influences and, in turn, is influenced by various aspects of the interunit structure (e.g., frequency of interaction) and interunit attitudes (e.g., trust). (p. 445)

Resemblance to System 2 and System 4

As will be recognized, Walton's *integrative* type of lateral relationship is in agreement with an application of System 4 to lateral relationships. Similarly, his *distributive* type of relationship fits the System 1 or 2 pattern of interaction. The similarities between the integrative model and System 4 and between the distributive model and System 2 will become more evident as two studies, one conducted by Walton and the other by Walton and his colleagues, are described briefly. Quoting Walton (1967):

Table 16-1
Components and characteristics of
contrasting types of lateral relationships

| | Type of lateral relationship | |
Component of relationship	Integrative	Distributive
1. Form of joint decision process between units	Problem solving: Free exchange of information. Conscientious accuracy of information transmitted.	Bargaining: Careful rationing of information. Deliberate distortion of information.
2. Structure of interaction and interunit decision framework	Flexible, informal, and open.	Rigid, formal, and circumscribed.
3. Attitudes toward other unit	Positive attitudes; trust, friendliness, inclusion of other unit.	Negative attitudes; suspicion, hostility, disassociation from other unit.

From Walton, Dutton, & Fitch, 1966. Used with permission.

Walton studied the innovative efforts of one country director (i.e., the ambassador's counterpart in the Washington, D.C., organization of the State Department) who has tried to increase interdepartmental integration and coordination at his level. Beginning in May 1966, he scheduled meetings on a monthly basis, inviting representatives from about a dozen agencies—those persons directly concerned with the affairs of the same foreign country.

The country director, who did not have the power to compel membership or attendance, relied on his own skill in managing the sessions to make discussions productive and valuable to individual members. Many meetings featured informal presentations by persons with unique knowledge about the country, followed by round-table discussions of the issues raised. His method of handling meetings included relating himself to members directly and personally; urging continuity in the personnel representing an agency, differentiating onetime observers from regular members; encouraging, accepting, and helping develop views which differed from his own; and not keeping minutes of the meetings.

By the way he managed the sessions, he gradually achieved certain states that in turn improved the problem-solving and conflict resolution capacity of this interagency network. Common exposure of the agency representatives to experts and to each other, and their own mutual education and information exchange activities, decreased the likelihood of future interagency conflict based on differences in perceived facts and tended to break down many negative intergroup stereotypes that exist about Peace Corps, Military, CIA, and State, etc. The development of personal relationships among agency representatives increased their tendency to check with each other for specific advice, information, and to coordinate activities generally. Encouragement of dissent and challenge in the absence of compelling policy or action decisions was effective in setting a group norm of sharpening, accepting, and exploring differences—a norm which could carry over into solving specific problems. A corollary group norm was one of identifying the additional information which the group would need if it were to choose between the alternative views. The agency representatives not only achieved a better understanding from State Department officials of overall goals for U.S. relations with the country in question, but also became more committed to them by virtue of a sense of identification with the interagency group. This enhanced sense of membership in the group and commitment to superordinate goals increased a member's personal discomfort whenever his agency's actions ignored the interests of other agencies. (pp. 37–38)

As a part of this project, Walton also studied the coordination among agencies of a large overseas mission and how that mission was handled by the ambassador. His findings support the pattern found in Washington. This is illustrated nicely by his description of the operation of a "Think Tank"[1] which he found in the overseas mission (Walton, 1967):

An additional important experimental device for achieving a higher and more creative level of integration of the many strands of foreign affairs activities was referred to as the "Think Tank." It was an informal weekly meeting of a group drawn from many agencies to think imaginatively about problems of concern to the foreign affairs community as a whole. The ambassador's staff assistant had played a key role in initiating the idea. The group also included a second staff assistant to the ambassador, the deputy director of AID, two military men, and a second level official from USIS. A ground rule for members was that they were to address the problems rather than represent their respective agencies' viewpoints. Generally this group included bright young men below the country team level. Apparently group meetings not only weakened stereotypes, but also increased members' confidence in their similar goals and the complementary competencies of their respective agencies. At the time of the study, they had identified some new potential areas of collaboration which they intended to recommend pursuing. (p. 38)

In both Washington and the field, Walton found that face-to-face group problem solving guided by skillful leadership in a supportive atmosphere contributed significantly to reducing conflict and increasing effective cooperation. In addition, this highly innovative procedure, the "Think Tank," was used for keeping the problem solving of the field group focused clearly on problems dealing with the overall interests of the United States and not on maximizing

---

[1]The "Think Tank" is very similar to an informal problem-solving and strategic-thinking group at Case Institute of Technology which referred to itself as the "Hats Group" because each person was expected to leave his or her departmental hat at the door.

the selfish interests and well-being of a subordinate unit. This focus on what is best for the entire organization is, as will be recalled, an essential characteristic of System 4 problem solving.

A study of conflicts in plants

The second study of Walton's to be examined involved six plants and was done with colleagues (Walton, Dutton, & Fitch, 1966). The nature of the firm and plants was described as follows:

> The Peerless Company was a large decentralized manufacturer of fabricated metal door and window products. Each of the company's more than one dozen fabricating plants, together with its corresponding sales district, was a geographically decentralized unit responsible for obtaining and producing customer orders in a profitable manner. Top management established detailed instructions for company plant personnel regarding plant organization, pricing of products, purchasing of materials, and methods of selling and producing. Production and sales personnel were evaluated, in part, on how well they accomplished their respective assigned tasks and, in part, on the overall performance of their district.

> The general plan of organization, which was similar for all plants, established the principal positions, activities and interactions for the sales and production groups. Responsibility for district operations was formally divided between two major departments, sales and production, each headed by a district manager. No general manager was responsible for both these activities at the district level. In fact, these two functions had separate lines of authority for the next two higher levels of the organization. The plant production group was expected to produce orders in an economical, timely and defect-free manner. The district sales group was responsible for obtaining orders at profitable prices and for maintaining service contracts with customers.

> The formal organizational plan included forces toward both cooperation and competition between sales and production. On the one hand, the activities of production and sales at the district level had to be coordinated to achieve maximum sales at the least cost. The success of the district as a whole could be furthered by a mutually cooperative approach to the critical problems, such as the scheduling of orders and quality control. Top management expected such an approach. On the other hand, production and sales personnel did not report to a common superior below the vice-president level. Thus, each unit could devote its entire attention to its own task, even at the cost of excluding the task of the other unit. Also, the several executives who supervised district sales and production managers could make differing interpretations of the general organizational plan—e.g., with respect to performance criteria, their emphasis on the routing of information to the district, or their leadership style. Even subtle differences in interpretation could have significant influence on the tendencies toward conflict or collaboration at the district level.

In many areas the task interdependence of the two departments was such that decisions or activities which improved the performance of one department did so at the expense of the performance of the other department. For example, one sequence of orders through a plant might best accommodate the sales department's operating objective of servicing customers in a certain way, whereas another schedule of orders would minimize plant costs (a factor on which production was measured). (pp. 446–447)

Walton found that all the data for each of the six plants could be combined into a comparative ranking which placed each plant on a scale from highly integrative to highly distributive. As will be recalled, Walton's concept of integrative corresponds with the System 4 pattern of operation and his distributive with the System 1 end of the System 1 to 4 scale. To measure where the plants fall on his distributive-integrative scale, Walton used items similar to the items used to measure where an organization falls on the System 1 to 4 continuum. The positions of the plants on Walton's distributive-integrative scale are shown in Figure 16-1.

In view of the similarities in the concepts of the two scales, i.e., (1) integrative-distributive, and (2) System 1 to 4, one would expect the two extreme plants, Bowie and Elgin, on the integrative-distributive scale to show corresponding differences on the System 1 to 4 scale. Fortunately, Dutton and Walton (1966) have published an intensive clinical analysis of these two plants. This analysis contrasts the most integrative plant, Bowie, with the least integrative, most distributive plant, Elgin. This clinical analysis provides further evidence of the costs and inefficiencies of the win-lose bargaining approach as a method for managing conflict, especially in comparison with problem solving. The case material on the Bowie and Elgin plants enables one to score the two plants, at least approximately, on the System 1 to 4 scale. The following quotations contrast these two plants:[2]

THE ELGIN PLANT—A CONFLICT RELATIONSHIP

The Elgin plant was the largest and one of the oldest plants in the company, with many employees of long-time service. Plant layout and equipment were typical and posed no particular problems, save in shipping, where space was cramped.

Bargaining and other dynamics of the conflict relationship. Maintenance of a bargaining approach to joint decision-making imposed particular requirements on the social system, as well as on the process of information handling and exchange in joint decisions. Each party required a conflict-oriented frame of reference consistent with a bargaining approach to joint decisions. Bargaining also imposed a need for particular, supporting patterns of attitudes and

[2]From J. M. Dutton and R. E. Walton, Interdepartmental conflict and cooperation: Two contrasting studies, *Human Organization,* 1966, *25*(3), 209–215, 219.

Integrative

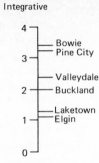

Figure 16-1 *Overall plant ranks.*

interaction. These Elgin behavior patterns can be analyzed in terms of strategy and tactics employed to implement a bargaining relationship.

Goals and orientation to decision-making. Officials in each of the two departments adopted narrowly defined objectives for their own department. That each department perceived the other as adopting divisive rather than unifying objectives can be seen in the comments of Elgin sales versus production officials.

> *Sales officials.* Sales is customer oriented. Production is interested only in cost. . . . Production only sees plant waste in costly orders and low output. . . . Sales' job is service—delivery when the customer wants it. . . . Sales' main job is to build volume in customer orders.

> *Production officials.* Our goal is to run orders efficiently. Many opportunities arise to reduce costs . . . but the salesmen don't know enough about production to recognize these things. . . . New items often give us problems. . . . Many times the salesmen try to sell ideas that cannot be produced economically or even at all!

These statements go beyond superficial confirmation of the departmental division of labor intended by top management. The two parties were aware of the existence of larger, overall district goals. But they chose not to adopt district goals as superordinate and not to coordinate their departments in the maximum interest of these goals.

Information-handling. Lack of understanding of each other's department problems characterized the approach to joint decision-making at Elgin. The parties also failed to communicate, or delayed communicating, relevant information to each other. These conditions at Elgin were legitimatized by the viewpoint of each party which saw problems of the other as "their problem, not ours."

Scheduling decisions, for example, were subject to mutual influence but were arrived at through demand-counterdemand, exaggeration, pressure maneuvers, and so on. Padding of needs for prompt and urgent handling of customer orders by sales officials was at the heart of the bargaining process. Production personnel, however, privately discounted sales requests as "obviously padded." On the other hand, production would exaggerate the difficulty it anticipated with a given request, whereas sales would assume that production constraints were more fanciful than real.

Quality control decisions exhibited the same bargaining pattern, including deliberate distortion and concealment. Sales engaged in overstatement of quality needs and production discounted sales quality requests.

The withholding of information stemmed in part from fear of raising future performance expectations and from fear of home office sanctions. If production (or sales) was too accommodating in scheduling decisions, they might create high expectations and, therefore, future problems for themselves. Similarly, full disclosure of quality defects might bring home office sanctions.

Because each department usually possessed more flexibility than it was willing to admit, it limited the number and type of contacts with the other, thus reducing the risk of revealing the true facts to the other.

Freedom of movement. At Elgin each party sought to gain maximum freedom for itself and to limit the other's freedom. On the one hand, each party attempted to fix future performance obligations and to establish jurisdictional limits *for* the other. On the other hand, each party engaged in tactical violations of limits imposed *by* the other.

Elgin sales was particularly active in circumventing formal procedures. Sales found production lacking in understanding, consideration, and competence and therefore attempted to take direct, unilateral action on their problems even when this violated procedures and usurped jurisdictional authority from production. This type of behavior is succinctly summarized in a sales official's comments:

> When production refuses, we have to act to satisfy customers. For instance, production often claims not to have material to produce an order. So we get on the phone to locate and purchase material. Production then, of course, claims that we are not within our rights. But we can't solve our problems by turning customers away.

To counteract this behavior, and to satisfy its generally felt need for caution and certainty in the conflict bargaining process, production further emphasized jurisdictional limits, restricted interaction, and formalized decision-rules to govern interdepartmental relations. The resulting oscillation between emphasis on rigid rules on the one hand, and unilateral action on the other, heightened the dilemma for each party of either choosing dependence on a reluctant peer or risking independent action. These tendencies are shown in the following comments by members of both units.

> Problems are resolved on a jurisdictional basis: "You take care of your part and we'll take care of ours." Each group decides who's responsible for what part of the problem and then goes its separate way; each party tries to hold out for the least possible action on his part.

The relationship between sales and production doesn't permit very much innovation on new orders. Production tends to resist, saying "Do it the old way," and finding lots of reasons not to try new ideas. However, sales needs new designs and depends on production for help. But if sales goes ahead with a new design alone, production feels their rights are infringed on.

The difficulties in joint decisions on scheduling resulted in a supreme attempt to formalize relationships between the parties on the handling of this problem. The parties at Elgin negotiated a written agreement which stipulated procedures for scheduling customer orders. The new scheduling agreement established the minimum production lead time on customer orders, and the plant capacity, and set forth a detailed plan of organization and procedures for scheduling customer orders. Under the plan two new expediters, plus the production control manager and service manager, were to constitute the sole contacts between sales, the production office, and the plant production floor.

This remarkably formal and explicit signed agreement was an expression of the two-unit relationship at Elgin. Its twofold significance was that it was produced by the bargaining relationship and that it was widely heralded at the plant as a forward step. Apparently the agreement controlled the tension and conflict between the departments. It strengthened tendencies already present to limit interaction between sales and production. Since members of the units found these exchanges both punitive and unrewarding, the plan provided welcome relief. The agreement delegated the scheduling problem to a small group and, as a consequence, numerous persons were able to withdraw from an uncomfortable relationship.

Sales was inclined to initiate more contacts than production. While the agreement tended to restrict interaction in scheduling, sales remained active in other areas, such as quality control. Here sales employed the tactic of circumventing formal procedures by exploiting special relationships with a person in production. Contrary to policy, this official permitted sales people into the plant to check on customer complaints.

Both parties frequently used pressure tactics to achieve their ends. The two types commonly employed were hierarchical relationships and "commitment tactics." At Elgin both sales and production turned to their regional and home office superiors as a means of resolving differences. For example, both managers frequently refused to accept responsibility for a given quality error. As a result disagreements were carried all the way up to the home office general sales and general production managers for a decision.

Another type of behavior, referred to in bargaining theory as "commitment tactics" was tactical to the conflict approach. One manager would attempt to influence a joint decision by structuring the situation so as to be seen by the other as irrevocably or maximally committed to his preferred position. For example, a sales official would often call the production planning manager to get a promise on delivery while holding the customer on another telephone line in order to "put the pressure on" production.

Production also used commitment tactics, sometimes by presenting sales with a *fait accompli*. This was not uncommon when an order cancellation or delay by the customer would be inconvenient to production. A sales official commented:

> Production will try to get a customer to take an order when the latter wants to cancel. Production has sometimes waited until the order was in production or has asked us to tell the customer the order was already in process.

> Production will also ship ahead of time when they have an order completed before the planned delivery date. They will do this even when they *know* the customer does not want the order early and has no place to store it.

Blaming was also tactically used both as a form of punishment and as a means of avoiding responsibility for failures in performance. The conflict about who was to blame for errors, losses, and delays was especially intense. The sales manager commented:

> Recently a customer received an order with oversize frames in it. He was willing to sort out the bad items himself if we could give him credit. But the production manager wouldn't do it. He wouldn't take the loss in production.

> We finally had to take the credit as sales expense. However, we delayed so long that the customer lost patience and we got the whole order back to rehandle ourselves.

At Elgin this pattern was often carried to the point of attributing every problem or negative result to the other fellow. Moreover, not only was the other party perceived as responsible for what was bad, but he was also seen as erroneously accepting credit for what was good! For example, production personnel charged that sales people took a lot of credit for work on new designs done in production.

Attitudes. The attitudes of the parties supported the bargaining approach to joint decision-making. Each department used the terms "we" and "they" to distinguish between the two groups and to compare "good" and "bad" motives. Each found occasion to report unfavorable attributes of the other, such as the lack of integrity of a plant foreman who expected personal gifts for helping a salesman. Also, each saw the other as lacking in understanding and competence. Vindictiveness was revealed in anecdotes in which one party expressed satisfaction at making the other "squirm."

The atmosphere at Elgin went beyond the use of stereotypes and obstructive behavior. Attitudes approached resignation and despair, and a lack of hope that any accommodation could be reached that would permit interdepartmental problem-solving. Efforts which had been made to improve relationships had failed. The service manager reported:

> The production planner and I tried business lunches together. But we quit after a while. We weren't getting anywhere. We also tried customer service meetings. These didn't work either. People's feelings got involved. There were personality conflicts. Production felt they weren't getting a hearing. They started to make these meetings gripe sessions against sales.

There was little or no interaction that was not related to work, and when members of sales and production did meet, the atmosphere was cautious and hostile. It was apparent at these meetings that the parties were holding back information. It was also apparent that each party brought up topics and made statements that were designed to make the other party feel uncomfortable. For instance, one party would point out errors and oversights by the other or would verbally reprimand the other for withholding information.

THE BOWIE PLANT—A COLLABORATIVE RELATIONSHIP

The Bowie plant had been acquired by the company within the past ten years. It had been purchased complete with equipment from its former owners, and many of the plant personnel had remained after the purchase. Bowie was somewhat smaller than the average plant but was fully equipped and could produce the company's complete line.

Problem-solving and other dynamics of the collaborative relationship. At Bowie members of the two groups interacted frequently to resolve problems that arose in the course of their work. They enjoyed these contacts, as the following scene indicates:

> The production manager burst into the sales manager's office and handed him a sample of a new part. "Try that," he said.
>
> "It certainly seems stronger," the sales manager replied. He tried to twist the sample in his hand and also tried to bend it under his foot. "It certainly is!" he exclaimed.
>
> "We'll run a trial on this in the plant and see how it works out," said the production manager, and then left.
>
> The sales manager explained the incident, saying "We were having trouble with this part. Frank, the production manager, got an idea from a toy he got for his kids and came to see me about it. He gave the idea to Tom, the designer, who worked it over to make it easier to produce. We think it is a very good idea."

In this incident a production man and a sales person cooperated with each other to develop an idea for an improved product. They saw the problem as a joint task for both sales and production and provided social support for each other in their attempts to solve the problem.

At Bowie problem-solving was the approach to joint decision-making used in all areas of interdependence, including new designs, scheduling, and quality control. Maintenance of this approach required a collaborative orientation from each party and a supporting pattern of interaction.

Goals and orientation to decision-making. Members of the Bowie organization tended to define objectives for themselves which embraced both production and marketing functions. The sales manager's comment was especially direct in this respect.

> You build a plant to make a certain product mix. Then you have to try to go out and sell this mix.
>
> In planning sales we try to develop a program to obtain business to keep all machines in the plant operating. There's a big capital investment out there and you can get terrible imbalances among departments if you don't exercise control.

> You also, however, have to sell what's there in the market. You can't tool up to produce what isn't there. The ideal is a balance between the market and the production setup.

The production manager had a similar view. For example, he indicated sufficient concern about missed deliveries that his remarks could have been confused with those emanating from sales.

Information-handling. In contrast with Elgin, both Bowie departments evidenced an understanding of the other's problems. For instance, the scheduling task at Bowie, as at Elgin, contained conflict potential: Customers tended to give short lead time and initiated requests for revised delivery dates; production officials had reasons peculiar to their task for preferring one schedule over another; breakdowns in bottleneck equipment occurred, etc. Distortion or rationing in the handling of information, however, did not develop. For example, the "padding" of sales requests which marked the scheduling process at Elgin occurred at Bowie only in a minor way, if at all. The salesmen at Bowie were more inclined than at Elgin to probe for the customer's real needs so that unnecessary demands were not passed on to production. The following salesman's comments are indicative of this understanding and consideration:

> The customers are educated not to expect delivery within a certain period of time. There are exceptions, but why foul up production scheduling to accommodate customers who don't anticipate their own needs?

> You do have to take the customer's needs into account. You can't be late. We have established an understanding with production. If our minimum delivery rule doesn't satisfy customers, then we contact production through the service manager.

Each party tried to anticipate problems, not only for itself but also for the other. Recall that at Elgin production was reluctant to inform sales of errors or slightly defective product runs. At Bowie, production people were encouraged to go to the service manager and tell him about an error. Sales would then phone to see if the customer was willing to accept the product anyway. The customer frequently cooperated if he was approached this way. The production manager commented on other areas in which he was benefited by sales:

> We have few problems in avoiding uneconomical or unprofitable orders. The sales manager is good about this. He gives me a look-see on possible problem orders insofar as cost is concerned. We look at these together and compare revenue and cost considerations.

> I also go to sales to *ask* for certain types of business. We may need finishing work of a particular type, for instance.

This degree of understanding at Bowie had not always existed. In the past salesmen had obtained every order they could. Certain current steps were being taken to further increase salesmen's understanding of production problems, including giving young salesmen firsthand experience in production.

Constraints at Bowie limited the degree to which the parties could be helpful to one another in jointly solving problems. One constraint was a lack of relevant cost information. The sales manager cited specific orders for small lots and complex items which were of doubtful profitability, but in the absence of cost information he could not be certain. This situation was viewed as a mutual problem rather than an intergroup issue, however.

Freedom of movement. At Bowie the parties generally tried to increase freedom of movement. Cooperation and procedures were adequate enough so that there was little or no incentive to circumvent the rules or formal procedures. Where deviations did exist, they did not present an issue. A member of the production organization said:

> Sales people are not supposed to come out on the floor but sometimes they do. I don't think there's anything wrong with it as long as the salesmen don't stop and talk to the machine operators. And they don't do this as far as I know.

There was flexibility in decision-making rules. No arrangement existed at Bowie comparable to the Elgin scheduling agreement. No minimum delivery rule was established. It was generally understood that quick delivery promises were risky, but the service manager was delegated authority by both parties to "play-it-by-ear."

In more general terms, there was a complete absence of attempts by either party to fix future performance for the other party or to force commitments from the other that would limit its future freedom. This freedom was accompanied by a relatively open interactional pattern. The sales and production managers met daily several times, as did their office subordinates, the service manager and production control manager. There were few restrictions on the movements of any member of the plant organization.

Although Bowie's interaction system was more open than Elgin's, there were certain restrictions in selected decision areas at Bowie. These limits were, however, pursuant to the collaboration pattern rather than exceptions to it. Limited interaction was especially notable in day-to-day scheduling decisions, as shown by a sales official's comment:

> People are generally free to come and go in the plant and office. However, we don't want salesmen to try to persuade the foreman to get their orders. By the same token we don't want foremen to ask salesmen for changes in orders. We do have lines of communication on scheduling matters through the service manager.

> We confine our scheduling contacts with production to the service manager. As soon as you have a number of people doing it, you lose control.

These comments indicated conditions where limited interaction could be beneficial to the collaborative relationship. Successful collaboration on scheduling required both cooperative criteria and adequate decision-rules. Scheduling was an extremely complex cognitive task. Limited interaction was beneficial to the scheduling system for the following reasons: First, it enabled the service manager to reject untimely distractions for the production scheduler when the latter was involved in the intricate task of constructing a schedule. Second, it kept the information on scheduling channeled through the position where cooperative criteria were applied. Influence exerted in a non-controlled pattern was often suboptimal in effect; for instance, when a salesman operated with incomplete data and inadequate rules in seeking to persuade a foreman to give preference to a particular order.

Closely related to open interaction patterns and freedom of movement was flexibility at Bowie in the establishment of positions and the performance of tasks. The leading instance of flexibility was a quality control plan. This plan, which had been devised at the Bowie plant and was unique within the company, employed a quality control man who rotated continuously through all departments in the plant watching for errors. Although the system contained the normal instances of laxness, and although this person, in performing his difficult tasks, encountered instances of friction from individuals, he was generally supported by both departments.

Another instance of organizational innovation was the establishment of the office of general manager serving both sales and production personnel. Home office approval had been secured for this move but the plant had taken the initiative on this change. The appointed official, the service manager, had extensive experience in production control as well as sales service and, in this smaller plant with its collaborative patterns, was well-qualified for an overall coordinating position.

Bowie presented a further contrast to Elgin in searching for solutions in lieu of using pressure tactics. Whereas at Elgin the sales official held the customer on the phone while making requests of production, in order to increase his own commitment to this request, at Bowie the sales official did not need this leverage to find out what production could or could not do. Therefore, he was free to try to influence the customer—or at least to test the customer's real needs.

> Because production tells us in advance that we will not make our schedule on a particular order, we can call the customer and ask for an extra few days. You find that 90 percent of the time if you call him first, you can get extra time. It's when he has to call you that you get in trouble. The customer is apt to wait until about 4 P.M. on the promised delivery date and then call and say, "Where are you?" If he learns then that no delivery is to be made, he loses confidence. If you call him, he will go to bat for you. If you don't, you embarrass him; he may not need the order but his attitude will be that he does!

There were hierarchical appeals within the plant. But it appeared that the issues which were bucked up raised appropriate questions for plant officials. They were not cases where power was needed to accomplish the obvious, as was the tendency at Elgin. Similarly extra-plant relations were largely used to implement the *jointly* developed policies of the sales and production managers. By working closely with the home office, the sales and production managers had jointly secured transfer orders from other districts to level production through low periods and had obtained home approval for the production of certain items for inventory, also a unique arrangement within the company.

Regional and home office sales and production officials were not used as courts of appeal. Superiors set budget goals and cost controls and established payoffs for performance but they were not feared or seen as arbitrators. The sales manager stated:

I have little contact with the regional manager and the home office. We don't depend on them. There is very little contact, on my part at least, and I feel there is little contact by the production manager.

The production manager's views on the use of the regional manager were similar to those of sales. He was a younger manager in training; nevertheless, he acknowledged the importance of working with sales, perhaps at some cost to his training relationship. He said:

I don't use the regional manager as a court of appeal. The regional manager is training me. But it has never reached the point where I can't work out any problems with the sales manager. We feel we can reach an equitable solution together.

The tendency at Bowie was to attempt to diagnose problems regarding defective joint decision-rules rather than to find a "scapegoat" or to place blame on the other party. This pattern contrasted sharply with that at Elgin. Although much less was dissipated over the question of who was to blame, this was not because there was no penalty associated with accepting responsibility. There was as much penalty at Bowie as at Elgin.

The sales manager opposed pinpointing responsibility for errors because of the defensive atmosphere created by this procedure.

We have a company quality control program. Its aim is to pinpoint losses. This aim can work against you because your people then try to avoid getting pinned for the error. However, we're not so interested in who created the problem as in what practices created the problem and how to correct these practices.

Not all officials wholly agreed with this position. The production manager was more inclined to support formal home office procedure—but for internal control purposes, not as an interdepartmental weapon. The quality control manager was still more favorably disposed to this procedure as an additional support for him in his task of maintaining quality. He also provided the researchers with information which, while it didn't change the general impression reported above, did confirm that the departments at Bowie were not always successful in avoiding the question of "blame."

Attitudes. The attitudes of both sales and production at Bowie have already been seen to support the problem-solving approach used in joint decision-making. Statements of members of the Bowie plant-district organization indicated that production and sales got along well. Personal relationships developed from work relationships. Members shared an interest in one another's affairs and saw each other off the job. Instances were revealed where members went out of their way to help another person.

The fact that liaison members at Bowie showed less strain than at Elgin was perhaps an indication of the differences in attitudes at the two plants. The Bowie service manager was well aware of the differences and potential conflict between sales and production in his district. However, he found his situation quite tolerable. And the quality control manager, who would be caught in the interdepartmental cross-pressure if anyone was, expressed the desire for *more* informal contacts.

Thus, the attitudes supported the blurring of departmental lines; encouraged trust and support between the two parties, and avoidance of punishing contacts; and furthered attempts to integrate the two units.

STRATEGY AND TACTICS: A COMPARATIVE SUMMARY

The patterns of behavior at Bowie were in sharp contrast with those at Elgin. Elgin employed a bargaining, and Bowie a problem-solving, approach to joint decisions. The patterns of goal orientation, information-handling, interaction and attitudinal structure strategical to these contrasting approaches are summarized in Table 1 [16-2]. . . .

CONFLICT IN LATERAL RELATIONSHIPS

Consequences for organizational performance. Negative consequences of conflict for performance were widespread and pronounced in all areas of interdependence in the lateral relationship. Conflict was accompanied by relatively fewer new designs, more frequent acceptance of unprofitable orders, loss of profitable orders, greater plant congestion, poorer customer delivery service, dismissal of crews for lack of work, refusal of overtime when customer orders were unfinished, shipment of orders of marginal and substandard quality to customers, and return of defective orders by customers. Some of these consequences were attributable rather directly to a competitive orientation to decision-making. Other consequences, such as the acceptance of new, unprofitable orders resulting from a lack of information exchange on prospective new designs, stemmed from behavior tactical to the maintenance of competitive goal orientation. Still other consequences were the result of behavior that was retaliatory. Attempts by sales, for example, to blame production for quality defects led production to refuse to accept customer inspection for defects. Loss of orders and extra charges for return freight were the result. . . .

Consequences for individuals. Conflict had apparent psychological and professional consequences for the principals and their leading subordinates. Participants in the conflict relationship showed greater anxiety and frustration. Such reaction may well be a function of individual tolerance for conflict and deserves further study.

Professional consequences also appeared to stem from the relationship. Participants in the conflict relationship were criticized by their superiors both at the plant and at the home office, and during interviews a number reported contemplating leaving the company. By contrast, at the integrative plant a number of persons commented on their prospects for being moved to more responsible company positions in the future. (pp. 209–215, 219)

Scoring Bowie and Elgin on the System 1 to 4 continuum

It is a revealing exercise to score Elgin and Bowie plants using Table 2-3. Fortunately, enough information is provided by the case histories to score each

Table 16-2

Summary of two contrasting approaches to interdepartmental relations

	Elgin: A bargaining approach	Bowie: A problem-solving approach
1. Goals and orientation to decision-making	1. With regard to respective goals and orientation to decision-making, each department emphasized the requirements of its own particular task, rather than the combined task of the plant sales district as a whole.	1. Each department stressed common goals whenever possible and otherwise sought to balance goals. Each party perceived the potentials for interdepartmental conflict in the separate task structures but nevertheless stressed the existence of superordinate district goals and the benefits of full collaboration for each party. Each saw the relationship as cooperative.
2. Information-handling	2. With respect to the strategic question of information exchange, each department (a) minimized the other's problems or tended to ignore such considerations as it did recognize; and (b) attempted to minimize or distort certain kinds of information communicated.	2. Each department (a) sought to understand the other's problems and to give consideration to problems of immediate concern to the other; and (b) endeavored to provide the other with full, timely, and accurate information relevant to joint decisions.
3. Freedom of movement	3. Several tactics were employed which related to the strategic question of freedom of movement. Each department sought to gain maximum freedom for itself and to limit the degrees of freedom for the other by the use of the following tactics: (a) attempting to circumvent formal procedures when advantageous; (b)	3. Each department explored ways it could increase its freedom of movement toward its goals with the following behavior: (a) accepting informal procedures which facilitated the task; (b) blurring the division between production and sales in tasks and positions; (c) refraining from attempts to fix the other's future performance; (d)

emphasizing jurisdictional rules; (c) attempting to fix the other's future performance obligations; (d) attempting to restrict interaction patterns; (e) employing pressure tactics—hierarchical appeals and commitment tactics—whenever possible; (f) blaming the other for past failures in performance.

Relations were laden with threats, hostility, and the desire for retaliation. Interdepartmental interactions were experienced as punishing by both sides. Contacts were limited to a few formal channels, and behavior within these channels circumscribed by a rigid rule structure. Department officials depended on higher authority. Home-office managers were called upon to resolve opposing views, to suggest solutions, and to support one party against the other.

structuring relatively open interaction patterns; (e) searching for solutions rather than employing pressure tactics; (f) attempting to diagnose defects in rules for decision-making rather than worrying about placing blame.

Relations were characterized by mutual support. Department officials were independent of higher authority. Home office was asked to support initiatives of joint proposals from the plant.

4. Attitudes

4. Each department developed attitudes in support of the above bargaining strategy and tactics.

4. Each department adopted positive inclusive and trusting attitudes regarding the other.

From J. M. Dutton and R. E. Walton, Interdepartmental Conflict and Cooperation: Two Contrasting Studies. *Human Organization*, 1966, 25, p. 216. Used by permission.

plant on virtually every item in this table. The scores for the two plants display wide differences. For example on item 3 of Table 2-3: "How open, candid, and unguarded is the communication and interaction between the opposing parties?" Elgin would score approximately in the upper part of System 1 and Bowie about in the middle of System 4. This would be the case also on question 4 in Table 2-3: "To what extent do the opposing parties seek to deceive or to inform the other correctly?" The profiles for the two plants made by lines connecting each plant's score on each item would not overlap at any point. Elgin consistently scores toward the System 1 end, Bowie toward System 4 on *every* item in Table 2-3.

The two plants can be scored also on many of the items in Table 2-2 and also on the items in the Appendix. When this is done, the two plants differ markedly. Elgin continues to be toward the System 1 end, usually falling in the System 1 or 2 range, whereas Bowie is much more toward System 4. This seems to be the case also for the few causal items on which the plants can be scored. Bowie's leadership, for example, is more supportive and makes more use of group problem solving than does Elgin's.

The clinical case histories elaborating Walton's integrative model versus his distributive model provide dramatic evidence of the costs of trying to use the Systems 1 or 2 model for coping with conflict. These costs are summarized briefly in the last paragraphs above of the case histories. In contrast with Bowie, the costs at Elgin were high both for the plant as a whole and for its various personnel, especially those most involved in the conflicts.

This study provides impressive evidence of the greater capacity of the integrative, or System 4, approach to manage conflicts constructively, compared with the distributive, or System 1, approach. Moreover, it is very likely that the relationships among the variables for all six plants would prove to be even more marked were it possible to measure and examine the relationships over time among the causal, intervening, and end-result variables. (The necessity of examining relationships over time was discussed in previous chapters.)

System 4: A guide to action

The two scales for viewing conflicts, namely the integrative-distributive and the System 1 to 4, have much in common. Walton's theory of lateral relationships in organizations appears to be congruent with the more general organizational theory encompassed in the System 1 to 4 model. This compatibility is advantageous to anyone wishing to apply the System 4 model to improve lateral coordination. Walton has elaborated quite fully the nature of his integrative pattern. This material along with his extensive research findings can be used to help guide any effort to reduce conflicts occurring in lateral relationships.

Similarly, the System 4 theory can be of value to those who wish to apply Walton's findings. The organizational climate of a firm has a marked effect on the extent to which a manager can use Walton's integrative or distributive approach to handling conflicts in lateral relationships. For example, it would be difficult, if not impossible, for a manager in a System 2 firm to adhere to the integrative approach to lateral relationships over an extended period. When a firm's top management uses System 2, it creates a System 2 organizational climate throughout the firm. This climate is too highly charged with distrust and hostility to enable an integrative pattern of relationships to survive for very long.

In contrast, a System 3½ or System 4 pattern of management in a firm would provide an organizational climate in which the integrative approach would flourish. Moreover, there would be forces in this climate encouraging the distributive patterns of lateral relationships, wherever they exist in the firm, to shift over time to the integrative pattern, and the members of the organization would have the skills to make this shift.

There is another, and probably more important, contribution that the System 4 theory can make. The System 4T model provides a guide to the action steps required to create the organizational climate needed for the integrative approach. The System 4T model specifies both the causal variables that must be altered and the character of the changes needed in these variables if an organizational climate conducive to the integrative approach is to be built. (See table 3-1.) The causal variables suggest both entry points and promising strategies to use in efforts to create the organizational climate desired.

As the extensive quotations from Walton clearly demonstrate, he, with his colleagues, is doing valuable research on the dynamics of conflict. All persons interested in coping with conflict would be well advised to read all Walton's publications dealing with conflict, including his books (Walton & McKersie, 1965; Walton, 1969) and his many journal articles. To facilitate locating these important contributions, the references list under Walton's name all the relevant publications of which he is either a senior or a junior author.

An earlier study

Another excellent case study providing substantial evidence to support the view that the System 4T model is far more effective in resolving conflicts constructively than are other kinds of social systems is Guest's study, *Organizational Change* (1962).[3] This study reveals that by shifting to a System 4T interaction-influence network, an organization can improve its capacity to resolve both intraorganizational conflicts between departments or hierarchical levels, and interorganizational conflicts between union and plant.

---

[3]A revised, shortened edition of Guest's original study is being published by Prentice-Hall in 1976 entitled *Organizational Change: Case Study and Analysis of Effective Leadership,* with coauthors Paul Hersey and K. H. Blanchard.

Guest reports the case so fully that the management system used by plant Y under the former manager and under the new manager can be scored readily. The plant shifted from about System 1½ to low System 4.

The clear description by Guest of the steps the new manager took to make this shift gives valuable insights concerning effective ways to bring about changes in the management system of a firm or to build an effective interaction-influence network between organizations locked in conflict.

17
Taking action

Conflicts can be arrayed along an important dimension. At one extreme are conflicts of sufficiently new or recent origin that sustained, continuing hostile attitudes on the part of each party toward the other have not yet had an opportunity to be established. At the other extreme of the continuum are conflicts in which the attitudes of each party toward the other are extremely bitter and hostile. Some feuds among clans or families display such extreme hostility that with no current provocation a member of one clan will seek to kill a member of the other. Warfare among some street gangs also shows this extreme form of established hostile attitudes. There is a continuum, consequently, which extends from a situation in which the parties to the conflict feel no continuing hostility toward the other, to one in which there is extremely bitter and unrelenting hostility.

It is necessary to know where a particular conflict falls along this continuum when an effort is to be made to help resolve the conflict constructively by building a System 4T interaction-influence network between the conflicting organizations. If, for example, there are little or no continuing hostile attitudes among the parties, it is relatively easy to arrange well-attended group meetings consisting of persons from each conflicting party who can provide appropriate linkage between the parties. It also is about as easy to get agreement on the integrative goals held or sought by both parties and on the situational requirements that both parties recognize and accept. All the steps proposed below as well as those in previous chapters for building a System 4T interaction-influence network can be executed with relative ease. The situation is quite different where strong, bitterly hostile attitudes exist. We will suggest ways of taking action under these circumstances in the latter part of this chapter.

The specific steps that need to be taken in applying System 4 principles obviously will vary greatly in the widely different kinds of situations where conflicts occur. Moreover, the nature of the application must fit the unique characteristics of that particular situation. Nevertheless, a general plan for change, based on the survey-feedback method for organizational improvement, can be described from which the specific steps appropriate for a particular situation can be derived.

The following discussion of an overall plan for bringing change is necessarily quite general. It is impossible to cover a subject that requires at least a full-length book in a single chapter. In any substantial effort to apply the concepts proposed in this volume, it will be desirable to go beyond what is stated here and draw fully on the body of knowledge being developed on achieving change in organizations, institutions, and total societies. Useful material will be found in such volumes as Beckhard, 1969; Bennis, 1969; Bowers, 1973; Lawrence and Lorsch, 1969; Mann and Neff, 1961; McCullough, 1975; Schein, 1969.

The general plan proposed assumes that a substantial proportion of the influential persons involved in the conflict are dissatisfied with the present situation and want to take action to bring about significant improvement. If only a few key leaders feel the need for change, a more widespread desire for the improvement will need to be created before starting a program to build an interaction-influence network better equipped to resolve the conflict. Existing problems along with situational requirements can be used to bring about the recognition of the need for improvement in the way the conflict is dealt with and the opportunities that can be realized when improvement occurs.

The process of change (fig. 17-1) begins with the selection of a desired or ideal model. Frequently, this step is overlooked in efforts to bring improvement. But, as Casey Stengel said, "If you don't know where you're going, you'll wind up somewhere else." The participation in the search and selection of a better model increases the motivation for change among those involved in the conflict and, as the desired model is found and as the gaps between what it can accomplish and present experience become more obvious, further motivation for change is generated.

The second step in the cycle is the measurement of the key human organiza-

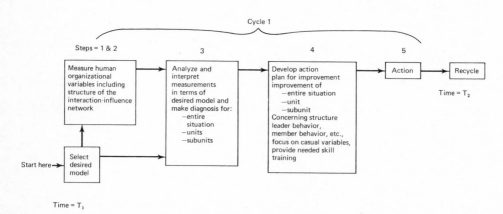

Figure 17-1 *Organizational improvement cycle.*

tional variables to discover how closely the present interaction-influence network approaches the desired model. In the process, as in the selection of the model, the persons affected must be involved. They should know why the data are being obtained and how the data will be used. They must be guaranteed anonymity, when they desire it, in responding to the measuring instruments; they must be convinced that the measurements will be used to bring about improvement and not to punish anyone. Everyone should feel secure about the use of the data.

The various measuring instruments that will be required in most situations have been described in preceding chapters and appear there or in the Appendix. The instruments most appropriate for the particular situation should be used. They should measure the particular variables important in that situation with the accuracy desired. Sometimes in the early phases of an improvement program, only general estimates are needed and not precise measurements. When this is the case, it is wasteful to use the time and resources required to obtain highly accurate data.

In planning what data to collect and how they will be used to bring improvement, consideration should be given to asking the respondents to answer the questionnaire in two ways: first, to describe the situation as they now see it, and second, to tell how they would like it to be. Virtually without exception, what persons would *like* calls for the same changes as those needed to move toward the System 4 model. The discrepancy between the present situation and what persons would like can be used, consequently, in developing action plans and in motivating behavior to bring the desired improvement.

As Figure 17-1 shows, the third step is analysis, interpretation, and diagnosis based on the measurements, particularly in relation to the dimensions specified by the desired model. When persons have planned for the measurements, they are eager to see the results and what the data suggest. They may, however, be somewhat apprehensive. The feedback of the measurements, therefore, should be done in a supportive, nonthreatening manner. The climate should be one that encourages the constructive use of the data, not a defensive response.

In hierarchical organizations such as corporations, a precaution should be taken to assure that the measurements will be used to bring about improvement and not be used punitively. All supervisors can be given the data that show how their own subordinates view the supervisors' behavior and how they react to it. No one else should be given the data that measure a particular supervisor's behavior. As soon as the supervisors become familiar with the implications and feel comfortable about them, they should share the data with their subordinates in sessions devoted to problem solving focused on where and how to bring needed improvement. Supervisors also should be encouraged to share the data with their own supervisor when they feel that they are making progress in achieving improvement and feel secure in sharing the information.

In a conflict situation, it is important to provide leaders or supervisors and their groups with the assistance they need to interpret fully and correctly the measurements obtained, their meaning, and their implications for action. This is especially desirable the first time measurements of the kind proposed here are used. This coaching should be done with a supportive orientation and should recognize fully the positive aspects of the measurements. Data that suggest the need for improvement should be treated as evidence that there is an *opportunity* to be embraced and *not* as evidence of current inadequacies. Insofar as supervisors need coaching in how to use the data in problem-solving sessions to bring improvement, they should be given it. This suggestion assumes that an external consultant (change agent) is aiding in the improvement program or is available to provide the needed expertise. If this is not the case, some provision for this kind of help should be made.

In analyzing the measurements of the human organization and assessing opportunities for improvement, attention should be devoted to the strengths and weaknesses in the operations caused by the strengths and weaknesses in the human organization. Weaknesses in the human organization cause corresponding weaknesses in operations. The best diagnoses make effective use of the data revealing both kinds of weaknesses.

The analysis, interpretation, and diagnosis step should be carried out for all levels and all parts of the interaction-influence network where improvement is being attempted. For example, if the improvement effort is focused on more constructive handling of the conflict between marketing and manufacturing in a firm, the measurements and analysis will have to deal with the interaction-influence network within each department, between the departments, and above the departments. If the improvement effort is focused on union-management relationships, the interaction-influence networks within the company and the union need to be analyzed as well as the network between them.

No questionnaires are presented in this book for measuring the structure of a particular interaction-influence network. However, the general characteristics that any structure should possess are discussed in Chapter 10 of this volume and much more fully in Chapter 10 of *The Human Organization* (Likert, 1967). These characteristics can be used to analyze the structure of the interaction-influence networks undergoing improvement, and deficiencies can be discovered by the discrepancy between the existing structure and the structure specified in Chapter 10.

Planning the action to be taken is step 4 (fig. 17-1). This is based on the analysis, interpretation, and diagnosis of step 3. If the diagnostic step had shown weaknesses in the actual operations corresponding to the weaknesses in the human organization, the action steps should be planned so as to focus on correcting the weaknesses in the operations as well as on improving the human organization. For example, poor performance may be occurring because of poor decisions caused by the supervisor or leader failing to share relevant information with those who made the decision. If this occurred, the action steps should seek to improve the sharing of information by the leader.

Similarly, if the diagnosis had shown inadequacies of a structural character, the action plan should seek to correct them. An example of a structural weakness is the absence of an effective interaction-influence network directly linking persons or groups whose behavior and activities need to be coordinated. This occurs frequently in all kinds of conflicts, as the chapters on structure have indicated. In industry, for example, a common source of unnecessary conflict is the widespread existence of functional lines from the top hierarchical levels of the firm to the bottom levels with little or no cross-functional linkages. Telephone companies commonly have no formal linking structure, such as cross-functional teams, between their various functional departments, such as traffic, plant, commercial, and engineering, except at the very top of the company. This lack of cross-functional linkage results in excessive interdepartmental conflict and has serious adverse effects on productivity and all other aspects of performance.

In planning the action to be taken, the principles and concepts presented in previous chapters should be applied. Some of the more relevant principles are:

1. *Focus the action efforts on the causal variables,* such as leadership behavior and structure. Do not try to change by direct action the intervening variables, such as motivation and control. If the causal variables are improved, there will be subsequent gains in the intervening variables. But if efforts to improve the intervening variables are made by focusing direct action on them, any improvement that occurs is likely to be minor and transitory, and there often is a deterioration in the causal variables with long-range, adverse consequences (Likert, 1973a).

2. *Move to the System 4 model gradually.* Do not attempt one big jump, such as from System 1 to System 4. Move, rather, from System 1 to System 2, from System 2 to System 3, from System 3 to System 4. Both leaders and members lack the skills and find it difficult to make a sudden, sizable shift to System 4. In moving toward it, a leader should make no greater shift at any one time than subordinates or members can adjust to comfortably and respond to positively. If a leader suddenly makes a sizable shift, the members do not have the interaction skills to respond appropriately and usually are made insecure or frightened by the shift and respond to it negatively.

3. *Involve those whose behavior has to change to bring the desired improvement in planning the action to be taken.* It is, of course, important to involve all the persons affected in all the steps of the improvement cycle, but it is especially important to involve them in planning the action effort.

4. *Use objective, impersonal evidence as much as possible in the action-planning process.* This includes using the situational requirements and the discrepancies between the measurements describing the current situation and the desired model. If measurements are available showing what people would like, they also can be used.

5. *Use integrative goals and mutual interests in the decision making that produces the action plan.*

6. *Insofar as the circumstances permit, have those persons who are in the most powerful and influential positions take the most initiative and become most active in the improvement program.* In a corporation, for example, the change programs that are

initiated and supported by top management are more likely to be successful than those started by middle management. Any program started by a middle-level manager that encounters top management's displeasure typically comes to a halt.

7. *Conduct the action planning in a supportive atmosphere* and seek to apply the principle of supportive relationships at every opportunity.

To enable the action plans to be executed well, it is highly likely that some training will be required. The need for training should be assessed carefully. Training may be needed in leadership and interaction skills, in group problem solving, and in the concepts and application of System 4 principles.

In step 5 (fig. 17-1), the action plans are put into operation. At some reasonable interval after the action has started, usually about one year after the first set of measurements was obtained, the improvement cycle should be repeated. The second cycle starts with the remeasurement of the interaction-influence network. Comparison of the remeasurement results with the original measurements reveals whether the action plan, when put into operation, produced the improvement sought. Any discrepancies between the remeasurement results and the desired changes point to areas where further improvement should be attempted by using the improvement cycle. Moreover, the remeasurement data, when compared with the desired model, also reveal opportunities to be embraced in the second improvement cycle for further strengthening the interaction-influence network and its capacity for resolving conflicts constructively.

After the action plans have been developed for the second cycle, they should be put into operation. The third improvement cycle should start with a third wave of measurements taken about one year after the second measurements were obtained.

Preventive action

One effective way to cope with conflict is to anticipate it and take steps, prior to any outbreak, to create forces that will lead to constructive action as was done in the following case:

Two organizations facing economic pressure found that it would be to their mutual benefit if they could develop and operate a major joint venture. It was not feasible for them to establish a separate entity for this undertaking. They had to use their joint facilities and personnel for it. Each organization appointed a coordinator for the new venture. Together these coordinators were to manage the personnel, physical facilities, and all the resources required. The chief executive officers of these two organizations recognized that the joint enterprise would be likely to experience conflict between the personnel. This was especially likely since many of these persons were highly specialized professionals. Rather than wait until conflict erupted, the two executives agreed in advance to approach any conflict that might be appealed to them with the determination and commitment that an acceptable solution could be found, that they would find it, and that they would not let a breakdown occur. They did not use the term, but they agreed to use win-win problem solving until they found a mutually acceptable solution. These two chief executive officers adhered to their agreement, resolved differences constructively, and several years after the joint venture was over, still had excellent working relationships with no unresolved conflicts.

Another way of taking preventive action is to build a highly effective interaction-influence network among parties where a major conflict is likely to occur. Such a network should be in place well in advance of any conflict. It might link union and management prior to negotiations, black and white populations in an urban area, students and the administration in large universities. Wherever a bitter conflict is likely or where even mild differences exist that may escalate into hostility, it is distinctly advantageous to build a System 4 interaction-influence network before conflict erupts.

Avoid built-in conflict

An additional way to minimize conflict is to avoid building the adversary relationship into potentially conflictual situations. The adversary role is win-lose in character. The United States legal system is built on an adversary pattern. This is the prevailing orientation in the teaching of most law schools. Recently, however, some lawyers have been moving from an adversary, win-lose approach to a win-win orientation, resulting in a mutually beneficial solution for all conflicting parties. It is hoped that this trend will continue and spread and that law schools will teach young lawyers this more effective philosophy and technique.

The adversary orientation is being built into a variety of relationships through regulations and legislation. This is occurring, for example, in some situations involving units of federal, state, and local governments and the unions they deal with. The entire pattern of prescribed interaction has an adversary, win-lose orientation often including strict rules as to who may talk to whom about what.

Steps to avoid regression under pressure

At times when individuals encounter problems that they are unable to resolve in a satisfactory way, they become angry. When anger is present, behavior is no longer controlled by that part of the brain most highly developed and most capable of intelligent action. Instead, it is dominated by a primitive part of the brain much less capable of performing intelligent functions.

This kind of regression also occurs in conflicts. When the parties are unable to resolve a conflict in a mutually acceptable manner because of the lack of an effective interaction-influence network, one or both parties may regress. They then resort to a more primitive form of social interaction, such as the use of violence or punitive action.

Examples of this phenomenon are legion. When bargaining breaks down, the union or management, or both, are apt to resort to punitive action or violence. When students, minority groups, or other segments of the society are unable to get the action that they feel is fair and needed, they often riot; in turn, the riots are often countered by brutal punitive action. The Palestinians, being unable to resolve their differences with the Israelis, support guerrillas that engage in acts of violence against the Israelis. The Israelis, in turn, regress to the primitive punitive behavior of "an eye for an eye, a tooth for a tooth" and strike back to "cut off the hand that has killed our youth."

Regression to more primitive social systems is no more effective in solving conflict than is regression to the use of primitive parts of the brain in solving personal problems. It aggravates and intensifies the conflict. It contributes nothing to a constructive resolution of the conflict.

Regression is most likely to occur when conflicts are serious and need, more than others, the most socially evolved and effective interaction-influence network to solve them. Unimportant and minor conflicts are likely to be resolved easily without regression.

Regression can be minimized if the parties to a conflict recognize its likelihood and conscientiously monitor their behavior to prevent it.

Well-established habits can reduce regression

The likelihood that regression will occur in a serious conflict is decreased if the parties involved are highly skilled in using System 4 principles and win-win problem solving and if a System 4T interaction-influence network links the parties. Parties to a conflict who are just learning System 4 principles and problem solving are much more likely to revert to more primitive forms of conflict resolution than are those for whom System 4 is a well-established habit.

The reversion phenomenon has important implications for any major effort to shift to the use of System 4T interaction-influence networks in resolving conflicts. It will be necessary to help persons likely to be involved in conflicts to learn to use this resource with a level of skill that makes its use habitual.

Obtaining professional assistance

In many conflict situations there may be sufficient financial resources available to obtain trained professional help in carrying out the organizational improvement cycle both initially and in subsequent cycles. When this is possible, substantially greater improvement is likely to be achieved in resolving the conflict constructively.

The professionals employed should have the following qualifications:

1. They should be thoroughly familiar with System 4, its structure, and its leadership and interaction processes.

2. They should be highly skilled in conducting every phase of the improvement cycle and in coaching and helping the parties to the conflict become fully involved in every step of the improvement cycle.

3. They should understand the dynamics of organizational or institutional change and be capable of facilitating it.

4. They should have the competence to provide through experiential training the substantive knowledge and the skills required for the successful completion of the organizational improvement cycle.

5. They should be seen by parties to the conflict as being completely impartial, as professionals who are seeking to help resolve the conflict but who are not identified with either party to the conflict. When professionals serve in this capacity, they are serving as third parties who are providing positive intervention in helping to resolve the conflict constructively. (See chap 9.)

Coping with conflicts when bitterly hostile attitudes exist

Let us turn now to some of the approaches that can be used when strong hostility exists between the parties. Strongly held, bitter attitudes are not created overnight, and they cannot be abolished rapidly. Such attitudes make it very difficult to take any of the steps required to build a System 4T interaction-influence network between the parties. It is impossible even to start building an effective interaction-influence network if the parties refuse to meet. The Arab-Israeli conflict displays this pattern; it has proved difficult, if not impossible, to get the leaders to meet personally. Similarly, until the Chinese initiated "Ping-Pong diplomacy" there was no meeting of top governmental leaders of the People's Republic of China and the United States. Some presidents of well-known firms have been heard to state firmly that they would not stay in the same room with the international president of the union with which their firm has its only or major contract. There are leaders among both blacks and whites in the United States who also have displayed this behavior of refusing to meet with leaders of the other party. These are examples of intensely bitter conflict in which it is difficult to bring the parties together to start building a System 4T interaction-influence network.

In some situations, when the leaders refuse to meet, the cause is personal animosity held by one or more of the leaders. In other situations, their refusal to meet is caused by the pressure the leaders feel from the members of their organizations. Some leaders believe that their lives would be threatened were they to meet with leaders of the other party to the conflict.

What steps can be taken, what strategies should be used, to build a System 4T interaction-influence network when these enduring, bitterly hostile attitudes among the parties are present?

Using a third party to help build an interaction-influence network

The use of a third party applies the balance theory of Heider (1958) and the theorems of Harary, Norman, and Cartwright (1965). When the conflicting parties refuse to meet or when there may be a real hazard in attempting to bring them together, an attempt is made to find a third party toward whom each of the conflicting parties has a favorable attitude. An invitation to meet from a disinterested outsider trusted by both sides often results in bringing the parties together in the same room. They may not like each other, but at least they have come together. If the hostility between conflicting parties is especially bitter, the third party may have to conduct some preparatory discussions with each party prior to the meeting.

An example of this approach might be a firm's president (*F*), and the president of an international union (*U*) who hold strongly hostile attitudes toward one another. The third party (*T*) who plays the cohesive role might be a widely respected community leader, such as a university president, a political leader, or a leading lawyer.

Balance theory as extended by the theorems of graph theory shows the direction of influence the third, cohesive, party brings to the situation. As shown in Figure 17-2, the relationships between *T* and *F* and between *T* and *U*

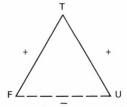

Figure 17-2 *Balance theory as extended by graph theory shows the influence of a third party in a conflict situation (F = firm president, U = union president, T = third party).*

are both positive (+) since they reflect favorable attitudes between the parties. The unfavorable attitudes between *F* and *U* are shown by the negative (−) sign. Any cycle or situation in which there is an *odd* number of negative signs is, according to graph theory, negative in sign and unbalanced. Since an unbalanced state lacks equilibrium, the forces in the situation are toward achieving a balanced state in which there is not an odd number of negative signs; i.e., all signs are positive (+), or there is an even number of negative (−) signs. In the case of our example, the favorable attitudes toward the third, cohesive-role party create pressures in *F* and *U* to shift their attitudes toward one another in a favorable direction.

Balance and equilibrium could be established, of course, if either *F* or *U* were to shift their attitude toward *T* from the + to −. An important part of *T*'s task, consequently, in the cohesive role, is to be sure that neither *F* nor *U* develops unfavorable attitudes toward *T* and to take corrective steps if this starts to occur. Here, again, the principles of supportive relationships can provide useful clues to appropriate behavior by *T*. Even more important and effective will be the use under *T*'s stimulation and leadership of problem solving by *T, F,* and *U* of problems where strong integrative goals exist and are recognized by both *F* and *U*.

Successful problem solving on problems of joint concern to *F* and *U* can vastly accelerate the shift on their part from unfavorable to favorable attitudes toward one another. The problems tackled initially by them should be problems, preferably, where strong integrative goals are clear and persuasive and where compelling situational requirements exist. These initial problems, moreover, should not involve any of the basic issues underlying the bitter, existing hostility because of the strong emotional forces associated with those issues. Other things being equal, the problems tackled first should be those which are most likely to be solved readily to the mutual satisfaction of *F* and *U*.

Needless to say, all the principles, techniques, and suggestions proposed in previous chapters for constructive problem solving to help resolve conflicts should be used by the group as they work on a particular problem. Some of these have been mentioned briefly again in this chapter.

Knowledgeable persons feel that group meetings initiated by such neutral third parties can be of genuine help in union-management conflicts when the interaction-influence network is seriously deficient, especially between the leaders of the two parties. A nationally recognized labor leader favors such action. He feels on the basis of personal experience and observations that serious perceptual distortions occur when there is a gap in the interaction-influence network between union leaders and management. These distortions have serious adverse effects upon the capacity of these leaders to engage in efficient problem solving to resolve the differences between their organizations. He stated quite frankly that until he was 35, he, himself, believed strongly that all foremen and higher levels of management "wore horns." He despised and distrusted all of them. As he has come to know management personnel reasonably well in more recent years through personal contact, he has come to realize how biased his earlier perceptions were and what a block they were to constructive interaction and productive problem solving. He feels that the kind of meetings proposed would help correct biased perceptions and lead to much greater capacity to solve bitter, difficult differences constructively.

A similar point of view exists also among top managers. One cited the case of a colleague who was amazed to find that the hourly employees of the firm were really "decent people." This colleague, a top vice-president in one of the world's largest corporations, had had his hostility toward union members increased greatly by his experiences during a long and costly strike. Several months later he read statements written by several hundred of the firm's employees concerning their jobs and the reasons they liked them. He was greatly surprised by the favorable tone of the statements. The morning after he had spent a long evening reading these statements, he told his colleagues in the office, "Our employees are really fine, decent people. They don't have hostile attitudes toward the company; they are actually interested in the company and its reputation and want to help keep it a leader in its field. You know, we really ought to do much more for these employees of ours."

Third parties can withdraw when their cohesive role is no longer needed

In the situations discussed above, the basic causes of the hostility would not be topics for discussion or group problem solving in the initial sessions of the group. Only after the group had met often enough to become a reasonably effective System 4 interaction-influence network would it be wise to consider examining the major problems underlying the original, bitter hostility. It is probable, however, that there never would be a need for this larger group to work on these problems. The change in the relationships and the beginning of open candid communication which would occur as a result of the initial meetings would enable the parties to the conflict to engage in productive problem solving on their differences without the continuing assistance of third parties.

Other use of third parties

Other techniques can be used in the early phase of the cohesive, third-party approach to help start building an effective interaction-influence network between bitterly hostile parties. One such technique is the T-group laboratory, which is also referred to as "sensitivity training." If conflicting parties can be brought together by a third party in meetings which last several sessions and preferably occur over several consecutive days in pleasant surroundings, T-groups combined with sessions on relevant substantive material often can be effective in starting to change relationships from hostility and distrust to the beginning of open, candid communication (leveling) and the development of trust. It is necessary, however, for the trainer or trainers who provide general direction for such sessions to be highly skilled, sensitive persons. They need to apply the principle of supportive relationships, to understand the role of integrative goals and the processes for recognizing and explicitly stating them, and to be skilled in the use of situational requirements. Personal and group psychotherapy rarely, if ever, have a place in these sessions.

This sensitivity laboratory procedure has been used by Doob (1970) and several colleagues in an effort to "contribute to the solution of two costly, misery-producing conflicts in the Horn of Africa between Ethiopia and Somalia and between Kenya and Somalia" (p. ix). Publications describing the laboratory and subsequent results tell an interesting story. (See Doob, 1970, 1971; Doob, Foltz, and Stevens, 1969; Walton, 1970.)

The *Journal of Applied Behavioral Science* is one of the best sources of papers describing the use of T-groups and the laboratory method for helping to resolve conflicts.

In considering the use of sensitivity traning to resolve conflict, it is well to keep in mind that this training usually deals with only a small part of the social structure required to cope with large and complicated conflicts. Establishing better interpersonal relations with even a few members of conflicting parties is useful. But if conflicts of any magnitude or extent are to be resolved, comprehensive interaction-influence networks linking all parts of the conflicting social systems—industrial, agricultural, cultural, political, economic—must be built and put into operation.

Blake and colleagues have used instrumental laboratories and grid laboratories both to do research on conflict as described in Chapter 4 and also to resolve conflict. Conflicts between headquarters and field, between departments, and between labor and management have been dealt with constructively by applying Blake's grid model (Blake et al., 1964).

Walton has an excellent small volume on the role of the third party in resolving conflicts (Walton, 1969). Persons interested in using this approach will find his book highly useful.

Multiple parties may be needed to perform cohesive role

In many bitter conflicts, it will be necessary to extend the cohesive-party approach to include more than one third party. A fourth, a fifth, or even more parties often may be required when no single third party sufficiently trusted by both of the bitterly hostile conflicting parties can be found.

In such situations, the following may be a workable strategy. Suppose, as shown in Figure 17-3a, that A and B are the bitterly hostile parties and that A has relatively favorable attitudes toward C and trusts C. And suppose that B has

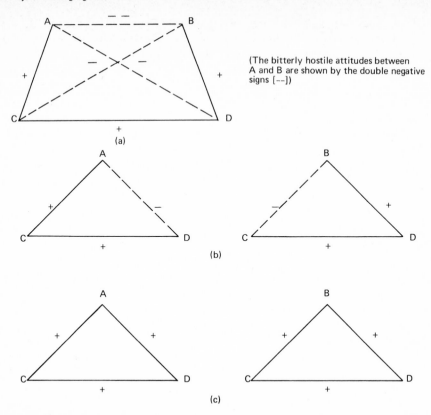

(The bitterly hostile attitudes between A and B are shown by the double negative signs [--])

Figure 17-3 *Balance theory as extended by graph theory shows the influence of more than one third party in a conflict situation (A and B = hostile parties, C and D = third parties). The marked hostility of A and B (a) gives way (b) and (c) to mutual confidence in C and D.*

comparably favorable attitudes toward *D* and trusts *D*, but *B* does not trust or have favorable attitudes toward *C*. And *A* does not trust or have favorable attitudes toward *D*. *C* and *D*, however, have mutually favorable attitudes and reciprocal trust. In such a situation the cohesive third-party approach would be started by building a reasonably effective interaction-influence network embracing *A*, *C*, and *D*. *C*, of course, would be the cohesive third party and would take the initiative in this effort. At about the same time, *D* would start building a reasonably effective interaction-influence network including *B*, *D*, and *C*. In this case *D* is the cohesive third party and would initiate the activity.

In suggesting topics to be worked on, *C* in the *ACD* meetings and *D* in the *BDC* meetings, would endeavor to propose problems which are of importance and concern to both *A* and *B*. *C* and *D* might, for example, be nations or committees or specialized agencies of the United Nations. The problem could be a problem of great concern to *A* and *B*. In the case of the Arab-Israeli difficulties, it might be the development of water resources through such processes as desalinization. By means of all the principles and procedures proposed in this and previous chapters, C would endeavor to build a reasonably effective interaction-influence network linking ACD, and D would endeavor to do the same for BDC. In these efforts, C and D should, of course, keep each other well informed and their activities coordinated since they are performing the third-party function as a team.

The next phase of the cohesive-party process can start after C has successfully built a reasonably effective interaction-influence network linking ACD, and D has done the same for BDC. This change is shown in Figure 17-3 in the shift from 17-3b to 17-3c. Although A and B are still bitterly hostile toward each other, their mutual confidence and favorable attitudes now toward both C and D would enable C and D to bring A and B together in a meeting. In this meeting both A and B would feel, in accordance with graph theory (see fig. 17-4a) forces acting on them to shift their attitudes from hostility toward friendship as shown in Figure 17-4b. It would be necessary, of course, to do much preparatory work prior to this meeting in separate sessions of ACD and BDC. This second phase involving face-to-face meetings of $A, B, C,$ and D would go through the same cycle of problem-solving activity suggested previously and normally used in the cohesive third-party approach. In this second phase, the pacing would probably be slower and C and D would probably have to work harder than in situations where only a single third party is required.

Closing the interaction-influence gap

Whenever the cohesive-party approach is used, there is always a final phase to be executed when the situation is ripe for it: the substitution of a newly built interaction-influence network linking A and B for the larger more complex and circuitous interaction-influence network which includes C and D.

This weaning from the larger interaction-influence network to the newly created shorter linkage has to be done, of course, in a careful, sensitive manner.

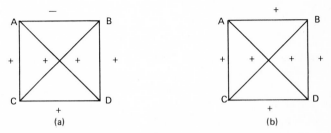

Figure 17-4 *Graph theory shows the shift from hostility (a) to friendship (b) between A and B brought about by third parties C and D.*

Any relatively new interaction-influence network, especially when it provides linkage among bitterly conflicting parties, is a delicate social fabric easily torn. Consequently, *C* and *D* would do well to watch, insofar as possible, the use of the new short linkage and encourage its use first for dealing with less intense problems likely to be resolved with relative ease. As this new short interaction-influence network grows in strength from successful use, it will develop the capability of resolving progressively more difficult and complex issues and conflicts.

During this weaning process, *C* and *D* can help maintain and increase the strength of the interaction-influence network linking *A* and *B* as well as keep informed on developments by continuing to use the total interaction-influence network to work on problems of concern to all four parties.

When an intensely bitter conflict involves large organizations, institutions, or nations, the process just described should be undertaken also to create many other linkages in addition to that linking the formal leaders of the conflicting parties. If the conflicting parties are nations, a maximum number of strong linkages should be built (1) between the governments and governmental units of these nations, and (2) between the organizations and influential citizens of these nations. These strong interaction-influence networks should be established between every important unit of these governments. These include, of course, the links between the heads of the governments and between their foreign offices or departments of state. But highly effective interaction-influence networks should be established also between every relevant branch of these governments, such as branches concerned with agriculture, education, labor, commerce, science, and transportation. Every one of these interaction-influence networks would help to provide additional channels for communication, problem solving, and influence which would perform important functions in efforts to resolve conflicts between these nations. For the same reasons and to perform the same functions, strong interaction-influence networks should be established between the nongovernmental organizations and the influential citizens of one nation and those of the others. This activity should include such organizations as labor unions, professional and scientific societies, business and trade groups, and educational associations. Multinational companies can make constructive contributions to this linkage process if they choose to do so.

Building these highly effective interaction-influence networks between conflicting nations and between the influential citizens and organizations of these nations will not provide the tough social fabric needed to resolve bitter conflicts unless the social fabric within each nation is strengthened correspondingly. The internal interaction-influence networks within each nation's government and its total society need to be as highly effective as the interaction-influence networks between nations. Otherwise, the social fabric will tear and the communication, influence, and problem-solving processes will fail at their weakest point within the nation. Such failures will prevent the coordinated problem solving and action required to resolve the bitter conflicts between the nations.

Stronger party should take initiative in using System 4

In most conflicts, one party is somewhat stronger than the other and has the capability and opportunity of determining how the conflict will be waged. The stronger party can and usually does select whether to use a System 1, 2, 3, or 4 model of interaction for dealing with the conflict. If System 1 or 2 is used, the conflict is suppressed by force and the weaker party is compelled to knuckle under and overtly comply with the pattern set by the stronger party. This has been the pattern of black-white and other race and minority relations in the United States and the rest of the world. This pattern does not resolve the conflict, it only drives it underground and intensifies it and the emotions associated with it. In despair, the weaker party may resort to violence. Violence occasionally enables a weaker party to make some gains, however temporary, which are beneficial to it. Much more often, the results are all negative, including a marked increase in the bitterness of the conflict.

Gandhi, Martin Luther King, and others have shown the weaker party how to use nonaggression in various forms to compel the stronger party to deal with the weaker in a System 3 or 4 pattern. Nonagression does not seem to intensify hostility but, rather, to create forces leading to solutions acceptable to both parties.

Since the use of the System 1 or 2 pattern intensifies a conflict, the stronger party, with its capacity to set the pattern, should use System 4 and the win-win approach. This will greatly increase the likelihood of achieving constructive solutions acceptable to the conflicting parties.

In many conflicts, third or fourth parties also can play a crucial role by taking the initiative to start building a System 4 interaction-influence network for resolving the conflict. Often anyone willing to act can start constructive action. In the case of third- and fourth-party role activity, the more prestigious persons usually are in a better position to initiate action. Nevertheless, in any conflict situation, the initiative in building the needed interaction-influence networks can be taken by anyone sufficiently concerned to undertake it.

In weighing the pros and cons of making the effort to use the System 4 approach to resolving a serious conflict, it is well to consider the time, costs, frustrations, and suffering involved in alternate ways of handling such major conflicts as those among nations. The major international conflicts have shown little improvement in decades with the approaches now being used. In the meantime, the tremendous increase in the power of weapons makes these conflicts much more serious for all humanity.

The label does not matter

As the material in this volume indicates, there is substantial evidence that the use in conflicts of the more socially evolved and effective system, System 4T, would be likely to resolve conflicts much more constructively than is now the case. In applying System 4T, it is unimportant, and at times it may be disadvantageous, to use the label. All that is necessary is to have the problem solving and interaction-influence processes approximate, as closely as possible, the characteristics of what we call, for convenience, "System 4T."

18
Looking to the future

Scientific knowledge has provided us with the tools to master our physical environment, but in doing so has greatly aggravated the problems man faces with himself, so that his welfare and probably his continued existence depend upon the outcome of a race between the achievement of his greater and greater ability to manipulate the physical world and the evolution of a social and political structure capable of controlling the great forces that have been unleashed.

Jerome B. Wiesner (1965, p. 28)

The vast sums of money that we are spending and have spent on research in the physical and biological sciences have yielded benefits to humanity, but this research also has created resources and developments that can destroy humankind. Nuclear bombs, guided missiles, biological warfare, nerve gas, and pollution of air and water are examples.

We have produced these powerful weapons and forces, but we have not developed the social systems and international problem-solving resources to control them. Support of social science research in the United States and other countries has been far too niggardly to create the quantum leaps in the development of more effective social institutions to parallel the great advances in the physical and biological sciences. Since 1945 the expenditures in the United States for social science research have been only about 2 percent of the total funds spent on all research.

At the present time our expenditures for research and development are still out of balance. We continue to spend too little on social science research to learn how to control the problems that other research is creating. Great sums are being spent on the physical and biological research which will produce still more complex and interdependent societies and even greater conflict. An illustration of the growing problems is the following excerpt from an article "World Water Supply Threatened . . . ," which appeared in the February 1972, issue of the *Survey of International Development:*

> The world is threatened by depletion of its fresh water resources, a Food and Agriculture Organization (FAO) study warns, because of the combined impact of such major factors as population increase, relentlessly demanding more water use; global industrial development; intensified agricultural methods of cultivation, requiring growing reliance on irrigation; and water pollution, caused particularly by massive fouling of the world's oceans as well as of inland fresh water resources. . . .
>
> The study notes that without drastic measures for conservation and rational use of fresh water, the world is likely to run short of this vital life maintenance source within the next century. . . .
>
> The FAO study's conclusions point to disaster for the world if it continues its present reckless course of not conserving fresh water. At the same time, the study also examines a broad range of corrective measures. (pp. 1–2)

This FAO report on water indicates that the technical knowledge to solve the problem exists or can be readily developed by relevant technical research. The serious side of the problem is getting action, especially on those aspects of the problem such as ocean pollution where cooperative, coordinated action from many nations is needed. We have the technical resources to solve the problem but lack the structure and the problem-solving mechanism to reach a win-win, cooperative solution, that is, a solution acceptable to all nations and one that they will willingly implement. The present problem solving is typically competitive win-lose (zero sum) in character. One nation gains at the expense of the other. Win-lose competitive problem solving is incapable of achieving the worldwide cooperative coordination required for the successful solution of the world's water problems.

In his syndicated column on March 20, 1974, James Reston[1] made the following statement:

> Helmut Schmidt, minister of finance of the Federal Republic of Germany, is almost as gloomy about the divisions among the advanced nations at a time when the world economy, despite recent boom conditions, is entering a phase of extraordinary instability.
>
> Writing in Foreign Affairs for April, he sees a struggle for the distribution of essential raw materials developing in the world, with most nations looking to their own selfish interests and avoiding the cooperative planning necessary to meet their common problems.
>
> Again the nations are misjudging the magnitude of the coming problems and the fragility of the present system of distributing world goods and paying for them. What remains, Schmidt asserts, "are resourceful bickerings over the results of joint efforts, a game full of ruses and little tricks, with strategies of threats, attrition and fatigue, of overnight conferences and dissolved meetings, a game of coalitions and cartels. . . .

"It is a struggle for the distribution and use of the national product, a struggle for the world product. . . ." Schmidt says. "The struggle over oil prices may be followed tomorrow by a similar struggle over the prices of other import raw materials. And since what is at stake is not just pawns on a chessboard, but the peaceful evolution of the world economy and the prosperity of the nations of the world, we need a politically sound philosphy if we are to win this dangerous fight."

This same situation is true also for many other growing problems that call for worldwide, coordinated solutions. Air pollution, food shortages, shortages in raw materials and minerals, energy crises, and over-population cannot be solved effectively by the win-lose method of problem solving. A problem can be suppressed for a period of time by the win-lose method, but this leads to a fear-charged stalemate accompanied usually by growing hatred. The win-lose method, consequently, aggravates and intensifies conflicts but does not resolve them. Enduring solutions to these serious, complex problems can be achieved only by problem-solving methods that yield solutions acceptable to all parties to the conflict.

There is urgent need for research and application efforts to discover and make operational use of more effective institutions at the national and international levels capable of achieving agreements on serious problems acceptable to all. The marked superiority of System 4T over existing systems demonstrates that much more powerful models for building and operating our social institutions can be discovered through research and made operational.

When the United States decided it needed the atomic bomb, it poured many billions of dollars into the research and development to create it and within a few years had it. Similarly, when the decision was made to put a man on the moon within a decade, tens of billions of dollars under the direction of the National Aeronautics and Space Administration (NASA) were poured into research, development, building the hardware, and training the personnel. The mission was accomplished on schedule. This same massive-effort approach could be used to accelerate the creation of the interaction-influence networks among nations and within nations required to resolve international conflicts constructively. It would need a large research and development program to discover the nature of the interaction-influence networks required and the most efficient ways of shifting to these better networks both within nations and among them. To apply this knowledge, there must be a large cadre of trained personnel. They would train the relevant persons within nations and in international organizations to build and use the much more effective interaction-influence networks that are required. This effort would be likely to receive support in each nation since these networks and the skills to use them would be of great value to nations. The nations possessing them would be able to perform much more efficiently all such activities as industrial production, education, health care, and government.

The sum required for this research and action program could be provided by a single nation, such as the United States, or by a consortium of nations acting either directly or through the United Nations. A consortium of nations financing the undertaking, rather than a single nation, would be likely to decrease nationalistic resistance.

To ensure enduring peace, some nations might need to spend on this research and action program as much as they put into their annual defense budgets. (The defense budget of the United States was $80 billion in 1974.)

Initially, the expenditures could not be at this rate, for there is a lack of trained researchers and action persons. As more personnel with the required research and action skills become available, the rate of expenditures should be increased accordingly.

The administration of the research and development effort and the action phases should be handled, as in the case of NASA, by persons thoroughly competent to conduct these activities. The undertaking should be funded and organized in a manner to assure highly competent administration.

The United States and other nations are spending vast sums on the physical and biological sciences and should continue to do so. The knowledge gained from this research and development, however, is creating many of the world's most serious conflicts and problems. We are now faced with the decision of spending equal or greater sums on the social sciences to create the problem-solving resources needed to resolve our serious social and political problems. We clearly need to do so.

Appendix

The bulk of the items in the table below, "Profile of Organizational Characteristics," were first published as Table 14-1 in *New Patterns of Management* (Likert, 1961) with the title "Organizational and Performance Characteristics of Different Management Systems Based on a Comparative Analysis." After Dr. William Swartley suggested that Table 14-1 could be used to measure the management system being employed by an organization or unit within it, the table was enlarged by adding leadership items and a few other items to it.

This enlarged table was published as Appendix II in *The Human Organization: Its Management and Value* (Likert, 1967) and was entitled "Profile of Organizational Characteristics." The table was accompanied by instructions to be used in administering it whenever it was to be used to measure the management system of an organization or organizational subunit.

The original purpose of the items in the "Profile of Organizational Characteristics" was, consequently, to describe the nature of different management systems, not to measure them. The use of the "Profile" to measure management systems was a later development.

An examination of the items in the table below will reveal that many of the items are better for describing and defining a management system than they are for measuring it. The wording of the alternatives is too complex and too long to serve the measurement function well.

This complex wording is retained in the Appendix since the primary purpose of the "Profile" in this volume is to define the different management systems, not to measure them. Although this "Profile" can be used with suitable instructions to measure the management system of an organization, it is rather cumbersome and inefficient. The table below is a slightly revised version of Appendix II in *The Human Organization: Its Management and Value.*

A shorter and much simpler form of the "Profile of Organizational Characteristics" is already available. This is form S (S for short) and appears in Chapter 5 as Figure 5-2.

A long form of the "Profile of Organizational Characteristics" with short, simple wording of the alternatives is being developed. It will be available after field tests, inter-item correlations, and factor analyses reveal that it is satisfactory for general use. Both this new long form and the S form can be used with both supervisory and nonsupervisory personnel.

Table A-1

Profile of organizational characteristics

Organizational variables	Item no.	System 1	System 2	System 3	System 4
LEADERSHIP PROCESSES USED Extent to which your supervisor has confidence and trust in *subordinates*	1	Has very little confidence and trust in subordinates ① ②	Has some confidence and trust ③ ④	Has quite a bit of confidence and trust ⑤ ⑥	Has a very great deal of confidence and trust ⑦ ⑧
Extent to which you, in turn, have confidence and trust in your supervisor	2	Have very little confidence and trust in my supervisor ① ②	Have some confidence and trust ③ ④	Have quite a bit of confidence and trust ⑤ ⑥	Have a very great deal of confidence and trust ⑦ ⑧
Extent to which your supervisor displays supportive behavior toward others	3	Displays virtually no supportive behavior ① ②	Displays supportive behavior in a few situations ③ ④	Displays supportive behavior in a moderate number of situations ⑤ ⑥	Displays supportive behavior quite generally and consistently ⑦ ⑧
Extent to which your supervisor behaves so that subordinates feel free to discuss important things about their jobs with him or her	4	Subordinates do not feel at all free to discuss things about the job with their supervisor ① ②	Subordinates feel slightly free to discuss things about the job with their supervisor, but discuss things guardedly ③ ④	Subordinates feel quite free to discuss things about the job with their supervisor, but with some caution ⑤ ⑥	Subordinates feel completely free to discuss things about the job with their supervisor and do so candidly ⑦ ⑧

Profile of organizational characteristics

Organizational variables	Item no.	System 1	System 2	System 3	System 4
Extent to which your supervisor in solving job problems generally tries to get subordinates' ideas and opinions and make constructive use of them	5	Virtually never gets ideas and opinions of subordinates in solving job problems ① ②	Occasionally gets ideas and opinions of subordinates in solving job problems ③ ④	Usually gets ideas and opinions and usually tries to make constructive use of them ⑤ ⑥	Virtually always gets ideas and opinions and tries to make constructive use of them ⑦ ⑧

CHARACTER OF MOTIVATIONAL FORCES

Organizational variables	Item no.	System 1	System 2	System 3	System 4
Underlying motives tapped: (A) *Desire for physical security* (B) *Economic motives* (C) *Desire to achieve and maintain a sense of personal worth and importance* (D) *Desire for new experience*	6	Major use of (A); moderate use of (B); slight use of (C) in form of desire for status and power ① ②	Some use of (A); extensive use of (B); some use of (C) in form of desire for status and power and by recognition and by achievement ③ ④	(A) Fulfilled; extensive use of (B); moderate use of (C) in form of desire for recognition and achievement and some use of (C) in form of power and status; some use of (D) ⑤ ⑥	(A) Fulfilled. Highly effective use of (B) achieved by involvement in decisions on how best to use economic motivations fully. Extensive use of (C) through group problem solving and resulting desire for achievement and self-actualization. Effective use of (D) ⑦ ⑧

Organizational variable	1	2	3	4	5	6	7	8
7. Manner in which motives are used	Fear, threats, punishment, and occasional rewards		Rewards and some actual or potential punishment		Rewards, occasional punishment, and some involvement		Economic rewards based on compensation system developed through participation: group participation and involvement in setting goals, improving methods, appraising progress toward goals, etc. Full recognition of achievement	
8. Kinds of attitudes developed toward organization and its goals	Attitudes usually are hostile and counter to organization's goals		Attitudes sometimes are hostile and counter to organization's goals and sometimes are favorable to the organization's goals and support the behavior necessary to achieve them		Attitudes usually are favorable and support behavior implementing organization's goals		Attitudes are strongly favorable and provide powerful stimulation to behavior implementing organization's goals	

Profile of organizational characteristics (Continued)

Organizational variables	Item no.	System 1	System 2	System 3	System 4
Extent to which motivational forces conflict with or reinforce one another	9	Marked conflict of forces substantially reducing those motivational forces leading to behavior in support of the organization's goals ① ②	Conflict usually exists; occasionally some forces will reinforce each other in support of the organization's goals at least partially ③ ④	Some conflict, but often motivational forces in support of the organization's goals will reinforce each other ⑤ ⑥	Motivational forces in support of the organization's goals generally reinforce each other in a substantial and cumulative manner ⑦ ⑧
Amount of responsibility felt by each member of organization for achieving organization's goals	10	High levels of management feel responsibility; lower levels feel less; rank and file feel little and often welcome opportunity to behave in ways to defeat organization's goals ① ②	Managerial personnel usually feel responsibility; rank and file usually feel relatively little responsibility for achieving organization's goals ③ ④	Substantial proportion of personnel, especially at higher levels, feel responsibility and generally behave in ways to achieve the organization's goals ⑤ ⑥	Personnel at all levels feel real responsibility for organization's goals and behave in ways to implement them ⑦ ⑧

Organizational variable	1 2	3 4	5 6	7 8
11 Attitudes toward other members of the organization	Subservient attitudes toward supervisors coupled with hostility; hostility toward peers and contempt for subordinates; distrust is widespread ① ②	Subservient attitudes toward supervisors; competition for status resulting in hostility toward peers; condescension toward subordinates ③ ④	Cooperative, reasonably favorable attitudes toward others in organization; may be some competition between peers with resulting hostility and some condescension toward subordinates ⑤ ⑥	Favorable, cooperative attitudes throughout the organization with mutual trust and confidence ⑦ ⑧
12 Satisfaction derived	Usually dissatisfaction with membership in the organization, with supervision, and with one's own achievements ① ②	Dissatisfaction to moderate satisfaction with regard to membership in the organization, supervision, and one's own achievements ③ ④	Some dissatisfaction to moderately high satisfaction with regard to membership in the organization, supervision, and one's own achievements ⑤ ⑥	Relatively high satisfaction throughout the organization with regard to membership in the organization, supervision, and one's own achievements ⑦ ⑧

CHARACTER OF COMMUNICATION PROCESS

Organizational variable	1 2	3 4	5 6	7 8
13 Amount of interaction and communication aimed at achieving organization's objectives	Very little ① ②	Little ③ ④	Quite a bit ⑤ ⑥	Much with both individual and groups ⑦ ⑧

Profile of organizational characteristics (Continued)

Organizational variables	Item no.	System 1	System 2	System 3	System 4
Direction of information flow	14	Downward ① ②	Mostly downward ③ ④	Down and up ⑤ ⑥	Down, up, and with peers ⑦ ⑧
Downward communication where initiated	15	At top of organization or to implement top directive ① ②	Primarily at top or patterned on communication from top ③ ④	Patterned on communication from top but with some initiative at lower levels ⑤ ⑥	Initiated at all levels ⑦ ⑧
Extent to which supervisors willingly share information with subordinates	16	Provide minimum of information ① ②	Give subordinates only information supervisors feel they need ③ ④	Give information needed and answer most questions ⑤ ⑥	Seek to give subordinates all relevant information and all information they want ⑦ ⑧
Extent to which downward communications are accepted by subordinates	17	Viewed with great suspicion ① ②	Some accepted and some viewed with suspicion ③ ④	Often accepted but, if not, may or may not be openly questioned ⑤ ⑥	Generally accepted, but if not, openly and candidly questioned ⑦ ⑧
Adequacy of upward communication via line organization	18	Very little ① ②	Limited ③ ④	Some ⑤ ⑥	A great deal ⑦ ⑧

		(1) (2)	(3) (4)	(5) (6)	(7) (8)
Subordinates' feeling of responsibility for initiating accurate upward communication	19	Virtually none	Relatively little, usually communicates "filtered" information and only when requested; may "yes" the boss	Some to moderate degree of responsibility to initiate accurate upward communication	Considerable responsibility felt and much initiative; group communicates all relevant information
Forces leading to accurate or distorted upward information	20	Powerful forces to distort information and deceive supervisors	Many forces to distort; also forces for honest communication	Occasional forces to distort along with many forces to communicate accurately	Virtually no forces to distort and powerful forces to communicate accurately
Accuracy of upward communication via line	21	Tends to be inaccurate	Information that boss wants to hear flows; other information is restricted and often inaccurate	Information that boss wants to hear flows; other information fairly to reasonably accurate	Accurate
Need for supplementary upward communication system	22	Great need to supplement upward communication by spy system, suggestion system, and similar devices	Upward communication often supplemented by suggestion system and similar devices	Some need for supplementary system; suggestion systems may be used	No need for any supplementary system

Profile of organizational characteristics (Continued)

Organizational variables	Item no.	System 1	System 2	System 3	System 4
Sideward communication: its adequacy and accuracy	23	Usually poor because of competition between peers, corresponding hostility ① ②	Fairly poor because of competition between peers ③ ④	Fair to good ⑤ ⑥	Good to excellent ⑦ ⑧
Psychological closeness of supervisors to subordinates (i.e., friendly, sincere, frank interaction between supervisors and subordinates)	24	Far apart ① ②	Moderately close if proper roles are kept ③ ④	Fairly close ⑤ ⑥	Usually very close ⑦ ⑧
How well do supervisors know and understand problems faced by subordinates?	25	Has no knowledge or understanding of problems of subordinates ① ②	Has some knowledge and understanding of problems of subordinates ③ ④	Knows and understands problems of subordinates quite well ⑤ ⑥	Knows and understands problems of subordinates very well ⑦ ⑧
How accurate are the perceptions by supervisors and subordinates of each other?	26	Often in error ① ②	Often in error on some points ③ ④	Moderately accurate ⑤ ⑥	Usually quite accurate ⑦ ⑧

CHARACTER OF INTERACTION-INFLUENCE PROCESS

		System 1	System 2	System 3	System 4
		Little	Little interaction and usually with some condescension by	Moderate interaction, often	Extensive, friendly interaction with

#	Question	1	2	3	4	5	6	7	8
27	Amount and character of interaction	interaction and always with fear and distrust		supervisors; fear and caution by subordinates		with fair amount of confidence and trust		high degree of confidence and trust	
28	Amount of cooperative teamwork present to achieve organization's goals	Virtually none		Relatively little		A moderate amount		Very substantial amount throughout the organization	
29	Extent to which subordinates can influence the goals, methods, and activity of their units and departments as seen by supervisors	Practically none		A slight amount		Moderate amount		A great deal	
30	Extent to which subordinates can influence the goals, methods, and activity of their units and departments as seen by subordinates	Practically none except through "informal organization" or via unionization		Little except through "informal organization" or via unionization		Moderate amount both directly and via unionization		Substantial amount both directly and via unionization	
31	Amount of actual influence which supervisors can exercise over the goals, activity, and methods of their units and departments	Believed to be substantial but actually moderate unless capacity to exercise severe punishment is present		Moderate to somewhat more than moderate, especially for higher levels in organization		Moderate to substantial, especially for higher levels in organization		Substantial but often done indirectly, as, for example, by supervisor building effective interaction-influence system	

Table A-1

Profile of organizational characteristics (Continued)

Organizational variables	Item no.	System 1	System 2	System 3	System 4
Extent to which an effective structure exists enabling one part of organization to exert lateral influence upon other parts	32	Effective structure virtually absent ① ②	Limited capacity exists; influence exerted vertically and primarily downward ③ ④	Moderately effective structure exists; influence vertically ⑤ ⑥	Highly effective structure exists enabling exercise of influence in all directions ⑦ ⑧
CHARACTER OF DECISION-MAKING PROCESS					
To what extent are decisions made by supervisors or by group participation and consensus?	33	By supervisors (or higher levels) with practically no opportunity for discussion ① ②	By supervisors, but with some opportunity for discussion ③ ④	By supervisors, but following discussion of problems ⑤ ⑥	By group participation and usually with consensus ⑦ ⑧
How adequate and accurate is the information available for decision making at *the place where decisions are made?*	34	Information is generally inadequate and inaccurate ① ②	Information is often somewhat inadequate and inaccurate ③ ④	Moderately adequate and accurate information available ⑤ ⑥	Relatively complete and accurate information available based both on measurements and efficient flow of information in organizations ⑦ ⑧

35. To what extent are decision makers aware of problems, particularly those at lower levels in the organization?

Often are unaware or only partially aware		Aware of some, unaware of others		Moderately aware of problems		Generally quite well aware of problems	
①	②	③	④	⑤	⑥	⑦	⑧

36. To what extent are technical and professional knowledge used in decision making?

Used only if possessed at higher levels		Much of the knowledge available in higher and middle levels is used		Much of the knowledge available in higher, middle, and lower levels is used		Most of the knowledge available within the organization is used	
①	②	③	④	⑤	⑥	⑦	⑧

37. Are decisions made at the best level in the organization as far as availability of the most adequate information bearing on the decision?

Decisions usually made at levels appreciably higher than levels where most adequate and accurate information exists		Decisions often made at levels appreciably higher than levels where most adequate and accurate information exists		Some tendency for decisions to be made at higher levels than where most adequate and accurate information exists		Overlapping groups and group decision processes tend to push decisions to point where information is most adequate or to pass the relevant information to the decision-making point	
①	②	③	④	⑤	⑥	⑦	⑧

Profile of organizational characteristics

Organizational variables	Item no.	System 1	System 2	System 3	System 4
Are decisions made at the best level in the organization as far as the motivational consequences (i.e., does the decision-making process help to create the necessary motivations in those persons who have to carry out the decisions)?	38	Decision making contributes little or nothing to the motivation to implement the decision, usually yields adverse motivation ① ②	Decision making contributes relatively little motivation ③ ④	Some contribution by decision making to motivation to implement ⑤ ⑥	Substantial contribution by decision-making processes to motivation to implement ⑦ ⑧
To what extent are subordinates involved in decisions related to their work?	39	Virtually none ① ②	Rarely involved in decisions; occasionally consulted ③ ④	Usually are consulted but ordinarily not involved in the decision making ⑤ ⑥	Are almost always involved in all decisions related to their work ⑦ ⑧
Are decisions made in person-to-person or group interaction and with limited or open discussion?	40	By superior in person-to-person, little discussion ① ②	By superior in person-to-person, some discussion ③ ④	By superior in person-to-person, with quite open discussion ⑤ ⑥	By group with very open and candid discussion ⑦ ⑧

CHARACTER OF GOAL SETTING OR ORDERING

System 3: Except in emergencies, goals are set or

System 4: Except in

41 In what manner is it usually done?

Orders issued		Orders issued, opportunity to comment may or may not exist		orders issued after discussion with subordinates of problems and planned action		emergencies, goals are established by means of group participation
①	②	③	④	⑤	⑥	⑦ ⑧

42 To what extent do the different hierarchical levels tend to strive for high performance goals?

High goals pressed by top, generally resisted by subordinates		High goals sought by top and often resisted moderately by subordinates		High goals sought by higher levels but with occasional resistance by lower levels		High goals sought by all levels, with lower levels sometimes pressing for higher goals than top levels
①	②	③	④	⑤	⑥	⑦ ⑧

43 Are there forces to accept, resist, or reject goals?

Goals are overtly accepted but are covertly resisted strongly		Goals are overtly accepted but often covertly resisted to at least a moderate degree		Goals are overtly accepted but at times with some covert resistance		Goals are fully accepted both overtly and covertly
①	②	③	④	⑤	⑥	⑦ ⑧

CHARACTER OF CONTROL PROCESSES

44 At what hierarchical levels in organization does major or primary concern exist with regard to the performance of the control function?

At the very top only		Primarily or largely at the top		Primarily at the top but some shared feeling of responsibility at middle and to a less extent at lower levels		Concern for performance of control functions likely to be felt throughout organization
①	②	③	④	⑤	⑥	⑦ ⑧

Table A-1

Profile of organizational characteristics (Continued)

Organizational variables	Item no.	System 1	System 2	System 3	System 4
How accurate are the measurements and information used to guide and perform the control function, and to what extent do forces exist in the organization to distort and falsify this information?	45	Very strong forces exist to distort and falsify; as a consequence, measurements and information are usually incomplete and often inaccurate ① ②	Fairly strong forces exist to distort and falsify; hence measurements and information are often incomplete and inaccurate ③ ④	Some pressure to protect self and colleagues and hence some pressures to distort; information is only moderately complete and contains some inaccuracies ⑤ ⑥	Strong pressures to obtain complete and accurate information to guide own behavior and behavior of own and related work groups; hence information and measurements tend to be complete and accurate ⑦ ⑧
To what extent are the review and control functions concentrated?	46	Highly concentrated in top management ① ②	Relatively highly concentrated, with some delegated control to middle and lower levels ③ ④	Moderate downward delegation of review and control processes; lower as well as higher levels perform these tasks ⑤ ⑥	Review and control done at all levels with lower units at times imposing more vigorous reviews and tighter controls than top management ⑦ ⑧

47

To what extent is there an informal organization present supporting or opposing goals of formal organization?

Informal organization present and opposing goals of formal organization		Informal organization usually present and partially resisting goals		Informal organization may be present and may either support or partially resist goals of formal organization		Informal and formal organization are one and the same; hence all social forces support efforts to achieve organization's goals	
①	②	③	④	⑤	⑥	⑦	⑧

48

To what extent are accounting, productivity, cost, and similar data used for self-guidance or group problem solving by managers and nonsupervisory employees, or used by supervisors in a punitive, policing manner?

Used for policing and in punitive manner		Used for policing coupled with reward and punishment, sometimes punitively; used somewhat for guidance but in accord with orders		Used for policing with emphasis usually on reward but with some punishment; used for guidance in accord with orders; some use also for self-guidance		Used for self-guidance and for coordinated problem solving and guidance; not used punitively	
①	②	③	④	⑤	⑥	⑦	⑧

49

To what extent are the human organization measurements and performance measurements needed for efficient planning and action obtained regularly at the most useful intervals and fed back rapidly to the members of the organization for their decision making and the guidance of their operations?

Very little		Some		Considerable		Very great	
①	②	③	④	⑤	⑥	⑦	⑧

Table A-1

Profile of organizational characteristics *(Continued)*

PERFORMANCE GOALS AND TRAINING*

Organizational variables	Item no.							
Level of performance goals which supervisors seek to have organization achieve	50*	Seek average goals ① ②	Seek high goals ③ ④	Seek very high goals ⑤ ⑥	Seek to achieve extremely high goals ⑦ ⑧
Extent to which you have been given the kind of management training you desire	51*	Have received no management training of kind I desire ① ②	Have received some management training of kind I desire ③ ④	Have received quite a bit of management training of kind I desire ⑤ ⑥	Have received a great deal of management training of kind I desire ⑦ ⑧
Adequacy of training resources provided to assist you in training your subordinates	52*	Training resources provided are only fairly good ① ②	Training resources provided are good ③ ④	Training resources provided are very good ⑤ ⑥	Training resources provided are excellent ⑦ ⑧

* These items do not measure the System 1 to 4 continuum but do measure other variables that affect the performance level of an organization. (See table 3-1.)

References

Adizes, I. *The effect of decentralization on organizational behavior.* (Doctoral dissertation, Columbia University) Ann Arbor: University Microfilms, 1971, No. 71-17, 563.

Alger, C., Decision-making theory and human conflict. In E. McNeil (Ed.), *The Nature of human conflict.* Englewood Cliffs, N.J.: Prentice-Hall, 1965, pp. 274–292.

Almond, G. A., & Verba, S. *The civic culture.* Princeton, N.J.: Princeton, 1963.

Andrews, F. M., & Farris, G. G. Supervisory practices and innovation in scientific terms. *Personnel Psychology,* 1967, *20*(4), 497–515.

Argyris, C. *Personality and organization: The conflict between system and the individual.* New York: Harper, 1957.

Argyris, C. *Integrating the individual and the organization.* New York: Wiley, 1964.

Asch, S. E. Effects of group pressure upon the modification and distortion of judgments. In H. Guetzkow (Ed.), *Groups, leadership, and men.* Pittsburgh: Carnegie Press, 1951, pp. 177–190.

The Associated Press. Dispatch from Warsaw, Poland. January 8, 1970.

Atkinson, J. W. *Introduction to motivation.* New York: Van Nostrand–Reinhold, 1964.

Atkinson, J. W., & Feather, N. T. *A theory of achievement motivation.* New York: Wiley, 1966.

Bailey, S. K. *Disruption in urban public secondary schools.* Washington, D.C.: National Association of Secondary School Principals, 1970.

Bales, R. F. *Interaction process analysis.* Cambridge, Mass.: Addison-Wesley, 1950.

Barnlund, D.C. A comparative study of individual, majority, and group judgment. *Journal of Abnormal and Social Psychology,* 1959, *58*, 55–60.

Barrett, J. H. Individual goals and organizational objectives: A study of integration mechanisms. Ann Arbor: University of Michigan Institute·for Social Research, 1970.

Bass, B. U., & Wurster, C. R. Effects of comparing rank on LGD performance of oil refinery supervisors. *Journal of Applied Psychology,* 1953, *37,* 100–104. (a)

Bass, B. U., & Wurster, C. R. Effects of the nature of the problem on LGD performance. *Journal of Applied Psychology,* 1953, *37,* 96–99. (b)

Beckhard, R. *Organization development: Strategies and models.* Reading, Mass.: Addison-Wesley, 1969.

Beier, E. G. The effect of induced anxiety on flexibility of intellectual functioning. *Psychological Monographs,* 1951, *65*(9), 3–26.

Benne, K. D., & Sheates, P. Functional roles of group members. *Journal of Social Issues,* 1948, *4*(2), 42–45.

Bennis, W. G. *Organization development: Its nature, origins, and prospects.* Reading, Mass.: Addison-Wesley, 1969.

Berkowitz, L. *Advances in experimental social psychology* (4 vols.). New York: Academic, 1964, 1965, 1967, 1969.

Bernhardt, R. G. *A study of the relationships between teachers' attitudes toward militancy and their perceptions of selected organizational characteristics of their schools.* (Doctoral dissertation, Syracuse University) Ann Arbor: University Microfilms, 1972. No. 72-11, 825.

Blake, R. R., & Mouton, J. S. Comprehension of own and outgroup positions under intergroup competition. *Journal of Conflict Resolution,* September 1961, *5,* 304–310.

Blake, R. R., & Mouton, J. S. *Corporate excellence through grid organization development.* Houston: Gulf Publishing, 1968.

Blake, R. R., Shepard, H. A., & Mouton, J. S. *Managing intergroup conflict in industry.* Houston: Gulf Publishing, 1964.

Blankenship, L. V., & Miles, R. E. Organization structure and managerial decision behavior. *Administrative Science Quarterly,* 1968, *13,* 106–120.

Blau, P. M. Cooperation and competition in a bureaucracy. *American Journal of Sociology,* 1954, *59,* 530–535.

Bondurant, J. V., & Fisher, M. W. (Eds.). *Conflict: Violence and nonviolence.* New York: Atherton, 1971.

Bose, S. K. *A psychological approach to productivity improvement.* Bombay: Conference of Psychologists, 1957.

Bose, S. K. Group cohesiveness as a factor in industrial morale and productivity. *J. Sci. Club* (Bangalore, India), 1958, Vol. 11. (a)

Bose, S. K. Industrial motivation for higher productivity. Lecture, Indian Institute of Technology, Kharagpur, India, 1958. (b)

Bowers, D. G. *Self-esteem and the diffusion of leadership style.* Ann Arbor: University of Michigan Institute for Social Research, 1962.

Bowers, D. G. *Applying modern management principles to sales organizations.* Ann Arbor: Foundation for Research on Human Behavior, 1963.

Bowers, D. G. Organizational control in an insurance company. *Sociometry,* June 1964, *27*(2), 230–244. (a)

Bowers, D. G. Self-esteem and supervision. *Personnel Administration,* July–August 1964, *27*(4), 23–36; 39. (b)

Bowers, D. G. O. D. techniques and their results in 23 organizations: The Michigan ICL study. *Journal of Applied Behavioral Science,* 1973, *9*(1), 21–43.

Bowers, D. G., & Seashore, S. E. Predicting organizational effectiveness with a four-factor theory of leadership. *Administrative Science Quarterly,* September 1966, *10*(2), 238–263.

Bowers, D. G., & Seashore, S. E. Peer leadership within work groups. *Personnel Administration,* September–October 1967.

Bradford, L. P., Jibb, J. R., & Benne, K. D. *T-group theory and laboratory method.* New York: Wiley, 1964.

Brehm, J. W. *A theory of psychological reactance.* New York: Academic, 1966.

Burke, R. J. Methods of resolving interpersonal conflict. *Personnel Administration,* July–August 1969, *32*(4), 48–55.

Burns, T. The directions of activity and communicating in a departmental executive group. *Human Relations,* 1954, *7,* 73–97.

Burns, T., & Stalker, G. M. *The management of innovation.* London: Tavistock Publications, 1961.

Byrnes, J. L. *A study of certain relationships among perceived supervisory style, participativeness, and teacher job satisfaction.* (Doctoral dissertation, Syracuse University) Ann Arbor: University Microfilms, 1973. No. 73-7790.

Cafferty, T. P., & Streufert, S. Conflict and attitudes toward the opponent: An application of the Collins and Hoyt attitude change theory to groups in interorganizational conflict. *Journal of Applied Psychology,* 1974, *59*(1), 48–53.

Caplan, R. D. *Organizational stress and individual strain: A social-psychological study of risk factors in coronary heart disease among administrators, engineers, and scientists.* Ann Arbor: University of Michigan Institute for Social Research, 1971.

Carr, R. W. *A study of the job satisfaction of high school principals.* (Doctoral dissertation, The University of Michigan) Ann Arbor: University Microfilms, 1971. No. 71-23, 719.

Cartwright, D. P. *Surveys of the war finance program* (Conference of Consumers' Interests, Proceedings). Philadelphia: University of Pennsylvania Press, 1947.

Cartwright, D. P. Some principles of mass persuasion: Selected findings of research on the sale of United States war bonds. *Human Relations,* 1949, *2,* 253–267.

Cartwright, D. P. Achieving change in people: Some applications of group dynamics theory. *Human Relations,* 1951, *4,* 381–392.

Cartwright, D. P. (Ed.). *Studies in social power.* Ann Arbor: University of Michigan Institute for Social Research, 1959, 155–156.

Cartwright, D. P., & Zander, A. F. (Eds.). *Group Dynamics: Research and theory* (3rd ed.). New York: Harper & Row, 1968.

Chapple, E. D., & Sayles, L. R. *The measure of management: Designing organizations for human effectiveness.* New York: Macmillan, 1961.

Chase S. *Roads to agreements.* New York: Harper, 1951.

Chowdhry, K. An analysis of the attitudes of textile workers and the effect of these attitudes on working efficiency. *ATIRA Res. Note* (Ahmedabad, India), 1953.

Chowdhry, K. *Human relations, a review: Background and current trends.* Ahmedabad, India: ATIRA Human Relations Division, 1960.

Chowdhry, K., & Pal, A. K. Production planning and organization morale: A case from India. *Human Organization,* 1957, *15*(5).

Chowdhry, K. & Trivedi, V. R. Motivation to work: Improvement in motivation to work of winders and warpers and its effect on loomshed efficiency. *ATIRA Res. Note* (Ahmedabad, India), 1953.

Christie, R. & Geis, F. *Studies in Machiavellianism.* New York: Academic, 1970.

Cleveland, H. *The future executive: A guide for tomorrow's managers.* New York: Harper & Row, 1972, 17–29.

Coch, L., & French, J. R. P., Jr. Overcoming resistance to change. *Human Relations,* 1948, *1,* 512–532.

Collins, B. E., & Raven, B. H. Group structure: Attraction, coalitions, communication, and power. In G. Lindzey & E. Aronson (Eds.), *The Handbook of social psychology* (2nd ed. Vol. 4). Reading, Mass.: Addison-Wesley, 1969, pp. 102–204.

Cooper, M. R. & Wood, M. T. Effects of member participation and commitment in group decision making on influence, satisfaction, and decision riskiness. *Journal of Applied Psychology,* 1974, *59*(2) 127–134.

Coser, L. A. *The functions of social conflict.* New York: Free Press, 1956.

Crombag, H. F. Cooperation and competition in means-interdependent triads: A replication. *Journal of Personality and Social Psychology,* 1966, *4,* 692–695.

Croome, H. *Human problems of innovation.* London: Department of Scientific and Industrial Reserach, 1959.

Crozier, M. Human relations at the management level in a bureaucratic system of organization. *Human Organization,* 1961, *20,* 51–64.

Crozier, W. J. Notes on some problems of adaptation. *Biological Bulletin,* 1920, *39,* 116–129.

Cruthchfield, R. S. Conformity and character. *American Psychologist,* 1955, *10,* 191–198.

Cullers, B., Hughes, C., & McGreal, T. Administrative behavior and student dissatisfaction: A possible relationship. *Peabody Journal of Education,* January 1973, pp. 155–163.

Dale, E. Delegation. *Enterprise,* April 1957, *7*(10), 36–37.

Dale, E. *Organization: An illustrated outline.* New York: privately published, 1960.

Dale, E. *Management: Theory and practice* (3rd ed.). New York: McGraw-Hill, 1973, pp. 193–194.

Dalton, M. *Men who manage.* New York: Wiley, 1959.

Derr, C. B. Conflict resolution in organizations: Views from the field of educational administration. *Public Administration Review,* 1972, *32*(5), 495–501.

Deutsch, M. *The resolution of conflict.* New Haven: Yale, 1973.

Dewey, J. *How we think.* Boston: Heath, 1910.

Doob, L. W. (Ed.). *Resolving conflict in Africa: The Fermeda work shop.* New Haven: Yale, 1970.

Doob, L. W. The impact of the Fermeda workshop on the conflicts in the Horn of Africa. *International Journal of Group Tensions,* 1971, *1*(1), 91–101.

Doob, L. W., & Foltz, W. J. The Belfast workshop. *Journal of Conflict Resolution,* 1973, *17*, 489–512.

Doob, L. W., Foltz, W. J., & Stevens, R. B. The Fermeda Workshop: A different approach to border conflicts in eastern Africa. *Journal of Psychology,* 1969, *73*, 249–266.

Douglas, A. G. *Industrial peacemaking.* New York: Columbia, 1962.

Dunlop, J. T. *Industrial relations systems.* New York: Holt, 1959, chap. 8.

Dunlop, J. T. *Consensus and national labor policy,* IRRA Presidential Address, 1960, pp. 14–15.

Dunnette, M. D., Campbell, J., & Jaastad, K. The effect of group participation on brainstorming effectiveness for two industrial samples. *Journal of Applied Psychology,* 1963, *47*, 30–37.

Dutton, J. M. *Analysis of interdepartmental decision making.* Academy of Management Proceedings of December 27–29, 1967. Reprinted at Lafayette, Ind.: Purdue University, Krannert Grad. School of Ind. Admin., Reprint Series No. 245.

Dutton, J. M. Interdepartmental decision-making in theory and practice: An overview. *Int. J. Prod. Res.,* 1971, *9*(1), 53–63.

Dutton, J. M., & Walton, R. E. Interdepartmental conflict and cooperation: Two contrasting studies. *Human Organization,* 1966, *25*(3), 207–220.

Evan, W. M. Conflict and performance in R & D organizations: Some preliminary findings. *Industrial Review,* 1965, *7*(1), 37–46.

Farris, G. F. *A causal analysis of scientific performance.* (Doctoral dissertation, The University of Michigan) Ann Arbor: University Microfilms, 1966. No. 66-14, 517.

Farris, G. F. Organizational factors and individual performance. *Journal Applied Psychology,* 1969, *53*, 87–92.

Feitler, F., & Blumberg, A. Changing the organizational character of a school. *The Elementary School Journal,* January 1971, pp. 206–215.

Ferris, A. E. *Organizational relationships in two selected secondary schools: A comparative study.* (Doctoral dissertation, Columbia University) Ann Arbor: University Microfilms, 1965. No 65-8839.

Festinger, L. Informal social communication. *Psych Review,* 1950, *57*, 271–282.

Festinger, L., Schachter, S., & Back, K. *Social pressures in informal groups: A study of human factors in housing.* Stanford, Calif.: Stanford, 1950.

Fiedler, F. E. *A theory of leadership effectiveness.* New York: McGraw-Hill, 1967.

Fink, C. F. Some conceptual difficulties in the theory of social conflict. *Journal of Conflict Resolution,* December 1968, *12*(4).

Follett, M. P. *Freedom and co-ordination, Lectures in business organization* (L. Urwick Ed.). London: Management Publications Trust, Ltd., 1949.

Foundation for Research on Human Behavior. *Creativity and conformity a problem for organizations.* Ann Arbor, 1958.

Fox, E. M., & Urwick, L. *Dynamic administration: The collected papers of May Parker Follett* (2nd ed.). London: Pitman Publishing, 1973. (Page citations from 1st ed., Metcalf, H. C., & Urwick, L, eds., New York: Harper, 1940.)

French, J. R. P., Jr., Israel, J., & As, D. An experiment on participation in a Norwegian factory. *Human Relations,* 1960, *13*(1), 3–19.

Frohman, M. A. *An empirical study of a model and strategies for planned organizational change.* (Doctoral dissertation, The University of Michigan) Ann Arbor: University Microfilms, 1971. No. 71-15, 153.

Ganguli, H. C. *Structures and processes of organization.* New York & Bombay: Asia Publishing, 1963.

Gardner, J. W. *Excellence: Can we be equal and excellent too?* New York: Harper & Row, 1961.

Georgopoulos, B. S., & Mann, F. C. *The community general hospital.* New York: Macmillan, 1962.

Georgopoulos, B. S., & Matejko, A. The American general hospital as a complex social system. *Health Services Research,* spring 1967, *2*(1), 76–112.

Georgopoulos, B. S., & Tannenbaum, A. S. A study of organizational effectiveness. *American Sociological Review,* 1957, *22*, 534–540.

Gibb, J. R. Defensive communication. *Journal of Communication,* September 1961, *11*, 141–148.

Gibson, A. K. *The achievement of sixth grade students in a Midwestern city.* (Doctoral dissertation, The University of Michigan) Ann Arbor: University Microfilms, 1974. No. 74-15, 729.

Gilbert, E. D. *Teaching styles prevalent in satisfying and dissatisfying college credit courses as perceived by adult students.* (Doctoral dissertation, Ohio State University) Ann Arbor, Mich.: University Microfilms, 1972. No. 72-27, 010.

Glidewell, J. C. Work-emotionality characteristics of total group and their relation to group problem solving. In Stock D., & Thelen, H. A. (Eds.), *Emotional dynamics and group culture* (Research Training Series #2). Washington, D.C.: National Training Labs (NEA), 1958.

Gregson, R. A. M. Interrelation of attitudes and communications in a sub-divided working group. *Occupational Psychology,* 1957, *31*, 104–112.

Guest, R. H. *Organizational change: The effect of successful leadership.* Homewood, Ill.: Dorsey-Irwin, 1962.

Guetzkow, H., & Gyr, J. An analysis of conflict in decision-making groups. *Human Relations,* 1954, *7*, 367–382.

Habibullah, M. *Employee-centered supervision and productivity in the jute industry of Pakistan.* Unpublished doctoral dissertation, Dacca University, 1967.

Hamilton, W. F. Coordination in the star fish. III. The righting reaction as a phase of locomotion (righting and locomotion), *Journal of Comparative Psychology,* 1922, *2,* 81–94.

Hammond, K. R., Todd, F. J., Wilkins, M., & Mitchell, T. O. Cognitive conflict between persons: Application of the "Lens Model" paradigm. *Journal of Experimental Social Psychology,* 1966, *2,* 343–360.

Harary, F., Norman, R., & Cartwright, D. *Structural models.* New York: Wiley, 1965.

Hare, A. P. *Handbook of small group research.* Glencoe, Ill.: Free Press, 1962.

Havelock, R. G., & Mann, F. C. *Research and development laboratory management knowledge utilization study.* Ann Arbor: University of Michigan Institute for Social Research, 1968.

Haynes, P. *A comparison of perceived organizational characteristics between selected work stoppage and nonwork stoppage school districts in the state of Michigan.* (Doctoral dissertation, Western Michigan University) Ann Arbor, Mich.: University Microfilms, 1972. No. 72-14, 182.

Heider, F. *The psychology of interpersonal relations.* New York: Wiley, 1958.

Hoffman, G. W., & Neal, F. W. *Yugoslavia and the new communism.* New York: Twentieth Century Fund, 1962.

Hoffman, L. R., & Maier, N. R. F. Valence in the adoption of solutions by problem solving groups: Concept, method, and results. *Journal of Abnormal and Social Psychology,* 1964, *69,* 264–271.

Hovland, C. I. et al. *The order of presentation in persuasion.* New Haven: Yale, 1957.

Hovland, C. I., Harvey, O. J., & Sherif, M. Assimilation and contrast effects in reactions to communication and attitude change. *Journal of Abnormal and Social Psychology,* 1957, *55*(2), 244–252.

Jerovsek, J., Mozina, S., Tannenbaum, A. S., & Likert, R. Testing a management style. *European Business,* autumn 1970, *27,* 60–68.

Johnson, D. E. *A comparison between the Likert management systems and performance in Air Force ROTC detachments.* (Doctoral dissertation, University of Minnesota) Ann Arbor: University Microfilms, 1969. No. 69-11, 409.

Julian, J. W., Bishop, D. W., & Fiedler, F. E. Quasi-therapeutic effects of intergroup competition. *Journal of Personality and Social Psychology,* 1966, *3,* 321–327.

Kahn, R. L. Two kinds of learning and their implications. New York: American Management Association, Personnel Series, #155, 1953, pp. 25–29.

Kahn, R. L., Wolfe, D. M., Quinn, R. P., Snoek, J. D., & Rosenthal, R. A. *Organizational stress: Studies in role conflict and ambiguity.* New York: Wiley, 1964.

Katz, D., & Kahn, R. L. *The social psychology of organizations.* New York: Wiley, 1966.

Katz, D., Maccoby, N., & Morse, N. C. *Productivity, supervision and morale in an office situation, part I.* Ann Arbor: University of Michigan Institute for Social Research, 1950.

Kavcic, B., Rus, V., & Tannenbaum, A. Control, participation, and effectiveness in four Yugoslav industrial organizations. *Administrative Science Quarterly,* March 1971, *16,* 74–86.

Kelley, H. H., & Thibaut, J. W. Group problem solving. In G. Lindzey & E. Aronson, *The handbook of social psychology* (2nd ed., Vol. 4). Reading, Mass.: Addison-Wesley, 1969, pp. 1–101.

Kepner, C. H., & Tregoe, B. B. *The rational manager.* New York: McGraw-Hill, 1965.

Ketchel, J. M. *The development of methodology for evaluating the effectiveness of a volunteer health planning organization.* (Doctoral dissertation, Ohio State University) Ann Arbor: University Microfilms, 1972. No. 72-27, 039.

Kolaja, J. *Workers' councils: The Yugoslav experience.* London: Tavistock Publications, 1965.

Lammers, C. J. Power and participation in decision making in formal organizations. *The American Journal of Sociology,* September 1967, *73*(2), 201–216.

Landsberger, H. A. The horizontal dimension in a bureaucracy. *Administrative Science Quarterly,* 1961, *6*, 298–332.

Lawrence, P. R., & Lorsch, J. W. *Organizations and environment.* Cambridge, Mass.: Harvard, 1967.

Lawrence. P. R., & Lorsch, J. W. *Developing organizations: Diagnosis and action.* Reading, Mass.: Addison-Wesley, 1969.

Lawson P. 1863–1959. *National Civic Review,* October 1959, *98*(9), 452.

Lepkowski, Sister M. L. *Cooperative decision making as related to supportive relations and communication in the senior high school.* (Doctoral dissertation, University of Buffalo) Ann Arbor: University Microfilms, 1970.

Lesieur, F. G. *The Scanlon Plan.* Cambridge: M.I.T. Press, 1958.

Levine, S., & White, P. E. Exchange as a conceptual framework for the study of interorganizational relationships. *Administrative Science Quarterly,* 1961, *5*, 583–601.

Lewin, K. Group decision and social change. In T. M. Newcomb and E. L. Hartley (Eds.), *Readings in Social Psychology.* New York: Henry Holt, 1947. (b)

Lewin, K. Frontiers in group dynamics. *Human Relations,* 1947, *1*, 5–41. (a)

Lewin, K. *Field theory in social science.* New York: Harper, 1951.

Likert, R. A technique for the measurement of attitudes. *Arch. Psychol.,* 1932, *140*, 1–55.

Likert, R. Motivation: The core of management. New York: American Management Association, Personnel Series, #155, 1953, pp. 3–21.

Likert, R. *New patterns of management.* New York: McGraw-Hill, 1961.

Likert, R. *The human organization: Its management and value.* New York: McGraw-Hill, 1967.

Likert, R. The relationship between management behavior and social structure— Improving human performance: Better theory, more accurate accounting. *Proceedings of the 15th International Management Congress, Toyko,* November 1969, pp. 136–146.

Likert, R. Human resource accounting: Building and assessing productive organizations. *Personnel,* May/June 1973, pp. 8–24. (a)

Likert, R. *Organizational improvement and human resource accounting.* Paper presented at American Psychological Association Meeting, Montreal, August 1973. (b)

Likert, R., & Bowers, D. G. Organizational theory and human resource accounting. *American Psychologist,* June 1969, *24*(6), 585–592.

Likert, R., & Bowers, D. G. Improving the accuracy of P/L reports by estimating the change in dollar value of the human organization. *Michigan Business Review,* 1973, *25*(2), 15–24.

Likert, R., Bowers, D. G., & Norman, R. M. How to increase a firm's lead time in recognizing and dealing with problems of managing its human organization. *Michigan Business Review,* January 1969, pp. 12–17.

Likert, R., & Willits, J. M. *Morale and agency development* (4 vols.) Hartford, Conn.: Life Insurance Agency Management Association, 1940. (Vol. 4).

Lindzey, G., & Aronson, E. *The Handbook of social psychology* (Vol. 4). Reading, Mass.: Addison-Wesley, 1969.

Litwak, E., & Hylton, L. F. Interorganizational analysis: A hypothesis on co-ordinating agencies. *Administrative Science Quarterly,* 1962, *6*, 395–420.

Loomis, C. P. *Social systems.* Princeton, N.J.: Van Nostrand, 1960.

Loomis, C.P. In praise of conflict and its resolution. *American Sociological Review,* 1967, *32*(6), 875–890.

Loomis, C. P. In defense of integration: For one nation and for one world. *The Centennial Review,* spring 1970, *14*(2), 125–165.

Loomis, C. P., Loomis, A. L., & Gullahorn, J. E. *Linkages of Mexico and the United States* Michigan State University Research Bulletin 14, 1966.

Loomis, C. P., & Loomis, Z. K. *Socio-economic change and the religious factor in India.* New Delhi, 1969.

Lorge, I., Davitz, D., Fox, D., & Herrold, K. *Evaluation of instruction in staff action and decision making,* (Air Research and Development Command Technological Report No. 16). Maxwell Air Force Base, Alabama: Human Resources Institute, 1953.

Lorge, I., & Solomon, H. Individual performance and group performance in problem solving related to group size and previous exposure to the problem. *Journal of Psychology,* 1959, *48*, 107–114.

Lowin, A. Participative decision making: A model, literature critique, and prescriptions for research. *Organizational Behavior and Human Performance,* 1968, *3*, 68–106.

Lundstedt, S. Conflict management: Preeminent challenge. *Bulletin of Business Research,* Ohio State University, January 1969, *44*(1), 1–5.

Lundstedt, S. Conflict management: Preeminent challenge. *Mental Hygiene,* October 1970, *54*(4), 584–588.

Maclean, F. *Tito.* New York: Ballantine Books, 1957.

Maier, N. R. F. The quality of group decisions as influenced by the discussion leader. *Human Relations,* 1950, *3*, 155–174.

Maier, N. R. F. *Principles of human relations.* New York: Wiley, 1952.

Maier, N. R.F. *Frustration: The study of behavior without a goal.* Ann Arbor: The University of Michigan Press, 1961.

Maier, N. R. F. *Problem solving discussions and conferences: Leadership methods and skills.* New York: McGraw-Hill, 1963.

Maier, N. R. F. Assets and liabilities in group problem solving: The need for an integrative function. *Psychological Review,* 1967, *74*, 239–249.

Maier, N. R. F., & Hayes, J. J. *Creative management.* New York: Wiley, 1962.

Maier, N. R. F., & Hoffman, L. R. Quality of first and second solutions in group problem solving. *Journal of Applied Psychology,* 1960, *44*, 278–283. (a)

Maier, N. R. F., & Hoffman, L. R. Using trained "developmental" discussion leaders to improve further the quality of group decisions. *Journal of Applied Psychology,* 1960, *44*, 247–257. (b)

Maier, N. R. F. & Hoffman, L. R. Group decision in England and the United States. *Personnel Psychology,* 1962, *15,* 75–87.

Maier, N. R. F., & Hoffman, L. R. Acceptance and quality of solutions as related to leaders' attitudes toward disagreement in group problem solving. *Journal of Applied Behavioral Science,* 1965, *1*, 373–386.

Maier, N. R. F., & Maier, R. A. An experimental test of the effects of "developmental" vs. "free" discussions on the quality of group decisions. *Journal of Applied Psychology,* 1957, *41*, 320–323.

Maier, N. R. F., & Sashkin, M. Specific leadership behaviors that promote problem solving. *Personnel Psychology,* 1971, *24*, 35–44.

Maier, N. R. F., & Solem, A. R. The contribution of a discussion leader to the quality of group thinking. *Human Relations,* 1952, *5*, 277–288.

Maier, N. R. F., & Zerfoss, L. F. MRP: A technique for training large groups of supervisors and its potential for use in social research. *Human Relations,* 1952, *5*, 177–186.

Mann, F. C. Toward an understanding of the leadership role in formal organizations. In R. Dubin, G. Homans, & D. Miller (Eds.), *Leadership and productivity.* San Francisco: Chandler, 1965.

Mann, F. C. & Neff, F. W. *Managing major change in organizations.* Ann Arbor: Foundation for Research on Human Behavior, 1961.

March, J. G. & Simon, H. A. *Organizations.* New York: Wiley, 1958.

Marchant, M. P. *The effects of the decision-making process and related organizational factors on alternative measures of performance in university libraries.* (Doctoral dissertation, The University of Michigan) Ann Arbor: University Microfilms, 1971. No. 71-15, 228.

Marquis, D. Individual responsibility and group decision involving risk. *Industrial Management Review,* 1962, *3*, 8–23.

Marquis, D. G., Guetzkow, H., & Heyns, R. W. A social psychological study of the decision-making conference. In H. Guetzkow (Ed.), *Groups, leadership, and men: Research in human relations.* Pittsburgh: Carnegie Press, 1951, pp. 55–67.

Marrow, A. J. *Making management human.* New York: McGraw-Hill, 1957.

Marrow, A. J., Bowers, D. G., & Seashore, S. E. *Management by participation: Creating a climate for personal and organizational development.* New York: Harper & Row, 1967.

Marshall, J. *Swords & symbols: The technique of sovereignty.* New York: Funk & Wagnalls, 1969.

Marshall, J., Marquis, K. H., & Oskámp, S. Effects of kind of question and atmosphere of interrogation on accuracy and completeness of testimony. *Harvard Law Review,* May 1971, *84*(7), 1620–1643.

Mathewson, S. B. *Restriction of output among unorganized workers.* New York: Viking, 1931.

McClelland, D. C. *The achieving society.* Princeton, N.J.: Van Nostrand, 1961.

McClelland, D., Atkinson, J. W., Clark, R. W., & Lowell, E. L. *The achievement motive.* New York: Appleton-Century-Crofts, 1953.

McCullough, G. E. The effects of changes in organizational structure: Demonstration projects in an oil refinery. In L. E. Davis and A. B. Cherns. *The quality of working life Volume Two: Cases and commentary.* New York: Free Press, 1975.

McCullough, G. E., & Likert, R. Effective human organizations: Their characteristics and value. *The Certified General Accountant,* October 1972, *6*(4), 15–19.

McGregor, D. *The human side of enterprise.* New York: McGraw-Hill, 1960.

McGregor, D. *The professional manager.* New York: McGraw-Hill, 1967.

McKersie, R. B., Perry, C., & Walton, R. E. Intra-organizational bargaining in labor negotiations. *The Journal of Conflict Resolution,* December 1965.

McVicker, C. P. *Titoism: Pattern for international communism.* London: Macmillan, 1967.

Mellinger, G. D. Interpersonal trust as a factor in communication. *Journal of Abnormal and Social Psychology,* 1959, *52*(3), 304–309.

Miles R. E. Conflicting elements in managerial ideologies. *Industrial Relations,* 1964, *4*, 77–91.

Miles, R. E. Human relations or human resources? *Harvard Business Review,* 1965, *43*, 148–163.

Miles, R. E. The affluent organization. *Harvard Business Review,* 1966, *44*, 106–115.

Miles, R. E., Porter, L. W., & Craft, J. A. Leadership attitudes among public health officials. *American Journal of Public Health,* 1966, *56*, 1990–2005.

Miles, R. E., & Ritchie, J. B. Leadership attitudes among union officials. *Industrial Relations,* 1968, *8*, 108–117.

Misumi, J. (Ed.). *Group dynamics in Japan.* Fukuoka, Japan: Kyushu University, Japanese Group Dynamics Association, 1973.

Misumi, J., & Seki, F. Effects of achievement motivation on the effectiveness of leadership patterns. *Administrative Science Quarterly,* March 1971, *16*, 51–60.

Misumi, J., & Shirakashi, S. An experimental study of the effects of supervisory behavior on productivity and morale in a hierarchical organization. *Human Relations,* 1966, *19*(3), 297–306.

Misumi, J., & Tasaki, T. A field study of the effectiveness of supervisory patterns in a Japanese hierarchical organization. *Japanese Journal of Education and Social Psychology,* 1965. *4*, 1–13.

Mohr, L. B. Organizational technology and organizational structures. *Administrative Science Quarterly,* December 1971, *16*(4), 444–449.

Moscovici, S., Lage, E., & Naffrechoux, M. Influence of a consistent minority on the responses of a majority in a color perception task. *Sociometry,* December 1969, *32*(4), 365–380.

Mulder, M., & Stemerding, A. Threat, attraction to group, and need for strong leadership. *Human Relations,* November 1963, *16*(4), 317–334.

Myers, A. E. Team competition, success, and adjustment of group members. *Journal of Abnormal and Social Psychology,* 1962, *65,* 325–332.

Myers, M. S. *Every employee a manager.* New York: McGraw-Hill, 1970.

National Civic Review. October 1959, p. 452.

National Commission on the Causes and Prevention of Violence. *The Congressional Record,* December 23, 1969, *115*(215), 2.

NTRDA. *A report of findings from the NTRDA outpatient research and demonstration project.* New York: National Tuberculosis and Respiratory Disease Association, 1970.

NTRDA. *National outpatient research and demonstration project.* New York: National Tuberculosis & Respiratory Disease Association, 1970.

Pelz, D. C. *Motivation of the engineering and research specialist.* New York: American Management Association, General Management Series #186, 1957, pp. 25–46.

Pelz, D. C. Creative tensions in the research and development climate. *Science,* July 14, 1967, *157*(3,785) 160–165.

Pelz, D., & Andrews, F. *Scientists in organizations: Productive climates for research and development.* New York: Wiley, 1966.

Perrucci, R., & Pilisuk, M. Leaders and ruling elites: The interorganizational bases of community power. *American Sociological Review,* 1970, *35,* 1040–1057.

Price, J. L. The impact of departmentalization on interoccupational cooperation. *Human Organization,* 1968, *27,* 362–368.

Public Administration News. Vol. 9, November 1959.

Pyle, W. C. An accounting system for human resources. *Innovation,* 1970, *10,* 46–54.

Pyle, W. C. Monitoring human resources—"On line." *Michigan Business Review,* July 1970, *22*(4), 19–32.

Pyle, W. C. Human resource accounting. *Financial Analysts Journal,* September–October 1970.

Raven, B. H. Social influence and power. In I. D. Steiner and M. Fishbein (Eds.), *Current studies in social psychology.* New York: Holt, 1965, pp. 371–382.

Raven, B. H., & Eachus, H. T. Cooperation and competition in means-interdependence triads. *Journal of Abnormal and Social Psychology,* 1963, *67,* 307–316.

Rensis Likert Associates, Inc. *Improving organizational performance: A brief progress report.* Ann Arbor: RLA, Inc., July 1971.

Rensis Likert Associates, Inc. *The Likert profile of a school: New survey instruments for public schools to improve organizational effectiveness manual for questionnaire use* (rev. ed.). Ann Arbor: RLA, Inc., 1975.

Reston, J. The shadow of starvation. *New York Times,* March 20, 1974.

Riedel, J. E. *A comparison of principal, teacher and student perceptions of selected elementary school principals' effectiveness* (Doctoral dissertation, University of Southern California) Ann Arbor: University Microfilms, 1974. No. 74-2104.

Roberts, K., Miles, R. E., & Blankenship, L. V. Organizational leadership, satisfaction, and productivity: A comparative analysis. *Academy of Management Journal,* December 1968, pp. 401–414.

Robert's rules of order, newly revised. Glenview, Ill.: Scott, Foresman, 1970.

Roethlisberger, F. J., & Dickson, W. J. *Management and the worker.* Cambridge, Mass.: Harvard University, 1939.

Rogers, C. R. *Client-centered therapy.* Boston: Houghton Mifflin, 1951.

Rogers, C. R. *On becoming a person.* Boston: Houghton-Mifflin, 1961.

Rogers, C. R., & Roethlisberger, F. J. Barriers and gateways to communication. *Harvard Business Review,* 1952, *30*(4), 46–52.

Ross, A. M. Rhetoric and reality in manpower. In I. H. Siegel (Ed.), *Manpower tomorrow: Prospects and priorities.* New York: A. M. Kelley, Publishers, 1967.

Samuel, Y. Organizational climate: Concept and measurement. In J. C. Taylor and D. G. Bowers (Eds.), *The survey of organizations: Toward a machine-scored, standardized questionnaire instrument.* Ann Arbor: University of Michigan Institute for Social Research, 1970, pp. 97–117.

Samuel, Y. *The role of social consensus as a conditioner in organizational planned change,* (Technical Report). Ann Arbor: University of Michigan Institute for Social Research, 1971.

Sanford, F. H. *Authoritarianism and leadership.* Philadelphia: Institute for Research in Human Relations, 1950.

Schachter, S. Deviation, rejection, and communication. In D. Cartwright and A. Zander (Eds.), *Group dynamics* (3rd ed.). New York: Harper & Row, 1968, pp. 165–181.

Schein, E. H. *Process consultation: Its role in organization development.* Reading, Mass.: Addison-Wesley, 1969.

Schmidt, W., & Tannenbaum, R. The management of differences. *Harvard Business Review,* December 1960, *38*, 107–115.

Schneirla, T. C., & Maier, N. R. F. Concerning the status of the star fish. *Journal of Comparative Psychology,* 1940, *40*, 103–110.

Seashore, S. E., & Bowers, D. G. *Changing the structure and functioning of an organization: Report of a field experiment.* Ann Arbor: The University of Michigan, Survey Research Center, 1963.

Seashore, S. E., & Bowers, D. G. The durability of organizational change. *American Psychologist,* March 1970, *25*(3), 227–233.

Seiler, J. A. Diagnosing interdepartmental conflict. *Harvard Business Review,* 1963, *5*, 121–132.

Shepard, H. A. In R. L. Kahn and E. Boulding (Eds.), *Power and conflict in organizations.* New York: Basic Books, 1964, pp. 134–135.

Shepherd, C. & Weschler, I. R. The relation between three interpersonal variables and communication effectiveness. *Sociometry,* 1955, *18*, 103–110.

Sherif, M. Experiments on group conflict and cooperation. *Scientific American,* November 1956, *195*, 54–58.

Sherif, M. (Ed.). *Intergroup relations and leadership: Approaches and research in industrial, ethnic, cultural, and political areas.* New York: Wiley, 1962.

Sherif, M. *Social interaction.* Chicago: Aldine, 1967.

Sherif, M., Harvey, O. J., White, B. J., Hood, W. R., & Sherif, C. W. *Intergroup conflict and cooperation: the robbers cave experiment.* Norman, Okla.: University of Oklahoma Book Exchange, 1961.

Sherif, M., & Sherif, C. W. *Groups in harmony and tension.* New York: Harper, 1953.

Simon, H. A. *The new science of management decisions.* New York: Harper & Row, 1960.

Simpson, R. L. Vertical and horizontal communication in organization. *Adminstrative Science Quarterly,* 1959, *4*, 188–196.

Smallridge, R. *A study of relationships between the perceived management system of elementary schools and the personal needs satisfaction of teachers.* (Doctoral dissertation, George Peabody College for Teachers) Ann Arbor: University Microfilms, 1972. No 72-25, 404.

Smith, E. D. *Psychology for executives.* New York: Harper, 1928.

Solem, A. R. Almost anything I can do, we can do better. *Personal Administration,* 1965, *28*, 6–16.

Sonquist, J. A., & Morgan, J. N. *The detection of interaction effects: A report of a computer program for the selection of optimal combinations of explanatory variables.* Ann Arbor: University of Michigan, Institute for Social Research, 1964.

Sonquist, J. A. *Multivariate model building: The validation of a search strategy.* Ann Arbor: University of Michigan, Survey Research Center, 1970.

Stagner, R. *The psychology of industrial conflict.* New York: Wiley, 1956.

A social profile of Detroit: 1952. (A report of the Detroit Area Study of the University of Michigan.) Ann Arbor: University of Michigan, Institute for Social Research, 1952.

Stock, Dorothy, & Thelen, H. A. *Emotional dynamics and group culture* (Research Training Series No. 2). Washington, D.C.: National Training Laboratories, 1958.

Strauss, G. Tactics of lateral relationship. *Administrative Science Quarterly,* 1962, *7*, 161–186.

Strauss, G. Work-flow frictions, interfunctional rivalry, and professionalism: A case study of purchasing agents. *Human Organizations,* 1964, *23*, 137–149.

Sturmthal, A. *Workers' councils.* Cambridge, Mass.: Harvard, 1964.

Swingle, P. G. (Ed.) *The structure of conflict.* New York: Academic, 1970.

Tagiuri, R. & Litwin, G. H. (Eds.). *Organizational climate: Explorations of a concept.* Boston: Harvard University, Boston Division of Research, Graduate School of Business Administration, 1968.

Tannenbaum, A. S. *The relationship between personality and group structure.* (Doctoral dissertation, Syracuse University) Ann Arbor: University Microfilms, 1954. No. 8183.

Tannenbaum, A. S. *A study of the League of Women Voters of the United States: Factors in League effectiveness.* Ann Arbor: University of Michigan Institute for Social Research, 1958.

Tannenbaum, A. S. (Ed.). *Control in organizations.* New York: McGraw-Hill, 1968.

Tannenbaum, A. S., & Allport, F. H. Personality structure and group structure: An interpretative study of their relationship through an event-structure hypothesis. *Journal of Abnormal and Social Psychology,* 1956, *53*, 272–280.

Tannenbaum, A. S., & Donald, M. N. *A study of the League of Women Voters of the United States: Factors in League functioning.* Ann Arbor: University of Michigan, Institute for Social Research, 1957.

Tannenbaum, A. S. & Georgopoulos, B. S. The distribution of control in formal organizations. *Social Forces,* October 1957, *36*(1), 44–50.

Taylor, D. W. Decision making and problem solving. In J. G. March (Ed.), *Handbook of organizations.* Chicago: Rand McNally, 1965, pp. 48–86.

Taylor, D. W., Berry, P. C., & Block, C. H. Does group participation when using brainstorming facilitate or inhibit creative thinking? *Administrative Science Quarterly,* 1958, *3*, 23–47.

Taylor, J. C. *The conditioning effects of technology on organizational behavior in planned social change.* (Doctoral dissertation, The University of Michigan) Ann Arbor: University Microfilms, 1970. No. 70-14, 659.

Taylor, J. C., & Bowers, D. G. *Survey of organizations: Toward a machine-scored, standardized questionnaire instrument.* Ann Arbor: University of Michigan, Institute for Social Research, 1972.

Thibaut, J. W., & Kelley, H. H. *The social psychology of groups.* New York: Wiley, 1959.

Thomas, E. J. Effects of facilitative role interdependence on group functioning. *Human Relations,* 1957, *10,* 347–366.

Thomas, J. M., & Bennis, W. G. *Management of change and conflict.* Baltimore: Penguin, 1972.

Thompson, D. E. Favorable self-perception, perceived supervisory style, and job satisfaction. *Journal of Applied Psychology,* 1971, *55*, 349–352.

Throop, R. K. *An explanatory survey of teacher job satisfaction: A path analysis.* (Doctoral dissertation, Syracuse University) Ann Arbor: University Microfilms, 1972. No. 72-6636.

Thurstone, L. L., & Chave, E. J. *The measurement of attitude.* Chicago: University of Chicago Press, 1929.

Todd, F. J., Hammond, K. R., & Wilkins, M. M. Differential effects of ambiguous and exact feedback on two-person conflict and compromise. *Journal of Conflict Resolution,* 1966, *10*(1), 88–97.

Toronto, R. S. *General systems theory applied to the study of organizational change.* (Doctoral dissertation, The University of Michigan) Ann Arbor: University Microfilms, 1972. No. 72-15, 019.

Triandis, H. C. Categories of thought of managers, clerks, and workers about jobs and people in industry. *Journal of Applied Psychology,* 1959, *43,* 338–344. (a)

Triandis, H. C. *Some cognitive factors affecting communication.* (Doctoral dissertation, Cornell University) Ann Arbor: University Microfilms, 1959. No. 59-977. (b)

Vroom, V. H. *Some personality determinants of the effects of participation.* Englewood Cliffs, N.J.: Prentice-Hall, 1960.

Wagstaff, L. H. *The relationship between administrative systems and interpersonal needs of teachers.* (Doctoral dissertation, University of Oklahoma) Ann Arbor: University Microfilms, 1970. No. 70-2343.

Walton, R. E. Theory of conflict in lateral organizational relationships. In J. R. Lawrence (Ed.), *Operational research and the social sciences.* London: Tavistock, 1966, 409–428.

Walton, R. E. Third party roles in interdepartmental conflict. *Industrial Relations,* October 1967, *1*(1), 29–43.

Walton, R. E. *Interpersonal peacemaking: Confrontations and third-party consultation.* Reading, Mass.: Addison-Wesley, 1969.

Walton, R. E. A problem-solving workshop on border conflicts in East Africa. *Journal of Applied Behavioral Sciences,* 1970, *6*, 453–496.

[Dutton, J. M., &] Walton, R. E. Interdepartmental conflict and cooperation: Two contrasting studies. *Human Organization,* 1966, *25*(3), 207–220.

Walton, R. E., & Dutton, J. M. The management of interdepartmental conflict: A model and review. *Administrative Science Quarterly,* March 1969, *14*(1), 73–84.

Walton, R. E., Dutton, J. M., & Cafferty, T. P. Organizational context and interdepartmental conflict. *Administrative Science Quarterly,* 1969, *14*(4), 522–542.

Walton, R. E., Dutton, J. M., & Fitch, H. S. A study of conflict in the process, structure, and attitudes of lateral relationships. In *Some theories of organization,* Homewood, Ill.: Irwin, revised 1966, pp. 444–465.

Walton, R. E., & McKersie, R. B. *A behavioral theory of labor negotiations: An analysis of a social interaction system.* New York: McGraw-Hill, 1965.

Walton, R. E., & McKersie, R. B. Behavioral dilemmas in mixed motive decision making. *Behavioral Science,* 1966, *11*, 370–384.

Warwick, D. P., Meade, M., & Reed, T. *A public bureaucracy: politics, personality, and organization in the U.S. State Department.* Cambridge, Mass.: Harvard, 1975.

Weaver, W. Dither. *Science,* 1959. *130*(3,371), 301.

White, H. Management conflict and social structure. *American Journal of Sociology,* 1961, *67*, 185–191.

White, H. C. Some perceived behavior and attitudes of hospital employees under effective and ineffective supervisors. *Journal of Nursing Administration,* 1971, *1*(1), 49–54. (a)

White, H. C. Perceptions of leadership styles by nurses in supervisory positions. *Journal of Nursing Administration.* 1971, *1*(2), 44–51. (b)

White, H. C. Leadership: Some behaviors and attitudes of hospital employees. *Hospital Progress,* 1971, *52*(1), 46–50. (c)

White, H. C. Leadership: Some behaviors and attitudes of hospital supervisors. *Hospital Progress,* 1971, *52*(2), 41–45. (d)

White, K. K. *Understanding the company organization chart.* New York: American Management Association, 1963.

White, R. K. & Lippitt, R. O. *Autocracy and democracy: Experiments in group leadership.* New York: Harper, 1960.

Whyte, W. F. (Ed.) *Money and motivation.* New York: Harper & Row, 1955.

Whyte, W. F. *Organizational behavior: Theory and application.* Homewood, Ill.: Irwin, 1969.

Wierzynski, G. H. A student declaration: "Our most wrenching problem." *Fortune,* January 1969, *79*(1), 114–116, 146.

Wiesner, J. B. *Where science and politics meet.* New York: McGraw-Hill, 1965.

Woodward, J. *Industrial organization: Theory and practice.* London: Oxford University Press, 1965.

Work in America: Report of a special task force to the Secretary of Health, Education, and Welfare. Cambridge, Mass.: The M.I.T. Press, 1973.

World water supply threatened—drastic remedial action advocated. *Survey of International Development,* February 1972, 1–2.

Zand, D. E. Trust and managerial problem solving. *Administrative Science Quarterly,* 1972, *17*(2), 229–239.

Zander, A. F. The effects of prestige on the behavior of group members: An audience demonstration. New York: American Management Association, Personnel Series, #155. 1953, pp. 22–25.

Zander, A. F. *Motives and goals in groups.* New York: Academic, 1971.

Zander, A. F., Forward, J. R., & Albert, R. Adaptation of board members to repeated failure or success by their organization. *Organizational Behavior and Human Performance,* February 1969, *4*(1), 56–76.

Zupanov, J., & Tannenbaum, A. The distribution of control in some Yugoslav industrial organizations as perceived by members. In A. S. Tannenbaum (Ed.), *Control in organizations.* New York: McGraw-Hill, 1968, pp. 91–109.

Name index

Aas, D., 51
Alger, C., 55n.
Almond, G. A., 120
Andrews, F. M., 5, 61, 133, 154, 248
Argyris, C., 82, 120, 208n.
Aronson, E., 177
Asch, S. E., 186
Atkinson, J. W., 19n.

Back, K., 61
Bailey, S. K., 217, 218
Bales, R. F., 106
Barnlund, D. C., 100
Bass, B. U., 157
Beckhard, R., 308
Beier, E. G., 124
Benne, K. D., 125, 127
Bennis, W. G., 308
Berkowitz, L., 106
Bernhardt, R. G., 17n., 55n., 239
Bishop, D. W., 279
Blake, R. R., 59–64, 66, 124, 141, 319
Blanchard, K. H., 305n.
Blankenship, L. V., 17n., 87, 88
Blumberg, A., 55n., 239
Bose, S. K., 95
Boulding, Elise, 64n.
Bowers, D. G., 16, 17, 46, 51, 71, 86, 87, 99, 101, 102,
    108, 208, 281, 308
Bowie plant, 291, 292, 296–301, 303, 304
Bradford, L. P., 127
Brehm, J. W., 162
Burns, T., 214
Byrnes, J. L., 17n., 55n., 239

Campbell, J., 100
Caplan, R. D., 17
Carr, R. W., 17n., 55n., 239
Cartwright, D. P., 5, 100, 106, 137, 165, 183, 209,
    259, 270, 271, 274–279, 281, 316
Case Institute of Technology, 289n.
Chowdhry, K., 95
Clark, R. W., 19n.
Cleveland, Harlan, 5
Coch, L., 17, 51
Collins, R. E., 271
Cooper, M. R., 99, 274
Crombag, H. F., 279
Croome, H., 214
Crutchfield, R. S., 186
Cullers, B., 55n., 239

Dale, Ernest, 11, 19
Detroit, 261–266

Detroit Area Study, 264n.
Deutsch, M., 279
Dewey, J., 126
Dickson, W. J., 208n.
Donald, M. N., 55n.
Doob, L. W., 319
Dunlop, J. T., 151
Dunnette, M. D., 100, 177
Dutton, J. M., 287, 288, 290, 291, 303

Eachus, H. T., 279
Elgin plant, 291–295, 297–302, 304
Elofsson, N., 94
Evan, W. M., 134

Farris, G. F., 153
Faucheux, Claude, 186
Feather, N. T., 19n.
Feitler, F., 55n., 239
Ferris, A. E., 17n., 55n., 239
Festinger, L., 61, 137
Fiedler, F. E., 110, 279
Fitch, H. S., 287, 288, 290
Follett, M. P., 141, 162, 193
Foltz, W. J., 319
Food and Agriculture Organization (FAO), 326
Foundation for Research on Human Behavior, 186
Fox, D., 100
Fox, E. M., 141, 162, 193
French, J. R. P., Jr., 17, 51, 270, 271

Gamble, T. W., 163, 164
Gandhi, Mahatma, 323
Ganguli, H. C., 95
Gardner, J. W., 122
General Motors Corporation, 71
Georgopoulos, B. S., 17n., 55n., 205, 272
Gibb, J. R., 63, 123, 124, 127
Gibson, A. K., 17n., 55n., 239
Gilbert, E. D., 17n., 55n., 239
Glidewell, J. C., 124
Golden, C., 143
Guest, R. H., 99, 108, 305, 306
Guetzkow, H., 8, 147
Gullahorn, J. E., 120
Gyr, J., 8, 147

Habibullah, M., 17n., 95
Harary, F., 316
Hare, A. P., 106
Harvey, O. J., 59–62, 67, 142, 191
Harwood Manufacturing Company, 86
Havelock, R. G., 176

Subject index